The *Oriental Music* Broadcasts, 1936–1937

Recent Researches in Music

A-R Editions publishes seven series of critical editions, spanning the history of Western music, American music, and oral traditions.

Recent Researches in the Music of the Middle Ages and Early Renaissance
Charles M. Atkinson, general editor

Recent Researches in the Music of the Renaissance
David Crook, general editor

Recent Researches in the Music of the Baroque Era
Steven Saunders, general editor

Recent Researches in the Music of the Classical Era
Neal Zaslaw, general editor

Recent Researches in the Music of the Nineteenth and Early Twentieth Centuries
Rufus Hallmark, general editor

Recent Researches in American Music
John M. Graziano, general editor

Recent Researches in the Oral Traditions of Music
Philip V. Bohlman, general editor

Each edition in *Recent Researches* is devoted to works by a single composer or to a single genre. The content is chosen for its high quality and historical importance and is edited according to the scholarly standards that govern the making of all reliable editions.

For information on establishing a standing order to any of our series, or for editorial guidelines on submitting proposals, please contact:

A-R Editions, Inc.
Middleton, Wisconsin

800 736-0070 (North American book orders)
608 836-9000 (phone)
608 831-8200 (fax)
http://www.areditions.com

Recent Researches in the Oral Traditions of Music, 10

Robert Lachmann

The *Oriental Music* Broadcasts, 1936–1937

A Musical Ethnography of Mandatory Palestine

Edited by Ruth F. Davis

A-R Editions, Inc.
Middleton, Wisconsin

To the memory of my grandmother, Helene Begleiter

A-R Editions, Inc., Middleton, Wisconsin

Printed in the United States of America

ISBN 978-0-89579-776-6
ISSN 0147-0086

♾ The paper used in this publication meets the minimum requirements of the American National Standard for Information Sciences—Permanence of Paper for Printed Library Materials, ANSI Z39.48-1992.

Contents

Figures

Tables

Compact Disc Tracks

On the accompanying audio CDs, each of the following selections appears twice: in restored form (odd track numbers) and in original form (even track numbers; see "Notes on the Restoration Process" in "About the Edition").

CD 1

1–2. Recitation 2.1, D354, *Shirat ha-yam* (Song of the Sea, excerpt, Exod. 15:1–4). Performed by Sa'adiya Nahum, 2 December 1936.

3–4. Recitation 2.3, D356, Proverbs 1:1–7. Performed by Sa'adiya Nahum, 2 December 1936.

5–6. Recitation 3.1, D382, *Laḥn* (hymn), from the Liturgy of St. Cyril. Performed by four priests with *trianto* (metal triangle) and *nāqūs* (pair of small metal cymbals), 11 December 1936.

7–8. Recitation 3.3, D393, "Peklaos gar," from the Liturgy of St. Gregory. Performed by two priests, 16 December 1936.

9–10. Recitation 4.1, D413, *Aseret ha-dibberot* (Ten Commandments, excerpt, Exod. 20:2–7). Performed by Eliahu Yahye Mizrahi, 4 January 1937.

11–12. Recitation 5.2, D452, *Qaṣīdit Nimr Ibn 'Adwān:* "Aw lamīn." Performed by Bājis Afandī Im' addī (voice and *rabāba*), 12 January 1937.

13–14. Recitation 6.1, D529, *Shirat ha-yam* (Song of the Sea, excerpt, Exod. 15:1). Performed by Ibrahim Kohen, 3 February 1937.

15–16. Recitation 6.5, D540, "Sukkāni dhāk al-wādī." Performed by Ibrahim Kohen (solo), Taufiq Kohen and Amram Kohen (chorus), 3 February 1937.

17–18. Recitation 7.1, D588, Judah Halevi (ca. 1080–1141), " 'At ben 'aṣe 'eden." Performed by Sa'adiya Nahum (solo), Yahya Nahari and Hayyim Mahbub (chorus), 17 February 1937.

19–20. Recitation 7.4, D587, Shalem Shabazi (1619–1720), " 'Ayelet ḥen." Performed by Sa'adiya Nahum (solo), Hayyim Mahbub and Yahya Nahari (chorus), 11 February 1937.

21–22. Recitation 8.1, D596, "Sā'at r-raḥmān dalḥīn." Performed by two Yemenite Jewish women with percussion (medium-sized drum without jingles; cymbals), 23 February 1937.

23–24. Recitation 8.3, D599, "Allāh yā Allāh, yā 'ālem bi-ḥālī." Same performers as recitation 8.1, 23 February 1937.

25–26. Recitation 8.4, D600, "Yā Allāh hal-yōm." Same performers as recitation 8.1, 23 February 1937.

27–28. Recitation 8.5, D601, "Yā-llāh 'na salak." Same performers as recitation 8.1, 23 February 1937.

CD 2

1–2. Recitation 9.1, *Taqsīm ḥijāz*. Performed by Ezra Aharon (*'ūd*), 16 March 1937.

3–4. Recitation 9.2, *Taqsīm ṣabā*. Performed by Ezra Aharon (*'ūd*), 16 March 1937.

5–6. Record 10.3, Moroccan song: "Ṣaḥbi l-awwal." Performed by Al-Touhami bin Omar. Baidaphon 093364.

7–8. Record 11.1, Egyptian song: "Qad ḥarrakat aydī n-nasīmi." Performed by Shaykh Sayyid al-Ṣafṭī. Odeon O-5168b (reissued on Hornbostel 1931, no. 20).

9–10. Record 11.2, "Shet araban saz semaisi." Composed and performed by Tanburî Cemil Bey (*tanbur*). Orfeon 10524.

11–12. Recitation 12.3, *Zaffa hamasiyya*. Performed by Mḥammed 'Abd ar-Raḥūn Abu Msellem and group, 28 April 1937.

13–14. Recitation 12.4, *'Ala dal'ūnā dabke*. Performed by 'Abd al-Fattaḥ as-Sahāda (voice) and Aḥmed Smīr (*shabbāba*), 28 April 1937.

15–16. Recitation 12.5, " 'A-l-hāma 'a-l-hāma." Same performers as recitation 12.3, with *zaghrūda* (ululation) by Aḥmed Smīr, 28 April 1937.

Preface

I discovered Robert Lachmann's *Oriental Music* broadcasts through a series of serendipitous encounters. In December 1990 I gave a seminar to the Music Department of the Hebrew University of Jerusalem on the then newly reconstructed campus on Mount Scopus. Following my talk, my hosts asked me if there was anything I wished to see. Without hesitation, I asked to see the collection of cylinder recordings the German-Jewish scholar Robert Lachmann had brought to Palestine in the 1930s.

I had a longstanding interest in Lachmann's ideas and work ever since I came across his monograph *Jewish Cantillation and Song in the Isle of Djerba* (1940)[1] in the library of the "Jaap Kunst" Ethnomusicology Centre at the University of Amsterdam, where I began my graduate studies in the late 1970s. It was this work that informed my initial fieldwork on Djerba some fifty years after Lachmann's visit in 1929 (see Davis 1986 and Davis 2002). I knew from Judah L. Magnes's foreword to the monograph that Lachmann had spent the last years of his life at the Hebrew University and that he had deposited there copies of his entire collection of cylinder recordings, the originals of which remained in the Berlin Phonogramm-Archiv. I was curious to hear the recordings on which the transcriptions, which formed the kernel of the study, were based.

The "Lachmann collection" was housed in a back room of the Jewish Music Research Centre (JMRC) at the Israel National Library, on the Givat Ram campus in West Jerusalem. The director of the Centre, Professor Israel Adler, greeted us enthusiastically. Apparently, Lachmann's English relatives Professor Peter Lachmann and Lady Irene Engle had recently donated a small grant to be made available for a project relating to his research. Professor Adler wanted my advice, as a scholar interested in Lachmann's work, as to how the funds could best be used. He took us to the room adjoining his office where the collection was housed. As he opened a drawer, cylinders rolled about desultorily. Stacked on the top shelf of a metal cabinet were piles of metal discs wrapped in brown paper sleeves. Clearly the recordings had not been touched for a long time—perhaps not since Edith Gerson-Kiwi catalogued them in the mid-1960s (Gerson-Kiwi 1974, 103).[2] Apparently the equipment needed to play them no longer existed in Israel. My advice was unequivocal: I suggested that, as a matter of priority, the JMRC explore means of making Lachmann's recordings accessible. Professor Adler took out a disc randomly (it turned out to be a double-sided record of two Yemenite Jewish women's songs) and placed it in a cardboard tape box. We agreed that I would take it back with me to England, where I would look into having it digitally copied. My unexpected visit had clearly highlighted the vulnerability and insecurity of the collection, not to mention its unusability, in its current state. At the same time, Professor Adler gave me an introduction to Lachmann's nephew Peter Lachmann, professor of immunology and a fellow of Christ's College, Cambridge.

In England, Philip Farlow of Audio Services, Surrey, produced a sample analog copy of the Yemenite women's song: their voices were clearly audible beneath the surface hiss and crackle, yet it seemed doubtful that the quality of the recording would support the sustained, intensive listening necessary for transcription. Peter Copeland, conservation manager at the British Library National Sound Archive, offered helpful initial suggestions, but subsequent enquiries confirmed that the logistics of transferring the entire collection to England for digital copying would be all but insurmountable and the cost prohibitive. Yet the seed had been sown, and the following year the JMRC launched a project in collaboration with the Vienna Phonogrammarchiv and the Austrian Friends of the Hebrew University that was both more ambitious and more realistic: to transfer all the disc and cylinder recordings of the Israel National Sound Archive to digital media in Jerusalem.[3]

Meanwhile, thanks to Professor Adler's introduction, I received an invitation to tea with Peter Lachmann and his family at his home in Cambridge. Peter, the son of Robert's younger brother, Heinz, was born in Berlin in 1931; he vaguely recalled his uncle's fleeting visit to the family home in 1935 to bid farewell before his departure for Jerusalem.[4] Delving among the family memorabilia, Peter showed me photographs and newspaper cuttings relating to Lachmann's work at the 1932 Cairo Congress. He asked me if I knew about Lachmann's radio programs for the Palestine Broadcasting Service. When I responded that I did not, he retrieved a pile of twelve scripts and promised to copy them for me. Each of the scripts bore the title "Oriental Music—A Talk [or 'A Series of Talks'] by Robert Lachmann," a roman numeral indicating its order in the series, a reference to the "Palestine Broadcasting Station" or "Jerusalem Station," and the date of transmission. Perusing the contents, I noticed that all the lectures except the first, which was essentially introductory, were interspersed with music examples, and that in all but two lectures (programs 10 and 11), these "recitations," as Lachmann called them, were performed live in the studio by musicians representing different communities of Palestine. Ideas and expressions familiar to me from Lachmann's Djerba monograph leapt from the pages: this was clearly more than a series of musical portraits of the individual communities. I knew of no other work by Lachmann based on his research in Palestine; indeed, apart from his Djerba monograph and two posthumously published essays edited by Edith Gerson-Kiwi, I knew of no other writings from his Palestine years. Thus, over tea, the idea for this edition was born: I would locate the recordings of the live radio performances or, if none had been made, of equivalent items in the Lachmann collection at JMRC, make musical and textual transcriptions from the recordings, and produce an edition of the radio programs with the recordings presented on accompanying compact discs.[5]

In July 2001 I had the good fortune to meet Edwin Seroussi, who was subsequently to succeed Israel Adler as director of the JMRC, on a visit to Cambridge. At Edwin's suggestion I compiled a list providing details of each musical item in *Oriental Music* according to the information given in Lachmann's lectures. By matching the details I provided with the information in Lachmann's recording diaries, he managed to locate the recordings of the live performances, which were marked "Radio" in the diaries. My subsequent perusal of the diaries revealed that, in each case, Lachmann had recorded the same performers and repertory at least once within the previous week, sometimes even on the same day, and often on other occasions too. Thus the musical content of the radio programs effectively tracked the progress of his recording activities in Palestine through the winter months of 1936–37. Between program 9 (16 March 1937) and program 11 (24 April 1937), Lachmann limited his recording sessions to performers and repertory featured in program 8 (songs of Yemenite Jewish women) and program 9 (solo improvisations performed on the *'ūd* by Ezra Aharon); thus programs 10 and 11, which survey urban musical traditions from Morocco to Hindustan and are illustrated by commercial recordings, filled the gap when Lachmann had no new local performers to introduce. It was not until 21 April—the week before the last program—that he turned his attention to a new repertory, the wedding songs of the Palestinian village musicians who would feature in program 12.

On a visit to Jerusalem in September 1995, Avi Nahmias, principal recording engineer of the Israel National Sound Archive, helped me locate the commercial records used for programs 10 and 11. At the time of my visit, Lachmann's metal disc recordings were undergoing specialist cleaning in preparation for copying. When I returned to Jerusalem in 2000 (see below), I worked with Nahmias to produce the final selection of recordings, which he copied according to the specifications required for the restoration process.

A Kreitmann Visiting Fellowship at Ben-Gurion University of the Negev in spring 2000 gave me the opportunity to spend three weeks in Jerusalem exploring the Lachmann Archive in the Israel National Library Music Department. This collection contains a wealth of professional and personal documentation from Lachmann's Berlin and Palestine years, including manuscripts of his various lectures and scholarly writings. Gila Flam, director of the Music Department, generously allowed me to make copies of all the sources I needed. Many but not all of the documents I consulted were subsequently reproduced in full by Ruth Katz in her exhaustive study of Lachmann's troubled relationship with the Hebrew University (Katz 2003); I give citations of Katz's study for such documents where appropriate.

Research grants awarded by the Arts and Humanities Research Council and the British Academy for the years 2002–3 provided both the time and the initial funding needed to embark on the lengthy process of seeking out, identifying, and enlisting the various specialists—technical, musical, and linguistic—that would enable me to put together this multifaceted project. Subsequent work was supported by research funds from Corpus Christi College, Cambridge; the Cambridge University Travel Fund; the Cambridge University Newton Trust Small Research Grants Scheme; and the Yale Institute of Sacred Music, where I held a visiting fellowship in 2010–11. A Rockefeller Foundation residency at the Bellagio Center on Lake Como, Italy, in spring 2010, gave me an oasis of tranquility in which to synthesize much of this data and write the first draft of this edition.

The sound restoration of the digitally transferred recordings was carried out jointly with Simon Godsill, professor of statistical signal processing at the University of Cambridge, using the facilities of the Department of Engineering. Simon Godsill is responsible for all the technical aspects of the work, while I take ultimate responsibility for our joint sound-editing decisions.

My former student Cheryl Frances-Hoad undertook the initial drafting and subsequent digital copying of music transcriptions. Her astute ear, her technical savviness, and, above all, her patience and humor proved invaluable as she worked with me through multiple versions of the transcriptions and devised ever more ingenious methods of adapting the recalcitrant Sibelius software to my ever-changing requirements. Ben Outhwaite, head of the Taylor-Schechter Genizah Research Unit at the University of Cambridge, assisted me in identifying the biblical sources of the Yemenite, Kurdish, and Samaritan cantillation in programs 2, 4, and 6 and transcribed the Hebrew texts from the recordings. Dr. Outhwaite also produced the transliterations and translations of the Yemenite Jewish wedding songs taken from the Yemenite-Jewish diwan, in program 7. The Judeo-Arabic lyrics of the Yemenite Jewish women's songs were transcribed from the recordings and translated by Avihai Shivtiel, also of the Taylor-Schechter Genizah Research Unit. The Coptic liturgical texts in program 3 were identified by Dr. George Bebawi of the Institute for Orthodox Christian Studies, Cambridge, who also gave freely of his time to provide me with working transcriptions, transliterations, and translations of the texts. Raafat Tadros of the Coptic Orthodox Church Centre in Stevenage, Hertfordshire, referred me to published sources of the Coptic texts and their translations and explained the various Coptic transliteration systems. Peter J. Williams, Warden of Tyndale House, Cambridge, provided the final transliterations of the Coptic texts and produced the transliteration table.

A chance encounter with Abeer Faada in the canteen of the Israel National Library led to her offering to transcribe and translate the Palestinian wedding songs in program 12 from the unprocessed recordings, thus providing me with my first working copies. Working from the processed recordings, my doctoral student Merav Rosenfeld-Hadad, Said Salman Abu Athera, and George Bebawi gave generously and freely of their time to produce working transcriptions and translations of the various Arabic songs in programs 5, 6, and 12. The text transcriptions and translations used in this volume were produced by Makram Khoury-Machool, with amendments provided by Yousef Meri of the Woolf Institute, University of Cambridge, and Esther-Miriam Wagner of the Taylor-Schechter Genizah Research Unit. The words of the Moroccan song in program 10 (record 10.3) were transcribed by Saad Souissi with additional contributions from Mohamed Kharbach. Finally, Miriam Wagner gave me invaluable advice on coordinating the different transliteration systems originally used for the individual Arabic dialects (Palestinian, Samaritan, Moroccan, and Yemenite) in programs 5, 6, 8, 10, and 12. The transcriptions in this edition use a slightly adapted version of her system, as shown in table 5.

At the 2010 conference of the Society for Ethnomusicology in Los Angeles, Jihad Racy eagerly took time to listen to and identify the Egyptian *tawshīh* in program 11 (record 11.1), and he subsequently provided me with the source of the Arabic text along with his own transliteration and translation. Philip Ball of Cambridge University's Photography and Illustration Service (PandIS) reproduced the images provided by Peter Lachmann and the Israel National Library (plates 1–6 and figures 6.1, 11.1, and 11.2); Jill Furmanovsky of Rockarchive, London, photographed the double-sided disc illustrated in plates 8 and 9; and Gerda Lechtleitner of the Vienna Phonogramm-Archiv provided the copies of Idelsohn's transcriptions (figure 2.1).

It would be impossible to thank individually all those who have contributed to this project with their generosity, encouragement, and support. My first thanks must go to Peter Lachmann, whose gift to the JMRC, donated jointly with his sister, Lady Irene Engle, was the catalyst for this project; who alerted me to the existence of the *Oriental Music* broadcasts and provided me with copies of the lecture texts and other documents from his private collection; and whose support, encouragement, and enthusiasm have been unwavering to the end. Sylvia Lachmann's gracious hospitality and interest made our encounters all the more productive and enjoyable. I am no less indebted to my colleagues at the JMRC, the Music Department of the Israel National Library, and the Israel National Sound Archive for generously sharing their materials with me and contributing their resources and expertise. I owe special thanks to (the now late) Israel Adler, Gila Flam, Avi Nahmias, and Edwin Seroussi, each of whom has, at various stages, provided indispensable support, and to Jehoash Hirshberg of the Music Department of the Hebrew University for his encouragement and support from the wings.

A snatched breakfast meeting with Philip Bohlman as I passed through the University of Chicago in the late 1990s led to his suggestion that I consider A-R Editions' Recent Researches in the Oral Traditions of Music series as the venue for this project. Phil's continuing interest and encouragement, his timely interjections with vital research leads, advice, and opportunities, and above all, his unwavering commitment to this edition throughout its long genesis, have been indispensable in enabling me to keep it afloat and steer it to completion. I thank Christine Bohlman for her encouragement, delivered with her inimitable directness and pragmatic wisdom, and both Phil and Christine for their hospitality.

Various invitations to present this material at conferences, seminars, and lectures provided invaluable opportunities to consolidate my research, hone my ideas, and benefit from the input of colleagues. For our discussions on these and on different occasions, I thank in particular Steve Blum, Philip Bohlman, Issa Boulos, Salwa el-Shawan Castelo-Branco, Philip Ciantar, Nick Cook, Ian Cross, Tina Frühauf, Sandy and Amira Goehr, Peter Jeffery, Nori Jacobi, Morris Kahn, Margaret Kartomi, Vasileios Marinis, Yoram Meital, Maryam Meri, Yousef Meri, Delphone Mordey, Bruno Nettl, Laudan Nooshin, John O'Connell, Margaret Olin, Goffredo Plastino, Jihad Racy, Carmel Raz, Dina Roginsky, Mark Slobin, Marcello Sorce Keller, Andrea Stanton, Martin Stokes, Sarah Weiss, and Susanne Ziegler. I owe special thanks to Taiseer Elias for clarifying the modal progressions of Ezra Aharon's performances in program 9; to Morris Kahn for his interest and support in the early stages of this project; and to Ateş Orga for his technical advice on the recordings and his magical way with words.

Much of the research and writing of this work was carried out away from home—in Jerusalem and Omer, Israel, and during residencies I held at various times in 2010 and 2011 at the Mediterranean Institute; the University of Malta; the Rockefeller Foundation Center in Bellagio, Italy; and at Yale University. I thank Sandy and Amira Goehr for making their beautiful home in Ein Kerem, Jerusalem, available to me and Abigail Wood, then my graduate student, as we embarked on our respective projects at the Hebrew University in spring 2000; I am grateful to Abbi for embracing my enthusiasms and sharing the excitement of that initial research. I thank Ilana and Eran Bryn for their hospitality and care in Jerusalem. I thank Pilar Palaciá and Elena Ongania for making my stay at the Villa Serbelloni, Bellagio, both pleasurable and productive; to Marcello Sorce Keller for welcoming me to his home in Swieqi, Malta, and entrusting me with its care; and to Martin Jean and his team—especially Andrea Hart, Jacque Campoli, Derek Greten-Harrison, and Glen Segger—at the Institute for Sacred

Music (ISM), and Dan Harrison in the Music Department, for the supportive framework they provided for my research at Yale. Most of my writing was completed through the long winter of 2010–11, which I spent virtually snowbound in a small house on Prospect Hill, New Haven. The ISM fellows' colloquia and the weekly graduate seminar I taught in the Yale Music Department were lifelines, ensuring ongoing dialogue. I thank Angharad Davis, Micah Hendler, Erin Johnson-Hill, Devin Race, Carmel Raz, and Kamala Schelling for acting as willing soundboards and for their honest reactions. Individually, my Cambridge students Emma Ainsley, Stephen Millar, Angela Moran, Salvatore Morra, and Merav Rosenfeld-Hadad gave me valuable feedback.

The primary work for this edition was carried out by Robert Lachmann, his technician Walter Schur, and the musicians, cantors, and other specialists with whom he collaborated in Jerusalem. The broadcasts themselves were one-off events; only the musical performances were recorded for posterity. Delivered within time slots of typically twenty-five minutes, including the live musical performances, Lachmann's lectures for the most part summarize information and ideas he presents more extensively elsewhere. The concept of this edition—to present the lectures with their musical illustrations in the context of Lachmann's archive project as a whole—depended for its realization on the imaginative conception of the Recent Researches in the Oral Traditions of Music series and the flexibility of its format. I am grateful to Philip Bohlman as series editor and to the managing editors of A-R Editions for giving me this opportunity, and to the entire staff of A-R Editions for their patience and support.

Among the friends and family who have traveled with me through key stages of this project providing crucial encouragement, advice, and support, my first thanks are to my grandmother, Helene Begleiter, to whose memory I dedicate this book, and my parents, Rita and Harry Davis. I thank Deberah Davis-Klug, Betty Balcombe, Michele Esterman, Jill Furmanovsky, Cheryl Frances-Hoad, Aaron and Liebe Klug, Little Mouse, Ateş Orga, and Frank Perry. Most of all, I thank my daughter, Francesca D'Arcy-Orga, who has grown up in the shadow of this project and has been affected by it in ways only she can tell.

Notes

1. This work, translated from German into English under Lachmann's supervision, was published posthumously with incomplete musical transcriptions (Lachmann died in 1939). An edition of Lachmann's original German manuscript was published in 1978 by Edith Gerson-Kiwi (Lachmann 1978).

2. Gerson-Kiwi does not give a precise date for this work, stating only that "the cataloging of the [Lachmann] archive was one of the first projects of the Hebrew University's Jewish Music Research Centre," which was established at the same time as the National Sound Archive in 1964 (Gerson-Kiwi 1974, 103). She gives a summary of the catalogue on pp. 103–8.

3. Ruth Katz erroneously gives the date of "late eighties" for the copying of the cylinders (she makes no mention of the metal discs, the medium Lachmann used in Palestine), claiming that the copying only occurred after "much and prolonged effort" by Israel Adler (Katz 2003, 237). However, as Professor Adler indicates in a letter of 28 April 1992 to Peter Lachmann, with copy to me, the project was still no more than a possibility in the early 1990s:

> We have made some progress concerning the possibility of making transfers of the original wax cylinders and metal discs of the Robert Lachmann Collection. . . . Apart from British contacts . . . we have also been successful in forming ties with the Paris Phonothèque nationale and the Vienna Phonogramme Archive. . . . We are currently looking into possibilities of cooperating with Vienna. . . . Apparently we will have to bring one of their experts to Jerusalem and/or send our audio technician to Vienna.

From then on, however, the project quickly began to take shape. In a letter to Lady Engle of 2 May 1993, enclosed in her letter to me of 20 May, Israel Adler updated her on the latest developments:

> I am happy to report that thanks to the efforts of the Austrian Friends of the Hebrew University . . . and the cooperative spirit of the Vienna Phonogramm Archiv [*sic*]. . . . the project is well under way. Mr Franz Lechleitner of the Vienna Sound Archives paid a working visit for ten days last summer and examined the collection and electronic facilities in Jerusalem. He devised a detailed program for acquiring the necessary equipment and carrying out the work, establishing a total budget of approximately $50,000. A substantial part of this sum has already been raised by the Austrian Friends of the Hebrew University. The next step will find our own Sound Engineer, Mr Avi Nahmias, visiting Vienna this summer for two weeks in order to receive the special training necessary for carrying out the project, and for personally bringing to Jerusalem the auxiliary equipment essential to the work.

And in a letter of 12 April 1994 to Lady Engle, with copy to me, Edwin Seroussi wrote:

> Let me inform you that we have completed the transfer of all the wax cylinders from the Lachmann collection with the cooperation of the National Sound Archives in Vienna. The next step will be to transfer the metal discs and to catalogue the entire sound collection. For this purpose we will have recourse to the Lachmann Fund.

It subsequently transpired, however, that the metal discs needed to undergo specialist cleaning prior to copying—a process that was still underway on my visit to the JMRC in September 1995 (see below). Finally, on 17 November 1996, Israel Adler wrote to me confirming that he had authorized payment from the Lachmann family grant for copying the recordings relevant to my project.

4. Peter Lachmann's family moved to London in December 1938 to escape Nazi persecution.

5. At this point the Israel National Library did not possess the scripts for the twelve *Oriental Music* radio programs. Peter Lachmann subsequently provided the library with copies that, however, turned out to be incomplete. Ruth Katz has reproduced the incomplete texts, unedited, as an appendix to her study of Lachmann's career at Hebrew University (Katz 2003, 328–78), and she provides an accompanying compact disc with extracts of the live recordings (she does not include the commercial recordings from programs 10 and 11). In a note to the list of recordings, Katz acknowledges "Mr. Avi Nahmias—head of the sound laboratory of The National Sound Archive—for helping me locate the original examples in 'The Lachmann Collection' " (Katz 2003, 416 n. 1). Apart from the Yemenite women's songs in program 8, which are taken from a different session, Katz's list of recordings is identical to the list I prepared with Avi Nahmias in 2000; thus, far from being the "original examples," the majority are in fact substitute recordings made on different occasions, and some (e.g. Example 4, D382, and Example 13, D529) are different items of repertory. However, Katz's compact disc is extremely useful in that it provides examples corresponding to all the musical items performed live in lectures 2–9 and 12. Where sections of recordings were irrecoverable because of damage to the disc, the engineer has simply removed these.

Introduction

> In no other country, perhaps, the need for a sound understanding of [its music] and the opportunity of studying it answer each other so well as they do in Palestine. For the European, here, it is of vital interest to know the mind of his Oriental neighbour; well, music and singing, as being the most spontaneous outcome of it, will be his surest guide provided he listens to it with sympathy instead of disdain.
>
> —Robert Lachmann, *Oriental Music,* program 1

Thus Robert Lachmann introduced his series of twelve radio programs, entitled *Oriental Music,* transmitted by the Palestine Broadcasting Service between November 1936 and April 1937. Featuring live studio performances by musicians and singers of different ethnic and religious groups living in and around Jerusalem, which were simultaneously recorded onto metal disc, Lachmann's programs provide a unique focus on the highly diversified complexion of Palestinian society at the time, including, in some cases, the earliest documentation of its music. In two programs based on commercial records (10 and 11), he expands the musical and intellectual scope of the series to include urban traditions from North Africa and the wider Middle East. His stated aim was to introduce his European listeners to "some outstanding kinds of [traditional music] and to mention, in every case, a few points that need to be understood." Yet underlying his didactic purpose was a broader ideological vision: insisting that musical understanding could provide a vital key to human understanding, Lachmann believed that his work could contribute to better relations between Europeans and their "Oriental neighbours," and, crucially, between Jews and Arabs.

This edition presents the texts of Lachmann's twelve radio lectures, newly edited from the original scripts,[1] in conjunction with musical transcriptions of selected performances, transcriptions, and translations of the sung texts, and selected digitally restored musical recordings (provided on the accompanying audio CDs). In the editorial notes and in the commentaries to programs 2–9 and 12 I reflect on key topics presented in the lectures in relation to Lachmann's wider scholarship and his musical and scholarly environment. Written concurrently with his fieldwork in Palestine through the winter of 1936–37, the *Oriental Music* broadcasts are among Lachmann's last writings, and they are the only substantial body of his work to refer significantly to the extraordinary music-ethnographic project that occupied the last three years of his productive life. Yet the programs are not solely, or even primarily, an introduction to specific musical traditions of Palestine and the Middle East. The musical content provides a backdrop for an exposition and synthesis, in a relatively succinct and accessible format, of fundamental ideas about the nature and evolution of music in relation to its social and cultural environment—in short, an entire musical worldview, as developed by Lachmann over the course of his scholarly career.

Lachmann's radio programs were conceived as part of a project aimed at creating an archive of Oriental music in the newly established Hebrew University of Jerusalem. In September 1933 Lachmann was dismissed from the post of music librarian at the Prussian State Library (which he had held since 1927) because he was Jewish. By the following February, he had entered into correspondence with Judah L. Magnes, chancellor of the Hebrew University of Jerusalem, with a view to establishing a "musical section" there. It is unclear exactly how, or on whose initiative, the idea for the archive came about; however, in a letter to Magnes dated 4 February 1934, Johannes Wolf, director of music at the Berlin Staatsbibliothek, reveals that Magnes was actively seeking to appoint a comparative musicologist at the time and recommends Lachmann, "one of our most brilliant comparative musicologists," for the prospective post (Katz 2003, 65). Replying to Wolf, Magnes mentioned that there existed in America "a committee of well-known musicians, including Lazare Saminsky, Ernest Bloch, Ossip Gabrilowitsch, Arnold Schoenberg, Joseph Achron, and Joseph Yasser, who [were] interesting themselves in the development of music at the Hebrew University" (quoted in Katz 2003, 66). On 21 February Magnes wrote to the Russian émigré composer Lazare Saminsky, then living in New York, indicating that he considered Lachmann, with his special expertise in "music of the Orient," a more desirable prospect than his more established senior colleague Curt Sachs.[2]

Born in Berlin in 1892, the second of three brothers, Lachmann was raised in a cultivated, assimilated Jewish family. His father, Dr. Georg Lachmann, was a teacher in a humanistic gymnasium; his mother, née Jennie Händler, was English by birth and had attended the prestigious Queen's College in London.[3] A keen violinist, Lachmann studied modern languages (English, French, and German) at the University of Berlin. His first sustained encounter with non-European music came during World War I, when he served as an interpreter to North

African and Indian prisoners of war at Wünsdorf (Brandenburg). His doctoral dissertation for the University of Berlin focused on the music of the Tunisian prisoners (Lachmann 1923).

As a comparative musicologist, Lachmann was knowledgeable in a wide range of European and non-European traditions. His publications include articles on Haydn and Schubert manuscripts in the State Library, and his classic monograph *Musik des Orients* (1929) explores music cultures from North Africa to the Far East. In 1930 he cofounded the Gesellschaft zur Erforschung der Musik des Orients (Society for Oriental Music Research), subsequently renamed the Gesellschaft für Vergleichende Musikwissenschaft (Society for Comparative Musicology), with his Berlin colleagues Erich M. von Hornbostel and Johannes Wolf. Lachmann was the sole founding editor of the society's journal, *Zeitschrift für vergleichende Musikwissenschaft* (Journal of Comparative Musicology)—the first international journal in ethnomusicology. The journal ran to three volumes (1933, 1934, and 1935) before the dissolution of both the society and its journal at the end of 1935.

Yet Lachmann was primarily a scholar of Arab music. Fluent in spoken and written Arabic, he carried out extensive fieldwork across North Africa through the 1920s and early 1930s, equipped with an Edison phonograph. In 1931 he collaborated with his former doctoral student, the Egyptian musicologist Mahmoud el-Hefni, in translating and editing the ninth-century treatise *Risāla fī Khubr tā'līf al-alhān* (On the Composition of Melodies) by Abū Yūsuf Ya'qūb al-Kindī (ca. 801–ca. 866). The following year, Lachmann was elected chair of the Committee on Musical Recordings at the 1932 Congress of Arab Music held in Cairo; his fellow committee members included Béla Bartók, Erich von Hornbostel, and the specialist in Moroccan music Alexis Chottin.

In April 1935 Lachmann arrived in Jerusalem accompanied by his recording technician, Walter Schur. He brought with him his state-of-the-art recording equipment; his personal library of books, periodicals, and commercial records; copies of his own collection of some five hundred wax cylinder recordings; and copies of some fifty cylinder recordings made by Abraham Z. Idelsohn in Jerusalem in 1913.[4] Over the following three years, Lachmann made 956 metal disc recordings documenting the oral musical traditions of the different non-European communities of Palestine. His work was supported by a private donation from Mrs. Leonie Guinzburg of New York, supplemented by his personal funds.[5] Yet no more than about half of each year was spent in Palestine itself. Claiming that his income was insufficient to support his work there continuously, Lachmann established an annual pattern of spending the winter months in Jerusalem and the summer in Europe (Berlin and London), where he was initially supported by a pension from his former employment in Berlin. His original one-year appointment as *ḥaver meḥkar* (research associate) in the School of Oriental Studies at the Hebrew University was extended on his arrival for a further two years, but in May 1938, despite Magnes's vigorous attempts to secure Lachmann a permanent position, the university agreed to support his work for only three more years, without further commitment.

Lachmann's professional correspondence and diaries from his Palestine years describe an unrelenting stream of obstacles relating to inadequate and insecure finances and lack of institutional support. As the fledgling university struggled to absorb even a fraction of the Jewish scholars seeking refuge from Nazi Europe, Lachmann's persistent requests for recording materials, equipment accessories, specialist accommodation, and payments for musicians fell on deaf ears. His insistence on recording all the religious groups, without prioritizing any one of them, drew criticisms from both Muslim and Jewish quarters and alienated potential sponsors interested only in the Jewish element. With World War II on the horizon, pressures of Jewish immigration from Nazi Europe fuelling Jewish nationalist aspirations and Arabs staging a general strike and revolt, the times were hardly auspicious for convincing potential sponsors, whether in Palestine or abroad, of the value and urgency of his unique and eclectic project. Chronic vascular disease led to Lachmann's hospitalization in September 1938 and eventually to his death in May 1939, at age forty-six.

Lachmann, Magnes, and the Hebrew University of Jerusalem

> The immigrant who went to America was, for the most part, of lower social station. Went, for the most part, to better his economic position and usually rose in the economic social (intellectual) scale. The immigrant to Palestine, in large part, of high social position. Usually a more or less important man in his community. . . . Coming to Palestine, he finds other of his kind gathered in one community, and his is not of as much importance as at home. . . . Life is strange, difficult. Often a lowering in the social and economic scale.
>
> —Judah L. Magnes[6]

> Palestine—a *hard* country full of stone and rock, irrigation and dry farming, extremes of altitude and depth. People hard, struggling each one for his living. Whatever idealistic impulses may have brought them here, they are immersed in the daily struggle to maintain themselves, their work, or their organization. Not much mercy. People permitted to go their own way. . . . A small country, Jerusalem a small city. Yet one organization distinct from another with little coordination and cooperation. . . . Blinkers, blinders. Feverish, one-tracked as though this were indeed the "centre of the universe" and salvation depended upon this piece of work at this time. But little perspective. . . . Rain and mud and rocks in winter. Sun and heat and malaria in summer. Letters "by hand." . . . Water troubles generally: washing, drinking (boiling), gardens, courtyard, leaks, drains, barrels. . . .
>
> —Judah L. Magnes[7]

In *"The Lachmann Problem": An Unsung Chapter in Comparative Musicology*, Ruth Katz describes Lachmann's career in Palestine in quasi-dramatic terms. Structuring her study in dramatic form—a two-part prologue and a two-part epilogue framing a docudrama in three acts—she portrays him as "a heroic anti-hero" (Katz 2003, 274). In a concluding section subtitled "Tragedy, Religious

Drama, or History in the Making?," she reaffirms her opening position that " 'The Lachmann Case' . . . may be read as a personal tragedy, or as the pangs of the uprooted, or even as religious drama" (Katz 2003, 15):

> Fortified by new insights into the group whose fate he shared, Lachmann hurled himself towards a *"Liebestod"*—towards transmutation into a new spirituality with self-destruction as its highest rapture. The newly "converted," thus, departed from this world in true Germanic fashion. Even Wagner might have been proud of him. Most of us ordinary human beings only sense the aura emanating from Lachmann's departure. The atmosphere surrounding his death has a quasi religious [*sic*] character; it is permeated by Lachmann's devotion to what he firmly believed and unreservedly trusted. . . . In retrospect, Lachmann's behavior, during the toughest years of his life, reminds us of those who are generally portrayed as impregnated and guided by something greater than themselves, such as religious heroes, saints or true prophets (Katz 2003, 277).

Yet, as Katz acknowledges, Lachmann's case was hardly unique. Introducing his story, she concedes that, "having chosen to go to Palestine, Lachmann's predicament there adds a chapter to the predicament of many professionals who were betrayed by their native cultures but failed to be absorbed adequately by the culture to which they turned" (Katz 2003, 15).[8]

At a time when music was represented only sporadically in the established universities of Europe and in North America, the very fact that the fledgling Hebrew University, cash-strapped and struggling for survival in a climate of social, political, and economic turmoil, in a land moreover where disease was rife and basic material resources scarce, should even consider supporting an archive of Oriental music was surely in itself remarkable. That it should do so precisely at the moment when the entire community of Jewish scholars in Nazi Germany suddenly found themselves without jobs, and when the university found itself under increasing pressure but with insufficient means to absorb even a fraction of these and other Jewish scholars seeking refuge from fascist Europe, was all the more so. If, as Katz suggests, the university's reluctance to commit itself fully to Lachmann's project should be read as a personal tragedy, then the very fact that it was willing to support it at all must surely be recognized as an extraordinarily bold leap of faith, testifying to the ideological integrity, vision, and imagination of its founding chancellor, Judah L. Magnes.

A Californian-born Reform rabbi, Magnes was appointed the first chancellor of the Hebrew University in November 1925. He had been awakened to Zionism at the turn of the century while studying for his doctorate in Berlin and Heidelberg. Among the various competing strands of Zionist ideology he was attracted, in particular, to the teachings of Aḥad Ha'am (Hebrew, lit. "one of the people"), pen name of Asher Zvi Ginzberg, the Ukrainian Jewish philosopher and ideologue of cultural Zionism. A secular Jew steeped in orthodox Hasidic culture, Aḥad Ha'am sought to translate the ethical values of Judaism as embodied in the Torah and above all in the prophetic writings into the terms of a modern, secular Jewish society. For Aḥad Ha'am and his fellow cultural Zionists, the message of the Hebrew prophets constituted the ultimate expression of the Jewish spirit, and the perceived spiritual alienation, disintegration, and decay brought about by emancipation were even greater threats to modern diasporic Judaism than were the age-old problems of anti-Semitism and persecution. In their utopian vision, spiritual renewal through the creation of a just society based on Jewish cultural and ethical values was the primary goal of Zionism and a prerequisite for political emancipation: only thus Israel would become "a Light unto the nations" as prophesied by Isaiah (42:6, 49:6).

In 1906 Magnes was appointed associate rabbi at Temple Emanu-El in New York, the principal temple of Reform Judaism, where he established a reputation as an inspired orator and a charismatic and principled, if sometimes controversial, community leader. With America's entry into World War I, however, Magnes's pacifist stance and vigorous antiwar activities isolated him from the majority of the Jewish community. At the end of 1922 he immigrated to Palestine with his family and dedicated himself to the cause of the Hebrew University.

For Magnes and his cofounders, this was to be no ordinary university distinguished only by its use of the Hebrew language. Rather, the Hebrew University would embody the highest ethical values of Judaism, providing the spiritual foundations for Magnes's Zionist project. Reacting to the news of the laying of the university's foundation stone on Mount Scopus in July 1918 to the sound of Ottoman and British gunfire, Magnes's mentor Aḥad Ha'am wrote from London:

> We do not know what the future has in store for us, but this we do know: that the brighter the prospects for the reestablishment of our National home in Palestine, the more urgent is the need for laying the spiritual foundations of that home on a corresponding scale which can only be conceived in the form of a Hebrew University [that] will endeavor to become the true embodiment of the Hebrew spirit of old and to shake off the mental and moral servitude to which our people has been so long subjected in the Diaspora. Only so can we be justified in our ambitious hopes to the future universal influence of the "Teaching" that "will go forth out of Zion."[9]

With the collapse of the Ottoman Empire after World War I, Great Britain was assigned the mandate for Palestine.[10] The terms of the mandate, as laid down by the League of Nations, incorporated the declaration made in 1917 by the British foreign secretary, Arthur James Balfour, that

> His Majesty's Government viewed with favour the establishment in Palestine of a national home for the Jewish people . . . it being clearly understood that nothing shall be done which may prejudice the civil and religious rights of existing non-Jewish communities.

As Jewish immigration increased through the 1920s, Arab nationalists mounted acts of violent resistance. For Magnes and his fellow cultural Zionists, their reaction to the Arab demands and, more fundamentally, their approach to Jewish-Arab relations touched at the heart of their Jewish consciousness. In a letter of 6 February 1930 to the American Reform rabbi and Zionist leader Stephen S. Wise, Magnes declared:

> For me this is not so much the Arab question as it is the Jewish question. What is the nature and essence of Jewish nationalism? Is it like the nationalism of all the nations? The answer is given by our attitude towards the Arabs, so that the Arab question is not only of the utmost practical importance; it is also the touchstone and test of our Judaism (quoted in Goren 1982, 286).

So uncompromising was Magnes in this belief that it ultimately took precedence over his commitment to the Zionist project itself. In a letter of 7 September 1929 to Chaim Weizmann, president of the World Zionist Organization, in the wake of the Arab riots at the end of August, he spelled out the practical implications of his pacifist stance:

> The question is, do we want to conquer Palestine now as Joshua did in his day—with fire and sword? Or do we want to take cognizance of Jewish religious development since Joshua—our Prophets, Psalmists and Rabbis, and repeat the words: "Not by might, and not by violence, but by my spirit, saith the Lord"? The question is, can any country be entered, colonized, and built up pacifistically, and can we Jews do that in the Holy Land? . . . If we can not even attempt this, I should much rather see this eternal people without such a "National Home," with the wanderer's staff in hand and forming new ghettos among the peoples of the world (quoted in Goren 1982, 277).

Magnes's approach to the Arab question was reflected in microcosm in his vision for the Hebrew University.[11] In Europe, the committee concerned with establishing the university was dominated by scholars, notably Albert Einstein and Chaim Weizmann, who conceived the prospective institution after the model of a European research university. From his vantage point in Palestine, however, Magnes believed that the mission of the Hebrew University was first and foremost to instill Jewish consciousness into the Yishuv (the Jewish settlement there) and serve its needs. With Magnes's unique capacities to mobilize and win the support of wealthy American Jewish philanthropists, many of them former members of his New York community, it was his vision that prevailed. In 1923, he secured an endowment of $500,000 from the American Jewish banker and philanthropist Felix Warburg for the founding of the Institute for Jewish Studies, the Hebrew University's first institute. Immediately thereafter, convinced that Arab culture should be represented equally, Magnes sought support for a complementary institute in of Arab and Oriental studies. As a result, the School of Oriental Studies was established in 1925, the university's inaugural year (Bentwich 1961, 21–22, 28; Kotzin 2000, 7). It was against this institutional and ideological backdrop that a decade later, his convictions reinforced by the turbulence of the intervening years, Magnes invited Robert Lachmann, as a specialist in Arab and Jewish music, to establish a Department of Oriental Music.

For Magnes, the ideology of cultural Zionism translated logically into the politics of binationalism, according to which the whole of Palestine would belong equally to Jews and Arabs. In common with other leading Zionist personalities such as Aḥad Ha'am, the philosopher Martin Buber, and Henrietta Szold, founding president of Hadassah (the women's Zionist organization), but in opposition to the Zionist majority, Magnes opposed the Mandatory plans for dividing Palestine; even more controversially, in the interests of democracy, he at first favored conceding to Arab demands to restrict Jewish immigration.[12] However, as pressure to facilitate Jewish immigration from Europe mounted through the 1930s, and in the absence of reciprocal support on the part of any Arab leadership, the case of the cultural Zionists seemed to many both hopeless and morally unsustainable. In fall 1935, in the face of mounting criticism from the university's board of governors, his fundraising efforts thwarted by the global economic depression, Magnes resigned his position as chancellor and accepted instead the honorary position of president. From then on, his ability to influence Lachmann's university career was radically diminished; having succeeded in launching Lachmann's project, Magnes was no longer in a position to steer it through.

The "Oriental Music Archive" and Outreach Projects

Lachmann originally conceived his "Section for Non-European Music"[13] as a regular university music department, distinguished only by a special emphasis on local music. Outlining his concept in a letter of 6 March 1934 to Magnes,[14] he explained that his department would offer a broad training in "general musicology" comparable to "the usual training as provided at Western universities":

> Students would have to be taught the elements of musical acoustics, psychology, and aesthetics as well as the outlines of musical history in Europe from antiquity down to the present day. As to the past, it would be desirable that they should gain a good general knowledge not only of the music itself, but also of musical theory in its different stages and of the various ways of musical notation, the latter being essential for an independent study of musical document in the Middle Ages and later (instrumental tablatures). As to modern music from the 18th century onward, the university training should be in close touch with a training in musical practice as provided by conservatories like the one existing already at Jerusalem (quoted in Katz 2003, 73).

Given its particular location, however, his department would focus primarily on research and training in "non-European, and especially Jewish music":

> In fact, this part may be expected to find special attention and care at a musical section of the Hebrew University which, owing to the history and geographical situation of Jerusalem, might well develop into a centre of research in Eastern music (quoted in Katz 2003, 74).

And while such research would naturally include the study of literary sources, such as "medieval Hebrew and

Arabic treatises" on music, he considered such philological activity to be

> of minor importance as compared to the *study of musical practice*. While books and manuscripts can be read, in reproductions, throughout the world, Eastern musical practice has to be studied in its natural surroundings and as forming part of the life of the respective people. And while books and manuscripts can be preserved in libraries for an indefinite time, the unwritten music of the East, being the most volatile of utterances, is endangered by the rapid spread of Western civilisation (ibid.; emphasis in original).

For these reasons, the main concern of his institute would be

> to study the music still extant, and to collect as many specimens as possible of every class of it, both vocal and instrumental. The most reliable method is that of recording them by means of the phonograph (and if possible, the sound picture) (ibid.).

On receipt of Lachmann's letter, Magnes initiated an intensive correspondence with potentially interested parties in Jerusalem and the United States with the aim of both creating and funding a position for Lachmann (Katz 2003, 81–87). Meanwhile, in a letter of 27 March,[15] he urged Lachmann to make every effort to reduce his budget, since "the University has at the present time no funds that it could use in order to bring and maintain you here" and "we have not any guarantee of securing funds at the present time" (quoted in Katz 2003, 86–87). Responding to Magnes on 7 April,[16] Lachmann proposed to reduce the resources for "general musicology" and instead "direct his first efforts towards field and laboratory work." He offered to donate his own recording equipment to the university and to make his personal library available for general use. However, with regard to Magnes's question whether his technician, Walter Schur, was "an absolute necessity at this time," Lachmann was adamant:

> Collaboration with an all-round technician would ultimately save expenses instead of increasing them. The person I have in view would enable me to concentrate upon my study undisturbed by technicalities. He would not only carry out the different technical processes connected with the records (which otherwise would have to be done in Berlin) but also all the manipulations and frequent repairs occurring in the field and the laboratory: in fact, there would be no need to employ another workman in cases of emergency. Besides, he is trained to do photographic work, which, I think, might be a successful and appreciable side-issue and perhaps, become a source of income for the institute, pictures of musical practice being extremely rare (quoted in Katz 2003, 88).

And, preempting another possible cause for concern, he continued:

> Permit me to add a personal remark. While a difficulty might be seen in the fact the person referred to is not a Jew, I can warrant his perfect loyalty which, as you can easily imagine, has been tried on more than one occasion in the recent past (ibid.).

As it turned out, Schur's contribution to Lachmann's work proved indispensable. Among his inventions was a special pickup for copying from cylinder to disc and from disc to disc. As Lachmann explains in his report for the years 1935–36:

> After recording, each disc is at once played back, which is impossible with the recording methods of the phonograph factories. In this manner it can be verified if, technically, the recording was successful. At the same time, the musicians are offered the opportunity to hear the reproduction of their voices or their playing. Experience has shown that this encourages even the least cooperative to improve their efforts.
>
> Having been replayed, the originals are then only used to prepare copies. It is these copies that serve for demonstration and, primarily, for the scientific work (quoted in Katz 2003, 142).[17]

Lachmann describes the pickup process in more detail in a letter to Norman Bentwich, former attorney general of Palestine and honorary vice-president of the London-based Friends of the Hebrew University:

> The originals are never used except for making copies. This is done by means of a "pick-up" and as, on these occasions, the originals are played with fibres, their quality in this process is not impaired to any appreciable degree.[18]

Another of Schur's indispensable inventions was a battery-operated portable recording machine. In a document of 8 January 1936 outlining the budget for a "Recording Laboratory" and a "Music Library,"[19] Lachmann explains:

> The laboratory contains two machines for recording on discs, one of them to be used in the studio, and the other, which is independent of public electricity, for recording at any place, even in the desert. The second machine was specially constructed by Mr. Walter Schur, who is in charge of the laboratory and who has also constructed a highly sensitive microphone and a pick up [*sic*] for playing over records in cylinder form (Edison type) to discs (quoted in Katz 2003, 148).

And, in a report on the archive dated April 1937,[20] Lachmann states that, to his knowledge, "this is the only, and at any rate the first, Institute to use electric recording of discs in the field" (quoted in Katz 2003, 185).

Schur's role even extended to operating the recording and playback equipment. In his July 1937 letter to Norman Bentwich, Lachmann stresses the importance of the correct handling of the records in order to realize their optimum sound quality:

> The playing of these records requires some experience, and that I prefer not to have them handled by outsiders; as a matter of fact, not being a technician, I cannot promise to handle them adequately myself; I generally leave this to my technician. Above all, before playing them, an ordinary gramophone has to undergo certain adjustments. For demonstration, it is preferable to play the discs through a loud-speaker. This is always done at my Archive.[21]

Lachmann outlined his program for the archive in numerous reports for the Hebrew University in his wider correspondence with Magnes. Essentially, his work embraced the oral musical traditions of all ethnic and religious groups in Palestine; it was multidisciplinary, including music-historical, sociological, ethnological, and philological perspectives; its scope was boundless, potentially extending beyond Palestine to the neighboring Middle East; and, above all, it was urgent. This last consideration recurs like a mantra throughout his Palestine writings, fueling his repeated requests for additional funding and his insistence on prioritizing collecting above all other activities. In his annual report for 1935–36, Lachmann identifies his archive's "most urgent task" as "the collecting of the corpus of melodies threatened in their existence, and to ready them for scientific processing" (quoted in Katz 2003, 140). Following a step-by-step description of his method, from the preparatory work to the documentation and "scientific processing" of the results, he concludes:

> It should however, be borne in mind that, given the rapidly progressing decay of local music, collecting activities proper must have precedence over the literary evaluation of the collected items (quoted in Katz 2003, 142).

Yet it was this very sense of urgency—fuelled by financial necessity and the insecurity of his position—that drove Lachmann to seek opportunities for promoting his work more widely. In a letter to Magnes dated 7 July 1935,[22] scarcely more than two months after his arrival in Palestine, Lachmann proposed various ways of securing "additional funds by interesting a larger public in the work of the section, without for a moment straying from the lines as proposed in the original programme" (quoted in Katz 2003, 118). One suggestion was to give occasional public lectures with musical illustrations "perhaps three times a year, before a general audience on observations made in the course of the work" (quoted in Katz 2003, 119). Another, following the example of Egypt, where the government had instituted music teaching in schools along the lines recommended by the 1932 Congress of Arab Music, was to advise the Mandatory authorities on a comparable program in Palestine.[23] Finally, Lachmann proposed "to take an active influence on the programme of the future broadcasting station in as far as it is concerned with non-European music" (ibid.).

Plans to establish a national public broadcasting service had been underway since December 1933, when a special broadcasting committee, set up by the Mandatory government, delivered its recommendations for a service modeled closely on the BBC. Programs would aim to improve as well as entertain, and topics of a contentious nature—particularly political and religious—would be eschewed. The committee was particularly concerned that the radio should help to raise spirits: "Much could be done to widen interests and to add to the gaiety of life, in order to counteract a morbid outlook which appears to be endemic in the Near East" (quoted in Stanton 2012; see also Stanton, forthcoming). On 7 July 1935—the day Lachmann wrote to Magnes—an official government communiqué appeared on the front page of the *Palestine Post,* the country's main English-language newspaper, announcing the plans for the new station. A new transmitter in Ramallah would be connected by special landlines to the station in Jerusalem, which would initially be based in the former Palace Hotel near the city center. There would be five hours of broadcasting each evening, with special hours allotted for each of the official languages: English, Arabic, and Hebrew. Programs would be arranged by the "Programme Director," who would be guided by the recommendations of an independent "Programmes Advisory Committee" appointed by the High Commissioner. The communiqué added, "Criticisms and suggestions from listeners will of course be welcome."[24]

Magnes was clearly aware of the potential significance of these developments for Lachmann's project. On 1 June, at Magnes's request, Lachmann supplied him with a document entitled "Remarks on Broadcasting Music from the Jerusalem Station," in which he outlined his vision for the prospective station in relation to local music. Essentially, he envisaged that the new service would have an educational function, and that its programs would aim not only to please, but also to guide the tastes of listeners. Indeed, for Lachmann, the two goals were inseparable:

> The more the audience, and especially the younger generation, become aware of what pure and unspoiled tradition is, the more there is hope that they will become impatient with the mixtures and sham productions which crowd the market. In fact, the stronger appeal of the real thing is unmistakable whenever genuine music is recited in concerts side by side with imitations of it (Lachmann 1935a).

Much of the essay is devoted to identifying particular types of "pure and unspoiled tradition" that in his view deserved special attention. In the case of Arab and Jewish folk music, for example, he insists that

> the interest attached to these is not purely aesthetical. . . . If it is worthwhile becoming acquainted with the character and emotions of the Bedouins, the shortest way to them is to listen to their song which is their most typical and spontaneous expression, and reveals a beauty of its own to anybody who cares to attend to it (ibid.).

As for the broadcasting of "Oriental" Jewish folk music—the music of the Jewish communities of the Middle East—Lachmann argues that

> its appearance in the programme . . . may resolve, or at least help to resolve the question, often discussed nowadays, as to what is typically Jewish in music. Moreover, it may provide a basis for new attempts at Jewish folk-music (ibid.).

He even advocates broadcasting "occasional recitals of sacred music" because:

> At a period of experiments in musical liturgy like the present, these traditions must be held up against attempts at trespassing into the region of secular music. Hearing of the unshaken traditional music of the various Oriental Synagogues and Churches might keep alive, or revive, public consciousness as to the true aim of sacred music which is not prettiness, but concentration of mind (ibid.).

But the main thrust of Lachmann's document is devoted to denouncing the "mixtures and sham productions that crowd the market," which he insists that radio broadcasting should avoid. Listing as examples "taking an Oriental tune and adding patches of European harmony to it" and "executing Oriental music on European instruments," particularly the piano and the violin, Lachmann effectively disqualifies from the radio much of the commercially popular Arab music of the day (ibid.). Yet he was not against hybridization per se. Recognizing that Palestine's unique sociopolitical situation might legitimately give rise to new musical expressions, he opens his essay on a cautionary note:

> There are valuable and there may be hopeful productions using Western as well as Eastern elements, and one must take care not to stop these along with the worthless ones. . . . Young Jewish or Arab composers may find, one day, a new way of expressing themselves, however imperfectly or clumsily, in a musical language somewhere, possibly, between the Western and the Eastern tradition. It is difficult to foresee the directions which future creative forces may take and it is, therefore, advisable to examine every individual case, instead of barring the way to new possibilities by rash generalisations (ibid.).

Indeed, Lachmann was soon to discover and actively promote examples of just such a new musical language in the experimental compositions of the Iraqi-Jewish *'ūd* player Ezra Aharon (see program 9).

The Palestine Broadcasting Service began transmitting from Ramallah on 30 March 1936. While the director and senior administrators were seconded from the BBC in London, subdirectors were appointed from the local population. Thus Karl Salomon, recently arrived from Germany, was appointed music subdirector for the Hebrew and English programs, and the Palestinian singer Yahya Lababidi was appointed subdirector for Arabic music. From the outset, the English and Hebrew programs relied primarily on live performances by a ready supply of Jewish musicians from Europe and only minimally on recorded music (Hirshberg 1995, 141). Lachmann was anxious that the Arabic program adopt a similar policy. In a letter to Magnes of 13 November 1935, Lachmann alerted him to an announcement in the day's *Palestine Post* that "no less than five hundred records of Arabic songs [had] been acquired for the Wireless Programme of local music." Assuming they must be commercial records imported from Egypt or other foreign centers, Lachmann complains:

> Not only are records of this kind heard in Cafes, shops, and private houses through this country; the original musicians themselves who supply these records, are easily accessible by listening to the broadcasting stations of Cairo and of Istanbul, and are heard, as a matter of fact, by large masses of the population. I have witnessed concerts of this kind at Nablus, at Haifa, and at the Damascus Gate, Jerusalem, where they are transmitted in Arab Cafes by means of loudspeakers. The audience would, of course, much rather hear local music from their favourites, who are known to them personally, than the urban music of Egypt etc. on which they are being fed to weariness. As to the singers and players, urban, rural and Beduin [*sic*], of this country, among whom there are excellent and inspired performers, they would, I am sure, be deeply disappointed at being invited to hear records from other countries instead of being given a chance of displaying their own abilities. The hope of intensifying musical life in this country by encouraging local singers, and by holding out, to unknown singers, the possibility of being discovered by and for the wireless, would be extinguished (quoted in Katz 2003, 129).

Lachmann's commitment to supporting local talent was reflected in his efforts in bringing local musicians and singers to the attention of the Palestine Broadcasting Service (see, for example, the account by the Nadav brothers in "About the Edition") and in his reliance, as far as possible, on live musical performances to illustrate his own public lectures and broadcasts. Notable among Lachmann's protégés was Ezra Aharon, whose performances so impressed Karl Salomon that he placed Aharon in charge of a special section for Oriental Jewish music (see the editor's commentary to program 9). However, Lachmann's most ambitious attempt to support local live music was his proposal, made in the summer of 1938, to collaborate with the BBC. By that time his pension from Germany had ceased, and the senate of the Hebrew University had rejected Magnes's proposal to create a permanent postion for Lachmann. Responding to this news in an impassioned letter to Magnes dated 14 November 1937,[25] Lachmann made the radical proposal to dissociate his archive from the Hebrew University and share its directorship with an Arab colleague:

> To secure Arab cooperation I should be willing to share the direction of the Archives with an Arab provided that we can be sure of his fully understanding our intentions as regards both research work and cultural contacts (quoted in Katz 2003, 198).

Lachmann was convinced that it was above all the inclusiveness of his approach—and particularly his refusal to focus solely on Jewish music—that underlay the university's reluctance to support his project more fully. Yet it was that very inclusiveness, he assures Magnes, that lay at the heart of the potentially wider contribution his work could make in the strife-ridden, increasingly polarized society of late-1930s Palestine:

> I have been at pains, on many occasions, to explain that the investigation of traditional Jewish music cannot be carried out satisfactorily unless neighbouring subjects, the music of the Oriental Christian Churches as well as Arab music, are studied along with it. I cannot help feeling that, outside, of course, the School of Oriental Studies at the University, this point is not generally accepted and that the reasons why it is not accepted are irreconcilable with a disinterested attitude towards research work like my own, or, as a matter of fact, research of any kind.
>
> My work necessitates free intercourse with all the different ethnical groups in this country and the Near East generally. It may therefore be made to contribute, however modestly, towards aims beyond its immediate scope, towards a better understanding between Jews and Arabs. This contribution could be made or, at least, tried to be made with some hope of success in a neutral atmosphere rather than in my present surroundings. When I consider a change in my relations to the University this point rather than my personal interest would carry most weight in favour of a dissociation (quoted in Katz 2003, 197–98).

It was in search of just such a "neutral atmosphere" that led Lachmann to turn to the BBC as a possible alternative source of patronage. On a visit to London in the summer of 1938, he approached C. A. L. Cliffe, director of overseas programming, with the novel proposal that the BBC delegate the selection of music and musicians—for its overseas programs and for local radio stations throughout the Empire—to specialists such as himself. Such a policy, Lachmann argued, would help promote local musical cultures and would surely be welcomed by musicians and audiences alike. Lachmann's contact with Cliffe was facilitated by the BBC officer R. A. Rendall, the first Director of the Paletsine Broadcasting Service, who had returned to London at the end of 1936. On 5 August 1938 Rendall wrote to Lachmann attaching a copy of his memorandum to Cliffe, in which he summarizes Lachmann's position:[26]

> Dr Lachmann realises that a broadcasting authority which wishes to be in close contact with its audience should not rely on recordings but rather if possible on live performers . . . but since this can, on financial grounds, only be done occasionally, he suggests that recordings such as he and other [experts] might secure would be very much more valuable to the BBC on grounds of programme value and prestige than commercial recordings which deal only with a very limited field of Oriental music, most of them being not truly Oriental at all. . . . There is a necessity, therefore, to find musical experts who can by close collaboration with native musicians enable the broadcasting authorities . . . to suit the taste of the whole of the native audience and not merely of those who have been "educated" to Western ideas. In this way, broadcasts of Oriental music would consist of . . . balanced programmes representing all the different aspects of traditional and present day music, which would encourage musicians of all types.

Cliffe evidently took considerable interest in Lachmann's proposal; he met him several times at Broadcasting House and introduced him to various colleagues there.[27] Eventually, however, Cliffe rejected Lachmann's project on the grounds that it was "outside the scope of the BBC," and he advised Lachmann to approach American research-oriented organizations, such as the Rockefeller or Carnegie Foundations, instead. Commenting on Cliffe's reaction in a letter of 16 August to Ralphe T. Edge, a business associate of his brother Kurt, Lachmann touches on the wider implications of his proposal:

> I believe that in giving this advice Mr. Cliffe underrates the possible effects, on the populations concerned, of a reform of the musical programs. He evidently considers that my proposition is interesting from the point of view of research rather than a political point of view (Hebrew University of Jerusalem, Lachmann Archive [hereafter Lachmann Archive], B. II. 8. [4]).

In fact, Lachmann had already reached out to his North American colleagues for support. In early 1937 Harold Spivacke, head of the music division at the Library of Congress, had mobilized a number of American musicians and scholars, including the composer Joseph Yasser, the ethnomusicologist Helen Roberts, and the musicologists Charles Seeger and Oliver Strunk, to try to arrange a lecture tour for Lachmann. Reacting to the idea with cautious enthusiasm, Lachmann clarified his motives in a letter to Spivacke dated 1 April 1937:

> You can further imagine that anything I shall undertake in the present circumstances will have the sole object of saving the institute. I detest money matters; but I must say quite plainly that if I went to America now I should do so hoping to place my work [in Palestine] on a solid financial basis (Lachmann Archive, B. II. 7. 16a).[28]

And in a letter to Joseph Yasser on 25 May, he explained:

> You can easily see that the preservation of traditional music by means of discs is the all-important task of my institute and that I must do everything in my power to try and keep it going. I can therefore risk an expensive undertaking like a trip to the USA only if I can assure myself of its financial success or, at least, exclude a financial loss beforehand. . . . To express matters as plainly as possible: I can only go to America if the costs of my stay there could be fully covered by fees for lectures and if, possibly, beyond this . . . some hope could be held out towards raising funds for my institute (Lachmann Archive, B. II. 7. 21).

Yet as early as 29 January, in a letter to Joseph Yasser, Helen Roberts had expressed misgivings about the planned arrangements for Lachmann, recalling the difficulties she had encountered in arranging a similar tour the previous year for the Dutch musicologist Arnold Bake. Her letter highlights the marginal status of musicology in American public life at the time:

> About your letter which came yesterday about the prospects of having Dr Lachmann give lectures in this country, I would say that the chances of success for him a very slim. Times are better, it is true, but the interest in musicology is very limited. Dr Bake was here only a year ago last fall and a year ago this winter, and we had the greatest difficulty getting lectures for him.
>
> Personally, I would be glad to help Dr Lachmann, but I am afraid that the best we could do for him, with superhuman efforts, would not compensate him for coming. You know how blasé the large cities, and even the small ones, are about foreign lecturers. You can hardly blame them. The USA has been lectured to death, almost, by foreigners, on every subject under the sun, and is beginning to tire of it. And musicology, while it ought to be interesting to musicians, is not to the majority of them. Of course small groups like the NY chapter of the AMS [American Musicological Society] would turn out in full force, but there, there would be no compensation for him (Lachmann Archive, B. II. 7. 21c).

After an initially positive reaction, Charles Seeger expressed similar misgivings. Writing to Lachmann on 11 May, Harold Spivacke explained:

> Mr [Charles] Seeger is not so optimistic about the possibilities of your giving lectures at the New School for Social Research as he was at first. It seems that the school had great difficulty in assembling audiences for Hornbostel and other German professors so they are loath to continue in this direction without some outside assurance of an audience (Lachmann Archive, B. II. 7. 16a).

Finally, in a letter dated 28 June, Joseph Yasser advised Lachmann that he too, after having consulted various colleagues, had come to the conclusion "that your visit to the USA would hardly be a financial success—much to my regret, I may add—and I do not think it would be worth while to take a risk along these lines" (Lachmann Archive, B. II. 7. 21b). Accordingly, in August 1937, Lachmann informed Spivacke that for financial reasons, the proposed lecture tour "cannot come off, at least not this year" (Lachmann Archive, B. II. 7. 16b).

More promising was the reaction of his American colleagues to his plans to resume editorship of the *Zeitschrift für Musikwissenschaft,* which he had been forced to resign at the end of 1935. Lachmann announced his intentions to relaunch the journal in his first annual report (1935–36), where he envisaged it as a vehicle for disseminating the archive's work (Katz 2003, 141). At first the insecurity of his position deterred him, but in early 1938, with the backing of Magnes, he began to put his plans into action. Clearly, the question of language was an issue with the journal's American readership. In a letter to Lachmann dated 5 February 1937,[29] the ever forthright Helen Roberts had written:

> I can understand your not wishing to continue the Zeitschrift as it is. But I do wish you would consider giving the new journal an English title which would be a virtual translation of the German one, and would take it up where the other left off. . . . I feel quite sure that a number, if not all, of our American society members would be glad to have the substitution of a journal more in English than in German. That has been a stumbling block to many—the German articles (quoted in Katz 2003, 266–67).

And in his letter of 28 June 1937, Yasser confirmed:

> I do not think you would find any difficulties in getting back your American subscribers, and even in increasing their number, particularly if your journal will be published mostly in English (Americans are very poor linguists) (Lachmann Archive, B. II. 7. 21b).

Accordingly, in May 1938, Lachmann sent a draft prospectus for the "Journal of Comparative Musicology" to Magnes, requesting his advice on the arrangements for subscriptions. Ten leading scholars in Oriental music and comparative musicology were listed as members of the editorial committee: Johan Sebastiaan Brandts Buys (Java), Alexis Chottin (Morocco), Henry George Farmer (Scotland), P. R. Kirby (South Africa), Mieczyslaw Kolinski (Czechoslovakia), Jaap Kunst (Holland), Messud Cemil (Turkey), Helen H. Roberts (USA), Curt Sachs (USA), and André Schaeffner (France). Others were said to be under consideration.[30] In August 1938 the Azriel Press of Jerusalem mailed copies of the prospectus to the booksellers Otto Haas (formerly of Berlin) and Harold Reeves in London (Lachmann Archive, B. II. 8. 5). The December 1938 catalogue of Harold Reeves contained the following announcement:

> *Journal of Comparative Musicology.* Edited by R. Lachmann and M. El-Hefny. A magazine devoted to non-European Music, articles in all languages. The yearly total output is estimated to run to 128 pages of text and 32 pages of music, with occasional illustrations, probably in quarterly installments. Annual subscription 12/– [12 shillings].
>
> It is trusted that this journal may fill the gap left by the "Zeitschrift fur Musik Wissenschaft" which closed publication in 1935 (Lachmann Archive, B. II. 8. 11).

Apparently it was only Lachmann's protracted illness and death the following year that prevented the journal from materializing.

Aftermath and Legacy

On 19 September 1938, shortly after his return from London, Lachmann was admitted to the Bikur Holim Hospital in Jerusalem. A certificate issued by the hospital on 19 October states that he was "in a severe state of pseudouremia based on chronic vascular disease." Despite temporary remissions, Lachmann never recovered. He died in the early hours of 9 May 1939 and, according to Jewish custom, was buried the same day. The following day Magnes penned a note to Lachmann's elder brother, Kurt, in London:

> Dear Dr. Lachmann,
> We carried your brother to rest yesterday afternoon. He lies in the new cemetery of the Jewish Community on Mt. of Olives.
>
> Many of his friends & associates had gathered at the Bicur [*sic*] Holim Hospital, and, as is the Jewish custom here, we carried his bier a distance through the streets.
>
> At the grave the traditional prayers were said, and I spoke a few words, also remembering his mother and all his family, far away.
>
> He died at three o'clock yesterday morning. He had not regained consciousness. There was no more strength left. . . . From the medical reports you must have realized that the span of life for which he might hope was not very great. We had wanted to bring him that far along that he might spend his last months with his mother.
>
> Yesterday afternoon the lectures of the school of Oriental Studies at the University were suspended. A notice about him was placed on the bulletin board of the University, and a circular letter sent to all the University workers. On the thirtieth day after his death there will be a memorial meeting to him at the University.
>
> His death was announced by notices in various parts of the city, as is the custom here. A few words were said about him in the radio broadcast. There will be a longer appreciation of him at another time.
>
> This morning we are to meet at the School of Oriental Studies to discuss the state of his work. It seems to be in a condition that will allow of its publication.
>
> Some recent letters that have come for him are being sent to you. I shall write to you again about some of his things.
>
> He had many admirers because of his exceptional mind and his fine spirit. He suffered much. Alas for all of the knowledge and nobility that have gone.
>
> We think of the grief of his mother. May God comfort her.
> Sincerely yours J. L. Magnes

The Lachmann Archive is silent on the fate of Lachmann's technician, Walter Schur. As a German national in British-occupied Palestine on the eve of World War II, his position was vulnerable. In a diary entry of June 1988, Peter Lachmann recounts a conversation with the Israeli musicologist Edith Gerson-Kiwi, Lachmann's former research assistant, at her home in in Jerusalem, in which she told him what she knew. Apparently Schur was arrested by the British as a suspected spy (whether for the Arabs or the Germans Gerson-Kiwi could not say) and imprisoned in the fortress at Acre, from which he escaped twice, dressed in Arab women's clothes. After the second escape he was never heard of again.[31]

Following his death, Lachmann's archive was transferred from his rented accommodation in downtown Jerusalem to the university buildings on Mount Scopus. This location became inaccessible when, after the First Arab-Israeli War of 1948, East Jerusalem was annexed by Jordan. The collection was retrieved piecemeal by military convoy until in 1964 it was incorporated into the newly founded National Sound Archive (Phonotheque) of the Israel National Library in the new university campus in West Jerusalem (Gerson-Kiwi 1974, 103). Shortly afterward Gerson-Kiwi prepared a catalogue of the archive, identifying the recordings according to data in Lachmann's surviving recording diaries.[32] In the absence of appropriate playback equipment, however, the fragile cylinders and rusty discs languished in drawers and cupboards in the offices of the Jewish Music Research Centre in the Israel National Library. Around the mid-1990s the entire collection was transferred onto digital media in a project funded by the Austrian Friends of the Hebrew University with technical equipment and expertise provided by the Vienna Phonogrammarchiv.[33]

Yet even as his recordings lay mute, Lachmann's vision continued to inspire the work of his former students. In his letter to Magnes of 6 March 1934, Lachmann had described a program of "lectures and training courses," adding, "it is to be wished that a fair number of students will attend these courses; the subject is vast and requires as many trained specialists as can be had" (quoted in Katz 2003, 75). Despite its lack of formal teaching status, by the end of 1936 the archive had attracted "three female students" (quoted in Katz 2003, 167);[34] in his letter to Magnes of 14 November 1937, Lachmann indicates that a fourth student had joined the team.[35]

As it turned out, it was Gerson-Kiwi, a pianist and a scholar of Italian renaissance music with a doctorate from the University of Heidelberg, who picked up the threads of Lachmann's project after his death. She had originally met Lachmann in Berlin while conducting musicological research at the State Library. They met again by chance in Jerusalem in 1935 at a lecture Lachmann was giving to children, which Gerson-Kiwi was reviewing for a local newspaper. Captivated by his topic, she visited his archive and soon thereafter became his research assistant. Yet even as she absorbed his teaching, her interpretation of his project differed subtly but crucially from his own. While Lachmann insisted on collecting the traditional music of all the Oriental communities without discrimination, for Gerson-Kiwi "Oriental" referred essentially to Oriental Jewish music. In her account of Lachmann's archive in *Musica Hebraica*, the journal of the World Centre for Jewish Music in Palestine, in the year before his death, she accords the non-Jewish traditions a secondary status, necessary only "for comparison" and as part of a wider concept of Jewish music:

> The main purpose of the institute lies in the collection and scholarly study of the traditional melodies of the Near East. Above all, it is oriental Jewish music which is collected for the institute in its most authentic and complete forms. . . . Such scientific knowledge is based essentially on a wealth of comparison, and thus it is necessary to broaden the entire notion of Jewish musical traditions. At the very least, one must include for comparison the music of neighbouring peoples, for example the Christian Jacobites, Copts, Abyssinians, or the Islamic peoples of North Africa and Asia Minor, that is, the Arab and Turkish peoples (Gerson-Kiwi 1938, quoted in Bohlman 1992, 198; and Bohlman and Davis 2007, 123).[36]

In the late 1940s, the gift of a tape recorder made by American donors to the Rubin Academy of Music in Jerusalem catalyzed Gerson-Kiwi into resuming her collecting activities. She did so in the framework of the new Ethnomusicological Institute for Jewish Music, at first under the auspices of the Israeli Ministry of Education, and from 1953 the institute was absorbed into the university's School of Oriental Studies (Shiloah and Gerson-Kiwi 1981, 202–3). By that time, however, the scope of her collecting work was constrained by the ideological imperatives and the new political realities of Israeli statehood. As the neighboring Islamic countries closed their borders to Israel, refusing to recognize the new Jewish state, the oral musical traditions of the new Jewish immigrants from those countries became the principal focus of Gerson-Kiwi's recording and research.[37] Reflecting on her early initiatives three decades later, she writes:

> In 1950, Israel was at the peak of the mass immigration of refugees. A major goal was to undertake an investigation of this unbelievable assembly of Jewish communities from the four corners of the world. . . . The early collection and analysis projects of the Archive, located since 1953 at the Hebrew University, were of an even greater importance because the variety of Oriental traditions of the "Ingathering of Exiles" was likely to disappear as the exiles became integrated as Israeli citizens. The work of the Archive was and remains today a modest attempt at musical documentation of one of the great historical events in Jewish history (Shiloah and Gerson-Kiwi 1981, 203).

Gerson-Kiwi was joined by others, including the Latvian-born Holocaust survivor Johanna Spector, who collected the oral musical traditions of immigrant Jews from the Yemen, Tunisia, Morocco, Pakistan, and Iraq, and those of the indigenous Samaritan community (see the editor's commentary to program 6). Their work was consolidated with the founding in 1964 of the National Sound Archive (Phonotheque) at the Israel National Library and its research organ, the Jewish Music Research Centre. Focusing on oral musical traditions, the National Sound Archive was conceived primarily as "a laboratory for research of Jewish music." However, the comparative principle that was the hallmark of Lachmann's work—which insisted that the study of Jewish music must also include the music of coterritorial non-Jewish communities—was by then embedded in the national musicology. Introducing the National Sound Archive as "the central Phonotheque of recorded music, specifically Jewish," Amnon Shiloah and Gerson-Kiwi explain:

> No other archive is as well-equipped as the Phonotheque with regard to both the quantity and the quality of recorded

> examples of music of Jewish origin; nor does it ignore the surrounding traditions of Arabic music and Oriental-Christian liturgies, both of which manifest a strong attachment to ancient Hebrew music. As long as all of them, the Jewish, Arab and Christian liturgies, are preserved as oral and regional traditions, these collections in the Phonotheque are a lasting monument of the major musical contributions of ancient Israel to the evolving sacred chant of early Christianity, with all its multiple patterns of dissemination throughout the old Occident (Shiloah and Gerson-Kiwi 1981, 203).

And, echoing Gerson-Kiwi's 1938 description of Lachmann's Oriental Music Archive, the Jewish Music Research Centre claims as its fundamental tenet "the understanding that a full appreciation of the Jewish musical traditions is impossible without reference to the musical cultures of the non-Jewish societies with whom the Jews were in close contact for the past two millennia."[38]

Lachmann's Palestine Writings

The *Oriental Music* broadcasts belong to a wider collection of public lectures Lachmann gave in Palestine and abroad through 1936 and early 1937. These complement three substantial pieces of research he completed during his first year in Palestine: his monograph *Jewish Cantillation and Song in the Isle of Djerba* (*Gesänge der Juden auf der Insel Djerba*) based on his research there in 1929; his translation of another treatise by al-Kindī, *Risāla fī ajzā' khabariyya fī al-mūsīqī* (Treatise on Informative Sections on the Theory of Music); and a paper titled "Music of the Algerian Kabyles." All three works were planned for publication in his prospective *Journal for Comparative Musicology,* which in the event of his death never materialized.[39]

The lectures, in contrast, were conceived as part of Lachmann's wider strategy to promote the work of his Oriental Music Archive.[40] On 12 February 1936 he gave the lecture "National und International in der orientalischen Musik" to the College of Music "Bet Levi'im" in Tel Aviv, and in the same month he presented his *Four Lectures on Eastern Music* to the Palestine Branch of the International Association of University Women in Jerusalem.[41] He illustrated these lectures with a combination of his own recordings, including some dating from his Berlin years, commercial recordings, and live performances by local musicians. In May 1936 Lachmann gave several lectures in Basel, Switzerland, where he spent three weeks en route to Berlin. As he states in his 1936–37 report:

> My lecture before [the Geographic-Ethnological Society] took place on 8 May 1936 on the subject: "Oriental Music and Antiquity" ["Orientalische Musik und Antike," reproduced in Lachmann 1974]. At the University I gave a series of six lectures from 1 May to 16 May on the subject: "Musical Cultures of the Near East" ["Musikkulturen des vorderen Orients," Lachmann 1936b]. The musical examples used in order to explain the subjects on these two occasions were taken, amongst others, from the discs of the Archive (quoted in Katz 2003, 166).

On 18 November 1936 Lachmann gave the first of his twelve *Oriental Music* programs. The remaining programs were broadcast fortnightly on Wednesdays with a gap of three weeks between programs 3 (16 December) and 4 (6 January); exceptionally, program 9, featuring the Iraqi-Jewish musician Ezra Aharon, was broadcast a day early on a Tuesday (16 March). The broadcasts began at 9:20 pm (programs 1–4) or 9:30 pm (programs 5–12) and typically lasted twenty-five minutes each. Exceptions were program 1 (fifteen minutes), program 2 (twenty minutes), and program 12, which ran for half an hour. On 17 December 1936, the day after program 3 on Coptic chant, Lachmann spoke on "Musical Systems among the Present Arab Bedouins and Peasants" to the Palestine Oriental Society in Jerusalem (Lachmann 1936c).

On 27 May and 30 May 1937, a month after completing his radio series, Lachmann gave two illustrated lectures at the Jerusalem Conservatoire of Music and Dramatic Art: the first on "Secular Songs of the Oriental Jews" and the second on "Tendencies in Oriental Jewish music of the Present Day." Both lectures were announced under "Events and Entertainments" for Jerusalem in the *Palestine Post,*[42] and they almost certainly belong to the series listed as "Four lectures (in Hebrew) at the Jerusalem Conservatoire, 1937" in the catalogue of the Lachmann Archive (A. III, 47, 2). These appear to have been Lachmann's last lectures before returning to Berlin for the summer. Apart from an item in the *Palestine Post* of 1 July 1937 stating that, in the coming year, "lectures on Oriental and Jewish music will be given by Dr R. Lachman [*sic*], an expert in this field,"[43] there appears to be no evidence that Lachmann gave any further public lectures.

Oriental Music

Presented in the inaugural year of the Palestine Broadcasting Service, Lachmann's radio programs are unique among his lectures in being based almost entirely on live performances of music practiced in Palestine. Yet they are not only—or even primarily—an introduction to the different musical traditions. More fundamentally, they present an unfolding of a methodology—or rather, a web of interconnected and overlapping methodologies—reflecting the accumulation of Lachmann's knowledge and experience over the course of his scholarly career. As he explains in his summary of the series (epilogue), appended to program 12, his purpose was to expose his listeners to "as many and as various specimens of unadulterated Oriental music as possible" and to provide "ways towards understanding them and towards understanding, through them, Oriental music generally." Accordingly, the musical illustrations and the communities they represent are rarely the main focus of Lachmann's lectures but serve rather to illuminate fundamental principles that, in his view, apply to all Middle Eastern music or to music as a whole.

For Lachmann, the correlation between musical system and social function constitutes the primary principle of classification in Eastern music. Reminding his listeners in his epilogue of the many different kinds of music they have heard—"religious and secular, urban and rural, vocal and instrumental, male and female songs, lyrical recitations and choral entertainment songs"—he explains, "It has been one of my chief endeavours to show that these kinds different in their social functions also have musical systems and forms of their own." On a secondary level, Middle Eastern music could also be classified according to different "national and racial styles"; yet "this division," Lachmann insists, "is not superior to the division according to the social functions of music." Compounding the complexity, historical developments over centuries had resulted in a blending of musical characteristics that were originally separate. In particular, he observes that the "rational" musical systems (i.e., scales, rhythms, and forms) of urban secular music have tended to impose themselves on other types, such as rural music and liturgical cantillation. This apparent tendency toward rationalization provides Lachmann with a methodological basis for gauging the relative age of a musical tradition according to the degree it has assimilated elements of urban music (see "The Djerba Monograph" below). Thus, in Lachmann's musical worldview, the panoply of Eastern music unfolds as a multilayered musical archeology in which remnants of different historical strata provide windows onto their own and potentially other musical pasts. As he explains at the end of program 1:

> Present day Bedouins, in playing the fiddle, follow rules established by musicians at the court of the early Abbasid Khalifs; negroes of the Sudan can correct our notions about how the lyre of Ancient Egypt was handled; and who knows how much may possibly be learnt from Oriental Jews of today about the singing at the ancient temple in Jerusalem?

Yet, Lachmann claimed, this entire archeological edifice was threatened with imminent collapse by the onslaught of European influence. This idea, recurring throughout his Palestine writings, was not born simply of musical conservatism or a misplaced notion of musical purity. As he acknowledged in "National und International in der orientalischen Musik," musical encounters between different peoples had occurred throughout history, contributing to the very richness and complexity of the musical ecology he was so anxious to conserve. In the past, however, such encounters (he claimed) had occurred gradually and for the most part between musical traditions "within the family"—that is, between different "Oriental" traditions. The present-day encounter with Western music was unprecedented, not only in the intensity and the speed of the onslaught but also in the essentially "alien" nature of the music in question. Thus Lachmann closes his series by returning full circle to his opening theme, including a plea to his listeners to resist the relentless advance of Western music and to encourage instead "genuine local music."

The Djerba Monograph

Of his Palestine writings, Lachmann's classic monograph *Jewish Cantillation and Song in the Isle of Djerba,* based on just two weeks' research in the remote Tunisian Jewish village of Hara Sghira, is by far the most substantial. Completed only months before he embarked on the *Oriental Music* broadcasts, this groundbreaking study of a single community provides the methodological blueprint not only for the radio series but for his Palestine project as a whole. Lachmann states the purpose of his visit at the outset:

> The two [Jewish] communities claim to be of great age; they are said to have settled in Djerba shortly after the destruction of the Second Temple. This tradition suggested the present inquiry; it seemed worthwhile to find out whether their cantillation and song could be traced back to antiquity. (Lachmann 1940, 1).[44]

His conclusions were negative: "Jewish music on Djerba does not belong to an older stratum than Jewish music on the mainland" (ibid.). Yet it was distinctive in another respect. In their zeal to protect the community from secular influences, the rabbis of Hara Sghira forbade the presence of musical instruments in the village. As a result, Lachmann's transcriptions and analyses of his recordings provide the springboard for a full-scale investigation of music conceived for the unaccompanied voice.

His twenty-two musical examples represent three different repertory types: liturgical cantillation, festival songs, and women's songs. As Lachmann's study reveals, each repertory type is characterized by different principles of tonal and rhythmic organization, or—in Lachmann's terminology—a different "musical system." The three Jewish repertories from Djerba clearly correspond to the three Yemenite Jewish repertories in *Oriental Music:* liturgical cantillation (program 2), men's wedding songs (program 7), and women's wedding songs (program 8). On the more general level of musical system, however, they correspond to the different musical types presented in the series as a whole.

According to Lachmann's analysis, the festival songs—which include songs for religious holidays and life-cycle celebrations—adopt the tonal and rhythmic systems (*maqāmāt* and *iaq'at*) and melodic forms of Tunisian-Arab urban music. Thus, despite their purely vocal rendering in Hara Sghira, they belong to the larger sphere of Arab urban music (represented in programs 9, 10, and 11 of *Oriental Music*) with its basis in instrumental practice. The liturgical cantillation and the women's songs of Djerba, in contrast, exemplify "different tendencies of the musical voice" (Lachmann 1940, 2). The liturgical cantillation belongs to "that class of recitation which includes the emphatic rendering of magic formulae, of sacred texts, and of heroic poems" (Lachmann 1940, 7), in which "the voice, instead of following purely musical impulses . . . primarily serves to support speech; thus in place of consonant tonal relations . . . the voice travels along lines intermediary between speech and song" (Lachmann 1940, 3). Lachmann explores the fundamental principles of this musical tendency in his radio lectures on liturgical cantillation (programs 2, 3, 4, and 6) and Bedouin poetic recitation (program 5). In the latter program, and in his lectures on Kurdish Jewish cantillation (program 4) and Samaritan cantillation (program 6), he posits its origins with magical incantation.

Finally, Lachmann classifies the Djerban women's songs as "rhythmic" song, "the forms of which are essentially dependent not on the connection with the text, but on processes of movement. Thus we find here, in place of the free rhythm of cantillation, and its very intricate line of melody, a periodical up and down movement" (Lachmann 1940, 84). Lachmann includes in this category "primitive choral singing ... and individual singing when connected with bodily movement as in dance and occupational songs" (Lachmann 1940, 2). In the *Oriental Music* programs, the "rhythmic" tendency is exemplified by the Yemenite women's songs (program 8), the antiphonal choral singing of the Yemenite Jewish men (program 7, especially recitation 7.4), the "convivial" song of the Samaritan priests (program 6, recitation 6.5), and the dance songs and rhythmic chanting of the Palestinian Arab men (program 12).

In his Djerba monograph Lachmann introduces another basic division in Arab music: that between urban music, represented by the men's festival songs, and rural music—"the music of the Bedouin and the Fellahin" to which the women's songs belong (Lachmann 1940, 82). He elaborates on the rural-urban dichotomy in the lecture "Musical Systems among the Present Arab Bedouins and Peasants" (Lachmann 1936c) and again in his discussion of the Arab *maqāmāt* in program 9, where he classifies the *maqāmāt* as a specifically urban phenomenon.

But the fundamental quality that for Lachmann distinguishes all types of purely vocal music—regardless of their rhythmical character or social function—is the fact that "the unaccompanied voice, as against certain forms of musical instruments, neither prompts the vision of a scale nor does it yield clues for fixing intervals" (Lachmann 1940, 2). In his view, the concept of a musical scale made up of discrete pitches separated by standard intervals has its origins not in vocal music but in the construction and playing technique of certain musical instruments: citing as examples "panpipes, pipes with series of fingerholes, harps and lyres mounted with series of strings, lutes with frets, etc.," he concludes that "an interrelation exists between the construction of such instruments and the conception of a scale as consisting of a sequence of fixed intervals" (Lachmann 1940, 4). Echoing theories developed by Curt Sachs and Erich M. von Hornbostel in the 1920s, Lachmann attributes the notion of standard intervals to the magical beliefs of certain ancient civilizations of Asia, which ascribed to certain physical measurements powers of cosmological significance. Musical instruments, with their role in sacred ritual, were particularly implicated in these beliefs. In ancient China, for example,

> the fall of a dynasty was attributed to the pitch of the imperial orchestra being faulty and its re-tuning, therefore, was the first measure for the new government to take. The length of reed pipes found in the tombs of ancient Egyptian kings and dignitaries and the arrangement of their finger-holes show that their makers had definite ideas about the scales to be used, which were based on cosmological rather than musical notions. The music played in the temples of China, Samaria, Babylonia and Ancient Egypt was not a mere embellishment of the ritual; the adaptation of the instruments to cosmological measures was held to be indispensable for the bringing about of favourable results (Lachmann 1940, 4–5).

In time, the ancient musical cosmologies gave way to new mathematical formulations that took into account "the growing demands of the human ear" (Lachmann 1940, 5–6). Nevertheless he insists that "ancient Greek and Chinese musical theory and their Indian, Arabian and European offshoots ultimately go back to cosmological ideas as their common basis" (Lachmann 1940, 6). Lachmann discerns the remnants of this way of thinking in the Middle Eastern system of melody types, or *maqāmāt* (sing. *maqām*), "each of which is assigned to a particular hour of the day, and is believed to possess certain magical properties" (Lachmann 1940, 5–6); he gives examples of such properties with respect to the *maqāmāt* presented in program 9.

Lachmann similarly claims magical origins, albeit of a very different kind, for liturgical cantillation and poetic recitation. Despite the "deep gulf" that separates these forms from their alleged origins, he considered that both types of recitation "represent late stages in a [process of] development ultimately going back to magic incantation" (Lachmann 1940, 7). Thus in Jewish and Christian cantillation "the course of the voice has smoothed down so as to proceed in regular musical intervals as against the irrational steps and glides used in magic and similar recitation" (ibid.). In programs 4 (Kurdish Jewish cantillation), 5 (Bedouin poetic recitation), and 6 (Samaritan cantillation), Lachmann explores the musical and spiritual characteristics that, in his view, link liturgical cantillation and sung poetic recitation to the primeval chant of the magic ceremony.

Lachmann's theory of the instrumental origins of the musical scale and its basis in ancient systems of measurement leads logically to his theory of a relative chronology of musical traditions based on the degree to which they had been influenced by the "rational elements" of urban music (Lachmann 1940, 84). On Djerba, both the liturgical cantillation and the women's songs had absorbed rational norms in different ways and in varying degrees (Lachmann 1940, 83). The cantillation, in particular, had "without doubt, assimilated traces of Andalusian music of Tunisian stamp"; in this respect it was consistent with Jewish cantillation elsewhere, which "can be subjected, more or less easily, to the scale systems of urban music—in Oriental communities, to the Arab system, and in European communities, in spite of some reservations, to Major and Minor" (Lachmann 1940, 7). On the other hand, Samaritan cantillation, which Lachmann encountered for the first time in Palestine, represented an intermediary stage of development between the cantillation of the Jewish and Christian liturgies and the incantation of the medicine man. Thus, for Lachmann, the extraordinary vocalizations of the Samaritan priests (which he likened to the recitation of the Japanese Noh drama) were vestiges of the "disguised voice" of the shaman, which supposedly emanated from the spirit that possessed him (ibid.). Lachmann returns to this interpretation of Samaritan cantillation and its evolutionary significance in program 6 of *Oriental Music* and elsewhere in his Palestine writings.

Crucially, however, Lachmann cautions against equating musical development resulting from "rationalisation of tone and time conditions" with notions of musical value and progress; indeed, he considered the reverse to be the case:

> The grade of rationalisation of the usage gives us an indication of its historic position within each of the three species. On the other hand, we should not consider it an indication of musical value. Its pre-rational traits . . . are not to be regarded . . . as imperfections calling for correction. On the contrary, with the suppression of these traits—to be expected in view of the growing influence of urban music—a process of decline will set in as it has already through rationalisation in other species (Lachmann 1940, 85).

Lachmann gives an example of just such a decline in program 5 when, citing an unidentified student of Balkan epic recitation,[45] he claims that the tendency among Balkan bards to substitute the diatonic scale for the "irrational" intervals of the *gusle*—the traditional accompanying fiddle—"distorts the character of the recitation and . . . degrades the reciters of heroic feats to village tenors."

Summarizing his results from Djerba, Lachmann considers the question of "Jewish music" in relation to the music of the non-Jewish environment. In so doing, he distinguishes between "musical characteristics that are transmitted and those that are inherited" (Lachmann 1940, 85). To the former belong tonal and rhythmic systems and, to some extent, melodic material, which, he maintains, may in principle be taught. Hereditary characteristics, in contrast,

> introduce us into more deep-lying strata of musical interpretation. They are expressed less in the musical material as such than in what is made of it; thus, for example, a melody taken over from a neighbouring people, perhaps unconsciously, is re-adapted and becomes more general in its form of expression. The individuality of the interpretation has as yet baffled analysis; we are reduced to relying on impressions (Lachmann 1940, 85–86).

Lachmann explores the distinction between transmitted and hereditary qualities in his 1936 lecture "National und International in der orientalischen Musik," in which he differentiates between recordings of an Arab song from Tunis and a Jewish song from Djerba according to nuances of interpretation:

> Perhaps it is not the melodic formation at all that is behind the difference in impression. My own view is that, if not the, then at least one, essential difference is in the difference in performance. Such a moment, however, is difficult to grasp, difficult to express in words. To my ear the Jewish melodic singing is more intensive, more urgent, the Arab more carefree, more monologue-like. But that is a personal impression with no claim to general applicability (Lachmann 1936c).[46]

He elaborates on the distinction between "transmitted" and "hereditary" qualities in his exploration of the different national styles of Middle Eastern urban music in program 11 of *Oriental Music*.

In its method of systematically sampling the different musical repertories of a single community, Lachmann's research on Djerba laid the foundation for his more extensive collecting activities within the different communities of Palestine. That he envisaged producing similarly comprehensive studies of their music is clear from his statement in his report of 4 May 1937 for the *Information Bulletin* of the Hebrew University:[47]

> Several branches of oriental music have been studied closely with the object of publishing collections of tunes fully representative of each particular branch.
>
> I. Above all, a very full collection of *Yemenite Jewish* records has been made. . . . The songs and recitations collected make it possible to furnish a complete musical supplement to the study of the manners and customs of the Yemenite Jews. . . .
>
> It is proposed to make a similarly complete collection of *Kurdish Jewish* cantillation and song next winter. . . .
>
> The *Samaritan* collection . . . now numbers 250 records. This will be a sufficient basis for a monograph on a similar plan to that of Yemenite music, including liturgical cantillation as well as secular songs (quoted in Katz 2003, 192–93; emphasis in original).

Concluding his Djerba monograph Lachmann states "it is obvious . . . that there is a demand for further collections—as extensive as possible—of Jewish and other traditional music in the Near East and for a careful examination of the same" (Lachmann 1940, 86). His *Oriental Music* broadcasts—the only substantial body of his work to be based almost entirely on his research in Palestine—may be understood as a gesture toward the "careful examination" of his collections that he might have produced had he lived longer.

The Wider Intellectual Environment

Lachmann's approach to the Eastern (Mizraḥi) Jewish repertories in programs 2, 4, and 7 and to the Samaritan cantillation in program 6 was clearly modeled on the pioneering work of Abraham Z. Idelsohn, who carried out the first systematic investigation into these repertories in Jerusalem between 1906 and 1921. Lachmann acknowledges the extent of his debt to Idelsohn in "National und International in der orientalischen Musik":

> I believe that it is necessary to emphasize here how much gratitude we owe to this pioneer in the research of Jewish music, A. Z. Idelsohn. There is, firstly, the astonishingly rich material contained in his many writings, above all in the ten-volume Thesaurus of Hebrew-Oriental Melodies. Idelsohn was the first to study the melodies of the oriental Jews, working from the accurate recognition that the communities least influenced by their environment would have had to have preserved the purest types of musical tradition. This is also why the works on the music of the Yemeni and Babylonian Jews should be judged the most valuable in his output.
>
> There is also the fact that Idelsohn was the first to use the phonograph to record Jewish melodies. In this way, he was the very first to lay a foundation for a verifiable and valid scientific account.

> Lastly, Idelsohn took every opportunity to consider the music of the peoples neighboring the Jews, or those among whom the Jews lived, so as to be able to work out what was characteristic to Jewish music. . . . In particular, he gave us—once again as the first to do so—a usable account of Arab city music and its system.[48]

Yet while Lachmann followed Idelsohn in his selection of musical excerpts and his commentary on them, he does not merely replicate his approach. Rather, he integrated Idelsohn's observations and methods into a wider discussion of musical evolution, the relationship between music systems and their social function, and the role of music in social life. Lachmann's holistic approach to Jewish music guided the work of his students and their associates, notably Edith Gerson-Kiwi and Johanna Spector, and in so doing laid the the methodological foundations for the work of subsequent generations of Israeli ethnomusicologists.

At the 1932 Congress of Arab Music in Cairo, Lachmann first met the celebrated Iraqi-Jewish musician Ezra Aharon (featured in program 9), who was among the exclusively Jewish group of instrumentalists that represented Iraq at the congress. Lachmann's work with Aharon and his fellow instrumentalists provided the catalyst for his continuing work with Aharon in Jerusalem and for his systematic investigation of the melodic modes (*maqāmāt*) of Arab urban music. Lachmann's experiences in Cairo heightened his awareness of the distinctive national traditions and their division into Eastern and Western styles, and the fundamental division between rural and urban Arab music (see programs 9, 10, and 11). It was also in Cairo that Lachmann was introduced to Coptic music, whose foremost scholar and practitioner, Ragheb Moftah, was secretary to Lachmann's recording committee. Although he makes no mention of Moftah in his program on Coptic music (program 3), it seems inconceivable that Lachmann would have been unaware of Moftah's project to transcribe the entire Coptic repertory from oral tradition into Western notation, which was well underway at the time (see the editor's commentary to program 3).

In the early 1930s a canonization project of an entirely different kind was taking place in the Balkans, where the Harvard classical scholar Milman Parry and his student Albert B. Lord were recording performances of epic sung poetry with the aim of uncovering in contemporary practice the processes by which Homeric poetry was conceived and performed. However, it was not the work of Parry and Lord but that of Gustav Wilhelm Becking (1894–1945) on the musical structure of the epic songs of Montenegro (Becking 1933), and Walter Wünsch, whose book *Die Geigentechnik der südslavischen Guslaren* (1934) Lachmann had recently reviewed, that inspired Lachmann's comparative approach to the Bedouin poetic recitation he recorded in Palestine (see program 5). Extending his comparison to the fingering technique of the accompanying stringed instrument (the *rabāba* in the Bedouin tradition and the *gusle* in the Balkan) and drawing on theories of musical diffusion developed by Hornbostel, Lachmann claimed to have uncovered the process by which a scale described in the tenth-century *Kitāb al-aghānī* by al-Iṣfahānī—long defunct in urban practice—had apparently survived among the Bedouins, albeit on a different instrument (the *rabāba* rather than the *'ūd*). Offering themselves as a backdrop to Lachmann's research on Bedouin poetic recitation are the writings of the English Rev. Dr. Henry H. Spoer, who in the early years of the twentieth century traveled among the Bedouin tribes of Palestine and Transjordan, collecting their oral poetry and lore. Spoer's transcriptions and translations of the Bedouin poems (including those recorded by Lachmann) appeared over several decades in journals such as the *Zeitschrift der Deutschen Morgenländischen Gesellschaft* (1912) and the *Journal of the American Oriental Society* (1921, 1923, 1945).[49]

Studies of Middle Eastern music, including Idelsohn's, were generally confined to the public sphere of male performers. In his Djerba monograph, Lachmann opened the first window on the distinctive Judeo-Arabic song repertory practiced by Jewish women. Notwithstanding his disparaging remarks about women's compositional ability at the beginning of program 8, Lachmann took a special interest in their songs. In a letter to his parents describing a recording session at the home of a wealthy farmer in the village of Difra, near Tanta in the Nile Delta, he wrote, "What I mainly heard were women's songs which, naturally, I was particularly interested in" (quoted in Katz 2003, 320). His account of his recording session with the Djerban women, which took the form of a communal gathering—the women huddled up with their children in a room overflowing with onlookers—prompted comparisons with inhabitants of other remote places:

> The stranger is openly stared at and talked about; the women of Djerba, in fact, could not refrain from critically feeling the material of my suit when they thought I was not looking. . . . While one of the women sang in the trumpet, others signified by gesticulation or by whispering that they were not satisfied with the recitation (and that they could do it better); and this was repeated at every change of singer. . . . The climax of the performance is always reached when the record is reproduced by the trumpet—the singers then hearing their own voice fill the room without their participation. Speechless wonder is succeeded by an outbreak of uproarious merriment. The singer gives rein to his or her emotions and beats his neighbour on the knees or on the shoulder; the women laugh with their hands over their mouths. The mistrust which the strange machine inspires before the performance is replaced by a readiness to sing again and again in order to hear one's own voice again and again. In the case of the singers at Djerba the effect of the unusual impression was obvious. Their prematurely old faces—the faces of poor, careworn mothers—brightened: their lips moved, repeating in whispers with the utmost satisfaction the words of the text as the song sounded through the trumpet (Lachmann 1940, 67–68).

In his monograph, Lachmann makes special mention of the Djerban women's song texts, which "are concerned with the main events in the life of Oriental Jewish women; in this way they give a lively insight into their sphere of thought and feeling." In program 8 of *Oriental Music,* in contrast, he scarcely mentions the texts of the

Yemenite Jewish women's songs. Yet his interest in women's songs generally, whether in Tunisia, Egypt, or Palestine, was less as a specifically gendered form of expression than as a fundamental musical type: they belong, as he explains in program 8, to "that large class of songs which is connected with regular bodily movement," which includes work songs, children's songs, and lullabies.

In her research on Yemenite Jewish women's songs in the 1960s, Edith Gerson-Kiwi draws attention to the variety of their lyrics:

> Their poetry, in the Arabic folk language, is oral and often improvised. It reveals a wealth of poetic types, from pure lyrics and shrewd proverbs to story-telling and the epic narration of historical or current political events. The epic songs are especially featured in Yemenite Jewish women's songs, together with work- and love-songs, nursery rhymes, and dance and play tunes; foremost, however, are the various species of ceremonial wedding songs (Gerson-Kiwi 1965, 98).

Even so, it was not until the 1970s and 1980s—more than three decades after Lachmann's research—that Israeli scholars of Yemenite descent began to collect the songs of their mothers and grandmothers, portraying them as a unique oral literature based in real-life experience, complementing the erudite literary worlds of the men's songs (see, for example, Gamli'eli 1975 and Caspi 1985).

It was a woman, Louise Baldensperger, who introduced Lachmann to the music of rural Palestine—the topic of program 12—in the village of Artas where she lived, on his first recording session outside Jerusalem. The daughter of Alsatian missionaries, Baldensperger—known locally as "Sitt Louisa" (Miss Louisa)—had previously collaborated in the research of another extraordinary scholar, the Swedish-Finnish ethnographer Hilma Granqvist, who spent a total of three years in Artas between 1926 and 1931; of the five books that resulted from Granqvist's research, the second—volume 2 of *Marriage Conditions in a Palestinian Village* (1935)—is devoted entirely to the celebration of weddings. With its detailed descriptions of activities associated with men, women, and children, Granqvist's ethnographic account amplifies Lachmann's brief summary of the men's contribution to "what is ordinarily heard at a village wedding in Central Palestine." Lachmann envisaged that his recordings might be used to "add the indispensable element of sound to mute descriptions as given by others" (program 7). The appendix to program 12 illustrates the potential of such an approach by matching the five songs featured in the program with extracts from Lachmann's and Granqvist's accounts of the corresponding musical events.

Notes

1. Unedited, incomplete versions of the lecture texts appear as an appendix in Katz 2003, 328–78; these are illustrated by excerpts from selected recordings on an accompanying CD. See note 5 in the preface and "The Lecture Texts" in "About the Edition."

2. This letter is reproduced in Katz 2003, 72. In 1933 Nazi racial laws led to Sachs's dismissal from his various posts in Berlin, where he had directed the Staatliche Instrumentensammlung, held a university professorship, and taught at several other music institutions. He spent several years in Paris at the Musée du Trocadéro (Musée de l'Homme) and the Sorbonne before emigrating in 1937 to the United States, where he was appointed professor of music at New York University. He also gave regular lectures at Columbia University and served as adjunct professor there from 1953 until his death in 1959.

3. In one of a series of "Letters to my Grandchildren" (in the private collection of Peter Lachmann), Thea Lachmann, the wife of Robert's younger brother, Heinz, describes the other members of the Lachmann family, including Robert, on the occasion of her first meeting with them in May 1926:

> Kurt was the oldest of the three Lachmann boys and thirteen years older than Heinz. He was full of life, very intelligent, rather overpowering but never dull. His mind was always occupied with big ideas and big schemes, which he worked on with enormous energy and concentration. He was a first class lawyer, but much more an advocate than interested in the law itself, as Grandpa always was. He was an amusing and scintillating personality. . . . I had heard a lot about Granny, Jenny Lachmann, who seemed to be the dominant person in the family circle. . . . I was struck by her resemblance to Queen Victoria. She was tiny, stout, rather ugly, still with traces of red in her abundant, grey hair and she was absolutely regal. After 42 years in Germany she had a very strong English accent (she was born in Swallow Street, near Regent Street in London and was educated at Queens College) but her German was perfect. She was dressed in black, as she had been since her mother's death in 1905. She had perfect manners and, small as she was, she was in total command of her family. Grossvater Georg Lachmann was tall, very stout and full of genuine kindliness and friend-liness [*sic*]. He had laughing grey eyes, was full of humour and in his whole appearances was the typical German professor in the best sense. Although they were very different in temperament and character Georg and Jenny were a devoted couple. . . . With Georg and Jenny came Robert. He was very pale and fragile, with a sensitive, highly intelligent face. He was very quiet, but when he spoke everyone listened, and problems, which a minute ago were heatedly discussed, suddenly had an obvious solution. The afternoon we spent with Robert, walking along the shore of the Wannsee and everything felt calm, harmonious and right.

I thank Peter Lachmann for his permission to include this extract.

4. The original cylinders of both Lachmann's and Idelsohn's collections remained in the Berlin Phonogramm-Archiv. Founded in 1900, this institute had developed a unique technology for copying recordings. From 1906, incoming music recordings were galvanized to produce copper negatives of the original wax cylinders (galvanos), which constituted a more

durable medium for preserving musical information. The galvanos were never played but served as matrices for further copying (Ziegler 1994). In a report dated 17 November 1935 (reproduced in Katz 2003, 131–32), Lachmann describes how he and his technician, on a return visit to Berlin in the summer of 1935, used a specially designed pickup to transfer the original cylinder recordings that had not yet been galvanized directly onto disc. The remaining cylinders were transferred to disc in Jerusalem. Lachmann gives details of his Berlin recordings in his 1935–36 report:

> My activity began in the war years with prisoners-of-war colonial troops from North Africa, from whom I was able to write down about 300 pieces, including their texts. A number of these are phonographically supported.
>
> After the war, collections of Moroccan, Persian, Turkish and Japanese vocal and instrumental pieces were established with the help of reliable informants who were temporarily staying in Berlin. All of these collections consist of these phonographic recordings with the addition of material written down by ear and are accompanied by remarks concerning the system and practice of the respective music, as well as by collected texts. . . .
>
> Starting from 1925, I have undertaken further studies on occasion of various travels to North Africa: in 1925, in Tripoli; in 1927, in Tunisia and Algeria, and in 1932 in different parts of Egypt, including Sinai. On all of these travels numerous recordings were made, altogether over 400 examples of Jewish and Arabic music (quoted in Katz 2003, 140).

5. In gratitude to his sponsor, Lachmann dedicated the English translation of his Djerba monograph to her (Lachmann 1940).

6. Judah L. Magnes, diary notes, Jerusalem, 25 March 1928 (quoted in Goren 1982, 270).

7. Judah L. Magnes, diary notes, Jerusalem, 13 February 1923 (quoted in Goren 1982, 206).

8. Lachmann was never under any illusion as to the insecurities of his position. In their protracted correspondence before Lachmann's arrival, Magnes consistently emphasized that the university had no plans or resources to fund a position in music in the foreseeable future. Writing on 1 January 1935, Magnes warned Lachmann, "We are not, unfortunately, in a position to make extra efforts on behalf of music out of our regular budget. The situation may some day change but we cannot build upon that hope in view of the large number of lacunae in our regular University structure for which funds will have to be secured. All that we can hope for is that friends interested in music may from time to time place sums for this purpose at our disposal" (quoted in Katz 2003, 95).

9. A sense of historic mission and biblical destiny colored the speeches made by the various dignitaries at the University's opening ceremony on 1 April 1925. In his closing address, for example, the poet Ḥayyim Naḥman Bialik proclaimed:

> The eyes of the myriads of Israel are lifted from the dispersion of the exile to this hill. They realize that at this moment Israel has kindled on Mount Scopus the first candle of the inauguration of her intellectual life. This day the glad tidings will go to all the scattered families in their places of sojourning, that the first peg in the up-building of the Tabernacle has been driven in, never to be removed (quoted in Bentwich 1961, 26).

Other speakers included the former British Foreign Secretary Lord Arthur Balfour (then chancellor of the University of Cambridge); Rabbi Abraham I. Kook, chief rabbi of Palestine; Sir Herbert Samuel, High Commissioner for Palestine; and Dr. Chaim Weizmann, president of the World Zionist Organization. For full transcripts of their speeches, see Hebrew University 1925.

10. Mandatory Palestine originally included the regions west and east of the Jordan River, historically known as Cisjordan and Transjordan. Transjordan soon became a separate administrative unit and in 1946 achieved full independence as the Hashemite Kingdom of Jordan.

11. In his study of Magnes's unique contribution to the Yishuv (the Jewish settlement in Palestine), Daniel P. Kotzin (2000) argues that, for the Californian-born Reform rabbi, Zionist ideology was inseparable not only from pacifism and Jewish ethical ideals but also from progressive American ideals of cultural pluralism and democracy. It was a combination of these values, he maintains, that guided Magnes's vision both for the Hebrew University and for Palestine as a whole: "For Magnes, the Zionist program would only be achieved once there was pluralistic democracy in Palestine. Magnes constructed The Hebrew University as a crucible for a new Jewish culture based on his Zionist ideals, and he offered the binational proposal as its political realization" (Kotzin 2000, 2).

12. The events of World War II caused Magnes to reverse his stance on immigration and to question his long-held belief that compromise could be achieved through negotiations between Jews and Arabs. In the January 1943 issue of *Foreign Affairs,* he acknowledged that, to prevent Palestine from becoming "a menace to world's peace," an imposed compromise would have to be implemented by external powers, namely "the association of the US with Britain" (quoted in Goren 1982, 37).

13. The name of the institute remained fluid until some months after Lachmann's arrival in Jerusalem. In a letter to Lachmann of 17 May 1934, Magnes refers to it variously as a "section in non-European Musicology" (Katz 2003, 90) and as "the new department (Research of Oriental Music)" (Katz 2003, 97). Lachmann's first three reports, dated 14 June, 21 June, and 7 July 1935, are entitled "Section for the Study of Non-European Music" (Katz 2003, 111, 114, and 121). The name "Archive of Oriental Music" first appears as the title of his fourth report of 17 November 1935 (Katz 2003, 131) and is used consistently (with minor permutations such as "Archives" and "for") from then on.

14. Reproduced in full in Katz 2003, 73–78.

15. Reproduced in full in Katz 2003, 86–87.

16. Reproduced in full in Katz 2003, 87–89.

17. Lachmann's annual report for 1935–36 is reproduced in full, translated from the original German, in Katz 2003, 138–47. The report is undated; however, it is clear from references within the document that Lachmann wrote it before leaving Jerusalem for the summer on 1 May 1936. For Lachmann's justification for his use of inferior-quality metal discs for recording, see "The Recordings: History and Documentation" in "About the Edition."

18. Robert Lachmann to Norman Bentwich, July 1937. Hebrew University of Jerusalem, Lachmann Archive (hereafter simply Lachmann Archive), no shelfmark.

19. Reproduced in full in Katz 2003, 148–52. The document goes on to list several "urgent requirements for developing the Archives" (p. 149), including "batteries used for recording music in the field" (quoted in Katz 2003, 150).

20. Reproduced in full in Katz 2003, 182–86. The report is headed simply "The document."

21. Robert Lachmann to Norman Bentwich, July 1937. Lachmann Archive, no shelfmark.

22. Reproduced in full in Katz 2003, 118–20.

23. In his report of 4 May 1937 for the *Information Bulletin* of the Hebrew University, Lachmann states that he has established connections with the directors of two schools in Jerusalem, and that "several demonstrations of the recordings have been given, with explanations, and have found such ready response that it has been planned to continue this on a larger scale next winter" (quoted in Katz 2003, 194). He adds that, at the request of the director of the Arab school, he produced two articles outlining his program for musical education in Arab schools, which were published in the school journal (ibid.). The Lachmann Archive includes an incomplete handwritten draft lecture titled "Musical Education in Arab Schools" (Lachmann Archive, A. III. 47. 4).

24. "Broadcasting Station Opening in November," *Palestine Post,* 7 July 1935, 1. Available online at http://www.jpress.org.il/publications/ppost-en.asp.

25. Reproduced in full in Katz 2003, 195–98.

26. Lachmann Archive, B. II. 8.2. A copy of the undated memorandum is attached to a letter of 5 August from Rendall to Lachmann.

27. Cliffe confirmed the details of these introductions in letters to Lachmann of 25 July and 5 August (Lachmann Archive, B. II. 8.2).

28. The following unpublished correspondence relating to Lachmann's proposed lecture tour is taken from Lachmann Archive, B. II. 7.

29. Reproduced in full in Katz 2003, 263–68.

30. Reproduced in full in Katz 2003, 203–204. Names of committee members have been expanded where known.

31. I am grateful to Peter Lachmann for providing this information from his diary.

32. The first dated recording in the catalogue is D304, recorded on 24 March 1936; see "Dating and Cataloguing of Lachmann's Recordings" in "About the Edition."

33. See the preface for further details on the transfer of the recordings to digital media.

34. Lachmann identifies these students as Dr. Edith Gerson-Kiwi, "Western liturgical songs and instrumental music"; Kitt Flaxman, M.A., "The Yemenite Bible reading"; and Sofia Lentschner, "Oriental Urban Instrumental Music" (quoted in Katz 2003, 167).

35. Katz 2003, 196. Three of these students are presumably Edith Gerson-Kiwi, Kitt Flaxman, and Sofia Lentschner (see note 34 above); the fourth has not been identified.

36. Longer extracts of Gerson-Kiwi's account appear with further interpretation in Bohlman 1992, 196–98; and Bohlman and Davis 2007, 123–24.

37. Between 1948 and the early 1970s nearly 600,000 Jews from Arab lands settled in Israel, and a further 260,000 settled in Europe and the Americas (Gilbert 1992, 48).

38. From the mission statement of the Jewish Music Research Centre at the Hebrew University of Jerusalem (http://www.magnes.org/research/research-resources/jewish-music-research-center-—hebrew-university-jerusalem).

39. To date, only *Jewish Cantillation and Song in the Isle of Djerba* has been published, first in an English version prepared under Lachmann's supervision (Lachmann 1940) and subsequently in the original German, edited by Edith Gerson-Kiwi (Lachmann 1978).

40. Although not all of the manuscripts carry dates, these can generally be deduced, if only approximately, from internal evidence or from references in other sources.

41. The *Four Lectures on Eastern Music* are reproduced in Katz 2003, 379–415. Both the manuscript and the six recordings illustrating the lectures (D28b, D58a, D58b, D59a, D69, and D104a; on the numbering system, see "The Recordings: History and Documentation" in "About the Edition") are undated. However, the *Palestine Post* of 6 February 1936 includes a notice for "Beth Harav MiGur, Palestinian Association of University Women, Lecture on 'Oriental Music' by Dr Lachmann" ("Today's Events," *Palestine Post*, 6 February 1936, 8; available online at http://www.jpress.org.il/publications/ppost-en.asp). Reviews of the third and fourth lectures in the series appear in the *Palestine Post* on 21 February (p. 11) and 3 March (p. 7), although only the opening lines are legible since in each case the rest of the page is blacked out.

42. "Events and Entertainments," *Palestine Post*, 27 May 1937, 6; and 30 May 1937, 6; available online at http://www.jpress.org.il/publications/ppost-en.asp.

43. "Progress of the Conservatoire: Publication of Annual Report," *Palestine Post*, 1 July 1937, 2; available online at http://www.jpress.org.il/publications/ppost-en.asp.

44. The Jews of Djerba traditionally inhabited two villages: Hara Kebira (lit. "big Jewish quarter"), on the outskirts of Houmt Souk, the island's main port and market town, and Hara Sghira (lit. "little Jewish quarter"), about seven kilometers inland. Lachmann based his research in Hara Sghira because "owing to its remoteness, it seemed better secured against alien influence" (Lachmann 1940, 1).

45. Lachmann identifies his source as the musicologist Walther Wünsch (1936c). See also program 5, footnote 8.

46. "Vielleicht ist es auch gar nicht die Melodiebildung, die den verschiedenen Eindruck ausmacht. Mir selbst scheint, wenn nicht *der*, so doch *ein* wesentlicher Unterschied in der *Verschiedenheit des Vortrags* zu bestehen. Ein solches Moment ist aber schwer greifbar, schwer in Worten auszudrücken. Mir klingt das jüdische Melodiesingen intensiver, eindringlicher, das arabische unbekümmerter, monologhafter. Aber das ist ein persönlicher Eindruck, der keinen Anspruch auf Allgemeingültigkeit erheben will."

47. Reproduced in full in Katz 2003, 192–94.

48. "Ich glaube aber, daß es notwendig ist hervorzuheben, wieviel auf alle Fälle diesem Pionier in der Erforschung der jüdischen Musik, A. Z. Idelsohn, zu verdanken ist. Da ist zunächst das erstaunlich reiche Material, das in seiner vielen Schriften, aber vor allem in dem zehnbändigen Hebräisch-Orientalischen Melodienschatz, enthalten ist. Idelsohn ist als erster darauf gekommen, die Melodien der *orientalischen* Juden zu studieren, aus der richtigen Erkenntnis heraus, daß die von der Umwelt am wenigsten beeinflußten Gemeinden die verhältnismäßig reinsten Typen der musikalischen Tradition bewahrt haben müßten. So sind denn auch die Arbeiten über die Musik der jemenischen und babylonischen Juden als die wertvollsten aus seinem Gesamtwerk zu schätzen.

"Weiter besteht die Tatsache, daß er als erster für die Aufzeichnung jüdischer Melodien den Phonographen herausgezogen und so überhaupt erst eine Grundlage für eine nachprüfbare wissenschaftlich stichhaltige Darstellung gelegt hat.

"Schließlich hat Idelsohn jede Gelegenheit benutzt, auch auf die Musik der den Juden benachbarten oder mit ihnen zusammenlebenden Völker einzugehen, um auf diese Weise das Eigentümliche der jüdischen Musik herausarbeiten zu können. . . . und vor allem hat er, wiederum als erster, eine brauchbare Darstellung der arabischen Stadtmusik und ihres Systems geliefert" (Lachmann 1936c).

49. See references in Spoer 1945, 37.

About the Edition

The Lecture Texts

The texts of Lachmann's twelve lectures are transcribed in full directly from the complete handwritten and typed scripts given to me by his nephew, Peter Lachmann, in 1991.[1] The dates of the programs are taken from the headings of Lachmann's scripts. The descriptive titles are my own. Heading information common to all the lectures—including general titles such as "Oriental Music | A Series of Talks [*or* A Talk] | by Robert Lachmann" and references to the Palestine Broadcasting Service, such as "Jerusalem Broadcasting Station" or "Palestine Broadcasting Station"—has been omitted. All numbered footnotes are editiorial additions; they include both critical notes reporting differences between the edition and Lachmann's original scripts not covered by the methods outlined below, and detailed glosses on the text. The few footnotes originally present in Lachmann's scripts are identified by symbols (asterisk, dagger, etc.).

In general, Lachmann's orthography has been retained, including a few idiosyncratic spellings (e.g., "neums" instead of "neumes" in program 4); the edition reproduces all diacritics used in Lachmann's scripts and retains his transliteration of proper names within the programs. Spellings have been standardized within each lecture text, but no attempt has been made to standardize variant spellings of the same word that occur across programs (e.g., "Beduin" is used in programs 2 and 4, "Bedouin" in program 5). Words and syllables in the script that are partly cut off at the end of a line of text are filled in without comment, since the intended reading is clear; punctuation in such cases, where unclear, has been supplied at the editor's discretion. In transliterating Arabic and Hebrew names and terms, Lachmann occasionally uses spaces to indicate the letters alif hamza and 'ayn (in the former) and alef and 'ayin (in the latter); the appropriate symbols (' for alif hamza and alef, ' for 'ayn and 'ayin) have been substituted in the edition. Any other adjustments to the orthography of Lachmann's scripts are reported on a case-by-case basis in the notes to the text.

Occasional minor changes have been made to the formatting, spacing, and punctuation of Lachmann's script. In particular, italics replace underlining or spaced letters used to indicate emphasis, hyphens have been added where necessary to clarify compounds, and commas have been added occasionally to clarify unbalanced grammatical constructions. Commas that appear at the ends of sentences have been tacitly changed to periods. Capitalization has been added for proper nouns where missing in the script; extraneous capitalization has been removed. Spaces between words have been added tacitly where missing from the script. Extraneous punctuation and spaces, stray characters, and crossed-out or typed-over text have been eliminated without comment.

The rubric "Recitation," used in Lachmann's typescripts to indicate the point at which a live performance is to take place, is supplemented with precise references to the musical illustrations that in this edition are numbered consecutively within each program (e.g., "recitation 8.1" refers to the first musical performance within program 8). In Lachmann's typescripts for programs 10 and 11, which are illustrated by commercial recordings, either "Record" with information on the record label and catalogue number (e.g., Baidaphon 093364), or record label and catalogue number alone, is used instead of "Recitation" to cue musical performances. The same nomenclature is used in the edition (e.g., "record 11.1," followed by a precise reference to the record label information, refers to the first recorded musical illustration played in program 11). Track references are given for the selections included on the accompanying CDs (see below).

This edition pairs each of Lachmann's lecture texts for programs 2–12 with selected recordings of the live performances or commercial recordings featured in each program; program 1, which serves as a general introduction to the series, includes no music. The recordings are presented both in their raw transferred state as provided by the Israel National Sound Archive and in digitally restored versions (see below for technical details); on the criteria by which these recordings were chosen, see "The Recordings: Technical Notes" below. In the programs based on live musical performances (2–9 and 12), which relate directly to Lachmann's work in Palestine, the lecture texts and editorial glosses are followed by documentation of the musical recordings, transcriptions of the music and sung texts of the selections included on the accompanying compact discs, translations of the texts into English, and for each program, an editorial commentary that situates Lachmann's treatment of the musical topic in a wider scholarly and musical context. In the programs based on commercial records (10 and 11), which provide general surveys of urban traditions of

North Africa, the wider Middle East, and beyond, the lecture texts and editorial glosses are followed by documentation on the recordings and transcriptions and translations of the sung texts.

The Recordings: History and Documentation

The Original Recordings

In the early 1990s, Avi Nahmias, sound engineer of the Israel National Sound Archive, interviewed the Yemenite bothers Raphael and Natan Nadav, who had recorded for Lachmann as teenagers in the 1930s.[2] According to the Nadav brothers, the discs Lachmann used (examples of which are shown in plates 8 and 9) were made of aluminum mixed with zinc or tin and were cut from large metal sheets in his recording laboratory by his assistant, Walter Schur. Occasionally, when metal was scarce, Lachmann used celluloid discs cut from discarded X-ray film. While cost and availability were undoubtedly the decisive factors in determining Lachmann's choice of recording materials, his reliance on metal rather than commercial-quality wax discs had crucial practical advantages. As he explained in a letter to Norman Bentwich, former Attorney-General of Mandatory Palestine and chairman of the British Friends of the Hebrew University:[3]

> Apart from the financial impossibility to acquire an apparatus and to make discs like those used by commercial firms, there are two other reasons why an apparatus of this kind would not be suited to my purposes:
>
> 1. After recording on a wax disc it is not possible to play back the music at once. Not before the copies have been made can one find out whether the recording has been satisfactory. On the other hand, for an Archive it is of great importance to play the records at once after having made them; in the first place, one must know whether the record has turned out well enough because one may not get hold of the performers a second time and, secondly, experience shows that native performers are generally not too willing to sing or play into the microphone until they have heard their performance reproduced, but, after that, are ready for any number of recitals.
>
> 2. The commercial apparatus can be used in a laboratory only, whereas, for the purposes of an Archive like my own, it is necessary to have an apparatus which is portable as well as independent of public electricity.

As for the inferior sound quality of the metal discs, Lachmann argued that

> the main object of the records of an Archive is not to demonstrate records to an audience, but to study them, that is, to transcribe them into staff notation and to measure pitches and time-values. For these purposes the discs used at my Archive are thoroughly satisfactory.

Finally, metal had the advantage of durability:

> The material of the discs has been chosen after carefully trying a number of possibilities. While it is true that on gelatine discs the needle produces less noise, metal is far more durable and costs five times less. Other material as well has been tried unsuccessfully.

In addition to the live performances for *Oriental Music*, several other recordings, including some featuring the Nadav brothers, are marked with the rubric "Radio" in Lachmann's diaries, indicating that they too were taken from radio broadcasts. Since the Palestine Broadcasting Service (PBS) did not as a rule record its transmissions, Lachmann had to make his own arrangements for recording these items. The Nadav brothers recalled their experience of Lachmann's modus operandi. First, they explained, he arranged for them to meet Karl Salomon, head of music at the PBS, who offered them a few performances. One day, Lachmann invited the brothers to drop by his studio after their broadcast. To their astonishment, when they arrived, Lachmann played them his recording of the performance they had just given. The brothers give no technical details; however, their account suggests that the recordings marked "Radio," including those illustrating the *Oriental Music* lectures, were not made in the broadcasting studio itself but were taken, quite literally, from the radio receiver.[4]

Dating and Cataloguing of Lachmann's Recordings

Lachmann's recording catalogue was prepared from his recording diaries by Edith Gerson-Kiwi in the mid-1960s.[5] The Palestine recordings are listed chronologically according to the numbers assigned by Lachmann, prefaced by the letter D. Discs D1–D289 are listed without dates and with minimal musical information, since the diaries referring to them are lost. Discs D290–D303 are also undated, but both the repertory and the performers are identified. The first dated disc, D304, was recorded on 24 March 1936. The commercial recordings are listed in a separate catalogue, each with a number prefaced by the letter F.

According to the dates given in Lachmann's diaries and (in the case of the earlier, undated recordings) information given in his research reports, Lachmann's recording activities in Palestine fell into four distinct periods, separated by the summer months he spent in Europe (see table 1). On his return to Jerusalem in September 1938 he fell ill with vascular disease and was unable to resume his recording activities. His last documented recording session was that of 28 May 1938.

In this edition, each of Lachmann's lecture texts is followed by a section giving information on the recordings, including titles or descriptions of the musical content, information on the performers, the "D" or "F" catalogue numbers assigned by Edith Gerson-Kiwi, and, in the case of the commercial recordings, record label and catalogue number. For the live recordings, the titles of the musical items and names of the performers are taken from Lachmann's lecture texts and recording diaries, supplemented where necessary by information provided elsewhere in his writings; the orthography of the titles may thus differ from that of the transliterated sung texts (e.g., recitation 7.4, "'Ayelet ḥen," whose opening words are transliterated as "'Ayyalaṯ ḥen" according to the Yemenite pronunciation of Hebrew; see "The Sung Texts" below). Information on the commercial recordings is taken from the catalogue prepared by Edith Gerson-Kiwi (see above).

Table 1
Dates of Lachmann's Recording Activities in Palestine

Period	Start Date (with recording number, if known)*	End Date	Total Number of Discs
1	4 June 1935 (D1)	early July 1935†	330
2	November 1935	31 March 1936 (D330)‡	
3	8 November 1936 (D331)	27 May 1937 (D764)	434
4	23 November 1937 (D765)	28 May 1938 (D959)	195

* Recording catalogue numbers follow the system outlined in Gerson-Kiwi 1974.
† In his first Jerusalem report (14 June 1935), Lachmann states that he and Schur arrived in Jerusalem on 29 April 1935, that the recording equipment did not arrive until the end of May because of delays at customs, and that his first recording session was on 4 June of that year (Katz 2003, 111). In his fourth Jerusalem report (17 November 1935), Lachmann states that he left Jerusalem for the summer on 10 July (Katz 2003, 131).
‡ It is unclear exactly when Lachmann returned to Jerusalem in 1935. Reporting on his activities from May 1936 to January 1937, he states that he left Palestine at the beginning of May 1936 to spend the summer months in Germany (Katz 2003, 166). The last session before his departure is dated 31 March 1936.

The Recordings: Technical Notes

The Digitization Process

The recordings on the CDs accompanying this edition were transferred directly from the original metal discs to DAT by Avi Nahmias using the following equipment:

Turntable/arm: Diapason archive turntable, model 12, with speed control and readout based on Technics SL 1200 mk2

Cartridge: Shure M44-C (stereo)

Stylus: Expert Stylus

Preamplifier: AHE audio heritage equipment PA-02

DAT recorder: Tascam DA-30

The recordings were made directly and flat (two channels) from the cartridge with amplification (PA-02) at 44.1 kHz.[6]

The primary criteria in determining the selection of recordings for restoration were their physical state and sound quality (see "Notes on the Restoration Process" below). In certain cases, we chose to substitute recordings of superior quality featuring the same performers and the same or equivalent repertory, made either on the same day (in a different session) or on a nearby date. In such cases, details of both the original and the substitute recording are given in the edition. Severe breakages in the sound occurred at some point in nearly all the recordings, most commonly toward the end. In cases where the extent of continuous sound was sufficient to give a clear sense of the overall structure of the performance (e.g., several strophes or melodic cycles), we edited the original recording to end at the break and the processed version to end at a point slightly before the break, depending on musical criteria. In recitation 5.2 (Bedouin solo recitation with *rabāba*), severe breakages that occurred both near the start of the recording and about two-thirds of the way through were corrected in order to present the entire performance. In recitation 3.3, the severe breakage that occurs in the cadential passage following the long melisma was corrected in order to present the complete opening section of the performance. In recitations 2.1 and 2.3 (Yemenite Jewish cantillation), 6.5 (Samaritan Arabic song), 7.1 (Yemenite men's wedding song), and 12.3, 12.4, and 12.5 (Arab wedding songs), there were no severe breakages in the original recordings, and complete performances are given in both the original and restored versions. In all recordings, severe breakages occurring as the playback needle hit the recording groove before the start of the performance were removed. Extracts corresponding to nearly all the live musical performances featured in Lachmann's programs are provided in unrestored state on the compact disc accompanying Katz 2003.[7]

All technical aspects of the sound restoration were carried out in Cambridge by Simon Godsill, professor of statistical signal processing in the Department of Engineering at the University of Cambridge. Sound-editing decisions—particularly those regarding joins where there were breakages in sound and the degree of surface and background noise removal—were made jointly, with the final responsibility lying with me. Since such decisions are inevitably subjective, we include both restored and unrestored versions of each track on the accompanying compact discs.

Notes on the Restoration Process, by Simon Godsill

The material was provided digitized at 16 bits and a sampling rate of 44.1 kHz onto DAT by the Israel National Sound Archive. All the subsequent processing was carried out entirely in digital format on a computer prior to transfer onto CD. The principal software used was Matlab, hosted on a standard Pentium-based Windows PC. All Matlab processing was carried out in double-precision floating-point format with quantization back to 16-bit fixed-point format only at the final stages. All Matlab code was developed by me during my research over many years to deal with a variety of challenging problems in sound restoration. The software was further developed to handle some of the major challenges presented by this particular project.[8] Final editing and equalization were carried out using the Adobe Audition editing package.

The source material survives in varying stages of degradation, but most of it exhibits large amounts of surface noise, including loud "pops," breakages, and smaller clicks and crackles. Lachmann's recordings have high noise levels and low signal bandwidth (with typically little present above 6 kHz). The material was processed in several stages. It is worth noting that each stage was carried out at a "microscopic" level and at times involved adjustments to noise signal values for events as short as 1/40,000 second (approximately the duration of a single digital sample value).

In the first stage, any severe breakages in sound were corrected—for example, when the playback needle jumped across several recording grooves and had to be moved back in order to access all of a recording. This process was carried out by a combination of careful editing (in Audition) and subsequent digital interpolation in Matlab over the resulting discontinuity at the "join."

In the second stage, clicks and crackles were removed, again in Matlab. This is a complex digital signal processing task that first requires a detection of all locations where the signal is disrupted, followed by a digital interpolation to fill in the "gap" left where a click was found. The principles behind both the detection and interpolation stages involve an acoustical modeling of the music/voice signal as a resonant tube (whose parameters are automatically determined); this model then allows the computer to distinguish between events generated by the acoustical model (assumed to be genuine music) and other extraneous events (assumed to be click noise). In signal processing terminology, we used an autoregressive acoustical model in this process and constructed an outlier test to determine which events to count as clicks. To give an idea of the scale of the processing, there may be between fifty and one thousand clicks to remove per *second* of recorded music. In fact, the processing methods had to be specially adapted in order to cope with the very high density of clicks and crackles found in the material from this archive.

In the third stage we performed general background noise, or "hiss" removal. This involved viewing the signal in the frequency domain over short time scales of around 1/40 second, or in other words, splitting the musical tones into their constituent fundamentals and partials. These dominant components were then passed largely unprocessed while other frequencies were attenuated to remove noise. Clearly there are tradeoffs involved in such a process, since transients and low-amplitude frequency components in the musical sound could be damaged by naive processing of this type. Thus there are many further details involved in the practical construction of such an algorithm. This is possibly the most subjective part of any audio processing system, and we chose not to remove the maximum amount of noise possible; rather, we pulled back the processing to a level we believed achieved a suitable compromise between maximum noise reduction and minimum loss of musical sound.

Finally, equalization was carried out in Audition. This was done on a track-by-track basis, making an appropriate judgment as to what sounded acceptable. In most cases the equalization was performed using a low-pass filter with a cutoff frequency somewhere between 4 kHz and 8 kHz, depending on the quality of the source material.

The Musical Transcriptions

Background: Lachmann's Transciption Methods

Lachmann described his recording activities in Palestine as part of a multistage process that began by systematically selecting the material to be collected and would ideally conclude with the "scientific processing" of the results.[9] He explained what he meant by "scientific processing" in his report of April 1937:

> The contents of the records are transcribed in staff-notation with all possible exactness, and with the help of a Metronome and a Tonometer for measuring the pitch. In the case of vocal music the texts are also noted.
>
> The material thus obtained is worked out as the basis of publications, and even at this stage it is possible to work out a number of subjects, each independent and complete in itself. . . . (quoted in Katz 2003, 184).

Lachmann's premature death, and his insistence on prioritizing collecting over all other activities, inevitably compromised such follow-up activity.[10] Yet the type of end product he envisaged, "independent and complete in itself," is amply exemplified by his monograph *Jewish Cantillation and Song in the Isle of Djerba* (Lachmann 1940), which he completed during the same period. In this study, Lachmann's general observations on the three different repertory types (liturgical cantillation, festival songs, and women's songs) outlined in the introduction to his book, are supported by complete music and text transcriptions and detailed musical analyses of each recorded item. At various points in his commentary Lachmann addresses the specific problems of representing melodies in free rhythm (liturgical cantillation) and fluctuating pitch (liturgical cantillation and women's songs) in Western staff notation.

Lachmann notates all the examples in his Djerba monograph in the treble clef. To facilitate comparison, he transposes the melodies belonging to each repertory type to a common scale, minimizing the use of accidentals. He uses only standard flat and sharp symbols, placing the same accidental above rather than before the note to indicate the raising or lowering of a pitch by a quarter tone. Even so, he does not aim for total accuracy; commenting on the variable intonation of the Djerban women's songs, he insists that "in reality, the impression of instability is even stronger than appears in the printed music" (Lachmann 1940, 69).

In his Djerba transcriptions, Lachmann indicates tempos and, if applicable, tempo changes as metronome values or ranges, which are frequently given as approximate. He uses precise rhythmic values to represent the free rhythm of the liturgical cantillation, including complex patterns of eighth notes, sixteenth notes, thirty-second notes, and dotted rhythms in alternating compound and duple groupings. In all three repertory types, Lachmann indicates phrase and section divisions by a hierarchy of double, single, and dotted barlines.

Acknowledging that "notation, by its very nature, rationalises time values" (Lachmann 1940, 35), Lachmann addresses the inherent anomalies involved in notating passages in free rhythm, especially where there is no stable pulse. Defending his use of precise values, he explains that these do at least offer an impression of accuracy, whereas simplifying the rhythm would result in distortion:

> The notation does not render the rhythmic vacillation with complete accuracy. . . . Yet . . . an attempt has been made to do justice to the variability of the time unit. Hence, complicated values have been used repeatedly where plain crotchets and quavers would have simplified, but also . . . slightly falsified the facts. . . . Thus the "irregular" rhythm of the cantillation as against scanning has at least been hinted at in the notation (Lachmann 1940, 37).

Moreover, even genres that are conceived in fixed rhythm, such as the festival songs and the women's songs, display a degree of rhythmic flexibility in performance:

> The fact that a tune is recognised as being in strict time does not depend on the performer handling the time units with mechanical strictness. In strict time as well as in free rhythm the time unit may vary considerably (Lachmann 1940, 36).

Transcription Methods

Except for the summary transcriptions in program 9, this edition adopts Lachmann's general approach to melodic detail. However, whereas in the Djerba monograph the transcriptions provide the basis for detailed and extensive musical analyses that in turn provide evidence for specific observations on the different repertories, in the *Oriental Music* broadcasts—as in his Palestine lectures generally—Lachmann provides only scant commentary on the individual performances. The musical examples serve rather as a backdrop to his general observations on the different repertory types, their musical systems, and their social functions. The musical transcriptions in this edition reflect the function of the performances in the lectures: essentially, they stand alone, and, apart from the summary transcriptions in program 9 and the tabular transcriptions in programs 3 and 6, they have no particular analytical focus. Conceived more generally as sound maps, tracing the tonal and rhythmic parameters of the individual performances on different structural levels, the transcriptions aim to guide and encapsulate the listener's aural experience, rendering aspects of structure and melodic detail more readily apparent than they would be to the ear alone. However, to the extent that Lachmann does comment on specific attributes of a performance, the transcriptions aim to reflect these. Thus, for example, the transcriptions of the Samaritan biblical cantillation (recitation 6.1) and the Samaritan Arabic song (recitation 6.5) attempt to indicate the "strange accents, glides, sudden stresses and sudden lapses into ordinary speech" that for Lachmann characterize both Samaritan liturgical cantillation and their general style of singing.

Musical transcriptions are provided for each of the selections from programs 2–9 and 12 that are included on the audio CDs; these selections, performed live in the broadcasting studio,[11] are of different kinds of music practiced in Palestine. The transcriptions were produced aurally, without mechanical or electronic aids other than a metronome and half-speed facility; all except the summary transcriptions in program 9 are based on preliminary drafts produced by Cheryl Frances-Hoad. The selections are transcribed in full with the following exceptions. For strophic songs, such as the Samaritan convivial song in program 6 and the Yemenite women's songs in program 8, only the opening strophe (with chorus, if applicable) is transcribed in full, with strophic repetition indicated by "etc."; the text of all strophes, however, is given in the text transcription. For the solo instrumental improvisations (*taqāsīm*) in program 9, I provide only summary transcriptions indicating the overall modal trajectory. For *Zaffa hamasiyya* in program 12 (recitation 12.3), in which each line is chanted repeatedly to the same basic melodic pattern, I give only the first few rounds of the pattern, with the full text transcribed separately. Where appropriate, editorial notes are provided before the transcriptions to describe any special issues related to the music transcriptions or to explain the purpose and placement of any supplementary music examples. For the selections taken from commercial records featured on programs 10 and 11 (CD 2, tracks 5–10), text transcriptions have been provided for the commercially recorded songs.

The following conventions apply to the transcriptions and the supplementary musical examples provided by the editor. Voices and melody instruments are transcribed on standard five-line staves, percussion instruments on one-line staves. Where a voice performs together with one or more instruments, each part is given a separate staff; the vocal staff is placed as the topmost staff of each system, with instrumental staves below. Differently from Lachmann's transcriptions, vocal passages are transcribed in transposing treble clef, and melody instruments are transcribed in treble clef or transposing treble clef depending on their range.

Dashed barlines are employed at the editor's discretion to delineate major rhythmic units, which may be of variable length. Repeat signs and ending brackets are employed as shorthands where appropriate. For pieces with a regular rhythmic pulse, initial tempos are given as metronome values. Standard vocal beaming is employed in vocal passages and standard metrical beaming in instrumental passages. Opposing stemming is used to indicate divergent pitches and/or rhythmic values between one or more performers in a group otherwise performing in unison.

The notated pitch may differ from the pitch sounded by up to a whole tone in order to minimize use of accidentals; where the difference is a halftone or more, the pitch equivalency is given on a small staff at the beginning of the transcription. Accidentals that occur consistently throughout a selection or section of it are indicated with key signatures. Both key signatures and temporary accidentals are indicated with the symbols ♯, ♭, ♮, 𝄳, and 𝄲. The symbol 𝄳 indicates a variable degree (i.e., a "half flat")

TABLE 2
Musical Symbols Used in the Transcriptions

Symbol	Description
𝄲	"half sharp," i.e., a variable degree between natural and sharp
𝄳	"half flat," i.e., a variable degree between natural and flat
∾	brief trill with adjacent note
● 〰〰 *	vibrato
x notehead (e.g., 𝅘𝅥 with x head)	vocalization of approximate pitch
small-size notes, notes in parentheses	unclear or approximate pitch, rhythm, or articulation
╱, ╲	slide between pitches
>, –	accented pitch
small-size 16th notes	ornamental anticipatory pitch(es)

* In the transcriptions in program 9, this symbol is used to represent the rapid repetition of a note; see table 6.

between natural and flat, and the symbol 𝄲 indicates a variable degree (i.e., a "half sharp") between natural and sharp. The handling of accidentals within individual transcriptions varies according to the presence or absence of dashed barlines:

1. In transcriptions involving dashed barlines (e.g., all selections in program 8), accidentals remain in effect until the end of a measure per standard engraving practice.

2. In transcriptions without barlines, accidentals are valid only for the note to which they apply, with courtesy cancellations added only the first time they are needed.

Slurs are used in vocal lines to clarify melismas but are omitted on the extremely long melisma on the word "gar" in recitation 3.3. The only articulation marks used are tenutos (–) and accent marks (>); tenutos are used in conjunction with repeated notes and slurs to indicate the smooth rearticulation of a note on a single syllable, and accent marks indicate a sudden, emphatic attack on a single note.

Noteheads in parentheses are used to indicate individual pitches that are only faintly articulated. Small noteheads are used in recitation 5.2 to indicate the faintly sounding sections in the *rabāba* passages. Elsewhere, small noteheads are used to indicate brief anticipatory pitches. *X* noteheads with stems indicate vocalizations (not necessarily intentional) of approximately the notated pitch; *x* noteheads without stems that are connected by a diagonal line to a main note indicate speech-like vocalizations following the main note. Mordent symbols (∾, ∾) indicate a short trill to the upper or lower note, respectively. A trill extension following a note indicates vibrato. A straight diagonal line joining two notes indicates a slide from one pitch to the next. Table 2 gives a summary of the notational symbols used in the transcriptions.

The Sung Texts

Text within the musical transcriptions is transcribed in roman script, using the transliteration systems outlined in tables 3–5. Texts based on written sources are given first in their original Hebrew, Arabic, or Coptic script, then in transliterated form and English translation.

The Hebrew biblical texts in programs 2, 4, and 6 were transcribed from the recordings according to the Yemenite, Kurdish, and Samaritan pronunciation systems by Ben Outhwaite. In the text transcriptions following the music of these selections, orthography and vowel pointing follow the Masoretic Text; the cantillation marks of the Masoretic Text have been omitted. The standard abbreviation יי has been substituted for the Tetragrammaton (rendered variously in the recordings depending on the performers' traditions). English translations of the biblical texts are taken from the Revised Standard Version (abbreviated RSV).

The Hebrew texts of the Yemenite Jewish wedding songs in program 7 are taken from the Jewish-Yemenite diwan (Yitzhary 1992), with translation by Ben Outhwaite. Table 3 presents the transliterated Hebrew alphabet according to the Yemenite, Kurdish, and Samaritan pronunciation systems.

The transliterations of the Coptic liturgical texts in program 3 were prepared by Peter J. Williams. In the text transcriptions following the music, the Coptic texts are given in their original Coptic script, with English translations taken from standard Coptic liturgical sources as referenced for each selection. Table 4 presents the transliterated Coptic alphabet.

The transliteration and translation of the Arabic text of the Egyptian *tawshīḥ* in program 11 (recitation 11.1) was prepared by Jihad Racy, with slight amendments to the translation made by Yousef Meri. The Arabic text of this song is reprinted from Lajnah al-Mūsīqīyah [1959?], volume 4 (unpaginated).

The colloquial Arabic and Judeo-Arabic song lyrics in programs 5, 6, 8, 10, and 12 were transcribed directly from the recordings in roman script, as is conventional for oral literature, along with English translation. The Judeo-Arabic lyrics of the Yemenite women's songs were transcribed and translated by Avi Shivtiel, and Makram Khoury-Machool transcribed and translated the Arabic lyrics of the Bedouin song in program 5, the Samaritan convivial song in program 6, and the Palestinian wedding songs in program 12 (see the preface), with slight amendments made by Yousef Meri and Esther-Miriam

TABLE 3

Hebrew Transliteration (Programs 2, 4, 6, and 7)

Provided by Ben Outhwaite

	Kurdish	Yemenite	Samaritan
Syllabary Characters			
א	ʼ	ʼ	zero; or ʼ medially
בּ/ב	b/v	b/v	b/f
גּ/ג	g/ḡ	g/ḡ	g
דּ/ד	d/ḏ	d/ḏ	d
ה	h	h	zero
ו	w	w	w
ז	z	z	z
ח	ḥ	ḥ	zero
ט	ṭ	ṭ	ṭ
י	y	y	y
כּ/כ/ך	k/ḵ	k/ḵ	k
ל	l	l	l
מ/ם	m	m	m
נ/ן	n	n	n
ס	s	s	s
ע	ʻ	ʻ	zero; or ʻ medially
פּ/פ/ף	p/f	p/f	f
צ/ץ	ṣ	ṣ	ṣ
ק	q	q	q
ר	r	r	r
שׁ/שׂ	š/s	š/s	š
תּ/ת	t/ṯ	t/ṯ	t
Vowels			
◌ָ	a	ɔ	a
◌ַ	a	a	a
◌ֶ	e	a	e
◌ֵ	e	e	e/i
◌ִ	i	i	i/e
◌ְ	ə	a	—
◌ֲ	a	a	—
◌ֳ or short ◌ָ	o	ɔ	a
◌ֱ	e	a	—
◌ֻ or וּ	u	u	u
וֹ or ◌ֹ	o	o	o

ʼ (*alef*) is a glottal stop.
ḏ, *ḡ*, *ḵ*, and *ṯ* are the fricative variants of *d*, *g*, *k*, and *t*.
ḥ is a voiceless pharyngeal fricative; ʻ (*ʻayin*) is a voiced pharyngeal fricative.
ṭ and *ṣ* are velarized forms of *t* and *s*.
š is a voiceless alveolar fricative like *sh* in the English "shop."
ə, the Kurdish pronunciation of the Hebrew *shewa* (◌ְ), is a short murmured vowel, such as that found in the first syllable of the English "potato."
ɔ, the Yemenite pronunciation of the vowel *qamets* (◌ָ), is a back vowel, midway between *a* and *o*, similar to the vowel in the English "saw."
Samaritan Hebrew has either no vowel or full vowels in place of the short *shewa* (◌ְ) and *ḥaṭef* vowels (◌ֲ, ◌ֳ, and ◌ֱ).

Wagner. The lyrics of the Moroccan song in program 10 were transcribed by Saad Souissi with additional contributions from Mohamed Kharbach. The final decisions in transcribing the Arabic texts were my own, and I take full responsibility for any errors and inconsistencies. The transliteration scheme used for the colloquial Arabic texts is given in table 5.

Finally, the following conventions apply to all texts:

1. Dialectical connecting syllables and bisyllables (such as *u-wa-nu-wa* in line 1 of recitation 6.1 and *haw-wa* and *aw-wa* in line 1 of recitation 8.1) and anaptyctic vowels (such as the *i* in the second syllable of "sub-*i*-ḥān" in the chorus of recitation 6.5) are set in italic type to distinguish them from main syllables of words. Depending on

the dialect, not all anaptyctic vowels that are underlaid in the music are included in the text transcriptions.

2. Syllables that are swallowed are placed in parentheses.

3. Nonverbal interjections such as coughs and trill-like ululations (*zagharīd*) are indicated with brackets in the text transcriptions (e.g., *[zaghrūda]*, *[cough]*) and are not accounted for in the musical transcriptions.

4. In the text transcriptions, the tag *[spoken]* precedes any text that is spoken rather than sung; spoken text is likewise not accounted for in the musical transcriptions. A return to sung text is indicated by *[sung]*.

TABLE 4
Coptic Transliteration (Program 3)
Provided by Peter J. Williams

Character	Transliteration
ⲁ	a
ⲃ	v
ⲅ	g
ⲉ	e
ⲏ	i
ⲓ	i
ⲕ	k
ⲗ	l
ⲙ	m
ⲛ	n
ⲟ	o
ⲡ	p
ⲣ	r
ⲥ	s
ⲧ	t
ⲟⲩ	u/w
ⲫ	f
ⲭ	k
ⲱ	ō
ϣ	sh
ϩ	h
ϫ	j
ϯ	ti
ⲁⲓ	ai
ⲟⲓ	oi

Notes

1. See the preface. Peter Lachmann later sent copies of these scripts—apparently in incomplete form—to the Jewish Music Research Centre at the Hebrew University of Jerusalem for incorporation into the Lachmann Archive. It is on these copies that the transcriptions of the lectures in Katz 2003, 328–78, are based.

2. I am grateful to Avi Nahmias for making me a copy of his recording of this interview.

3. Undated sketch written in Berlin between 21 May and 22 June 1937. Hebrew University of Jerusalem, Lachmann Archive, B. II; (2c).

4. Avi Nahmias has suggested that Schur could either have recorded directly from the radio receiver or placed a microphone in front of it. Avi Nahmias, personal communication.

5. A summary of this catalogue is available in Gerson-Kiwi 1974, 103–8. See note 2 in the preface.

6. This information was supplied by Avi Nahmias.

7. Katz does not include recordings for recitations 2.4, 8.1, 8.2, 12.1, or 12.2, nor does she include any of the commercial recordings for programs 10 and 11. Most of the extracts on Katz's audio CD are taken from recordings of similar repertory by the same performers made on different occasions. See note 5 in the preface.

8. For information on the scientific principles involved in audio restoration, see Godsill and Rayner 1998.

9. The various stages in this process are described in Lachmann's annual report of 1935–36 (reproduced in Katz 2003, 138–47) and, more concisely, in his report of April 1937 (reproduced in Katz 2003, 182–86).

10. The Lachmann Archive includes a notebook with texts handwritten in Arabic and Hebrew script for many of the Jerusalem recordings, including those for programs 5, 8, and 12 (Lachmann Archive, A. I. 20). However, the numerous discrepancies between the written and sung versions suggest that the texts were not transcribed directly from the recordings.

11. See above on the use of substitute recordings.

TABLE 5

Arabic Pronunciation (Programs 5, 6, 8, 10, and 12)

Letter(s)	Pronunciation*
Consonants	
'	glottal stop or short *e* depending on dialect
b	as *b* in "habit"
t	as *s* in "stop"
th	as *th* in "thick"
j	as *j* in French "jour"
ḥ	no European equivalent; similar to a stage whisper "ha" but formed further back with back of the tongue depressed.
kh	as *ch* in Scottish "loch"
d	as *l* in "leader"
dh	as *th* in English "either"
r	rolled, as *r* in Spanish or Italian "caro"
z	as *z* in "gazelle"
s	as *t* in "state"
sh	as *sh* in "push"
ṣ	emphatic *s*, similar to "son"
ḍ	emphatic *d*, similar to "done"
ṭ	emphatic *t*, similar to "tall"
ẓ	emphatic *z*, similar to "zoo"
'	'ayn; no European equivalent
gh	gargled, similar to *r* in French "rouge"
f	as *f* in "fast"
q	no European equivalent; formed by taking the point of contact with the soft palate for *k* further back; also as *g* in "go"
k	as *k* in "skate"
c	similar to *ch* in "church"
l	as *l* in "let"
m	as *m* in "moon"
n	as *n* in "nine"
h	as *h* in "head"†
w	as *w* in "well"
y	as *y* in "yes"
Vowels	
a (short)	as in "fat"
ā (long)	as in "father"
i (short)	as in "fit"
ī (long)	as *ee* in "feet"
u (short)	as in "put"
ū (long)	as *oo* in "food"
aw (diphthong)	as *ou* in "out"
ay (diphthong)	like "eye"

* This table is intended as a pragmatic guide only, since pronunciation varies between dialects and among different population groups. In addition, sung pronunciation may vary considerably from spoken, depending on, among other factors, musical context and performance situation.

† Also denotes feminine ending of nouns and adjectives, pronounced as *a* in "Pa" (or colloquially as *e* in "get"), or as *t* when linked.

Plates

Plate 1. Robert Lachmann, Germany, early 1930s.
Private collection of Peter Lachmann.

Plate 2. Georg and Jenny Lachmann (née Händler) and their three sons (from left to right), Heinz, Robert, and Kurt. Berlin, n.d. Private collection of Peter Lachmann.

האוניברסיטה העברית
THE HEBREW UNIVERSITY

Jerusalem, ירושלים,

April 12 th, 1935

Dr. Robert Lachmann
Klopstockstr. 20
Berlin, Germany

Dear Dr. Lachmann,

I am happy to say that we received your visa and that of your helper from the government, and they are being sent to you today.

Let me wish you a pleasant journey and a safe arrival. When you come, I am looking forward to your work with the greatest of interest.

With regards, I am

Sincerely yours,

J. L. Magnes

JLM/ieb

Plate 3. Letter from Judah. L. Magnes to Robert Lachmann, 12 April 1935. Music Department, Israel National Library, Jerusalem.

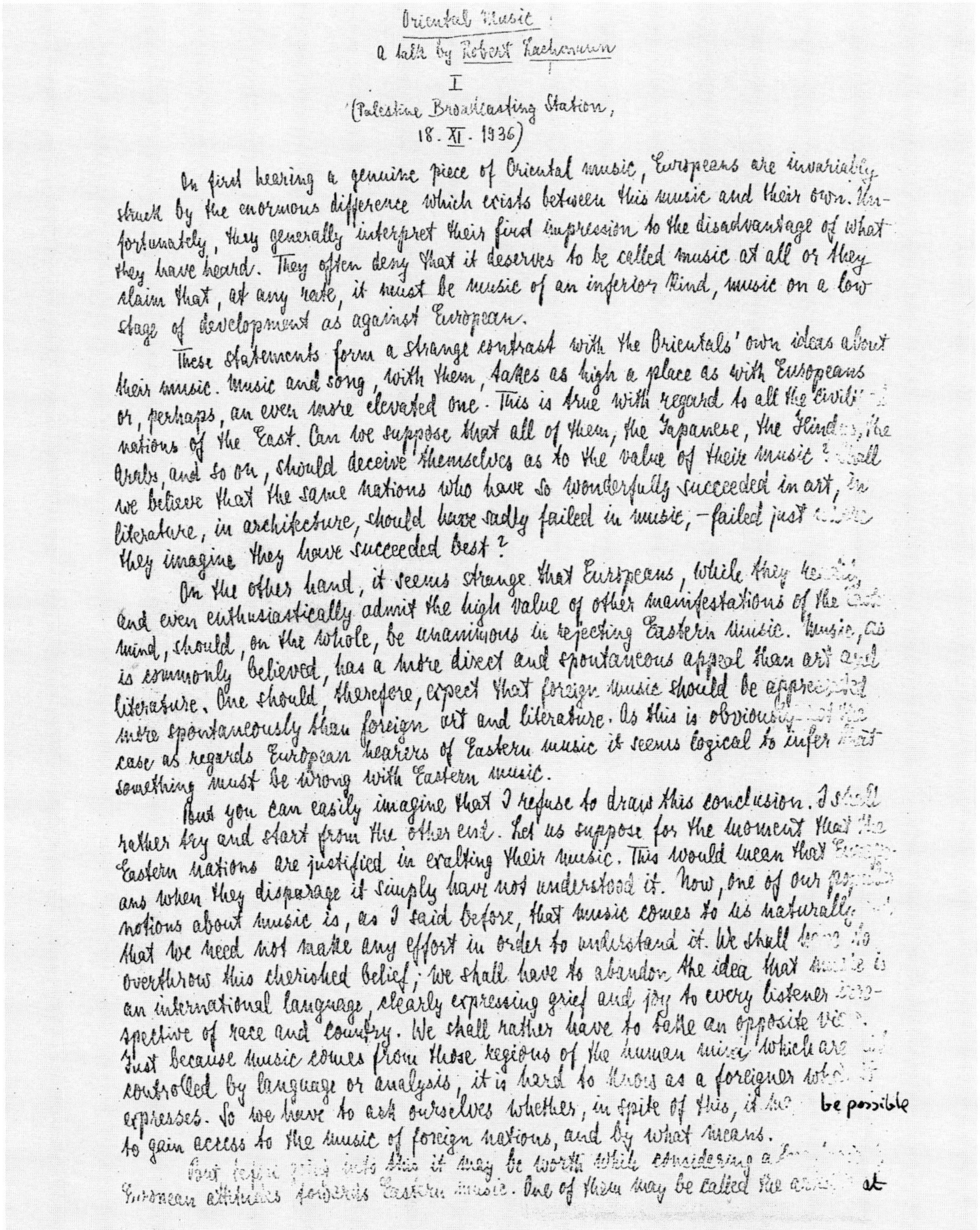

Oriental Music:
a talk by Robert Lachmann
I
(Palestine Broadcasting Station,
18. XI. 1936)

On first hearing a genuine piece of Oriental music, Europeans are invariably struck by the enormous difference which exists between this music and their own. Unfortunately, they generally interpret their first impression to the disadvantage of what they have heard. They often deny that it deserves to be called music at all or they claim that, at any rate, it must be music of an inferior kind, music on a low stage of development as against European.

These statements form a strange contrast with the Orientals' own ideas about their music. Music and song, with them, takes as high a place as with Europeans or, perhaps, an even more elevated one. This is true with regard to all the civilised nations of the East. Can we suppose that all of them, the Japanese, the Hindus, the Arabs, and so on, should deceive themselves as to the value of their music? Shall we believe that the same nations who have so wonderfully succeeded in art, in literature, in architecture, should have sadly failed in music, – failed just where they imagine they have succeeded best?

On the other hand, it seems strange that Europeans, while they readily and even enthusiastically admit the high value of other manifestations of the Eastern mind, should, on the whole, be unanimous in rejecting Eastern music. Music, as is commonly believed, has a more direct and spontaneous appeal than art and literature. One should, therefore, expect that foreign music should be appreciated more spontaneously than foreign art and literature. As this is obviously not the case as regards European hearers of Eastern music it seems logical to infer that something must be wrong with Eastern music.

But you can easily imagine that I refuse to draw this conclusion. I shall rather try and start from the other end. Let us suppose for the moment that the Eastern nations are justified in exalting their music. This would mean that Europeans when they disparage it simply have not understood it. Now, one of our popular notions about music is, as I said before, that music comes to us naturally, that we need not make any effort in order to understand it. We shall have to overthrow this cherished belief; we shall have to abandon the idea that music is an international language, clearly expressing grief and joy to every listener irrespective of race and country. We shall rather have to take an opposite view. Just because music comes from those regions of the human mind which are not controlled by language or analysis, it is hard to know as a foreigner what it expresses. So we have to ask ourselves whether, in spite of this, it will be possible to gain access to the music of foreign nations, and by what means.

But before going into this it may be worth while considering a few typical European attitudes towards Eastern music. One of them may be called the [illegible] at

Plate 4. Robert Lachmann's handwritten copy of program 1 of *Oriental Music,* page 1. Private collection of Peter Lachmann.

Printed in England. Sept., 1938. (6,500 pads.)

CABLE AND WIRELESS
LIMITED.

5/-152

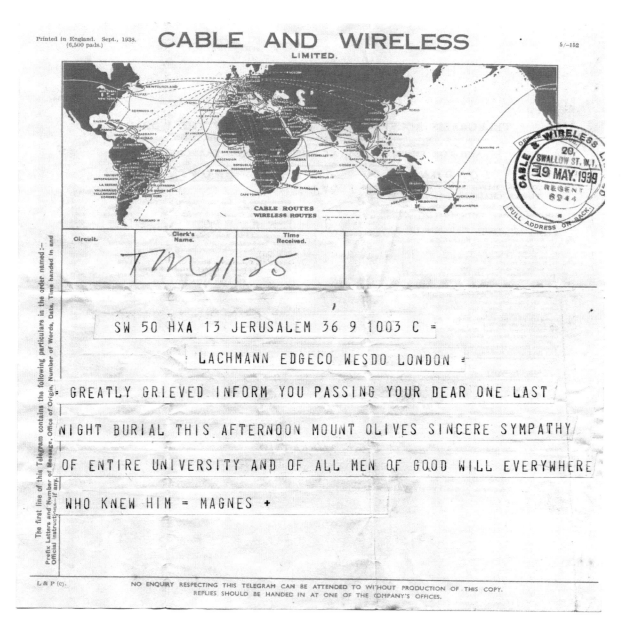

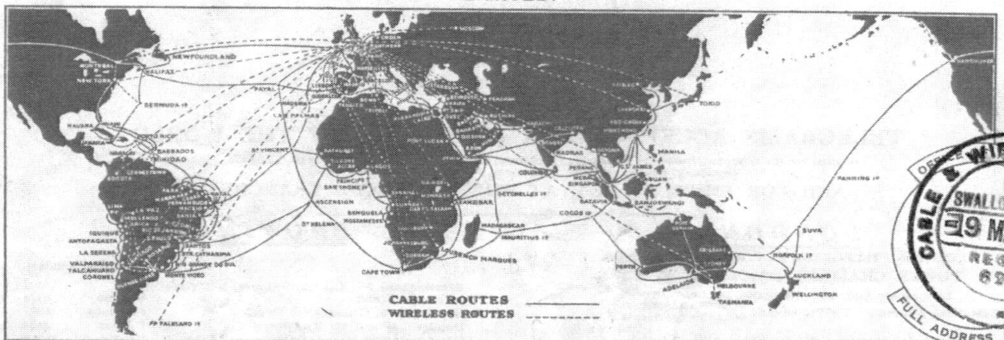

CABLE & WIRELESS LTD. 20, SWALLOW ST. W.1. 9 MAY 1939 REGENT 6944 FULL ADDRESS ON BACK

The first line of this Telegram contains the following particulars in the order named:— Prefix Letters and Number of Message, Office of Origin, Number of Words, Date, Time handed in and Official instructions—if any.

Circuit.	Clerk's Name.	Time Received.
TM	11	25

SW 50 HXA 13 JERUSALEM 36 9 1003 C =

LACHMANN EDGECO WESDO LONDON =

= GREATLY GRIEVED INFORM YOU PASSING YOUR DEAR ONE LAST

NIGHT BURIAL THIS AFTERNOON MOUNT OLIVES SINCERE SYMPATHY

OF ENTIRE UNIVERSITY AND OF ALL MEN OF GOOD WILL EVERYWHERE

WHO KNEW HIM = MAGNES +

L & P (c).

NO ENQUIRY RESPECTING THIS TELEGRAM CAN BE ATTENDED TO WITHOUT PRODUCTION OF THIS COPY.
REPLIES SHOULD BE HANDED IN AT ONE OF THE COMPANY'S OFFICES.

Plate 5. Telegram from Judah L. Magnes to Kurt Lachmann, 9 May 1939. Private collection of Peter Lachmann.

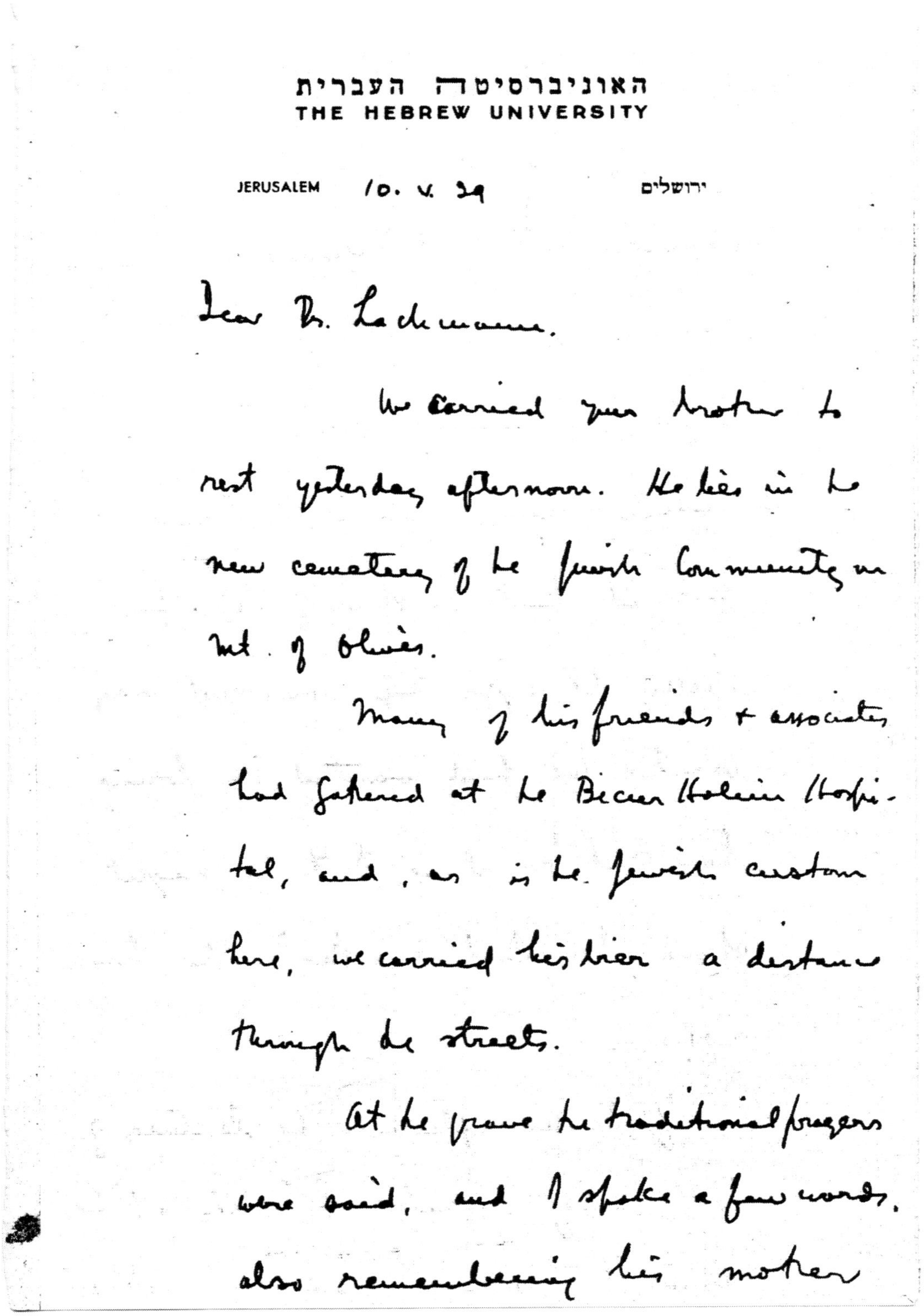

האוניברסיטה העברית
THE HEBREW UNIVERSITY

JERUSALEM 10. V. 39 ירושלים

Dear Dr. Lachmann,

We carried your brother to rest yesterday afternoon. He lies in the new cemetery of the Jewish Community on Mt. of Olives.

Many of his friends & associates had gathered at the Bicur Holim Hospital, and, as is the Jewish custom here, we carried his bier a distance through the streets.

At the grave the traditional prayers were said, and I spoke a few words, also remembering his mother

Plate 6. Letter from Judah L. Magnes to Kurt Lachmann reporting Robert Lachmann's death, 10 May 1939, page 1. Private collection of Peter Lachmann.

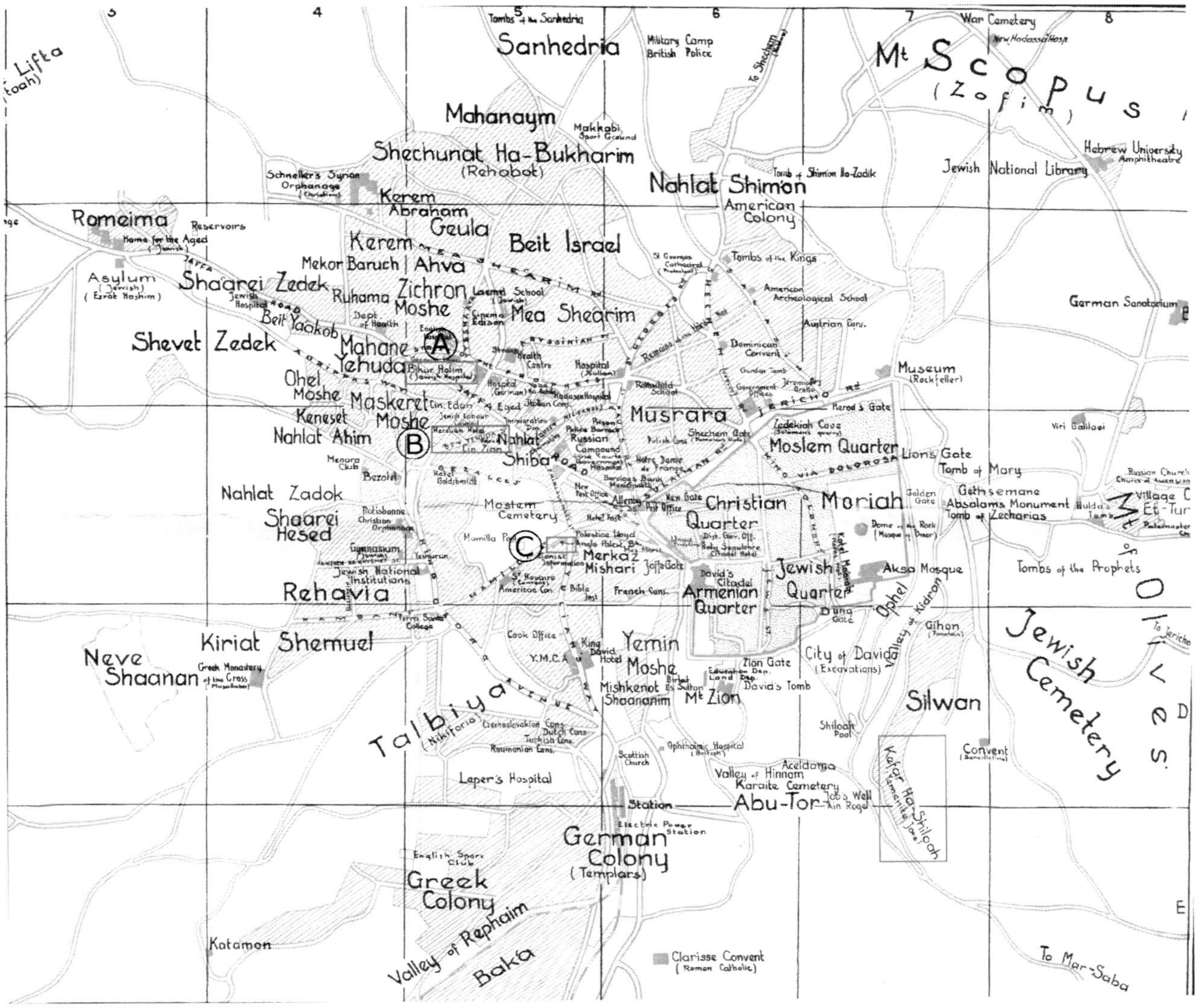

Plate 7. Map of Jerusalem, 1935, showing locations mentioned in the edition (A = Bikur Holim Hospital, B = Lachmann's Oriental Music Archive, C = Palestine Broadcasting Station).

Plate 8. Original disc of recording D596. Side A of two-sided disc. Photograph by Jill Furmanovsky.

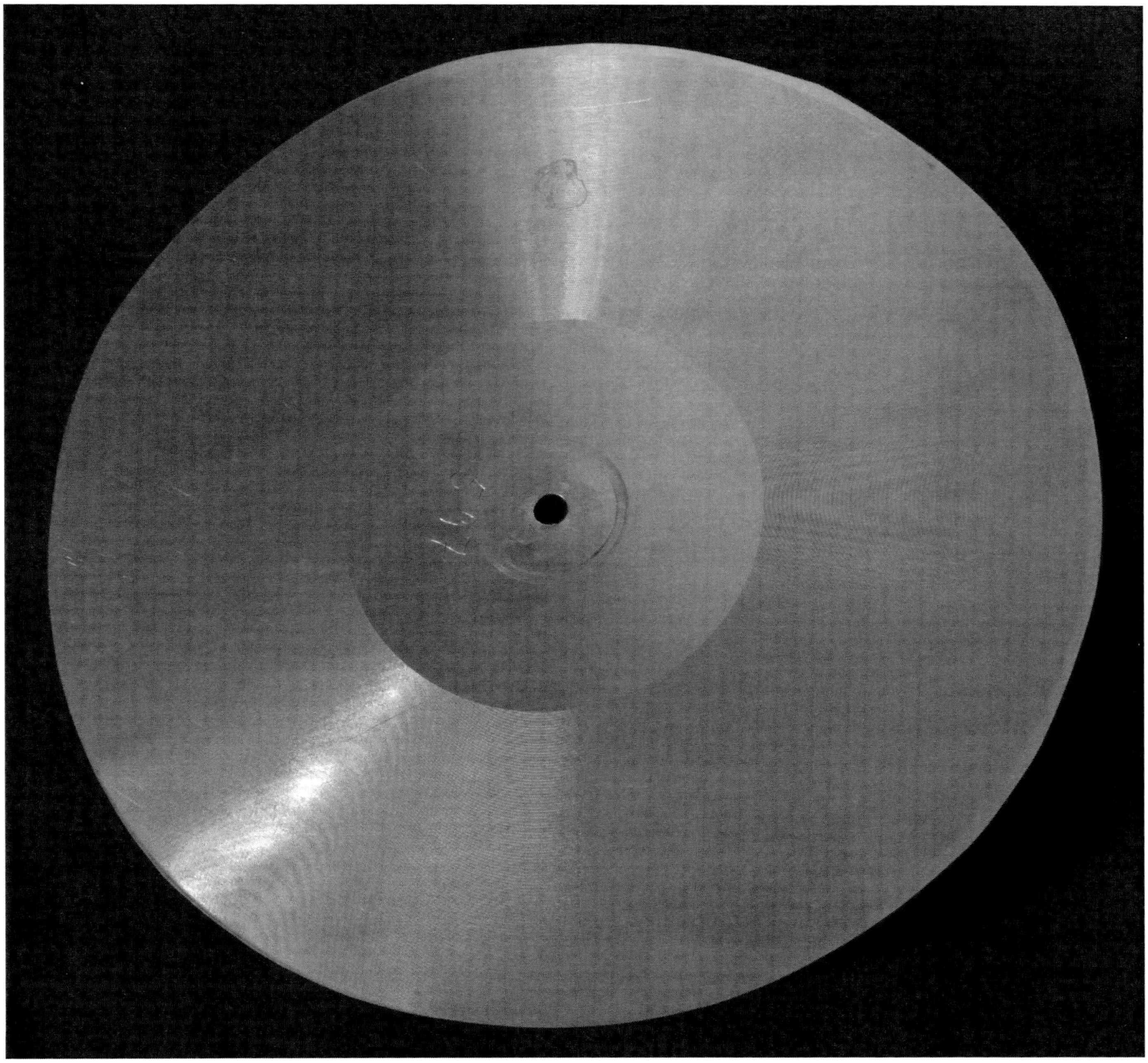

Plate 9. Original disc of recording D597. Side B of two-sided disc. Photograph by Jill Furmanovsky.

The *Oriental Music* Radio Broadcasts

Program 1

"On first hearing a genuine piece of Oriental music"
18 November 1936

On first hearing a genuine piece of Oriental music, Europeans are invariably struck by the enormous difference which exists between this music and their own. Unfortunately, they generally interpret their first impression to the disadvantage of what they have heard. They often deny that it deserves to be called music at all or they claim that, at any rate, it must be music of an inferior kind, music on a low stage of development as against European.

These statements form a strange contrast with the Orientals' own ideas about their music. Music and song, with them, takes a high place as with Europeans or, perhaps, an even more elevated one. This is true with regard to all the civilized nations of the East. Can we suppose that all of them, the Japanese, the Hindus, the Arabs, and so on, should deceive themselves as to the value of their music? Shall we believe that the same nations who have so wonderfully succeeded in art, in literature, in architecture, should have sadly failed in music,—failed just where they imagine they have succeeded best?[1]

On the other hand, it seems strange that Europeans, while they readily and even enthusiastically admit the high value of other manifestations of the Eastern mind, should, on the whole, be unanimous in rejecting Eastern music. Music, as is commonly believed, has a more direct and spontaneous appeal than art and literature. One should, therefore, expect that foreign music should be appreciated more spontaneously than foreign art and literature. As this is obviously not the case as regards European hearers of Eastern music it seems logical to infer that something must be wrong with Eastern music.

But you can easily imagine that I refuse to draw this conclusion. I shall rather try and start from the other end. Let us suppose for the moment that the Eastern nations are justified in exalting their music. This would mean that Europeans when they disparage it simply have not understood it. Now, one of our popular notions about music is, as I said before, that music comes to us naturally and that we need not make any effort in order to understand it. We shall have to overthrow this cherished belief; we shall have to abandon the idea that music is an international language, clearly expressing grief and joy to every listener irrespective of race and country. We shall

---

1. Lachmann's remarks on European attitudes toward Eastern music resonate with earlier firsthand accounts. In an account based on five years in Egypt between 1825 and 1835, the Englishman Edward William Lane confesses that the delight he experienced in listening to the "more refined types of music," which increased with familiarity, was rarely shared by other Europeans he met. He goes on to describe the rapturous responses displayed by "natives of Egypt" to performances of both vocal and instrumental musicians (Lane [1836] 1986, 369). And nearly a century before Lane, Charles Fonton (1725–93), a French *drogman* (interpreter) in the Levant, opened his pioneering study of Turkish music (1751) with a scathing attack on European prejudice, which he claimed was based on ignorance, a false sense of ethnic superiority, and a failure to appreciate that beauty exists only "within the context of the genius of each nation" (Shiloah 1991, 187). Fonton's study, which survives in manuscript form (Paris, Bibliothèque nationale de France, n.a. 4023), is reproduced in Neubauer 1985, with commentary and indices in Neubauer 1986.

Lachmann frequently began his public lectures on the defensive, preempting the expected negative reactions. Addressing the Geographical-Ethnological Society in Basel in May 1935, he warned his audience that:

> Im allgemeinen trifft orientalsiche Musik bei europäischen Hörern auf Ablehnung. Die Musk des Vorderen Orients bildet hiervon keine Ausnahme; im Gegenteil, sie stösst erfahrungsgemäss auf grössere Ablehnung als die Musik von Völkern, die Europa an sich ferner liegen (Lachmann 1974, 46).
>
> [In general Oriental music is received with rejection by European listeners. Music of the Near East is no exception to that rule; the opposite is true: experience tells us it is even more rejected than the music of peoples farther away from Europe.]

It is precisely for that reason, he suggested, that instead of focusing on its aesthetic qualities, they approach it "for its historical value: for its relationship with the past" (ibid.). See also footnote 9 below.

In his lecture "National und International in der orientalsichen Musik," addressed to a primarily Jewish audience at the College of Music "Bet Levi'im" in Tel Aviv, Lachmann defended his interest in non-Jewish music by insisting that only thus was it possible fully to understand "the essence of Jewish music" (Lachmann 1936c).

rather have to take an opposite view. Just because music comes from those regions of the human mind which are not controlled by language or analysis, it is hard to know as a foreigner what it expresses.[2] So we have to ask ourselves whether, in spite of this, it may be possible to gain access to the music of foreign nations, and by what means.

But before going into this it may be worth while considering a few typical European attitudes towards Eastern music. One of them may be called the artistic attitude. Many European composers, in past and present, have taken a fancy to Eastern music, to its atmosphere, to some tunes or fragments of tunes. Their impressions, sometimes quite vague, have inspired compositions some of which have attained great repute. But all these products of an exotic style in European music are interesting as part of their composers' work rather than as reproductions of Eastern music. Couperin's Les Chinois may have sounded very Chinese, and Beethoven's Turkish March, very Turkish, in their contemporaries' ears.[3] But to-day we have come to know that these pieces have no resemblance with their alleged originals and even the general exotic impression that they must have conveyed has faded away in the course of time.

It is particularly the French who tend towards spicing their music with a foreign flavour; think of Saint-Saëns' Suite Algérienne or of Bizet's Carmen.[4] To most of us, Spanish music is known only through Carmen; but then, Spaniards insist that the music in Carmen is not Spanish at all. It is but natural that the creative musician in catching up scraps of foreign music should at once transform them into something else, something essentially his own. The very qualities which distinguish him as a composer make him unfit for helping us towards a better understanding of foreign music.

A different attitude towards Eastern music is taken by those whom I would refer to as reformers. If Oriental music is less developed than European, why not improve upon it and raise it to a higher degree of perfection? As a matter of fact, this has been tried over and over again. Harmony, e.g., is either lacking in Eastern music altogether, or only exists in a rudimentary state while, in European music, it has come to be an indispensable element, and is used as a principal means of expression. Many people, therefore, have undertaken to provide Eastern music with chords and so to add that lustre to it which they felt to be missing.

Another offence found in Eastern music regards its scale. Very frequently the musical intervals of the voice as well as of the instruments deviate from the European scale. In all these cases, Eastern intonation strikes the European ear as faulty. This difficulty as well has attracted the active mind of the reformer. He simply replaces the original instruments of the East by others on which the European scale is fixed once for all and he so arrives at forcing European tuning on Eastern melody. The most suitable instrument for both these purposes, for harmonizing Eastern music and for re-tuning it, is the piano; and really, during the last century and the first decades of

---

2. Lachmann opened the first of his *Four Lectures on Eastern Music* with a similar argument:

> There is a wide-spread saying according to which music, as against speech, is an international language, mutually understood and appreciated by all. . . . On the whole, this is a wrong opinion. . . . We can, to a very high degree, arrive at understanding what is said in a foreign language; but we can hardly arrive at really understanding foreign music. The reason for this is evident. Language chiefly addresses itself to our intellect; words can, to a certain degree, be defined and translated. Music is a more direct mode of expression. But while its directness, its spontaneity, is generally considered as its chief claim to be an international language, it is precisely this quality which separates the musical expression of one people from that of another. Instead of saying, therefore, that music need not be translated we ought rather to say that it cannot be translated (quoted in Katz 2003, 381).

3. Ironically, neither Couperin's "Les Chinois" nor the theme of Beethoven's "Turkish March" was originally intended to sound Chinese or Turkish. In her penetrating study of Couperin's descriptive titles, Jane Clark identifies "Les Chinois," from Couperin's *Fourth Book of Harpsichord Pieces* (1730), as a reference to the play of the same name by Regnard and Dufresnay, which appeared in the popular compilation *Le theatre italien de Gherardi* (Gherardi 1683). These plays were enjoying great success in the Parisian fair theaters in the 1720s, and Couperin drew inspiration from several others too (Clark 1980, 166–69). As Clark demonstrates, not only are the Chinese references in Regnard and Dufresnay's play themselves merely incidental; Couperin's piece is clearly an imitation of the play's prologue, which is set not in China but on Mount Parnassus "with Apollo and the Muses. On the summit stands a winged ass representing Pegasus. An ensemble of comic instruments is heard; this is repeatedly interrupted by the ass braying" (Clark 1980, 169).

Beethoven's "Turkish March" belongs to his set of incidental music *Die Ruinen von Athen*, op. 113, composed in 1811 to accompany the play of the same name by August von Kotzebue for the opening of the new theater in Pest. Beethoven based the theme of the B-flat-major "Marcia alla turca" on the theme of his piano variations in D, op. 76. The march features an expanded percussion section with triangle, cymbals, and bass drum—orchestral code for the janissary (*mehterhane*) bands of the Ottoman court; unusally, though, the timpani is absent.

4. Saint-Saëns's tone poem *Suite algérienne*, op. 60 (ca. 1880) draws from the composer's experiences during the two months he spent in Algeria in 1873. Subtitled "Impressions pittoresques d'un Voyage en Algérie," its four movements carry the descriptive titles *Prélude (en vue d'Alger), Rhapsodie mauresque, Rêverie du soir (à Blidah),* and *Marche militaire française (de retour à Alger).* Beneath each title is a verbal sketch of the sounds, rhythms, and scenes depicted in the score.

In contrast, the extent to which *Carmen* (1875) is based on Spanish sources continues to be debated. The French libretto, by Henri Meilhac and Ludovic Halévy, which is based on the 1845 novel by Prosper Mérimée, is set in Seville, in the heart of what was once Moorish Spain; Carmen and her companions are described as "bohémiennes" (lit. "Bohemians," i.e., Gypsies). Arguing that Bizet's familiarity with Spanish music and its influence on the score of *Carmen* are generally underestimated, Theodore Beardsley has identified specific rhythms and tunes derived from Spanish folksongs and pieces by the Spanish composers Sebastián Yradier and Manuel Garcia (Beardsley 1989). *Carmen* has been the focus of numerous recent writings on musical exoticism; see, for example, Locke 2009, 150–74; McClary 1997, 115–29; McClary 1992, 29–35; and Parakilas 1993–94.

the present one, with the rise of European romantic interest in matters Oriental, a growing number of Eastern or would-be Eastern tunes and songs has been published to the accompaniment of the piano or the harmonium.

These attempts at reforming Eastern music have an interesting parallel in the tendencies of a certain class of Oriental musicians. With them, too, the questions of harmony and of European tuning are predominant. However little they may have done till now towards building up a new kind of Eastern music, they have set their minds on having the piano as its representative piece of furniture. It is, however, worth mentioning that the only official body which, up to now, has given an opinion as to these attempts, the Egyptian Ministry of Education, has rejected the piano as unsuitable for the performance of Eastern music, and has strictly excluded it from musical education.[5]

We cannot predict the future results of the various efforts and influences which contribute towards Europeanizing Oriental music. But the introduction of European harmony and tuning into present day Oriental music, if it is meant to raise it to a higher standard, certainly misses its aim. It is curious to note in what way the character of Oriental tunes is changed by imposing harmony and the European scale upon them. Above all, the application of European chords does not necessarily stress the main points of the melody, but may, on the contrary, detract our attention from them, and thus confuse rather than guide us when we try to understand its natural flow. An Eastern melody may, e.g., have the note D as its tonic. The accompaniment would, in this case, according to European rules of composition, have to strike a D-minor chord. But the notes F and A which belong to this chord may not be prominent, or may not even as much as occur in the melody. The accompaniment, therefore, would, instead of supporting the melody as it invariably does in European music, be at cross purposes with it. But even when the tune and the accompaniment do not actually contradict each other, Eastern melody is in no need of accompaniment. While in European music harmony is essential because it is conceived along with melody, the salient notes in Eastern tunes need not be stressed by chords; they are established in the course of the tune itself by purely melodical and not by harmonical devices.

This is an important point not only with respect to traditional Eastern music. It also concerns Europeans who try and compose unaccompanied tunes—for which there is a growing demand in this country at present. It will not do to compose unaccompanied tunes on an harmonic basis. If played or sung without an accompaniment they will always sound imperfect; the accompaniment, in such cases, is not superfluous, but is only suppressed. Instead of this, one should rather turn to traditional Eastern music as a model; there, we find everything that is necessary to know about the construction of unaccompanied melody as distinguished from European harmonic music.

As to the piano, it is easy to see why it is inadequate as a medium of Oriental music. Firstly, there is the question of scale. In many parts of the East, the notes of the scale do not coincide with those to be found on the keyboard; and in the Near East as well as in India, the number of notes in use exceeds those offered by the piano. So, to accept the piano for Eastern music, in many cases means to merge neighbouring notes which the Orientals have been careful to keep apart, following, evidently, the demands of their ear and their musical sense.[6] Nor is the piano capable of rendering all those delicate shades of tone which Oriental musicians manage to produce on their own instruments, especially on plucked strings.

No—we certainly do not bring Eastern music any nearer to our understanding by tampering with it. Nor does it benefit from it any other way; instead of the real

5. The ministry's opposition to the use of the piano reflects the official recommendation of the Committee on Musical Instruments at the 1932 Cairo Congress of Arab Music. The committee was headed by Dr. Mahmoud al-Ḥifnī (el-Hefni), who was Inspector of Music at the Ministry of Education. Al-Ḥifnī had completed his doctorate at the University of Berlin, and he had recently worked with Lachmann on a translation of a treatise on music by al-Kindī (Lachmann and el-Hefni 1931). It was hardly surprising, therefore, that al-Ḥifnī was sympathetic to Lachmann's views. Nevertheless, as Jihad Racy notes, "the committee's report did not conceal the disagreement between the Europeans, who expressed misgivings about the Arab use of the piano, and the overwhelming majority of the Egyptian participants, who voiced their enthusiasm for the instrument" (Racy 1991, 75).

In fact, by the 1930s, the piano was well-entrenched in Egyptian musical life. The eminent Egyptian theorist Kāmil al-Khulā'ī had advocated the use of *pyānū* (piano), *armūnīkah* (mouth organ), and *mūzīkah* (accordion) as early as 1904, in his *Kitāb al-mūsīqā al-sharqī* (The Book of Eastern Music) (al-Khulā'ī 1904, 58–59; quoted in Racy 1977, 62). Racy refers to the "hundreds of examples of piano sheet music—separate compositions transcribed and sold to Egyptian pianists during the 1920s and 1930s," and the numerous advertisements mentioning male and female piano teachers that appeared around the same time (Racy 1977, 38–39). The piano became a status symbol in middle- and upper-class homes, where it was particularly associated with women, both as performers (Racy 1977, 63) and as composers. Salwa El-Shawan Castelo-Branco, for example, writes of "a repertoire of 'salon music' . . . disseminated through sheet music and commercial recordings [consisting] of arrangements for piano of selected Arab compositions and a new Arab piano repertoire, most of which was created by a few women composers trained in Arab and Western music" (Castelo-Branco 2002, 610).

In 1930s Palestine, the Yemenite Jewish singer Bracha Zefira was giving recitals of Yemenite, Bedouin, and Sephardic songs accompanied on the piano by her Russian husband, Nahum Nardi, to popular acclaim. Such was her success that she was selected to perform her Yemenite song arrangements in the inaugural broadcast of the Palestine Broadcasting Service in March 1936. Zefira went on to commission arrangements for piano and various instrumental combinations, including full orchestra, from Paul Ben-Haim and other leading European immigrant composers (Hirshberg 1995, 189–96).

6. Lachmann elaborates on the modal-melodic character of Arab music in program 10, where he describes the evolution of the modern twenty-four-note-per-octave scale of Arab, Persian, and Turkish music and the melodic material derived from it. See program 10, footnotes 3–5.

thing, we obtain a hybrid production, typical neither of East nor West, and shallow like ditchwater.

If, on the other hand, we take it as it is, leaving all European prejudice behind, we may hope to penetrate to its core. In no other country, perhaps, the need for a sound understanding of it and the opportunity of studying it answer each other so well as they do in Palestine. For the European, here, it is of vital interest to know the mind of his Oriental neighbour; well, music and singing, as being the most spontaneous outcome of it,[7] will be his surest guide provided he listens to it with sympathy instead of disdain.

The opportunities, in this country, of hearing traditional music are most varied. I shall try, during this series, to give you examples of at least some outstanding kinds of it, and to mention, in every case, a few points that need to be understood.[8] I hope that in this way you will become acquainted with the main aspects of the present day music of the Near East and with the principles underlying it.

But this will not be all. It is almost impossible to discuss Eastern music without being led into the past. In fact, this is one of its highest claims to our interest; through the mouth of a present day musician we may hear tunes which have charmed audiences of a thousand years and more ago. Thus, the study of the music as found here and now may throw some light on what has been said about music by ancient and medieval authors, and would otherwise remain obscure; and it may revive the mute scenes of music which have come down to us as the work of ancient painters and sculptors.[9] Present day Bedouins, in playing the fiddle, follow rules established by musicians at the court of the early Abbasid Khalifs; negroes of the Sudan can correct our notions about how the lyre of Ancient Egypt was handled; and who knows how much may possibly be learnt from Oriental Jews of today about the singing at the ancient temple in Jerusalem?

---

7. The romantic belief that the anonymous oral musical traditions of rural communities—and, by extension, oral musical traditions generally—are spontaneous expressions of the collective psyche permeates nineteenth-century folk music scholarship and derives from the concept of the *Volkslied* as formulated by the eighteenth-century poet-philosopher Johann Gottfried Herder in his two-volume anthology *Stimmen der Völker in Liedern: Volkslieder* (1778, 2nd ed. 1779). This belief inspired countless musical nationalisms (see Bohlman 2011) and was widely adopted by comparative musicologists to justify their opposition to Western musical influence. In 1930s Palestine, Lachmann turned the case for musical nationalism on its head by promoting traditional music as a means of understanding the Other. Yet he was by no means the first to do so. In the preface to her popular book *The American Indians and Their Music,* published a decade earlier, the American ethnomusicologist Frances Densmore argued that:

> Music is closely intertwined with the life of every race. We understand the people better if we know their music, and we appreciate the music better if we understand the people themselves. . . . The chief purpose of the book is to assist an acquaintance with our nearest neighbour—the American Indian (Densmore 1926, 5).

8. Lachmann lifts this phrase from the opening of "the admirable book on 'The Music of Hindostan' by Mr. Fox Strangways," which he cites in the first of his *Four Lectures on Eastern Music:*

> People who have lived in India have often asked [me], with various inflections of the voice, "Do you like" or "do you really like Indian music?" The more one thinks what the answer to this should be, the more it seems to resolve itself into another—"Do you really understand it?"—to which there can, of course, be no final answer. Indeed it would be difficult with regard to our own music to reply satisfactorily to the question or to do more than put down a few of the points that need to be understood (Fox Strangways 1914, 1, quoted without citation in Katz 2003, 386).

9. In attempting to capitalize on the relative prestige of the music of the ancient and medieval (as opposed to present-day) Orient in contemporary European culture and scholarship, Lachmann perpetuates the myth—widespread among nineteenth- and early-twentieth-century European scholars and upheld by certain Eastern musical cultures themselves—of the long continuity and unchangeability of their oral musical traditions; see also Bohlman 1987 and Racy 1981, 7–8. Lachmann explores the implications of this premise for the contemporary understanding of topics such as medieval Arab music theory, the recitation of ancient Greek and Northern European epic poetry, and the performance of ancient Greek tragedy in several lectures written in 1936 and 1937, including "Orientalische Musik und Antike," delivered in Basel in May 1936 (reproduced in Lachmann 1974); "Musical Systems among the Present Arab Bedouins and Peasants," delivered in Jerusalem in December 1936 (Lachmann 1936a); and program 5 of *Oriental Music* (see "Editor's Commentary" to program 5).

Program 2

Liturgical Songs of the Yemenite Jews
2 December 1936

The three Yemenite Jews who will presently illustrate this talk with examples from their liturgical cantillation are sitting opposite me waiting for their turn and one cannot help reflecting on the strange contrast between these men who have been brought up in medieval ways of behaviour and thought and their present surroundings,—a modern broadcasting room with its technical outfit.[1] What, above all, may be in their minds as to the object of their recital? If they were told that they were being expected to perform what we call a concert of sacred music they would hardly understand; nor are they likely to realise the interest attached to it from the point of view of musical history.

As an introduction to the Oriental outlook on music and song I would mention an incident which occurred a few years ago. A friend of mine, when preparing for a research tour to Yemen, sought the advice of a number of persons who were considered to be authorities on the conditions in that country and on the manners and customs of its inhabitants. Among other things he mentioned his intention to carry a phonograph with him in order to record specimens of Yemenite music. The answer to this invariably was that music, in Yemen, was strictly prohibited and that it would, therefore, be useless to search for it and even dangerous to be found searching for it. Fortunately he did not act on this expert advice, and had the satisfaction of recording and bringing home a unique collection of Beduin and other songs from that remote part of the world.

It is quite true that in Yemen as well as in other parts of the East a ban[2] on music exists. This ban, however, does not affect everything that Europeans are used to call music. It only extends to certain branches of it, namely those which, from the point of view of Muslim orthodoxy, are discredited because of their connexion with immoral pleasures.

In this respect, the three great religions which originated in the Near East have a great deal in common. Each of them has a long record of pamphlets on the lawfulness of music and theologians have over and again denounced musical instruments as prompting evil instincts and dissipation.[3] I have myself, in connection with my work, come up against a situation which arose from this orthodox attitude. When I visited one of the Jewish communities on the isle of Djerba in order to study their Synagogue song they pointed out to me that I would not be permitted to make phonograph records. I first thought that the sacred nature of the cantillation was

1. The "three Yemenite Jews" are identified in Lachmann's recording diaries as Sa'adiya Nahum ("from Haca, Yemen"), Rafael Nadav, and David Dehari. Sa'adiya Nahum is the soloist in the readings from the Pentateuch and Proverbs (recitations 2.1 and 2.3).

2. Lachmann's script: *bann*.

3. Attitudes toward music and musical instruments evolved according to different frames of reference in Judaism, Christianity, and Islam. In Judaism, the reasons traditionally given for the proscription of instrumental music in the synagogue are mourning for the destruction of the Second Temple in 70 CE and the resultant exile. There is a precedent for this tradition in Psalm 137:1–4, in which the Jews lament their exile to Babylon following the destruction of the First Temple in the sixth century BCE: "By the waters of Babylon, there we sat down and wept, when we remembered Zion. On the willows there we hung up our lyres. . . . How shall we sing the Lord's song in a foreign land?" The only biblical instrument that has been consistently retained in synagogue worship is the *shofar* (ram's horn), which is blown on Rosh Hashanah and during the preparatory month of Elul, and whose original function, according to Idelsohn, is primarily symbolic (Idelsohn [1929] 1992, 10). For a general discussion of attitudes toward music and musical instruments in Judaism, see Shiloah 1992, 65–86; for approaches to music more broadly in both Judaism and Islam, see Shiloah 2007a. In Islam, the absence of unequivocal guidance in the Qur'an or hadith gave rise to a substantial polemical literature among medieval philosophers about the lawfulness of listening to any kind of music, particularly in religious contexts (*al-samā'*); see Farmer 1929, 20–38; Shehadi 1995, 95–162; and Nelson 2001, 32–51. Negative attitudes toward music and musical instruments in early Christianity were fueled by associations with pagan practices and sexual immorality. For source materials in patristic literature, and a succinct account of the polemics against pagan music and musical instruments, including their precedents in Greco-Roman and Jewish thought, see McKinnon 1987.

held to be incompatible with its reproduction by a machine. But what they really objected to was not the mechanical reproduction of sacred song, but the horn which was prefixed to my old-fashioned recording machine and which, in their opinion, gave it the character of a musical instrument. It was most difficult to overcome their scruples as they had never before tolerated musical instruments within their town.[4]

In Europe, the moral prejudice against professional musicians remained alive until little more than a century ago—remember the treatment Mozart suffered at the hands of his archbishop at Salzburg.[5] The old struggle against the evil influence of music was revived but recently when Argentine dances and, later on, jazz obsessed people's heads and bodies.

Still, the European[6] nations, in a long and complicated historical process, evolved a new outlook on music. The various branches of music, however different their function in life and their effect on the hearers, came to be considered as parts of one thing, that is to say, of music in the widest sense of the word. We cannot stop to discuss whether or to what extent this development was due to the influence of Ancient Greek thought and the Greeks' keenly artistic feeling. Even the Greek word music to which there is no equivalent in other languages may have contributed a great deal towards impressing upon us those qualities which are common to all the different branches of music. But the recognition of the unity of music would not have been brought about except for a material change in musical practice. Above all, the medieval church, endeavouring to make the power of secular music serviceable to religious ideals, came to accept musical instruments and the scales of secular music.[7] Thus, the difference between the various branches of music gradually diminished.

With the Orientals, on the other hand, the different kinds of music have, on the whole, remained separate. Dance music, e.g. to them is essentially different from the recitation of heroic poetry; and liturgical cantillation, again, stands by itself. They do not use a general term to obliterate the difference, and the instruments employed in one of the different kinds of music are generally particular to it and not liable to be transferred to another. A prohibition, therefore, of certain kinds of music or of musical instruments does not affect music as a whole; they do not think of music as a whole.[8]

So we have to regard the various groups in Oriental music as separate just as the Orientals themselves do, and have to judge each of them by its own standards and principles. Europeans are only too apt to miss this point; they apply the standards of any one kind of Oriental music to another or even the standards of European music to Oriental, and wonder why they do not fit. It does not occur to them that they might as well find fault with a pen-and-ink drawing for its lack of colour or with a water colour painting for its lack of neat outline. As a matter of fact, different kinds of music in the East do not only vary as to their moral effects or their function in life, but also in their musical system.

All this must be kept in mind when approaching the subject of Oriental liturgical cantillation. It is hardly an exaggeration to say that religious cantillation, in the East, is not a branch of music which happens to be connected with liturgy, but rather a part of liturgy which happens to be chant or akin to chant.

Oriental Synagogue song supplies a characteristic instance of this type of music—if it is to be called music. Its distinction from secular music, either purely instrumental or sung to the accompaniment of instruments, is self-evident.[9] Fixed intervals and scales, being a natural and visible result of the handling of musical instruments, are alien to it; the unaccompanied voice yields no standard intervals. Synagogue song, therefore, is not originally grouped according to a system of scales and whenever a Synagogue singer claims that his cantillation is based on some scale we may be sure that this is a modernization due to the influence of secular urban music.[10]

---

4. Lachmann describes having to pay a fee for a special expiatory prayer before carrying out research on Djerba (Lachmann 1940, 2; and Lachmann 1978, 28).

5. For German-reading scholars in the 1930s, the definitive Mozart study was Hermann Abert's *W. A. Mozart* (1919), based on Otto Jahn's classic text of 1856. Abert reserves judgment on the reasons for the breakdown of relations between the Mozarts and their former patron, Archbishop Hieronymus Colloredo of Salzburg, commenting only that "it was no act of capricious despotism on the prince's part that led to the final breach but the incompatibility of their characters and views" (Abert 2007, 258).

6. Lachmann's script: *Europeans*.

7. Of the instruments accepted into the medieval church, only the organ was used consistently from the middle of the eighth century onward; on the early use of the organ in church music, see Williams 1993, 1–16. Scholars have traditionally identified two main sources for the eight church modes, both of which derive from Hellenistic sources: (a) the eightfold Byzantine modal system (*oktōēchos*), which was transmitted from Byzantine sources to the Carolingian clergy during the eighth century (see Jeffery 1992, 107); and (b) ancient Greek music theory, particularly as transmitted to the medieval West in the sixth and seventh centuries by such scholars as Cassiodorus, Martianus Capella, and especially Boethius (see Powers and Wiering 2001).

8. On the conceptualization of the various branches of "music" in Islam and the corresponding Arabic terminology, see al-Faruqi 1985, 6–15.

9. Lachmann's script: *selfevident*.

10. Lachmann elaborates on these ideas in the first chapter of his Djerba monograph, which he completed during his first year in Jerusalem (Lachmann 1940 and 1978; see also "The Djerba Monograph" in the introduction). His argument has an immediate precursor in Erich M. von Hornbostel's discussion of the earliest tone systems, in which he distinguishes between musical systems characterized by definite scales, which were determined by the physical properties of musical instruments and their measurements, and the principles of "pure melody" that governed the singing of the unaccompanied voice (Hornbostel 1927, 447–49). Arguing that the interdependence of motor impulses and melodic movement was "rooted in the psychophysical constitution of man" (Hornbostel 1928a, 34), Horn-

In the cantillation of the Synagogue the word is all-important. The text dictates the course of the voice; the melodic element serves to enhance its impressiveness by reducing the fluctuations of speech to a definite number of melodic phrases and cadences. Nor is the cantillation regulated by any system of musical metre. There is no strict time as we find it marked in other kinds of music, by drums or plucked strings. In this respect, too, the text dominates; the musical time-values are in the service of syntax and rhetoric.

The cantillation is divided into groups which correspond to the different books of the Bible and other parts of the liturgy. Each of these parts has its particular set of melodic phrases and cadences which, used in the succession required by the text, constitute a melodic tone (in Hebrew, niggūn). Here, again, the preeminence of the text is worth remarking upon; the different melodic modes take their names from the books of the Bible and the other parts of the liturgy. Thus, the cantors distinguish a Pentateuch—, a Prophets'—, a Psalms'—, an Esther mode[11] and so on.[12]

You will now hear some specimens of this cantillation. The melodic element of Synagogue song varies considerably from one community to another. On the present occasion, the Yemenite tradition has been chosen; it may claim a more than ordinary interest because of the early seclusion of the Yemenite Jewish community. This and the frugal conditions of their life have their counterpart in the simple and archaic style of their cantillation.[13]

The first is from the Song of the Sea (šīrāt[14] ha-yam). Although forming part of the second book of the Pentateuch, this song, owing to its special character, is recited in a mode reserved to certain outstanding parts of the Pentateuch while the rest is in the ordinary Pentateuch mode. (Recitation 2.1, CD 1, tracks 1–2)

You are now going to hear the end of the book of Esther which is recited in a mode of its own. The last verse is repeated by the community who, of course, transform the cantor's free rhythm into strict time. (Recitation 2.2)

As a third and last specimen of Yemenite Synagogue cantillation the beginning of the book of Proverbs (mišlē) will follow. Its mode is the same as that of the Song of Songs.[15] (Recitation 2.3, CD 1, tracks 3–4)

The non-liturgical songs of the Yemenite[16] Jews which, again, fall into several groups are, of course, entirely different from their cantillation. I must refrain, now, from entering upon a description of the musical style of these non-liturgical songs; but as they are an important feature in the life of the community it is worth while hearing at least one specimen. The class of song to which this specimen belongs and which is simply called song (šīra[17]) is connected with dances. Its strict time is accentuated by clapping the hands; but the beats, instead of marking equal time-intervals, go off into rhythmical phrases of a definite form.[18] (Recitation 2.4)

---

bostel defines "pure melody" as "an undivided unity which [the singer] performs at one stroke as an athlete does an exercise" (Hornbostel 1928a, 35; both cited in Blum 1991, 11–12). Yet, as Stephen Blum has demonstrated in his penetrating discussion of the intellectual foundations of ethnomusicology, the concept of a fundamental dichotomy between vocal and instrumental music and its corollary—that between natural and artificial music—belongs to a far wider conversation that had been in progress since at least the late eighteenth century (Blum 1991, 13). Jean-Jacques Rousseau, who traced the origins of both language and music to spontaneous vocalizations of passion and the birth of human communication, described the gradual separation of music from words and the substitution of theory for the natural inflections of the voice, as a process of decline: "In proportion as language was perfected, melody imperceptibly lost its ancient energy by imposing new rules upon itself and the calculation of intervals was substituted for the subtlety of inflections. . . . Thus melody, beginning to no longer be so attached to discourse, imperceptibly assumed a separate existence, and music became more independent of the words" (Rousseau 1998, 329).

11. Lachmann's script: *Esthermode.*

12. In his essays introducing the individual volumes of the *Thesaurus,* Idelsohn identifies the "particular set of melodic phrases and cadences" used by each tradition for the different parts of the Bible or liturgy. He summarizes his observations in the comparative transcriptions and tables in chapters 3 and 4 of Idelsohn (1929) 1992.

13. Lachmann's characterization of the Yemenite style of cantillation is clearly based on Idelsohn, as is his selection of examples and commentary on them. See the editor's commentary below.

14. Lachmann's script: *sīrāt.*

15. On the relationship between the two books in the Hebrew Bible, see the editor's commentary below.

16. Lachmann's script: *Yeminite.*

17. Lachmann's script: *sīra.*

18. See program 7 for a more expansive treatment of songs sung by Yemenite Jewish men at weddings (also featuring Sa'adiya Nahum as the soloist; see program 7). Idelsohn, too, attached considerable importance to this nonliturgical repertory: seventy-three of his two hundred Yemenite transcriptions in the *Thesaurus* are of "non-synagogal song," and he includes several additional examples in his appendix to volume 1.

Recitation 2.1: Shirat ha-yam *(Song of the Sea, excerpt, Exod. 15:1–4)*

Recording number: D354

Performer: Sa'adiya Nahum

li- šu- ‘ɔ
za ’e- li wa- ’an- we- e- hu
’a- lo- he ’ɔ- vi
wa- ’a- ro- ma- man- hu:
haš- šem ’iš mil- ḥɔ- mɔ
haš- šem ša- mo:
mar- ka- vot̠ par- ‘o
we- ḥe- lo yɔ- rɔ vay- yɔm
u- miv- ḥar šɔ- li- šɔw ṭub- bu- ’u vi- yam- suf:

אָז יָשִׁיר־מֹשֶׁה וּבְנֵי יִשְׂרָאֵל אֶת־הַשִּׁירָה הַזֹּאת לַיי וַיֹּאמְרוּ לֵאמֹר אָשִׁירָה לַיי
כִּי־גָאֹה גָּאָה סוּס וְרֹכְבוֹ רָמָה בַיָּם׃
עָזִּי וְזִמְרָת יָהּ וַיְהִי־לִי לִישׁוּעָה זֶה אֵלִי וְאַנְוֵהוּ אֱלֹהֵי אָבִי וַאֲרֹמְמֶנְהוּ׃
יי אִישׁ מִלְחָמָה יי שְׁמוֹ׃
מַרְכְּבֹת פַּרְעֹה וְחֵילוֹ יָרָה בַיָּם וּמִבְחַר שָׁלִשָׁיו טֻבְּעוּ בְיַם־סוּף׃

(Exod. 15:1–4)

ʼɔz yɔšir-moša uvne yisrɔʼal ʼaṯ-hašširɔ hazzoṯ laššem wayyomaru lemor ʼɔširɔ laššem ki-ḡɔʼo ḡɔʼɔ sus waroḵavo rɔmɔ vayyɔm:

ʻɔzzi wazimrɔṯ yɔh wayhi-li lišuʻɔ za ʼeli waʼanwe-*e*-hu ʼalohe ʼɔvi waʼaromamanhu:

haššem ʼiš milḥɔmɔ haššem šamo:
markavoṯ parʻo weḥelo yɔrɔ vayyɔm umivḥar šɔlišɔw ṭubbuʻu viyam-suf:

Transliteration by Ben Outhwaite

Then Moses and the people of Israel sang this song to the Lord, saying, "I will sing to the Lord, for he has triumphed gloriously; the horse and his rider he has thrown into the sea.
The Lord is my strength and my song, and he has become my salvation; this is my God, and I will praise him, my father's God, and I will exalt him.
The Lord is a man of war; the Lord is his name.
Pharaoh's chariots and his host he cast into the sea; and his picked officers are sunk in the Red Sea."

(RSV)

Recitation 2.2: Esther 9:29–10:3

Recording number: D355

Performers: Sa'adiya Nahum, Rafael Nadav, and David Dehari

Recitation 2.3: Proverbs 1:1–7

Recording number: D356

Performer: Sa'adiya Nahum

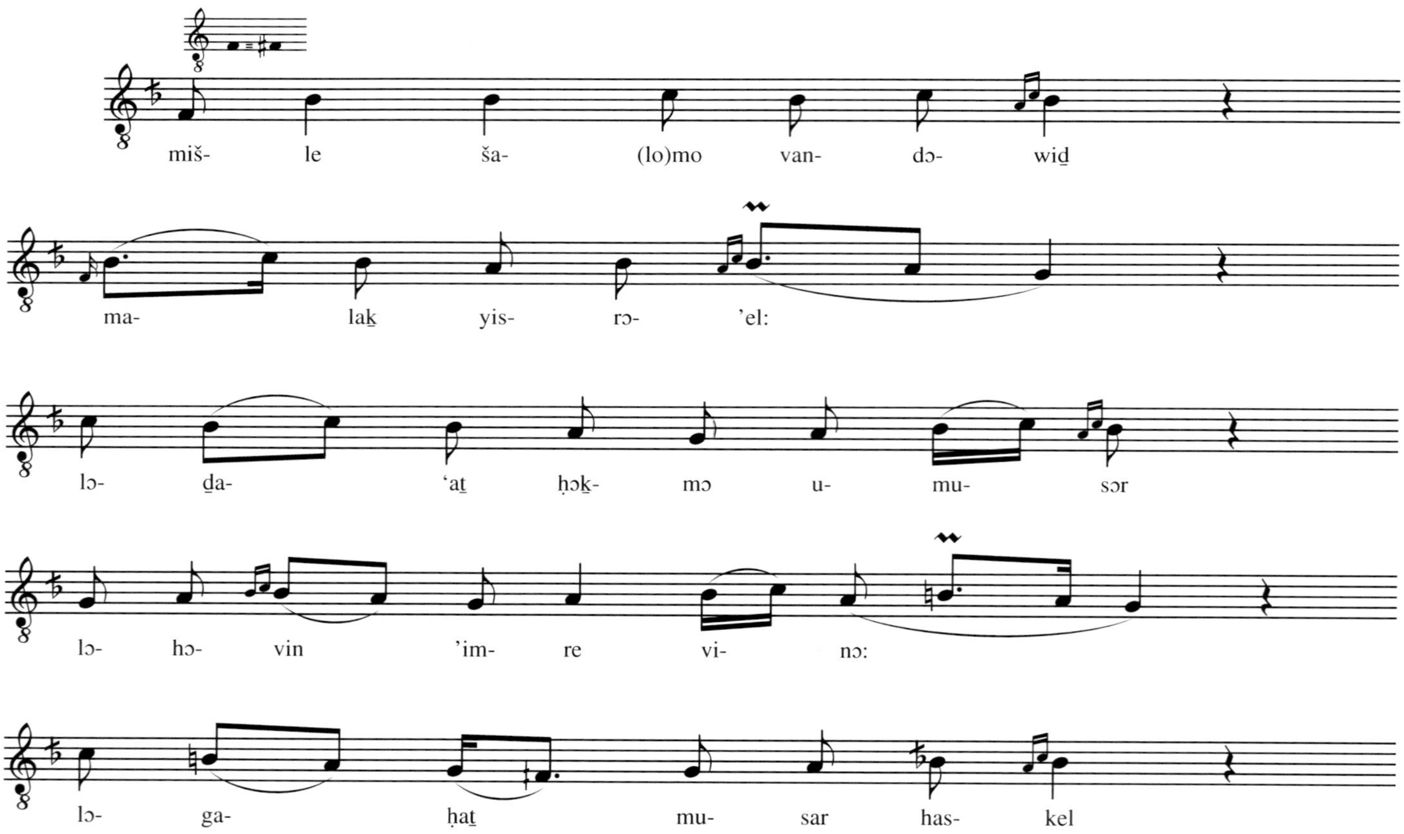

ṣa- ḏag u- miš- pɔṭ u- me- šɔ- rim:
lɔ- ṯeṯ lif- ṯɔ- yim ʻɔr- mɔ
la- na- ʻar da- ʻaṯ um- zim- mɔ:
yiš- maʻ ḥɔ- ḵɔm wi- yo- saf la- gaḥ
wa- nɔ- von taḥ- bu- loṯ yig- na:
lɔ- hɔ- vin mɔ- šɔl um- li- ṣɔ
div- re ḥa- ḵɔ- mim wi- ḥi- ḏo- ṯɔm:
yir- ʼaṯ ʼa- do- nɔy re- šiṯ dɔ- ʻaṯ
ḥɔḵ- mɔ u- mu- sɔr ʼa- vi- lim bɔ- zu:

מִשְׁלֵי שְׁלֹמֹה בֶן־דָּוִיד מֶלֶךְ יִשְׂרָאֵל:
לָדַעַת חָכְמָה וּמוּסָר לְהָבִין אִמְרֵי בִינָה:
לָקַחַת מוּסַר הַשְׂכֵּל צֶדֶק וּמִשְׁפָּט וּמֵישָׁרִים:
לָתֵת לִפְתָאִים עָרְמָה לְנַעַר דַּעַת וּמְזִמָּה:
יִשְׁמַע חָכָם וְיוֹסֶף לֶקַח וְנָבוֹן תַּחְבֻּלוֹת יִקְנֶה:
לְהָבִין מָשָׁל וּמְלִיצָה דִּבְרֵי חֲכָמִים וְחִידֹתָם:
יִרְאַת יי רֵאשִׁית דָּעַת חָכְמָה וּמוּסָר אֱוִילִים בָּזוּ:

(Prov. 1:1–7)

mišle šalomo van-dɔwid̲ malak̲ yisrɔ'el:	The proverbs of Solomon, son of David, king of Israel:
lɔd̲a'at̲ ḥɔk̲mɔ umusɔr lɔhɔvin 'imre vinɔ:	That men may know wisdom and instruction, understand words of insight,
lɔgaḥat̲ musar haskel ṣad̲ag umišpɔṭ umešɔrim:	receive instruction in wise dealing, righteousness, justice, and equity;
lɔt̲et̲ lift̲ɔyim 'ɔrmɔ lana'ar da'at̲ umzimmɔ:	that prudence may be given to the simple, knowledge and discretion to the youth—
yišma' ḥɔk̲ɔm wiyosaf lagaḥ wanɔvon taḥbulot̲ yigna:	the wise man may also hear and increase in learning, and the man of understanding acquire skill,
lɔhɔvin mɔšɔl umliṣɔ divre ḥak̲ɔmim wiḥid̲ot̲ɔm:	to understand a proverb and a figure, the words of the wise and their riddles.
yir'at̲ 'adonɔy rešit̲ dɔ'at̲ ḥɔk̲mɔ umusɔr 'avilim bɔzu:	The fear of the Lord is the beginning of knowledge; fools despise wisdom and instruction.
Transliteration by Ben Outhwaite	(RSV)

Recitation 2.4: Shira

Performers: Sa'adiya Nahum, Rafael Nadav, and David Dehari

Recording number: D357

Editor's Commentary

By opening his series with Yemenite Jewish song, Lachmann was clearly following in the footsteps of Abraham Z. Idelsohn, who launched his own ten-volume *Thesaurus of Hebrew-Oriental Melodies* (*Hebräisch-orientalischer Melodienschatz*) with "Songs of the Yemenite Jews" (Idelsohn [1914–32] 1973, vol. 1). Born in 1882 to an orthodox Jewish family in Foelixburg (Filzburg) in what is now Latvia, Idelsohn trained as a cantor before studying music history, theory, and composition at conservatories in Leipzig and Berlin.[1] While serving as a cantor—first in Regensburg, then in Johannesburg—he became increasingly disillusioned by what he perceived as the pervasive "Germanization" of diasporic Jewish life and music. In 1906 Idelsohn immigrated to Jerusalem, believing he would find, in the ancient Jewish homeland at the end of the Ottoman Empire, the authentic sources of Jewish song. What he actually found were the so-called Mizraḥi (Hebrew, "Eastern") Jewish communities who, driven by poverty, persecution, and messianic aspirations, had immigrated in waves from the wider Middle East since the late nineteenth century, in parallel with yet independently of the Zionist immigrations from Europe. It was among these "Eastern" Jews—who had essentially remained isolated from European diasporic influences—that Idelsohn honed his understanding of Jewish song as a distinctive branch of Oriental-Semitic music, sharing fundamental structural, aesthetic, and social qualities with the surrounding Arab music:

> We see that just as the Jew, being of Semitic stock, is a part of the Oriental world, so Jewish music—coming to life in the Near East—is, generally speaking, of one piece with the music of the Orient. It takes its trend of development through the Semitic race, and retains its SEMITIC-ORIENTAL CHARACTERISTICS in spite of non-Semitic—Altaic and European—influence. Jewish song achieves its unique qualities through the sentiments and the life of the Jewish people. Its DISTINGUISHING CHARACTERISTICS are the result of the spiritual life and struggle of that people (Idelsohn [1929] 1992, 24).[2]

From 1906 to 1922 Idelsohn lived in Jerusalem, transcribing the cantillation and songs of the Mizraḥi Jews from live performance.[3] His work resulted in the first five volumes of the *Thesaurus,* which document Yemenite, Babylonian, Persian, Oriental Sephardic, and Moroccan traditions. The remaining five volumes, representing various European traditions, were compiled from written sources after his emigration to America in 1922.[4] Each volume begins with a substantial literary introduction providing historical, ethnographic, and music-theoretical information and detailed comparative analyses of the individual examples, including the pronunciation of the Hebrew texts.

Unlike Lachmann, Idelsohn pursued his collecting activities independently, without local institutional support; when he left Jerusalem in 1922, he left no traces of his work there. However, between 1911 and 1913, he received a grant from the Imperial Academy of Sciences enabling him to record 109 *Phonogramme* using equipment beloging to the Vienna Phonogrammarchiv;[5] in 1913, he recorded seventy-one wax cylinders using equipment loaned by the Berlin Phonogramm-Archiv. While the Berlin collection is only sporadically documented, the Vienna recordings are accompanied by *Protokolle* providing essential details for each item, including forty-three musical transcriptions. As Edwin Seroussi has observed, the recordings themselves played only a minor role in Idelsohn's investigations, and the transcriptions based on them constitute only a very small fraction of his total output (Seroussi 2005, 53). Yet Idelsohn's use of recording technology had immense symbolic significance. By virtue of their very existence, the phonograms endowed his work with unprecedented authority and status, transforming his notations from mere subjective impressions into a "verifiable and scientific account" of the oral musical traditions (Idelsohn [1914–32] 1973, 1:3). In the summer of 1935, Lachmann supervised the transfer of Idelsohn's Berlin collection onto metal disc by means of Walter Schur's "specially constructed pick-up" (see "The 'Oriental Music Archive' and Outreach Projects" in the introduction). Returned thus to Jerusalem, Idelsohn's recordings were absorbed into Lachmann's Oriental Music Archive, forming its earliest historic layer.

Yet it was Idelsohn's writings that were to have the more direct impact on Lachmann's research, providing him with a conceptual framework and analytical models with which to hone his own understanding of Oriental Jewish song. The key to Idelsohn's representation of Jewish music as an "Oriental" tradition lay in his novel understanding of the concept of mode, which treated the motive, as opposed to the interval, as the fundamental structural unit: "A MODE . . . is composed of a number of MOTIVES (i.e. short music figures or groups of tones) within a certain scale" (Idelsohn [1929] 1992, 24). Paradoxically, it was this very analytical model—derived from Idelsohn's observations of the melodic principles underlying the surrounding Arab music—that informed Idelsohn's understanding of the fundamental unity of Jewish song. His insistence on the preeminence of "melody type" or "motive" over intervallic criteria enabled him to overlook differences of intonation between the Western and Oriental traditions in his comparative analyses and thus to conclude, as an "incontrovertible" fact, "that despite the resultant variance, Synagogue song remains identical the world over, because these differences in tonality are of sufficiently minor importance not to change the character of the music" (Idelsohn [1929] 1992, 26). Replicating itself faithfully through oral transmission, yet constantly absorbing new elements, Jewish music was for Idelsohn not only a source of national cultural history; it was a metaphor for the Jewish people itself, "the tonal expression of Jewish life and development over a period of more than two thousand years" (Idelsohn [1929] 1992, 24).

Idelsohn considered the songs of the Yemenite Jews to be a particularly ancient form of this tonal expression. As he explains in his introductory essay to the first volume of the *Thesaurus:*

> The Jews of southern Arabia, who for centuries lived in the southwestern province of the Arabian peninsula, in Yemen, shut off from the rest of the world, were gradually lost to the recollection of their co-religionists and kinsmen throughout the world. According to their tradition these Jews had immigrated into Arabia after the destruction of the first temple and continued to live there. . . . Their song is [therefore] of great importance to musical research in general and especially to the historical development of the synagogal as well as the ecclesiastical chant, since it remained uninfluenced from without and was spared the contact with Europe on the one hand and on the other with the Arabic-Persian art-music (Idelsohn [1914–32] 1973, 1:1–2).

Of the 109 recordings Idelsohn made for the Vienna Phonogrammarchiv, thirty-one are of Yemenite Jews—by far the largest number for any single group (the next most numerous are the twenty-one recordings of Persian Jews). Twenty-five of the forty-three musical transcriptions Idelsohn made from his recordings in the Phonogrammarchiv are of Yemenite Jewish song.

In program 2 Lachmann follows Idelsohn's example in his selection of illustrations by privileging those melodies that—according to Idelsohn's criteria—demonstrate special evidence of antiquity, whether by virtue of their "simple and archaic" character or because they are otherwise unique in the Jewish canon. In the section below I discuss Idelsohn's treatment of the same or similar liturgical passages in the first volume of the *Thesaurus,* comparing Idelsohn's transcriptions with Lachmann's recorded examples as presented in this edition. References to Idelsohn's recordings follow the citation system used by the Vienna Phonogrammarchiv in the CD anthology *The Collection of Abraham Zvi Idelsohn, 1911–1913* (Schüller and Lechtleitner 2005); *Protokolle* refers to the documentation Idelsohn provided to accompany his recordings for the Phonogrammarchiv (see Idelsohn 1917a).

Recitation 2.1: Shirat ha-yam *(Song of the Sea, excerpt, Exodus 15:1–4)*

Idelsohn attached particular importance to the recitation formulas used for the "songs" of the Pentateuch—those passages where the irregular biblical prose crystallizes into poetic form. In the Yemenite tradition, three such passages are recited in a special "song mode" (designated

Liedweise in the *Protokolle*). They are the Song of the Sea (Exod. 14:30–31, 15:1–21), the Ten Commandments (Exod. 20:1–17 and Deut. 5:6–18), and the narrative of the death of Moses (Deut. 34).

In Idelsohn's presentation, the Yemenite song mode is distinguished by its extreme simplicity. It encompasses only three tones, from a second above to a second below the keynote. Its melodies are composed of only two motives, one cadencing on the keynote and the other cadencing on the tone below (Idelsohn [1914–32] 1973, 1:27; see recitation 2.1 and example 2.1). For Idelsohn, these melodic traits are significant:

> The very smallness of compass of the Yemenite song mode testifies to its antiquity. It finds no further employment in the synagogal chant of the Yemenites. . . . Among the synagogal modes of the other Jews there is nothing similar to it (ibid.)

Indeed, the very fact that the Yemenites possessed a special mode for the songs of the Pentateuch, while all other Jewish communities sang the same passages "in the ordinary Pentateuch mode, though in a more solemn manner" (Idelsohn [1914–32] 1973, 1:27), was itself evidence of its antiquity for Idelsohn. He found support for his argument in the Samaritan tradition, believed to predate that of any of the Jewish communities: "It seems very likely that the Jews of antiquity had a special mode for the songs of the Pentateuch, for the Samaritans have preserved to this very day a special mode for the Song of the Sea" (ibid.).[6]

Idelsohn recorded two different melodic versions of the Yemenite Song of the Sea for the Vienna Phonogrammarchiv, sung by two cantors from different parts of Yemen. His transcriptions of both versions appear identically in the *Protokolle* and the first volume of the *Thesaurus*, where they appear in the appendix as nos. 205 and 206 respectively. The first version, Ph 1194 (Schüller and Lechtleitner 2005, CD 1, track 12) was recorded in Jerusalem on 20 August 1911 and consists of Exodus 15:1–4, though verse 4 is incomplete. The performer is Rafael Alschech, a thirty-two-year-old prayer leader from Sana'a, Yemen, who had "lived in Jerusalem for a long time" (Idelsohn [1922–32] 1973, 1:4). Idelsohn's transcription of this recording, shown at the beginning of figure 2.1, centers on B as its keynote; the CD recording sounds approximately a half tone higher.[7] The second version, Ph 1667 (Schüller and Lechtleitner 2005, CD 1, track 29), recorded in Petah Tikva on 24 March 1912, is of Exodus 15:1–8 (the eighth verse is incomplete). The performer is Jehuda Ben Schalom, a recent arrival from one of "the various provinces of Yemen" (Idelsohn [1922–32] 1973, 1:4). The transcription, which begins in the middle of figure 2.1, is based on F♮;[8] in this case, the CD recording sounds slightly lower. The recordings Ph 1194 and Ph 1667 are of approximately the same duration (1′46″ and 1′50″ respectively), although the latter contains nearly twice as much text; Jehuda Ben Schalom's declamation proceeds at a brisker tempo and is considerably less melismatic than the rendition by Rafael Alschech (Ph 1194). As shown in example 2.2, Lachmann's recording of

Example 2.1. Yemenite mode for the songs of the Pentateuch: motives 1 (descending to the lower second) and 2 (closing on the keynote). Idelsohn [1914–32] 1973, 1:27.

the Song of the Sea (recitation 2.1) corresponds approximately to Rafael Alschech's version.

A third version of the Yemenite Song of the Sea appears in the first volume of the *Thesaurus* (Idelsohn [1914–32] 1973, vol. 1, no. 9). This transcription contains a reference to "Platte 1194" (i.e., Vienna Phonogrammarchiv, Ph 1194, the version of Rafael Alschech from Sana'a); however, whereas Idelsohn's transcription of Alschech in the appendix to volume 1 (Idelsohn [1914–32] 1973, vol. 1, no. 205) is based on the keynote B, the transcription in the main body of the volume is based on C, and its melody only approximates that of Ph 1194. It is also considerably longer than the excerpt recorded by Alschech, comprising nineteen verses (Exod. 15:1–19) instead of four. Clearly, despite the reference to Ph 1194, the version of the Song of the Sea appearing in the main body of volume 1 was not taken from the recording made by Alschech. Instead, like most of Idelsohn's transcriptions in the *Thesaurus*, it was probably a composite of several repeated live performances, each corresponding only approximately to any given recording.[9]

Recitation 2.2: Esther 9:29–10:3

In the *Thesaurus* Idelsohn describes the special style of reciting the Book of Esther, remarking both on the difficulties involved in transcribing it, and the unique character of the Yemenite mode:

> According to a Talmudic rule the verses in the Book of Esther should be recited in public not in a detached way, but continuously in one sentence like a roll or a letter, which the precentor must execute though connection in the melody. This mode is recited in an incredibly quick tempo so that it is almost impossible to make an exact record of it. The specimen quoted in the collection is only an approximate delineation thereof. The declamatory modes of the Yemenite precentors differ from one another and agree only in the repetition of the second. The Esther modes of the other Jewish rites are totally different from the Yemenite (Idelsohn [1914–32] 1973, 1:28).

Idelsohn illustrates the Esther mode with one transcription taken from the opening of the book (1:1–4; Idelsohn [1922–32] 1973, vol. 1, no. 126). Lachmann's example in program 2, in contrast, consists of the end of the book of Esther, where the declamation is marked by a transition from free to fixed rhythm as the chorus repeats the final verse.

Recitation 2.3: Proverbs 1:1–7

Idelsohn provides no examples from the Book of Proverbs in the *Thesaurus*. He does, however, give two versions (one solo, the other choral) of the opening of the Song of Songs, which is recited in the same mode as

Figure 2.1. Idelsohn's transcriptions of *Shirat ha-yam* (Song of the Sea, Exod. 15:1–4) from recordings Ph 1194 and Ph 1667. Vienna Phonogrammarchiv, *Protokolle*, pages 70–72.

Example 2.2. Comparison between Lachmann's and Idelsohn's recordings of *Shirat ha-yam* (Song of the Sea, Exod. 15:1–4).

Example 2.2 continued

Proverbs; thus, while the melodies of the two books are different, their motivic material is similar.[10] According to Idelsohn, the Yemenite Song of Songs mode, like that of the Song of the Sea, is unique: "none of the modes of the other Jewish rites has any similarity to the Yemenite mode for the Song of Songs" (Idelsohn [1914–32] 1973, 1:28). Idelsohn's two versions of the Yemenite Song of Songs mode appear in the first volume of the *Thesaurus* as nos. 17 (designated "solo") and 18 ("choral"). Both versions span a range of a fourth, the choral (b♭–e♭) lying approximately a fourth higher than the solo (f–b♭). Idelsohn's transcription of the "choral" version, with text from Song of Songs 1:1–4, contains a reference to "Platte 1164" (i.e., Vienna Phonogrammarchiv, Ph 1164). Like the aforementioned third version of the Song of the Sea, however, the transcribed melody only approximates that of the corresponding recording. Idelsohn's actual transcription of the recording (Ph 1164; Schüller and Lechtleitner 2005, CD 1, track 6), with text from Song of Songs 1:1–6, appears in both the *Protokolle* and the appendix to the first volume of the *Thesaurus* (Idelsohn [1914–32] 1973, vol. 1, no. 209). In addition to these transcriptions, Idelsohn illustrates three characteristic motives for the Song of Songs mode: the first ascends to the fourth, the second descends from the fourth to the keynote before rising to the third, and the third closes with a descent to the keynote (Idelsohn [1914–32] 1973, 1:28; example 2.3).

In Lachmann's recording of Proverbs 1:1–7 as sung by Sa'adiya Nahum (recitation 2.3), the intonation is unsettled through the first verse. Even so, this verse clearly consists of two melodic phrases: the first approximating Idelsohn's motive 2 with an ascent to the third degree, and the second approximating Idelsohn's motive 3 with a descent to the keynote. From verse 2 to the end of the recitation, the cantor alternates each half-verse between motives 2 and 3.

Example 2.3. Yemenite mode for the Song of Songs: motives 1 (ascending to the fourth); 2 (descending from the fourth to the keynote before rising to the third; and 3 (closing on the keynote). Idelsohn [1914–32] 1973, 1:28.

Notes

1. For a brief autobiographical account, see Idelsohn (1935) 1986. For a critical comparison between this account, written in English, and its Hebrew counterpart, published six months earlier, see Schleifer 1986.

2. See Bohlman 2005, 47–49 for an overview and critical appraisal of Idelsohn's understanding of *maqām* structures in Jewish music.

3. In Jerusalem Idelsohn supported himself and his family as a freelance cantor, teacher, choir director, and composer. See Idelsohn (1935) 1986.

4. Idelsohn (1914–32) 1973, vols. 6–10. These volumes include German, Polish, Lithuanian, Hasidic, Judeo-German, and European Sephardic melodies.

5. Idelsohn's collection of recordings from the Vienna Phonogrammarchiv has been published in a complete CD edition by the Austrian Academy of Sciences (Schüller and Lechtleitner 2005).

6. Idelsohn recorded Samaritan priests of Nablus reciting the Song of the Sea for both the Vienna Phonogrammarchiv and the Berlin Phonogramm-Archiv. See editor's commentary to program 6.

7. The transcription also appears in Idelsohn (1914–32) 1973, vol. 1, no. 205.

8. The transcription also appears in Idelsohn (1914–32) 1973, vol. 1, no. 206.

9. For further views on this hypothesis, see Seroussi 2005, 52.

10. The similarity in recitation mode reflects the close relationship between the two books in the Hebrew canon: the Song of Songs follows closely after Proverbs, and both books are traditionally ascribed to King Solomon. The full Hebrew title of Proverbs is *Mishle Shlomo* (The Proverbs of Solomon), after the opening verse, "Mishle Shlomo ben David, melekh Yisrael" (The proverbs of Solomon the son of David, king of Israel). The Song of Songs begins, "Shir hashirim asher li-Shlomo" (The Song of Songs, which is Solomon's); hence the use of "Song of Solomon" as an alternative name for the book.

Program 3

Coptic Liturgical Chant and Hymns
16 December 1936

It is, perhaps, indiscreet to talk about the preparations of a performance to those who expect merely to hear and, possibly, appreciate the results. But the present case deserves to be an exception as throwing some light on the nature of the music to be performed, i.e., the chanting of Oriental Christian liturgy. Indeed, it has been difficult to provide illustrations from this chanting. We should not be complaining about this. Anybody who takes a deeper interest in this kind of music will in any case have to go and hear it in its legitimate place, the church, instead of contenting himself with the isolated specimens presented here to-night which, at best, can be no more than an incentive to further study. On the contrary, the attitude taken up by the Church authorities should command our respect. Their hesitation as to whether their liturgy should be performed at all outside its own sphere and, if so, what parts of it would be permissible for the present purpose shows that they are far from considering their chant as a mere musical entertainment; for them, as I pointed out in my previous talk, it is primarily and essentially part of their liturgy. You therefore have to consider the present programme of Coptic chant as a compromise resulting from an endeavour to present its main distinctions without surrendering, to a secular audience, the parts held to be most sacred.

A chief point of attraction in the chant of the different Christian Churches lies in its diversity. This is due to a main feature inherent in Christianity, namely its missionary character. In proportion as Christianity spread over a variety of peoples these came to colour its liturgy with their own special ways of singing. So the liturgy, musically as otherwise, differs from people to people and each variety in itself would merit special investigation.

As to research into the music of the Oriental Churches, little has hitherto been done. We should like to know how much, exactly, they have in common with each other and to what extent their common or[1] their separate tradition is indebted to Ancient Jewish cantillation; and we should, further, like to establish a kind of chronological order between them. But at present, our knowledge of them is too superficial for us to answer any of these questions. Particularly as regards the Coptic and Ethiopian Churches, we are unable to enter upon a discussion of technical detail.[2] I shall, therefore, confine myself to some main points of Coptic chanting.

Gregorian liturgical chant, i.e., the chant of the Latin Church, is divided into eight modes. But this neat grouping of melody into eight categories implying definite scales is the final outcome of centuries of development, and traceable to a system of secular music.[3] Gregorian chant, thus, has adopted a system originally alien to ecclesiastical cantillation. But even this European branch of Christian chant had never wholly succumbed to the secular instrumental conception which tends to dissolve a melody into the isolated notes visible, as a scale, on the instruments on which it is performed,—a conception which has ultimately led to using these notes for a free and untraditional invention of melodies.[4]

In the early period of Christianity, liturgical cantillation was not divided on a basis of scale, but of melody types depending, in their turn, on the different parts of the liturgical text.[5] Nor is the division into no more and no less than eight modes an inevitable consequence of liturgical demands. While some Oriental Churches, such as the Byzantine and the Armenian, have eight modes, the Coptic and the Abyssinian Church divide their liturgies in an altogether different way. Each of them distinguishes only three melody types which bear the names of the three Masses to which they are applied; but these Masses and their melody types are not the same in the Coptic and Abyssinian service.

You will hear examples from all the three Coptic melody types. Besides the cantillation of the Mass, each

1. Lachmann's script: *ot*.

2. For subsequent developments in Ethiopian chant scholarship, see Shelemay and Jeffery 1993–97.

3. See program 2, footnote 7.

4. See program 2, footnote 10.

5. In Byzantium, where the Christian chant melodies were classified according to the *oktōēchos* (system of eight melodic modes, or *ēchoi*) from at least the eighth century, each week in the eight-week liturgical cycle was assigned to a different melodic mode.

comprises a wealth of hymns which, contrary to the recitation of the Mass which is in free rhythm, are chanted in strict time and with the support of percussion instruments,—a triangle and a pair of cymbals. The use of these or similar instruments is current in the rituals of many ancient creeds and the Coptic Church may simply have kept it up; still, this preservation of a pagan usage is remarkable considering the insistence[6] of Christian fathers on the total exclusion of musical instruments and even of hand-clapping from the services which must be kept pure of any profane element.[7]

It is sometimes claimed that in the music of the Coptic service Ancient Egyptian music in the times of the Pharaohs[8] survives. This claim is based on the fact that the Copts themselves, or part of them, are descendants of the Ancient Egyptians. But at the present stage of our knowledge it is impossible to decide whether their use of percussion instruments or any other musical element in their service can really be regarded as a vestige of Ancient Egyptian practice.[9]

We now pass on to the musical illustrations which, with the kind permission of His Grace, the Coptic Bishop of Palestine, will be executed by priests of the Coptic Monastery in Jerusalem.[10] The first item is a hymn based on the mode of the Kyrillus Mass which is considered to be the most ancient of the three. Its place in the service is the time when the bishop or another dignitary enters the church on a solemn occasion. (Recitation 3.1, CD 1, tracks 5–6)

The following hymn is in honour of Virgin Mary, and is chanted in the middle of the Basilius Mass. This Mass is the most important of the three; it is performed at every ceremony whereas the performance of the two others is left to discretion.[11] (Recitation 3.2)

The last and final recitation is in the Gregorius mode. It is not a hymn, but forms part of the Mass itself. Unlike the hymns it is not accompanied by percussion. It consists of the priest's cantillation and the answer of the community. (Recitation 3.3, CD 1, tracks 7–8)

Editor's Note on the Music

A striking aspect of both recitations 3.1 and 3.3, characteristic of Coptic chant generally, is the independence of the melody from the text.[12] Lachmann makes no mention of this fundamental characteristic, which contradicts his observations in programs 2 and 4 on the primacy of the text, or word, in sacred cantillation generally. In Coptic chant a single vowel may be prolonged over several musical phrases—a practice known as "vocalise" when, as in recitation 3.1, the phrases have a definite pulse, and as "melisma" in the case of richly ornamented rubato phrases (as in recitation 3.3). The latter is a 1′36″ extract consisting almost entirely of an extended melisma (1′17″) on the second word of the text, *gar* (your); it begins with a more or less even duple-meter pulse that dissolves into an extended rubato toward the end. This melismatic passage is contrasted by the predominantly syllabic cadential phrase to which the remaining four words on the recording are sung.

Equally striking in these two recorded examples is the lack of correspondence between the textual and musical phrases. In both recordings, musical cadences fall randomly in the middle of lines, words, and even, in the case of recitation 3.3, a single prolonged syllable. In recitation 3.1, the cyclic melodic structure of the hymn—whose repetitions are indicated by roman numerals—bears no relation to the phrase divisions in the text.

---

6. Lachmann's script: *instance.*

7. Idelsohn gives a comparative survey of musical instruments and ritual in ancient Egypt, Phoenicia, Assyria, Babylon, and the Temple in Jerusalem in the first chapter of *Jewish Music* (Idelsohn [1929] 1992, 3–23). See McKinnon 1987 on the prohibition of musical instruments by the early Church.

8. Lachmann's script: *Pharaos.*

9. The belief that Coptic music is descended directly from ancient Egyptian practice is central to Coptic identity (see editor's commentary below). While the origins of Coptic chant remain obscure, this belief has attained some scholarly credibility. As Marian Robertson-Wilson writes:

> The music, in fact, probably derives from many regions of Egypt and from various centuries, and at the very least is a reflection of its ancient past. Certain practices appear to have persisted from ancient Egypt, such as the employment of professional blind singers, the use of percussion instruments echoing the sound of ancient sistra and bells, antiphonal singing, and the unusually long vocalises reminiscent of the "hymns of seven vowels" sung by Pharaonic priests (Robertson-Wilson 2001).

10. His Excellency Metropolitan Abraham, Archbishop of the Holy Archdiocese of Jerusalem, All Palestine, Philadelphia of Jordan, and All the Near East. St. Anthony's Monastery of the Coptic Patriarchate of Jerusalem is situated literally on the roof of the Church of the Holy Sepulchre.

11. The liturgy of St. Basil the Great is the only one that is sung throughout the year. The liturgy of St. Gregory Nazianzen is only sung at the four great feasts of Christmas, Epiphany, Easter, and Pentecost. Although the liturgy of St. Cyril is included in the principal Coptic prayer book (Euchologion; Arabic, *al-khulaji,* "kholagy"), it is rarely celebrated because so few melodies survive (Robertson-Wilson 2001, 413; and Moftah, Roy, and Tóth 1998, ix).

12. For a comprehensive account of the history, transmission, and character of Coptic church music, see Robertson-Wilson 2001; for a more general overview, see Moftah, Roy, and Tóth 1998, ix–xi. See also the essays on the Library of Congress website "Coptic Orthodox Liturgical Chant and Hymnody" (http://lcweb2.loc.gov/diglib/ihas/html/coptic/coptic-home.html).

Recitation 3.1: Laḥn *(hymn), Liturgy of St. Cyril*

Original recording number: D390

Substitute recording number: D382 (11 December 1936)

Performers: Four priests with *trianto* (metal triangle) and *nāqūs* (pair of small metal cymbals)

Note: Roman numerals I–IV indicate the four rounds of the cyclic melodic pattern (see "Editor's Note on the Music" above).

en- ni- ja- ji:
en- te ti-
- ek- kli- si- a: a-
IV
- ri- so- vt

ⲡ̀ⲟⲩⲣⲟ ⲛ̀ⲧⲉ ϯϩⲓⲣⲏⲛⲏ:
ⲙⲟⲓ ⲛⲁⲛ ⲛ̀ⲧⲉⲕϩⲓⲣⲏⲛⲏ:
ⲥⲉⲙⲛⲓ ⲛⲁⲛ ⲛ̀ⲧⲉⲕϩⲓⲣⲏⲛⲏ:
ⲭⲁ ⲛⲉⲛⲛⲟⲃⲓ ⲛⲁⲛ ⲉⲃⲟⲗ.

ϫⲱⲣ ⲉ̀ⲃⲟⲗ ⲛ̀ⲛⲓϫⲁϫⲓ:
ⲛ̀ⲧⲉ ϯⲉⲕⲕⲗⲏⲥⲓⲁ̀:
ⲁ̀ⲣⲓⲥⲟⲃⲧ ⟦ⲉ̀ⲣⲟⲥ:
ⲛ̀ⲛⲉⲥⲕⲓⲙ ϣⲁ ⲉ̀ⲛⲉϩ.⟧
(Coptic text from St. Mary and St. Shenouda 2002, 728)

epuro ente tihirini:
moi nan entekhirini:
semni nan entekhirini:
ka nen novi nan evol.

jōr evol ennijaji:
ente tiekklisia:
arisovt [eros:
enneskim sha eneh.]
Transliteration by Peter J. Williams

O King of peace,
give us your peace,
make firm for us your peace,
and forgive us our sins.

Disperse the enemies
of the Church,
fortify [her,
that she may not be shaken forever.]
(Adapted from St. Mary and St. Shenouda 2002, 728)

Recitation 3.2: Hymn to the Virgin Mary, Liturgy of St. Basil

Recording numbers: D391, D392

Performers: Same as recitation 3.1

Recitation 3.3: "Peklaos gar," Liturgy of St. Gregory

Recording number: D393

Performers: Two priests

ⲡⲉⲕⲗⲁⲟⲥ ⲅⲁⲣ ⲛⲉⲙ ⲧⲉⲕⲉⲕⲕⲗⲏⲥⲓⲁ ⲥⲉϯϩⲟ ⲉ̀ⲣⲟⲕ:
[ⲟⲩⲟϩ ⲉ̀ⲃⲟⲗϩⲓⲧⲟⲧⲕ ⲉ̀ⲫⲓⲱⲧ ⲛⲉⲙⲁⲕ:
ⲉⲩϫⲱ ‘ⲙⲟⲥ:
ϫⲉ ⲛⲁⲓ ⲛⲁⲛ ⲫⲛⲟⲩⲧⲓ ⲡⲉⲛⲥⲱⲧⲏⲣ.]
(St. Mark 1997, 236)

peklaos gar nem tekekklisia setiho erok:
[woh evolhitotk e-efyōt nemak:
eujō emmos:
je nai nan efnuti pensōtir.]
Transliteration by Peter J. Williams

For your people and your church call unto you
[and unto the Father through you
and with you saying
Have mercy upon us O God, our Savior.]
(Adapted from St. Mark 1997, 236)

Editor's Commentary

> I still remember this decisive instant in recording the Church Heritage as if I see it now! We were on a Golden ship in the Nile in front of El-Dobara Palace . . . Under us, still water of the Nile flowed in peace and we were surrounded by wonderful gardens on both banks. Mlm. [Mu'allim, i.e., cantor] Mikhail entered and behold two great musicians met! (Moftah 1975)

Thus Ragheb Moftah, ardent promoter, practitioner, and pioneering scholar of Coptic music, recalled the first encounter between the blind cantor Mikha'īl Jirgis al-Batanūnī (1873–1957) and the English musicologist Ernest Newlandsmith (b. 1875, d. unknown), on Moftah's houseboat in the winter of 1927. The encounter marked the start of the most comprehensive effort to date to notate the orally transmitted melodies of Coptic chant.

When Lachmann arrived in Cairo in 1932 to participate in the Congress of Arab Music, he took a special interest in Coptic music. In his letters to his parents, he reports on his visit to the Coptic quarter in the Old City (Katz 2003, 309), his plans to attend a Coptic mass (ibid.), his invitation to a private concert of church music at the home of "an immensely rich Copt" in Heliopolis (Katz 2003, 315), and his meeting with the patriarch to obtain permission to record (Katz 2003, 317). The secretary to the congress's recording committee, which Lachmann chaired, was none other than the young Coptic chant scholar Ragheb Moftah, and the twelve wax matrixes of Coptic chant Lachmann produced for the congress are the earliest recordings of the tradition.[1] Oddly, Lachmann makes no mention in program 3 of Moftah's own pioneering project to transcribe the entire corpus of orally transmitted melodies into Western notation.

Born into a wealthy Coptic landowning family in 1898, Moftah grew up in the Faggala district of Cairo at a time of mounting national resistance to the British occupation. In Coptic circles, this resistance was directed primarily against Protestant missionary influence, and Faggala was the center of a reform movement within the Church whose primary aim was to educate youth in the Coptic language and traditions. When Moftah was sent to Germany to study agriculture, he used this opportunity to study piano and music theory at the universities in Bonn and Munich. He also began to research ancient Egyptian and Coptic manuscripts in European libraries (including the British Library and the Bibliothèque nationale), seeking evidence of the pharaonic sources of Coptic chant.

On his return to Cairo in 1926, Moftah abandoned all plans for a career in agriculture and, with his family's support, devoted the rest of his life to the study, practice, and preservation of authentic Coptic music. For it was not only Protestant missionary influences that he perceived as a threat. Just as in Europe, two decades earlier, Abraham Z. Idelsohn had reacted against alien, Germanic influences in Jewish music, so Moftah opposed modernizing forces within the Coptic reform movement itself. Such tendencies, he felt, were epitomized by the work of the Egyptian army officer Kāmil Ibrāhīm Ghubriyāl, who, in the middle of World War I, when paper supplies were scarce and printing presses virtually at a standstill, had published a book of responses arranged for choir and congregation with piano accompaniment, transcribed into Western notation (Ghubriyāl 1916). As Ghubriyāl explained in his introductory essay (translated in Atalla n.d.), his underlying goal was to counteract the general decline in the moral, cultural, and communal life of Egyptian Copts; he spends much of the essay decrying the "shameful habits that became widely known as part of a trendy and modern-day living," such as "attending nightclubs to enjoy listening to singers, and when throwing wedding parties, having belly dancers that tend to be dangerous to virtues and morals" (ibid.). His own work represented an attempt to "remove this tumor before it overtakes us" and provide the "cure for this disease" (ibid.). Ghubriyāl recognized the crucial role played by women in upholding religious and family values, and he frequently addresses the interests of women and young girls.[2] Above all, he intended his work to be accessible:

> With attention to ladies' preferences the melodies combine religious traditions with modern tastes. To facilitate memorization, I transliterated the Coptic responses into roman letters that are widely known. . . . I could not write it in Coptic because so few people know it. . . . I translated every response into Arabic so that people can understand what is said in church (ibid.).

He recommended that music notation be used in teaching "so that preachers and future clergy are knowledgeable of this art, akin to European deacons and priests," and he advocated the use of the organ in churches to standardize variations in performance.[3] Finally, lest his intentions be misunderstood, he emphasized that it was for neither fame nor profit that he pursued this work, "but rather to my brewing passion and national idea that I accomplished it as a service to my country to raise its dignity" (ibid.).

Moftah took a diametrically opposing stance to Ghubriyāl, paralleling that of Idelsohn for Jewish music. Far from advocating their use, he considered the piano and organ in Coptic worship to be aberrations, just as Idelsohn had for Jewish worship.[4] His aim was to rid Coptic music of alien elements in order to rediscover its authentic Egyptian roots. For Moftah, as for Idelsohn before him, the primary function of notation was to record, canonize, and preserve the orally transmitted melodies: it was not intended to replace rote memorization in teaching or performance, and least of all was it intended as a means of popularization.

Moftah found a kindred spirit and an avid collaborator in the self-styled English "minstrel friar" Newlandsmith, whom he met passing through Cairo en route to the Holy Land. A professional violinist and composer, disillusioned with the increasing commercialization of European music, Newlandsmith had dedicated his life to promoting what he believed was the true purpose of music: to serve the divine.[5] From 1926 to 1936 he spent the winter months on Moftah's houseboat on the Nile, transcribing the orally transmitted melodies of the Coptic Church directly from live performance into Western staff notation. His chief source was Mikha'īl Jirgis al-Batanūnī, who was renowned for the clarity and plainness of his rendition. In order fully to eliminate the "appalling debris of Arabic ornamentation," Newlandsmith notated only basic melodic outlines, transposing the melodies to minimize the use of accidentals. By 1936 he had notated the complete Liturgy of St. Basil and twenty-five major seasonal hymns.

When illness prevented Newlandsmith from returning, Moftah directed his energies to the training of cantors and choirs, establishing the first teaching centers for Coptic music in Cairo and Alexandria. In 1954, two years after Egypt's independence, he became the founding director of the music division of the Higher Institute of Coptic Studies in Cairo. This provided the institutional framework for his new initiative to record the entire repertory of Coptic church music, as performed by al-Batanūnī and his students, on reel-to-reel tape. Whereas Moftah's sessions with Newlandsmith had provided the framework for honing his own understanding of the tradition, it was his recordings that established the canon of Coptic church music for posterity. To this day, they provide the authoritative reference and teaching aid for cantors and deacons in what has remained an essentially oral musical tradition.

In the early 1970s Moftah embarked on a collaborative project with the Hungarian folklorist Margit Tóth to transcribe his recordings of the Liturgy of St. Basil as sung by the Higher Institute's choir of deacons, led by Mu'allim Sādiq 'Atallah.[6] Trained in the Bartókian method, Tóth's approach could not have contrasted more with Newlandsmith's. With the benefit of repeated listening, she notated every melodic nuance of the recorded chant, distinguishing the embellishments from the basic melody through the use of differently sized of noteheads and different stem directions. Tóth's transcriptions, published with transliteration and English translation of the Coptic texts by Martha Roy, provide the standard scholarly reference for Coptic church music (Moftah, Roy, and Tóth 1998).

Toward the end of his long life (he died in 2001, aged 103), Moftah donated his collection of transcriptions, recordings, and other professional documents to the Library of Congress; these materials form the nucleus of the collection "Coptic Orthodox Liturgical Chant and Hymnody" available as part of the library's online *Performing Arts Encyclopedia*.[7] Yet for all his immense work in documenting Coptic music, Moftah remained rooted in its living, auditory practice. His niece, Laurence Moftah, provides a fitting epitaph:

> No doubt Moftah will be remembered for his masterly recordings of liturgies and chants which he bequeathed to Copts and the world at large. But he will also be remembered as the old man in a black suit, wearing a black beret on his bald head, standing in the front row among the choir, his ears attentive to every melisma rendered by the master cantor and deacons, as he conducted the Coptic Orthodox Easter celebration and all other Coptic feasts and festivities at St. Mark's Cathedral in Abbassiyya (Moftah 2006).

Notes

1. Only ten matrixes survived the journey to England to be reproduced on disc by His Master's Voice (HD 14–21; 145).

2. Ghubriyāl confirms that he will donate the profits from his book to support two projects: the building of "the Girls College and the Coptic Church in Heliopolis, as well as to the free Coptic school for girls and charitable organizations in Cairo and outlying suburbs," and he calls on "the dignitaries and leaders of the Coptic nation, as well as members of women's organizations . . . to teach this book and disseminate it throughout all of the Coptic schools for girls" so that "our daughters will grow to love our Church and tend to our language" (Atalla n.d.).

3. Ghubriyāl attributes the loss of most the Liturgy of St. Cyril to performance variations by priests and cantors "despite the opposition of church leaders": "This was one of the reasons that the hymns of the oldest Coptic liturgy of Saint Mark, as arranged by Pope Cyril the 24th Pope of Alexandria, was lost" (ibid.).

4. Idelsohn's attitude toward the use of organ and piano in Jewish worship is consistent with his attitude toward the Jewish Reform movement in general; see, for example, his chapter "The Influence of the Reform Movement on the Synagogue Song in the Beginning of the Nineteenth Century" in *Jewish Music* ([1929] 1992, 232–45).

5. On Newlandsmith, see his autobiography (Newlandsmith 1927); and Ramzy 2008, which includes an exhaustive list of references.

6. Moftah first became acquainted with Tóth in the late 1960s when her compatriot, the musicologist Ilona Borsai, made three research trips to Egypt on a UNESCO-funded project. On one such trip she met Moftah at the Institute of Coptic Studies in Cairo, where she recorded Coptic liturgical music. On returning to Hungary, Borsai invited Tóth, who was then head of the Folk Music department at the Museum of Ethnography, to transcribe some of the materials that she collected, including several hymns of the Liturgy of St. Basil. When Tóth sent her transcriptions to Moftah for review, he was so impressed that he sent her more recordings to transcribe; eventually, he invited her to Cairo for two six-month visits, in 1970–71 and 1975, to transcribe recordings he had made at the Institute for Coptic Studies. In 1980 Tóth returned to Egypt for good, where she taught ethnomusicology at the Cairo Music Conservatory while continuing to transcribe Coptic music.

7. Available at http://lcweb2.loc.gov/diglib/ihas/html/coptic/coptic-home.html.

Program 4

Liturgical Songs of the Kurdish Jews
6 January 1937

Before going into to-night's special subject, the religious song of the Kurdish Jews, it may be useful to say something more definite about the character of liturgical music than on previous occasions. It is not enough to point out that liturgical song is essentially different from secular song. It is necessary to determine, in addition, the various features which make it so different. We can conveniently divide these features into two groups the first of which concerns the spiritual, and the second the technical side of religious song.

The spiritual foundation of religious[1] ceremonies in general goes back to prehistoric conditions of life. In those times the usages of which have been preserved by primitive society, the salient feature of the cult lay in a magical ceremony intended to attract benefit to, and dispel misfortune from, the respective community. The sorcerer or medicine man of the tribe works himself into a trance by means of intoxicants and bodily movements. In this state, the voices of demons speak through him. After that, the community itself also takes an active part in the ceremony in song and dance. We must not imagine that this ceremony, in spite of the low standard of civilization of the tribe concerned, is wild and unorganized. From the magical point of view, nothing short of scrupulous precision can achieve the desired effect of the ceremony.

Perhaps the proposition that there should be any connection between those crude acts of superstition and the solemn service of religion may be repellent. But this connection cannot be overlooked by students of the history of civilization and I shall try to illustrate it with a few examples.

The name of shāman which means a medicine man is believed to go back to the same root as the first part of the word Sāma-Veda, the name of the book which contains the text used for chanting the Ancient Indian ritual.[2]

The elaborate curing rituals of a certain American Indian tribe are stated, in an ethnological study, to "involve a most detailed procedure lasting at times for eight nights. A single mistake in the place, wording, order of the hundreds of songs included would render the whole proceeding invalid."[3] Likewise the Yemenite and other Oriental Jews believe that mistakes in the cantillation of the liturgy deprive the religious service of its efficacy and even may have disastrous consequences for the culprit and his family. This accounts for the fact that the office of cantor is but reluctantly accepted in Yemenite communities.[4]

---

1. Lachmann's script: *relidious*.

2. The term *Sāmaveda* is derived from the Sanskrit words *sāman* (hymns, chants, melodies) and *veda* (knowledge). The word *shaman*, in contrast, is considered by most scholars to be a loanword from the Tungusic *šamán*, used to designate such a practitioner among the Tungusic and Turko-Mongol peoples of ancient Siberia. Imported to Europe by explorers, its use became more generalized (see, e.g., Lot-Falck 1977, 9; Rouget 1985, 18). Lachmann's association of the word *shaman* with the Sanskrit *Sāmaveda* may relate to a nineteenth-century tradition in which *shaman* was considered a derivative of the Sanskrit *çramana*, "a Buddhist ascetic or monk," via the Chinese *sa-men* or Pali *samana*. This myth was deconstructed some twenty years before Lachmann's broadcast by Bernard Laufer, who attributes it to the "romantic movement of pan-Indianism" (Laufer 1917, 371). It persists, however, in the work of Mircea Eliade, who suggests that the Sanskrit *çramana* "could be the origin of the Tungusic word" (Eliade 1989, 495).

3. Lachmann cites the same passage, also without attribution, in his February 1936 lecture "National und International in der Orientalischen Musik" (Lachmann 1936a). It is likely that he is referring to George Herzog's description of the healing rituals of the Navajo, "in which hundreds of songs follow each other in fixed order. Elaborate as are these procedures—some of them last for nine nights—, so elaborate are the song texts. And a single mistake, even in the order of the meaningless syllables which are the sole texts for certain groups of songs, will invalidate ceremony and cure" (Herzog 1934, 462). The American ethnographer Frances Densmore had previously made a similar observation in her book *The American Indians and their Music*, reporting on her systematic comparison of multiple recordings of the same song: "Whether sung by the same or different people, at the same session or several years apart, the renditions were uniform in every respect. . . . Accuracy is insisted upon so strongly that if a mistake is made in a ceremonial song of certain tribes the ceremony must be begun all over again and the careless singer must pay a heavy fine" (Densmore 1926, 131–32).

4. Here Lachmann paraphrases Idelsohn, who writes: "In contrast to the Ashkenazim and Sephardim, the Yemenites . . .

In primitive ritual the danger of evil spirits disturbing the force of the spell is obviated by the sound of rattles and clappers. This may throw some light on the use of bells, e.g. in Buddhist and in Christian service. It is interesting to think that the solemn peal of bells valued, nowadays, on aesthetical merits, should originally have served very practical purposes, namely, to keep away evil spirits from funerals, to avert the dangers of lightning and, on the other hand, to make a propitiatory noise on festive occasions such as births.[5]

The demon who is supposed to inhabit the medicine man's body cannot, of course, have a human voice. This explains the strange and, sometimes, incredible tones in which the magic formulae are pronounced and, I believe, opens up a perspective far beyond magic ceremonies. The disguised voice of the medicine man is probably responsible, to a certain extent, for the vocal technique, so obnoxious to Europeans, of Oriental singers generally, a technique which has also extended to secular singing.[6] You will hear particularly significant examples of this disguised voice on a later occasion when Samaritan priests will recite passages from the Bible.[7]

Jewish religious service represents an outstanding instance of the ways in which primitive musical usages have been gradually transformed and raised to a high level. While the shofar has retained the character of magical instruments[8] the reciter's voice has been moulded in accordance with the requirements of the complex and delicate structure of the scriptural text. The Lord's voice speaks through Moses to the community pronouncing the Ten Commandments. In Kurdish cantillation, this passage is made to stand out from the ordinary mode in which the Pentateuch is recited; it has a melody type of its own which you are now going to hear.[9] (Recitation 4.1, CD 1, tracks 9–10)[10]

As to the technical side of cult music, some traits are universal. Above all, the peculiar way of reciting sacred texts cannot be classed under a common heading with the singing of ordinary tunes. Strictly speaking, there are no tunes; the voice travels along lines established by the textual structure; the text determines its point of rest and the places where ornaments are inserted.[11] Therefore,

---

do not tolerate deviations from the traditional chant. The office of precentor, according to their view, is connected with dangers, for the precentor as intermediary between the congregation and God, like the high priest in ancient times, has the duty to render the prayers word for word and letter for letter. If, however, he makes a slight linguistic mistake and fails to emend it immediately, his prayer and at the same time the prayer of the entire congregation is rejected in heaven as defective and incorrect. But in that case the precentor bears the sins of the congregation and is also punished immediately. Hence many pious men are afraid to accept the office of precentor, and they interpret the mortality of their small children, which is unfortunately epidemic among them, as punishment for sins committed while they officiate as precentors" (Idelsohn [1914–32] 1973, 1:16).

5. Lachmann elaborates on this idea in his lecture "National und International in der Orientalischen Musik," where he cites the Latin motto "Vivos voco, mortuos plango, fulgura frango" (I call the living, I mourn the dead, I break the lightning), traditionally engraved on church bells, that appears as the epigraph to Friedrich von Schiller's *Das Lied von der Glocke* (1798). In this motto, Lachmann observes, "die moderne (sentimentale) und die alte (magische) Auffassung erscheinen nebeneinander" (the modern, sentimental understanding and the old, magical one appear together; Lachmann 1936a).

6. See Nelson 2001, 21, who notes that the rules of Qur'anic recitation (*tajwīd*) require that certain consonants are articulated with an intense nasal timbre (*gunnah*), imparting a nasal quality to the recitation as a whole. According to Virginia Danielson, nasality was considered a desirable quality and a marker of authenticity in the vocal styles of the legendary Egyptian singers (notably Sayyid Darwish, Muhammad ʻAbd al-Wahhab, and Umm Kulthūm) who rose to fame in the early part of the twentieth century and whose voices were revered and emulated throughout the Arab world (Danielson 1997, 138–39). The inextricable relationship between Qur'anic recitation, religious song, and Arab music was a fact acknowledged even by non-Muslim musicians (Danielson 1997, 26).

In his lecture "National und International in der Orientalischen Musik" (Lachmann 1936a), Lachmann cites (without referencing the source) Erich von Hornbostel's description of the "masked voice" of the medicine man among the Indian tribes of northern Brazil:

> So long as . . . the beseeched demon . . . speaks from the mouth of the medicine man, [the latter's] voice is masked with every means he could acquire in an apprenticeship of many years; superhuman lung power in the booming fortissimo and in the fermatas held for an all but infinite time without the slightest reduction in volume—in one case 18 seconds . . . uncanny wailing glissando and chromaticism otherwise unheard of among primitive peoples; ventriloquistic colouring of the voice with the mouth closed, the true-to-nature imitation of animal voices, namely that of the jaguar, linked in its being to the magician; and not least the grunting and groaning of the possessed man, the hissing exhalation of the tobacco smoke, and the gargling with the intoxicating tobacco juice (Lachmann 1936a).

7. See program 6.

8. Idelsohn discusses the various functions and beliefs associated with the *shofar* (ram's horn) in ancient Israel. Among these was "the magic power of frightening and dispersing evil spirits and gods of the enemies. . . . This belief was current among all primitive tribes, and it was, likewise, accepted in Israel, as many Biblical stories and phrases testify. The blowing of the Shofar was even attributed to Yahve himself, in order to frighten his enemies and to gather the scattered remnants of his people to his sanctuary" (Idelsohn [1929] 1992, 9; cf. Zech. 9:14). Curt Sachs also cites numerous examples of the magical attributes of the *shofar,* including the biblical story of the siege of Jericho, when the sound of the *shofarot* caused the walls to come tumbling down (Josh. 6:20; see Sachs 1940, 111–12).

9. Here Lachmann differs from Idelsohn, who states that the Yemenites are unique in having a special melody for the songs of the Pentateuch; the other Jews have "no special melody for the songs or lyrical pieces [which] are executed by them in the ordinary Pentateuch mode, though in a more solemn manner" (Idelsohn [1914–32] 1973, 1:27). See also footnote 13 below.

10. The performer of this recitation is identified in Lachmann's recording diaries as "Eliahu Yahye Mizrahi, Zaho (Kurdistan), nahe Mossul" (Eliahu Yahye Mizrahi from Zakho, Kurdistan, near Mosul). On Lachmann's comments on the performance, see the editor's commentary below.

11. Lachmann's assertion that this is a universal trait is contradicted by his own examples of Coptic and Samaritan

the cantillation sometimes comes near the accents of the speaking voice, and is invariably in free rhythm. Only on certain occasions does the melodic strain acquire some of the autonomous qualities of a set tune. In Jewish cantillation, this is mostly the case at such places where the text changes from its usual prose into a poetical form. The most important example of this is the Song of the Sea in Exodus[12] which is cantillated in another and more lyrical way than the rest of the Pentateuch. In Kurdish tradition, Deborah's song as well follows the melody type of the Song of the Sea, thus standing out from the ordinary Prophets' mode.[13] (Recitation 4.2)

In a similar way as the magic incantation of the medicine man is followed and contrasted by the song of the community, the various liturgies of the civilized world have, over and again, been enriched with hymns. These hymns, mostly sung to metrical texts, supply a welcome relief from the strain of the solo cantillation. Being sung by a chorus they are naturally in strict time; they have regular balanced tunes which are repeated strophically; in short, the prevalence of the word over the melody is here reversed.

In connection with the technicalities of sacred cantillation, short mention, at least, must be made of the curious fact that the textbooks are usually provided with signs of recitation. This is equally true of the Vedic books of Ancient India, further, of the medieval liturgical books of most Christian Churches and, likewise, of the sacred books of the Jews and Mohammedans. These signs have varying forms and functions. None of them are what we should call a musical notation such as the signs, alphabetic or similar to the alphabet, as used for Ancient Greek and for medieval European and Arab tunes; or such as European staff notation. Here, again, it comes into evidence that, in antiquity and in the Middle Ages, religious cantillation was an entirely separate thing as against tunes of a secular and instrumental nature. Secular notation is independent of texts; liturgical signs of recitation cannot do without them.

Among the signs which accompany liturgical texts, two groups have to be distinguished, one of them indicating the structure and the rhetoric of the text, the other—the neums of the Christian Churches and the numeric signs of the Sāman chant—delineating, roughly, the rise and fall and undulations of the voice. The Christian Churches as well as the Vedic liturgy use both forms side by side. The Jewish and the Mohammedan[14] sacred books employ only one form; and there has been, at least with regard to the Jewish signs, a great deal of dispute as to whether this form has to be interpreted as a distinct musical notation or as a guide to the textual structure which, in itself, has evolved certain melodic modulations of the voice.[15] The study of the Jewish accent marks, the ta'amīm, would, I think, profit greatly if an historical connection[16] between them and the Christian signs could be

chant in programs 3 and 6, which display a conspicuous lack of correspondence between the text and melodic structures. See the "Editor's Note on the Music" in programs 3 and 6.

12. Exodus 15:1–18; see program 2, especially recitation 2.1.

13. Judges 5:1–31. Idelsohn, in contrast to Lachmann, distinguishes between the "more solemn manner" of recitation reserved for the Songs of the Pentateuch and the musical mode itself, which for all Jews other than the Yemenites is "the ordinary Pentateuch mode." See footnote 9 above.

14. Lachmann's script: *Muhammedan*.

15. In this highly compressed passage, Lachmann suggests that, while the function of notation in all four liturgies (Christian, Vedic, Jewish, and Muslim) is essentially syntactical ("indicating the structure and rhetoric of the text"), in the Vedic and Christian traditions it also indicates melodic qualities ("delineating, roughly, the rise and fall and undulations of the voice"). Several decades later, Leo Treitler would challenge the very distinction between melodic and syntactical functions with respect to Christian chant, arguing instead for "a conception of melody for which the first notations were invented not so much as a sequence of pitches, but as a succession of vocal or melodic movements accompanying the declaiming of syllables of text" (Treitler 1982, 244 and 269–70).

In considering the "signs which accompany liturgical texts," scholars generally distinguish between (a) notation whose function is purely syntactical and has nothing to do with melodic aspects; and (b) ekphonetic notation, in which signs relating to the structural divisions of the text that do not themselves contain melodic information serve as mnemonic aids for corresponding melodic motives. The signs in the Qur'an, which guide the reader in *tajwīd*—the system of rules governing correct recitation—clearly belong to the first type. This system, which is believed to codify the sound of the recitation as revealed by the Angel Gabriel to the Prophet Muhammad, regulates the duration of syllables, divisions of the text, vocal timbre, and pronunciation, but specifically excludes melody (Nelson 2001, 5; 14–31). When the Qur'an is recited melodically, as in the performative style known as *mujawwad*, the melody must be executed spontaneously, since "fixity is expressly forbidden by religious authorities lest it infringe on the primacy of the text" (Nelson 2001, 110; see also Frischkopf 2009 for the development of different recitation styles). The proscription against melodic fixity in Qur'anic recitation is in striking contrast to the principle of "scrupulous precision" that governs the exact rendering of the Yemenite Jewish tradition (see footnote 4 above).

The Hebrew system of accents, known as *te'amim* (Hebrew, sing. *ta'am*, lit. "taste" or "sense"), is generally considered a type of ekphonetic notation, although, as in Lachmann's time, some scholars still consider it purely syntactical. In this system, which was codified in Tiberias between the late ninth and early tenth centuries CE, cantillation signs are applied to individual words and mark the syntactical divisions of the biblical text, thus bringing out the "sense" of the passage. The individual *te'amim* are named for their graphical shapes (e.g., *revi'i*, "square") or syntactical functions (e.g., *sof pasuq*, "end of verse") and contain no precise pitch or rhythmic information in themselves. Rather, they serve as mnemonic aids for corresponding melodic motives whose interpretation varies among different communities and according to different biblical books. As Idelsohn explains, "Only for those who know the mode and its motives and characteristics do the accents serve their purpose. . . . The fact that the same accents are set for all the twenty-one books, irrespective of the different modes, proves that they are only primitive reminding-signs of the rising and falling of a tune" (Idelsohn [1929] 1992, 69).

16. Lachmann's script: *connexion*.

established.[17] But even at the present stage of our knowledge we may safely say that, whereas the neums can be considered as a musical notation, some essential characteristics of such a notation are lacking in the ta'amīm.

It has thus been shown that the various religions,[18] in their liturgical chant, have some main features in common and that some of these can ultimately be traced back to primitive forms of cult. It might be attempted to establish a kind of chronological order between the different kinds of cantillation which now exist throughout the world, according to their more or less developed style. On the other hand, the distinguishing features must not be left out of consideration. There are strong points of difference not only between the chant of the various religions, but also between the chant of the various populations adhering to the same creed. In the case of Christianity, this musical diversity, as I mentioned in a former talk, is due to the large variety of nations which came to be Christianized. But Jewish cantillation, as well, has fallen into a number of separate traditions. The reason for this, obviously, is the dispersion of the Jewish people after the destruction of the Second Temple. It has therefore become a chief question for students of Jewish musical history, which one of these traditions may have kept closest to the original; but it is not yet possible to say the final word about this. Another question, closely linked up with the former one, concerns the different influences which have tainted the original. We know that, in the Near East as well as in Europe, Synagogue song has taken over musical traits of the nations among which the Jews came[19] to live. These traits are clearly marked as far as hymns are concerned. A Moroccan[20] Jewish sacred song, e.g., cannot be understood without the knowledge of the system of the Arab secular music of that country.[21] As to alien influence on the cantillation of the Bible, however, we must, again, profess our present inability to make definite statements although it is possible to say a great many vague things about Arab or Slav or German impregnation.[22]

Kurdish cantillation, at any rate, has a distinct character of its own which, I think, exactly conforms to other characteristics of the Jews of that region. It certainly lacks the intense strain and religious fervour inherent in Yemenite cantillation. Akin, in some way, to the Babylonian branch of tradition it is distinguished from it by its straightforward delivery and its male robust vigour.[23] The first chapter of the Book of Jonah as recited during the afternoon service of the day of atonement may serve as an example of this. (Recitation 4.3)

In conclusion, a passage from Zohar, the chief book of cabbalistic doctrine, will be recited.[24] Among the Kurdish Jews this book can be read in two different modes of which you will now hear the more ancient one. (Recitation 4.4)

---

17. Idelsohn had attempted to establish just such a connection, arguing that the Jewish system of accents is closely related both to the Greek *prosodia* of the second century CE and to the contemporaneous Byzantine and Armenian notation systems of the ninth century (Idelsohn [1929] 1992, 68–69).

18. Lachmann's script: *religious.*

19. Lachmann's script: *come.*

20. Lachmann's script: *Moroccon.*

21. Lachmann elaborates on this observation in his chapter on the festival songs (*piyyutim*) of the Jews of the island of Djerba, Tunisia, in which he identifies the melodic modes (*maqāmāt*, sing. *maqām*) and rhythmic-metric types of the six examples recorded (Lachmann 1940, 57–67; and Lachmann 1978, 125–53). In "National und International in der Orientalischen Musik," he illustrates the commonalities between the Jewish and Arab repertories with recorded examples of a *maqām* prelude and song from Tunis and a *piyyut* from Djerba (Lachmann 1936a). See also program 7, footnote 4.

22. Commenting on the cantillation of the Jews of Djerba, Lachmann concludes that "like that of all oriental-Sephardic communities, the cantillation of Djerba resembles Arab music in its tone relations and in its melody. . . . Nevertheless . . . some of the examples under consideration have turned out to be modally ambiguous; this fact may signify that the cantillation has . . . preserved to a certain extent the freedom of intonation originally characteristic of this species. It is a point of fact that the manner of cantillation—in Djerba as elsewhere—cannot be assigned to a rational system" (Lachmann 1940, 84; see also Lachmann 1978, 197).

23. Idelsohn describes the Kurdish tradition as "analogous to the Babylonian" (Idelsohn [19142–32] 1973, 2:32).

24. This passage, beginning "Pataḥ Eliahu ha-navi" (Elijah the Prophet opened), is taken from the introduction to Tikunei ha-Zohar 17a; it is sung at the beginning of each service in the Sephardic rite and in some Hasidic traditions.

Recitation 4.1: Aseret ha-dibberot *(Ten Commandments, excerpt, Exod. 20:2–7)*

Original recording number: D419 (Exod. 20:2–17)

Substitute recording number: D413 (Exod. 20:2–7, 4 January 1937)

Performer: Eliahu Yahye Mizrahi (on both original and substitute recordings)

אָנֹכִי יי אֱלֹהֶיךָ אֲשֶׁר הוֹצֵאתִיךָ מֵאֶרֶץ מִצְרַיִם מִבֵּית עֲבָדִים:
לֹא יִהְיֶה־לְךָ אֱלֹהִים אֲחֵרִים עַל־פָּנָי:
לֹא תַעֲשֶׂה־לְךָ פֶסֶל וְכָל־תְּמוּנָה אֲשֶׁר בַּשָּׁמַיִם מִמַּעַל וַאֲשֶׁר בָּאָרֶץ מִתָּחַת וַאֲשֶׁר
בַּמַּיִם מִתַּחַת לָאָרֶץ:
לֹא־תִשְׁתַּחֲוֶה לָהֶם וְלֹא תָעָבְדֵם כִּי אָנֹכִי יי אֱלֹהֶיךָ אֵל קַנָּא פֹּקֵד עֲוֹן אָבֹת
עַל־בָּנִים עַל־שִׁלֵּשִׁים וְעַל־רִבֵּעִים לְשֹׂנְאָי:
וְעֹשֶׂה חֶסֶד לַאֲלָפִים לְאֹהֲבַי וּלְשֹׁמְרֵי מִצְוֹתָי:
לֹא תִשָּׂא אֶת־שֵׁם־יי אֱלֹהֶיךָ לַשָּׁוְא כִּי לֹא יְנַקֶּה יי אֵת אֲשֶׁר־יִשָּׂא אֶת־שְׁמוֹ
לַשָּׁוְא:

(Exod. 20:2–7)

ʼanoḵi ʼaḏonay ʼeloheḵa ʼašer hoṣeṯiḵa meʼereṣ miṣrayim mibbeṯ ʻavaḏim:

lo-yihye ləḵa ʼelohim ʼaḥerim ʻal-panay:

lo-ṯaʻase ləḵa pesel wəḵol-təmuna ʼašer baššamayim mimmaʻal waʼašer baʼareṣ mittaḥaṯ waʼašer bammayim mittaḥaṯ laʼareṣ:

lo-ṯištaḥawe lahem wəlo ṯaʻovḏem kiʼ anoḵi ʼaḏonay ʼeloheḵa ʼel qanna poqeḏ ʻawon ʼavoṯ ʻal-banim ʻal-šillešim wəʻal-ribbeʻ-*ay*-im ləsonʼay:

"I am the Lord your God, who brought you out of the land of Egypt, out of the house of bondage.

"You shall have no other gods before me.

"You shall not make for yourself a graven image, or any likeness of anything that is in heaven above, or that is in the earth beneath, or that is in the water under the earth;

"you shall not bow down to them or serve them; for I the Lord your God am a jealous God, visiting the iniquity of the fathers upon the children to the third and the fourth generation of those who hate me,

wə'ose ḥesed la'alafim lə'ohavay ulšomre miṣwoṭay:

lo ṭissa 'eṯ-šem-'aḏonay 'eloheḵa laššaw ki lo yanaqqe 'aḏonay 'eṯ 'ašer-yissa 'eṯ-šəmo laššaw:

Transliteration by Ben Outhwaite

"but showing steadfast love to thousands of those who love me and keep my commandments.
"You shall not take the name of the Lord your God in vain; for the Lord will not hold him guiltless who takes his name in vain."

(RSV)

Recitation 4.2: Shirat Devorah *(Song of Deborah, Judg. 5:1–11)*

Recording number: D420

Performer: Eliahu Yahye Mizrahi

Recitation 4.3: Jonah 1:1–10

Recording number: D421

Performer: Eliahu Yahye Mizrahi

Recitation 4.4: "Pataḥ Eliyahu ha-navi" (Tikunei ha-Zohar 17a)

Recording number: D422

Performer: Eliahu Yahye Mizrahi

Editor's Commentary

Ideslohn devotes the second volume of his *Thesaurus of Hebrew Oriental Melodies* to "Songs of the Babylonian Jews," referring to the Jews who had settled in the lands of ancient Mesopotamia (present-day Iraq). Among these were the Aramaic-speaking or "Kurdish" Jews who inhabited the mountainous regions of the north and northeast, known as Kurdistan.[1] While the majority of the Babylonian Jews spoke Arabic, the Kurdish Jews, like their Nestorian Christian neighbors, still spoke "the so-called neo-Syrian dialect . . . a jargon composed of Persian, Kurdish, Turkish, Arabic and Hebrew elements with a basis, however, which has remained Aramaic" (Idelsohn [1914–32] 1973, 2:30–31).

For Idelsohn, the Babylonian tradition was "of special value," for the community had maintained a continuous presence there since the Babylonian exile in the sixth century BCE. Describing it as "the oldest [Jewish] settlement outside Palestine known to history, a settlement which has continued uninterruptedly and has been subjected to no important influences of other Jewish communities," he concluded that "it may therefore be assumed that in their traditional song ancient elements have been preserved" (Idelsohn [1914–32] 1973, 2:5).

Yet unlike the Yemenite Jews, who likewise claim ancient origins, the Babylonians could claim no comparable history of long isolation. On the contrary, in the first millennium following the destruction of the Second Temple, Babylon, with its famous Talmudic academies of Sura and Pumpedita, replaced Jerusalem as the center of Jewish intellectual and spiritual life. Nor were the Babylonians themselves a homogeneous community. Idelsohn identifies among them Persian Jews and "a large section" who were descendants of Jews who were expelled from Arabia by Caliph Omar in the early seventh century CE, shortly after the death of the Prophet Muhammad (Idelsohn [1914–32] 1973, 2:1). Against this background, the Jews of Kurdistan were of special interest to Idelsohn, since in his view they were "undoubtedly the direct descendants of the old Babylonians of Talmudic times" (Idelsohn [1914–32] 1973, 2:31). He includes ten transcriptions of Kurdish song in the *Thesaurus of Hebrew-Oriental Melodies* (Idelsohn [1914–32] 1973, vol. 2, nos. 165–74), taken from his recordings of a "scholar" from Sabulak on Lake Urmia. On examining them, however, he concluded that the Kurdish pronunciation of Hebrew was "the same as that of the Babylonians. Their synagogal songs are also similar" (Idelsohn [1914–32] 1973, 2:31).

Like Idelsohn, Lachmann considered the Kurdish tradition as "akin, in some way, to the Babylonian," distinguishing it only by "its straightforward delivery and its male robust vigour." It fell to his former research assistant Edith Gerson-Kiwi to assign a distinctive identity to Kurdish cantillation and recognize that the community's continuing use of the Aramaic vernacular had its analogy in their musical expression:

> It is certain that many aspects of their expression . . . in song preserve some remnants of an early pre-Christian style; in other words, here we seem to have some samples of a living antiquity . . . to a considerable extent connected with Jewish history of the biblical period (Gerson-Kiwi 1971, 60).

Specifically, she suggests that

> an ancient form of cantillation, not conforming to the Tiberian system and not even to the earlier more indigenous Babylonian one, can be observed in the reading of the prose books (Pentateuch, Prophets, and the Hagiographs) (Gerson-Kiwi 1971, 64).

In his Djerba monograph, Lachmann places Jewish cantillation squarely within "that class of recitation which includes the emphatic rendering of magic formulae, of sacred texts, and of heroic poems" (Lachmann 1940, 7). Elaborating upon this idea in the second of his "Four Lectures on Eastern Music," he identifies magical incantation as the common source of both epic poetic recitation and liturgical cantillation, which evolved along separate paths (Katz 2003, 393–396).[2] Thus Gerson-Kiwi does not deviate fundamentally from Lachmann when she interprets the Kurdish tradition of Jewish cantillation within the general conceptual framework of oral poetic recitation:

> The idea of narrating long stories . . . and, in particular, of immersing religious texts in an incessant stream of melody, as an esoteric medium of communication, was a common trend in most old Asiatic cultures. This is above all a distinctive constituent of oral folk literatures, as of the heroic epics of the East where a single proto-melody served a thousand verses (Gerson-Kiwi 1971, 62–63).

At first, Gerson-Kiwi suggests, the same manner of delivery was transferred to the intonation of the poetic books of the Bible, particularly

> the poetical Book of Psalms [which], with its many regular structures of parallelistic half-verses, the simple early melody scheme may have been enough to carry over hundreds of verses. But . . . when this proto-melody-line was adopted for the prose books of the Bible . . . it had to undergo a fundamental transformation which eventually led to the written symbols (reading accents) . . . and their final codification by the Tiberian school of Masoretes in the tenth century (Gerson-Kiwi 1971, 63).

Yet, just as the Arabic language failed to penetrate the clefts and ravines of the Kurdish mountains, so, too, she suggests, the newly codified system of biblical recitation was not accepted everywhere:

> In the remote and mountainous territories of northern Mesopotamia, the foreign Tiberian reading system probably never became firmly rooted, and the readers continued to chant in the older familiar Babylonian system, or even in a scheme in common use for story-telling and folk epics (Gerson-Kiwi 1971, 62–63).

Gerson-Kiwi discerned among her Israeli informants at least two different styles of Kurdish Jewish cantillation, which she associates with two historical phases: the earlier "Aramaic liturgical speech melody" or "indigenous mountain style," and the later Babylonian style conforming to the Masoretic system of text accents (Gerson-Kiwi 1971, 64–65). Indeed, she observes, "the more educated present-day Kurdish cantors . . . can, on request, produce the same liturgical text with a jebeli [Arabic: mountain] or with a sephardic melody" (Gerson-Kiwi 1971, 61). She characterizes the Aramaic style as "displaying a tendency to stretch over long tracts in a litany or parlando style, especially if the text is of a narrative nature (as in the chanting of the biblical books)" (Gerson-Kiwi 1971, 60). Elaborating on the relationship between text and melody, she explains:

> A fixed melodic frame serving one complete sentence may be considered as the skeleton of any of the following verses, and underlying the more individual realization of its single parts. The general disposition of a single sentence is marked by a clear declamation line, not unlike the psalmodic one, which however can be interrupted at any moment by prolonged and often dramatic melismata on the more significant words (Gerson-Kiwi 1971, 65).

It is surely just such a "clear declamation line . . . interrupted by prolonged and often dramatic melismata" that characterizes the recitation of the Ten Commandments by Eliahu Yahye Mizrahi on Lachmann's recording (recitation 4.1). In one respect, however, Mizrahi's delivery was evidently not typical. In his diary entry for the recording, Lachmann remarks: "Zehn Gebote in eigenen [*sic*] Niggun. Etwas zu schnell gesungen, um alles auf die Platte zu bekommen" (Ten Commandments in his own mode. Sung somewhat too fast, in order to get everything on one disc).

Notes

1. Roughly, the region from Mosul in present-day Iraq, northward to Zakho on the Turkish border, and eastward to Lake Urmia in present-day Iran.

2. Lachmann discusses specific cultural and musical commonalities between liturgical cantillation and poetic recitation in program 5. Elsewhere he posits that the origins not only of liturgical cantillation and the recitation of epic poetry but also of Greek tragedy and the Japanese Noh drama can ultimately be traced to the magic ceremony. As he explains in the second of his *Four Lectures in Eastern Music,* "the recitative tendency . . . has not remained within the limits of liturgy. . . . Out of the spirit of magical beliefs and of an ecstatic state of mind grew ancient tragedy and its musical belongings" (quoted in Katz 2003, 394). Positing "an historical connection with a probability bordering on certainty" between Noh drama and Greek tragedy, he concludes that "the Japanese drama . . . enables us to form at least an idea of what the recitation of the Greek drama may have been like. At the same time, the close resemblance of its chanting with liturgical cantillation bears witness of its ritualistic and magical origin" (cited in Katz 2003, 395). Lachmann discusses similar themes in his lecture "Orientalische Musik und Antike" (Lachmann 1974, 55–58).

Program 5

Bedouin Sung Poetry Accompanied by the Rabāba
20 January 1937

In the present series of talks this is the first one dealing with secular music. Its particular subject is Arab song and recitation accompanied by the Rabāba,[1] one of the two chief instruments in use among Beduins and peasants, the other being a reedflute.[2]

The Rabāba is a bowed instrument, a primitive fiddle with a rectangular body which consists of a wooden frame covered with parchment. The instrument has only one string made of horse hair. It is held upright like the European violoncello. The player usually sits on the ground in the Oriental fashion and so does the one whom you will hear presently.[3]

To European hearers, the peculiar charm of this kind of recitation is, perhaps, not easily accessible. The true way of approach is, of course, to let ourselves be captured by its genuine spirit and atmosphere. But it may be of help if we also try to understand its connections[4] with similar kinds of music and to fix its place in musical history. For this purpose, we shall pass, for a moment, from this country to Europe and from the present time back to antiquity.

We are inclined to think of the recitation of epic poetry as a custom belonging to a remote past. In this we are right as far as Greece and the Western part of Europe are concerned. We know that the great heroic epics, the Homeric poems, the Anglo-Saxon Beowulf, the lay of Hildebrand, were not delivered in ordinary speech, but were recited to the accompaniment of an instrument. In Ancient Greece the recitation was accompanied on a lyre or harp. As to Old English and German epics, we do not even know the precise character of the instrument. Besides, there are other important points of doubt regarding epic recitation. If the poems were not spoken in an ordinary tone of voice, what other kind of recitation was used? Were they sung? And, if so, to what kinds of melody? To sing thousands and ten thousands of lines not even grouped into stanzas means either constantly to introduce new tunes or to repeat one tune over and over again; the one would bewilder the hearers, the other fatigue them. Further: what part was assigned to the instrument? Were the tunes—if there were tunes—played in unison with the singer's voice or was the instrument only used for occasional interludes?

No satisfactory answer to any of these questions has been found in literary sources. Still, modern research in folk-music has shown a way towards forming at least an approximate idea of what epic recitation may have been like centuries and milleniums ago. In recent years, special attention has been given to the recitation of popular epic poems in Montenegro and the neighbouring regions.[5]

---

1. In Lachmann's script, the word *rabāba* appears sometimes with and sometimes without a macron over the second *a*. The spelling has been normalized throughout the program text to include the macron.

2. The *shabbāba* (also known as *qaṣaba*) is an end-blown reed pipe with finger holes and without a mouthpiece, traditionally played by shepherds. The instrument is featured in recitation 12.4.

3. A stick runs through the body of the instrument to form the neck, which holds the peg. Attached to the base of the instrument is a metal spike. For a description of the construction, playing technique, and musical function of the Bedouin *rabāba,* see Hassan 2002, 409.

4. Lachmann's script: *corrections.*

5. Lachmann is almost certainly referring here to the work of Gustav Wilhelm Becking (1896–1945), a fellow student of Johannes Wolf in Berlin, on the musical structure of the epic songs of Montenegro (Becking 1933). In the lecture "Orientalische Musik und Antike," presented the previous summer in Basel, Switzerland, Lachmann wrote, "In Montenegro and its surroundings we find still today the performance of poems from Slavic heroic sagas, which extend over up to ten thousand lines without segmentation into stanzas. Examples of this kind of performance had been recorded in Berlin a few years ago and were then analysed by Prof. Gustav Becking in Prague" (Lachmann 1974, 54).

Epic songs of the Balkans were also attracting the attention of classical scholars. Between 1933 and 1935, the Harvard scholar Milman Parry and his student Albert B. Lord led a field expedition to the former Yugoslavian territories (Herzegovina, Bosnia, Montenegro, and Southern Serbia) to research Southern Slav epic song. Believing that Homer's epic poems originated in an oral tradition that preceded literacy, Parry's aim was to record an experimental body of heroic song that would enable

They, too, like most ancient epic poems, consist of thousands of lines not grouped into stanzas; the normal duration is three quarters of an hour. The poems have a heroic character; they express the mental attitude of feudalism, thus leading us back to conditions of life prior to urban civilization and similarly those in which ancient epic poetry originated. These conditions are, obviously, indispensable for producing poetry of this kind and for keeping it alive. Since modern civilization has begun to penetrate even into this remote corner of Europe the practice of epic recitation is rapidly dying out there, or is undergoing reforms,—which practically means the same.

Epic poetry, in Montenegro, is neither sung nor spoken; it is difficult to find the adequate word for the way in which it is delivered. The recitation is distinguished from ordinary speech in the first place by the movement of the voice being restricted to a small number of more or less definite notes, mostly five. Moreover, the voice is highly strained; the reciter makes use of what, on a former occasion, had been called a disguised voice.[6]

You may remember that, on that occasion, the disguised voice was mentioned as one of the characteristics of magical incantation which passed into ritual service and even into secular song. In this as well as in other respects, epic recitation as represented by Balkan singers can be shown to be related to sacred cantillation. Other features common to both are the close dependence[7] of the melodic structure on the text, the strict limitation to a few melodic turns and cadences and, above all, the fact that in both cases a single person, priest or poet, keeps a large audience spellbound.

On the other hand we must be careful not to obliterate the difference between liturgical and epic recitation. The textual difference between liturgical prose and epic metre results, musically, in a contrast between free rhythm and unequal divisions as against a more or less regular sequence of stressed and unstressed notes. Another important distinction lies in the fact that while sacred cantillation is purely vocal epic poems are usually recited to the accompaniment of an instrument.

In Montenegro, the accompanying instrument is the Gusle, a bowed instrument which is distinguished from the Arab Rabāba mainly through the form of its wooden body, an elliptical bowl covered with parchment. The five notes of the recitation are produced on the open string and by the four fingers excluding the thumb. The places where the fingers stop the string are not indicated by frets nor do they yield rational tones and semitones. All the notes are used in the course of one recitation, but only four are substantive while the ringfinger always has a subordinate function.

In recent times, efforts are being made to reform this scale by substituting intervals of the diatonic scale for the irrational ones of popular tradition. The effect of this reform shows how closely the traditional scale which, to a modern European ear, sounds out of tune, is bound up with the epic style. The reformed scale distorts the character of the recitation and, as a student of it has rightly remarked, degrades the reciters of heroic feats to village tenors.[8]

The function of the Gusle consists not only in supporting the voice, but also in supplying a prelude and interludes. The prelude is a feature common to all Oriental music working up both the player's and his hearers' minds to the spirit of the recitation to come; we shall have to deal with it at greater length in connection with urban music.[9] The interludes are generally short; they serve to stress the metrical divisions, mostly between one verse and another and, at the same time, to give the reciter breathing space.

Arab literature, from pre-Islamic times onward, does not include epic poems. In spite of this, we are entitled to place the practice of singing to the Rabāba side by side with the epic recitation in Montenegro. The technique and function of the Rabāba coincide, on most points, exactly with those of the Gusle. Before going into details of this practice I want to let you hear a specimen of it. The singer and player, on this occasion, is Bāgis Ḥanna Ma'addi, a peasant from Ṭaiba in the Ramallah district.[10] He will first sing one of the poems which storytellers insert into their narratives. In order to be able to appreciate recitations of this kind it is, of course, indispensable to

---

him to discover, in the living oral traditions of epic song making, the processes by which Homer's poetry had been conceived and performed. Tragically, Parry's research was cut short in December 1935 by his death at age thirty-three from a shooting accident, and work on the musical part of his recordings did not begin until the spring of 1941, when Béla Bartók took up a visiting appointment at Columbia University for this purpose (Suchoff 1972, 568–70; Bartók and Lord 1951, x, xv–xvi). Lord's monograph *The Singer of Tales,* which took up the threads of the work Parry had begun under the same title, appeared in 1960; for a modern reprint, see Lord (1960) 2000.

6. See program 4 above.

7. Lachmann's script: *dependance.*

8. In the handwritten manuscript of his lecture "Musical Systems among the Present Arab Bedouins and Peasants," presented to the Palestine Oriental Society in Jerusalem in December 1936 (Lachmann 1936c), Lachmann credits this remark to Walther Wünsch, citing his book *Die Geigentechnik der sudslavischen Guslaren* (Wünsch 1934, 31), which Lachmann had recently reviewed in the third volume of *Zeitschrift für vergleichende Musikwissenschaft* (Lachmann 1935b, 45–46).

9. See program 9 and, for a more general treatment of urban music, programs 10 and 11.

10. This could have been the same *rabāba* player mentioned by Lachmann in "Musical Systems among the Present Arab Bedouins." Comparing the fingering techniques of several players, he singles out one "Christian Arab from Taiba in the Ramallah district" who "proved most conscious of all being able to account exactly for what he did. His thumb was left on the string almost permanently, but was released on certain occasions when the recitation dropped about a minor third to the note of the empty string. He always used his little finger, but, on the whole, merely for grace-notes. Above all his distinction between the qaṣīda and the other forms of song was particularly clear. In playing a qaṣīda the ringfinger, and in playing any other kind of song, the middlefinger was absolutely excluded" (Lachmann 1936c).

understand the meaning and context of the poem. These may, in the present case, be summarized as follows.

For eight years a feud was carried on between two Bedouin tribes. One of the two leaders planned to take possession of a place then in the other's hand. The place, represented as a bride, was given liberty to choose between them. The poem expresses the bride's answer in which she fervently favours her actual owner. (Recitation 5.1)

In this form of song, exactly the same notes are used on the Rabāba as those which constitute the scale of the Gusle. The ringfinger, used merely as a passing note on the Gusle, is here left out altogether.

You will now hear another form of recitation which, on certain points, contrasts with the former one. This song as well is connected with a story. A Bedouin chief has married a girl belonging to a hostile tribe. After a happy but short period of married life she dies and he spends every day of the year following her death in composing poems expressing his poignant grief. This is one of them. (Recitation 5.2, CD 1, tracks 11–12)

Unlike the former recitation the present one is in free rhythm. They also differ as to their scale. The ringfinger, formerly in disuse, has come into prominence and the note of the middlefinger, formerly a substantive note, has now dropped out.

For this alternative use of the middle- and the ringfinger which is the salient point of the present system of Rabāba playing, the Gusle presents no analogy. We have reason to believe that it represents a later stage of the Rabāba practice, and has to be attributed to the influence of an urban system of scale which was practised on the lute before the tenth century and which is known to us chiefly through indications in the Book of Songs, the Kitāb al-aghāni of Abu l-Faraǵ[11] al-Isbahānī. The prominence of the middlefinger would thus be the original stage during which the Rabāba was in total agreement with the Gusle.

Thus some light may have been thrown on Ancient epic recitation through present day practice. It is not proposed that they are identical. Instruments like the Gusle and the Rabāba are certainly not the same as those that were in the hands of Ancient Greek or Western reciters; the fiddle probably came from Central Asia and did not appear in the Near East before the later part of the first millenium after Christ. Yet the way in which epic poems are recited in the Balkans nowadays supplies a possible answer to the question as to how they may have been recited elsewhere in the far past. At any rate we have no other answer to give and no reason to reject the one which offers itself.

The Arab and Balkan practices of recitation are linked up by the striking similarity in the form and handling of the respective instruments, the Rabāba and the Gusle. It is quite possible that there is an historical connection between them. The fiddle may have been brought by wandering tribes from Central Asia as far as the Balkans, and its original practice preserved there whereas the Arabs, after taking it over from them, adapted it to their own purposes.[12] The recitation to the Rabāba, owing to the lyrical character of the poems recited, has to be set apart from epic recitation proper; but it still belongs to the same atmosphere of heroic feats and passions. The mental attitude from which it proceeds as well as the musical system which it preserves make it an invaluable inheritance of the past, all the more so as there is reason to doubt whether it will survive the growing influx of modern civilization.[13]

11. Lachmann's script: *Tarağ*.

12. Béla Bartók was likewise struck by similarities between Balkan and Arab practice as he worked on Milman Parry's collection of epic songs. Writing from Columbia University on 18 April 1941, Bartók remarked that "the [Balkan epic] chant itself is undoubtedly part of old European folk heritage, but the gusle accompaniment occasionally shows parallels with Arabic melodic treatment probably due to an influence during the long Turkish occupation" (quoted in Suchoff 1972, 570). Lachmann's hypothesis on the possible Central Asian origins of the *gusle* is supported by recent scholarship; see Forry 2000, 941.

13. For a multitextured ethnographic study of a continuing tradition of Arabic oral poetic recitation based on the Sirāt Banī Hilāl epic and its social dynamics in a Nile Delta village, see Reynolds 1995.

Recitation 5.1: Qaṣīdit al-Balqā'

Recording numbers: D480–D481 (= D451, 12 January 1937)

Performer: Bājis Afandī Im'addī, voice and *rabāba*

Recitation 5.2: Qaṣīdit Nimr Ibn ʻAdwān: *"Aw lamīn"*

Original recording numbers: B482–D482 (=D452, 12 January 1937)

Substitute recording number: D452 (12 January 1937)

Performer: Bājis Afandī Imʻaddī, voice and *rabāba* (on both original and substitute recordings)

Note: Passages where the *rabāba* approximately duplicates the voice are indicated in the *rabāba* staff by "etc."

uw sā-‘āt gal- gā- nin wa sā- ‘āt ghā- fī
uw sā-‘āt
etc.
ba- hīl ad- da- mi- ‘ min mig- lat al- ‘a- yn sā- ‘āt ‘a-l- khad-dayn bul- ṭum ik- fā- fī
etc.
aw sā- ‘āt fi l- baṭ- nān mi- thl al- ma- jā- nīn
etc.
aw dā- yir ma‘- l- ‘aj- yān ‘ar- yān ḥā- fī
etc.

aw wayn al- la- dhī kā- nū yi- sal- lū-al- ga- lib wayn
etc.
aw yit- raḥ- ḥa- bū bī ʻind mā- kūn lā- fī
wayn al-
etc.
etc.
la- dhī kā- nū yi- ḥay- yū al- gha- rī- bīn
Recording unclear here
(static)
wi zay- fū aẓ- ẓiy- fān bi- ʼaḥ- san ẓi- yā- fī
etc.

wa- ʻan- nā in- ta- ḥū wi-l- yawm ṣā- rū ba- ʻī- dīn
etc.
aw ghrī- bīn al- wa- ṭān lā- kin ba- ʻī- dīn al- ma- sā-
etc.
fī uw bi- frāg(i)- him wi- blīt yā rabb tish- fīn
etc.
ya- llī ʻa- layk al- ḥāl mā hūsh
etc.
khā- fī

uw min lām- nī yib- lā bi- jinn uw ʻa- zā- rīn
etc.
yij- ʻal ʻi- ẓā- mah dāyi- rāt likh- lā- fī
etc.

[spoken]
al-shāʻīr al-kabīr Bājis Afandī Imʻaddī.
qaṣīdit Nimr Ibn ʻIdwān, lammā tawaffat Waḍḥa imraʼtuh.

[sung]
aw lamīn ashkī mawjiʻ l-galib lamīn
wu-mā lī ʻalā l-balwāt ṣdīgin imwāfī

galbī ʻalā l-bica wi-l-jaẓẓ wi-n-nūḥ wi-n-nīn
uw sāʻāt galgānin wa sāʻāt ghāfī

uw sāʻāt bahīl ad-damiʻ min miglat al-ʻayn
sāʻāt ʻa-l-khaddayn bulṭum ikfāfī

aw sāʻāt fi l-baṭnān mithl al-majānīn
aw dāyir maʻ l-ʻajyān ʻaryān ḥāfī

aw wayn alladhī kānū yisallū al-galib wayn
aw yitraḥḥabū bī ʻind mākūn lāfī

wayn alladhī kānū yiḥayyū al-gharībīn
wi zayfū aẓ-ẓiyfān bi-ʼaḥsan ẓiyāfī

wa-ʼannā intaḥū wi-l-yawm ṣārū baʻīdīn
aw ghrībīn al-waṭān lākin baʻīdīn al-masāfī

uw bifrāgihim wi-blīt yā rabb tishfīn

ya-llī ʻalayk al-ḥāl mā hūsh khāfī

uw min lāmnī yiblā bi-jinn uw ʻazārīn

yijʻal ʻiẓāmah dāyirāt li-khlāfī

Transcribed by Makram Khoury-Machool

[spoken]
The great poet Bājis Afandī Imʻaddī.
Poem of Nimr Ibn ʻIdwān, on the death of his wife, Waḍḥa.

[sung]
To whom should I complain of my heartache, to whom,
since I have no loyal friend in times of calamities?

My heart continues to cry, lament, and wail.
At times I am anxious, and at others I doze.

At times the tears pour from the corner of my eye,
and at times I strike my cheeks with my hands.

At times I wander in the dunes, as do madmen,
wandering with vagabonds, barefoot and naked.

Where is she who consoled my heart, where,
she who welcomed me when I needed a remedy?

Where is she who used to greet strangers,
and hosted guests with the best hospitality?

She turned away from me and today is far away;
although she is near in the homeland, yet she is very distant.

O Lord, cure me from her departure, that brought me the worst of calamities,
you from whom nothing can be concealed.

Let him who blames me be visited by demons and the Angel of Death,
and may his bones be turned beneath the ground.

Translated by Makram Khoury-Machool

Editor's Note on Recitation 5.2

Nimr Ibn ʻAdwān (d. ca. 1823) was a warrior-poet of the ʻAdwān tribe, which traditionally inhabited the fertile land east of the Jordan River known as al-Balqaʻ. Toward the end of Nimr's life, the ʻAdwān were driven out of their lands into the mountains of Adjlūn by their enemy tribe, the Beni Ṣaḥr (Spoer 1923, 178). Nimr's wife, Waḍḥa, was presented to him by her family as a gift after he saved her sister from assault by a member of the Beni Ṣaḥr at the mouth of a cave where Nimr was hiding (Spoer 1923, 180–81). Waḍḥa died seventy days after giving birth to her only son, ʻAgāb. Inconsolable, Nimr poured out his grief in countless poems (*qaṣāyid,* sing.

qaṣīda) in Waḍḥa's memory. So devoted was Nimr to Waḍḥa that he never found another woman who could satisfy him: "Although he married many—according to some native authorities eighty—he divorced them all and returned them to their homes" (Spoer 1923, 184).

Nimr's poems and the traditions about him were collected by the Anglican cleric and orientalist Rev. Henry H. Spoer (1930), who made several trips to the lands of the 'Adwān, beginning in 1904, and published his material in various articles over the following decades. Spoer gives an account of Nimr's life, as recorded in oral lore and in his poems, in Spoer 1923, and he includes two versions of the poem "Aw lamīn ashkī mawji'-l-galib" (recitation 5.2), sung by different singers, in Spoer and Haddad 1945, 38 (English translation on p. 42). In his 1945 article, coauthored with Elias Nasrallah Haddad, Spoer gives an illuminating commentary on the processes of composition and memorization in performances of Bedouin sung poetry according to his own observations:

> We were often confronted with the fact, familiar among singers elsewhere, that those who found great difficulty in reciting a qaṣīda could sing it with perfect ease, probably due to the circumstance that in singing they could slur over a word or syllable which in speaking would have to be pronounced with greater precision (Spoer and Haddad 1945, 8).

He describes sessions in which variants were created communally, comparing the process to the way children's playground rhymes are varied, as the audience exploited lapses in the reciter's memory by substituting words of similar sounds or meaning:

> The oral memory of our Bedawi friends of the cadences was often to us a matter of great astonishment as sometimes there was no clear enunciation of a word or words in their recitatives, but what appeared to us to be mere imitative sounds of the unknown word. But it was evidently not so to the native audience, as in such a case someone would immediately call out "hāda mūš maṣbūṭ hāda mūš durri lāzim tgūl" [this is not exact, you're not supposed to say this now] and some word would be supplied giving substance to the imitative sound. This would lead to a general transdiscussion, and others would advance their knowledge of the poem. When at last the excitement was over and a word had been finally decided upon, as being the correct one, it would often transpire that it presented little more meaning to some of the hearers than the formless sound of the needed word (ibid., 37–38).

Editor's Commentary

> Present day Bedouins, in playing the fiddle, follow rules established by musicians at the court of the early Abbasid Khalifs.
>
> —Robert Lachmann, *Oriental Music,* program 5

The idea, posited in program 1, that the Bedouin *rabāba* could illuminate "rules" of medieval Arab urban music, occurred to Lachmann during his first recording sessions in Palestine. In his third Jerusalem report of 7 July 1935, he remarked that he had recorded

> a Bedouin singer who accompanied himself on the Rabab al-shair [Arabic *sha'ir,* "professional poet-singer"] [who] deservedly has the reputation of being one of the best musicians in his genre. Besides a number of characteristic songs I obtained some valuable information as to the system underlying the playing on this kind of Rabab, a system which is a more rudimentary form of that existing in the time of Al-Isbahānī's Kitāb al-Aghānī and, therefore, throws some light on medieval practice (quoted in Katz 2003, 122).

Over the following three years, Lachmann recorded several different *rabāba* players, noting their precise methods of fingering in his recording diaries. He discussed his preliminary findings, exploring their potential implications for music history, theory, and ethnography, in three lectures delivered between May 1936 and January 1937. The most substantial of the three is "Orientalische Musik und Antike" (published posthumously in Lachmann 1974, 55–59), which he presented in May 1936 to the Geographic-Ethnological Society in Basel, Switzerland. In this wide-ranging study of diverse musical practices, Lachmann posits a relationship between the different fingerings used for the *rabāba* and the system of melodic classification described in the tenth-century Arab music treatise *Kitāb al-aghānī* (Book of Songs) by the Persian scholar Abū al-Faraj al-Iṣfahānī (897–967).[1] Later in the same lecture, Lachmann explores the similarities between Bedouin and Balkan traditions of poetic recitation, speculating on the possible relationship of both practices to the recitation of epic poetry in ancient Greece and Northern Europe. He synthesizes these two thematic strands, the one focusing on the instrument, the other on the poetry, in "Musical Systems among the Present Arab Bedouins and Peasants," presented in December 1936 to the Palestine Oriental Society in Jerusalem. In this lecture, Lachmann pairs an elaborate discussion of the different scale systems of the *rabāba*—based on his fieldwork in Palestine—with an equally elaborate account of those of the *qaṣaba* (a reed flute without a mouthpiece, also known as *shabbāba*) based on his earlier fieldwork in Tunisia and Algeria (Lachmann 1936c). These two lectures provide the conceptual framework for his summary observations in program 5, which he broadcast just a month after his lecture to the Palestine Oriental Society.

Famous as a unique source of biographical information on individual poets and musicians from pre-Islamic times through the ninth century, the *Kitāb al-aghānī* contains nearly one hundred songs texts with information on their melodic settings, including their melodic modes (*nagham*) and rhythmic-metric patterns (*īqā'*; Sawa 1985 and Sawa 1989). Commenting on al-Iṣfahānī's presentation Lachmann explains:

> Curiously enough, a mode, here, is not defined in terms of scale, but by two places on the fingerboard of the lute. . . . the first of the two notes by which every mode is defined may be either the open string or any one of the four fingers while the second one is either the middle or the ringfinger [which cannot be used together]. . . . the alternative between the middle and the ringfinger on the 'ūd [four-stringed lute] means an alternative between B♭ and B (Lachmann 1936c).

Thus the melodies in the *Kitāb al-aghānī* fell into two basic modal groups according to whether they use B or B♭.

Al-Iṣfahānī's method of melodic classification was superseded in urban Arab music by the modal system known as *maqām*. It survives, however, according to Lachmann, in the Bedouin *rabāba*. Having observed the practice of "a number of players from Palestine and Trans-Jordan" (Lachmann 1936c), he concludes that, like the melodies in the *Kitāb al-aghānī,* those of the *rabāba* fall into two categories, according to whether the middle finger or ring finger is the more prominent. Furthermore, the choice of fingering depends on the type of poetry sung:

> In the form of recitation which includes all the romances, and has the generic name of Qasīda the middlefinger is more prominent; in all the other forms of song. . . . the functions of the two fingers are reversed (Lachmann 1936c).[2]

The full significance of this arrangement became apparent to Lachmann when he compared the technique of the *rabāba* with that of the *gusle,* the bowed string instrument used to accompany the recitation of Balkan epic poetry. While acknowledging that there was no precise analogy in Arab poetry to the epic poetry of the Balkans, he felt justified in considering the Bedouin *qaṣīda* (romance), with its pre-Islamic origins, to be the closest equivalent. And in terms of its construction, playing technique, musical function, and social functions, the *gusle* appeared to share almost all the essential characteristics of the *rabāba*. Like the *rabāba,* the *gusle* requires the use of all four fingers in addition to the open string. However, "in the course of one recitation . . . only four [pitches] are substantive while the ringfinger always has a subordinate function." In other words, the fingering of the *gusle* "corresponds exactly to the fingering employed on the *rabāba* for the recitation of the romances which, in Arab literature, are the nearest equivalent to the popular epic poems of the Balkans" (Lachmann 1936c).

In light of his observations, Lachmann deduced that, of the two types of *rabāba* fingering, the one it shared with the *gusle* was the older. In other words,

> the prevalence of the middle-finger over the ring-finger on the rabāba is older than the opposite practice. It would seem natural that the older practice was maintained for the accompaniment of romances, this is, for those kinds of recitation for which the instrument was originally intended whereas the newer technique, with the ring-finger prevailing, was left to purely lyrical forms of song which have no narrative as a background and which do not originally call for an instrumental accompaniment (Lachmann 1936c).[3]

In order to explain the introduction of the "newer technique" into Bedouin practice, Lachmann returned to al-Iṣfahānī's *Kitāb al-aghānī*. Convinced that the innovation could only have come from an external source, he concluded that

> the medieval system of Arab urban music [found] its way into the musical practice of Bedouins and peasants. . . . [The] change between B♭ and B [implied by finger position on the *'ūd*] is an established element in Ancient Greek and Ancient Indian theory and urban practice;[4] there is no need to try and find another source for its occurrence in Arab urban music. On the other hand, it would be difficult to explain why the Bedouin should, without any external influence, have added a new element to their traditional method of accompanying narratives while Balkan peasants who are in a similar social situation have kept it up unchanged (Lachmann 1936c).

In positing the influence of an urban source on Bedouin practice, Lachmann was drawing upon theories concerning the origin and diffusion of tone systems developed by his Berlin colleagues Curt Sachs and Erich von Hornbostel in the 1920s. The original focus of Sachs's and Hornbostel's observations, however, was not the fingering patterns of the one-stringed fiddle but rather the apparently arbitrary intervallic relations produced by the equidistant arrangement of the finger holes of "ancient, exotic and folk flutes." As Sachs was to explain in his posthumous *The Wellsprings of Music:*

> It is obvious—as every violinist or guitarist knows—that two musical steps of equal width require different strides on the instrument, with the second smaller than the first one, and so forth. This applies to finger holes as much as to frets. . . . [In flutes, however,] the holes are equidistant throughout or else arranged in two groups, either one with equidistant holes and separated from one another by a somewhat larger space. . . . This is a strange abdication of the aural to the visual sense (Sachs and Kunst 1962, 99–100).

Sachs first proposed an explanation for this apparently irrational musical phenomenon in his essay on the tuning of the ancient Egyptian pipes in the collection of the Berlin Museum (1921). Equating the distance between the finger holes of the pipes with the divisions of the ancient Egyptian foot, he concluded that it was the physical measurement itself—rather than any hypothetical acoustical criteria—that served as the basis for determining their scales (Sachs 1921, 82). Elaborating on Sachs's observations in a broad comparative study, Hornbostel explored the cultural-historical significance of the measurements and their roots in the cosmological systems of ancient Asian civilizations (Hornbostel 1928b). Lachmann summarizes Hornbostel's position in his Djerba monograph, with an attribution to his 1928 article: "The development of musical instruments is part of a process by which magical beliefs were widened out into an all-embracing conception of the universe. Things under the control of man—temples and fields as well as tools and instruments—came to be subjected to fixed standards of measurement; it was held that by these means they were made to conform to the cosmic dimensions ruling the structure and equilibrium of the world" (Lachmann 1940, 4). However, as musical instruments and their measurements passed across continents and epochs and from high to low social strata, their precise measurements lost their sacred significance, and their physical properties were adapted to local conditions. In such cases, "the flutes lost exactness to thoughtless copying and to casual measuring by the maker's digits and span" (Sachs and Kunst 1962, 100–101).

In his lecture "Musical Systems among the Present Arab Bedouins and Peasants," Lachmann's explanation of the principles underlying the tuning of the *qaṣaba* and of flutes with equidistant fingerholes generally virtually replicates the arguments of Sachs and Hornbostel, down to his account of "the discovery" of the tuning systems of the pharaonic and other ancient flutes (Lachmann 1936c). Like his colleagues, Lachmann identifies processes of adaptation and simplification as both fiddle and flute passed from higher to lower social spheres. The distance between the finger holes of the Bedouin *qaṣaba,* he explains, typically spans the breadth of about two fingers—a span which, while no longer conforming to ancient Egyptian measurements, results in a comfortable position for the player. Similarly, in the case of the *rabāba*:

> The medieval urban system of scales as implied by the Kitāb al-aghānī, in being transferred to a more primitive social sphere, has been simplified. While in urban music each of the two main groups [scales produced by the alternating middle- and ring-fingers] was subdivided into modes, rural practice has retained only the [two] main groups. . . . Besides, the system is no longer practiced on the four-stringed 'ūd, the representative instrument of the 'Abbasid court-musicians and of urban music ever since, but on the less ambitious one-stringed rabāba (Lachmann 1936c).

Notes

1. For a modern edition, see al-Iṣfahānī 1963–73.
2. Curiously, Lachmann's explanation is not borne out by his music examples, both of which he identifies as *qaṣīda* in his recording diaries, even though recitation 5.2 is supposed to represent the newer technique. Spoer also identifies the text of recitation 5.2, "Aw lamīn ashkī mawji' l-galib," as a *qaṣīda* (Spoer 1945, 38; English translation on p. 42).
3. See endnote 2 above.
4. Here Lachmann inserts a reference to *Musik des Orients* (Lachmann 1929, 50–51).

Program 6

Liturgical Cantillation and Songs of the Samaritans
3 February 1937

A survey of religious music in the Near East which did not include Samaritan cantillation would omit one of its most remarkable aspects. The importance of this type of religious chant is out of all proportion with the very small number of those who are keeping it alive,—members of a community which numbers less than 200 persons.[1] In trying to find out what makes Samaritan sacred music so interesting we shall have to ask what distinguishes it from the music of other Oriental liturgies, Jewish, Christian, and Muhammedan.

The Samaritans claim that their present cantillation of the Pentateuch has been preserved unchanged from antiquity like all the rest of their customs and traditions. With all due reserve towards claims of this kind—which are raised rather too frequently among Oriental nations—we must admit that the Samaritan claim carries a great deal of conviction. The Samaritans are a mixed population consisting of Jews who had remained in Palestine after the main bulk of the Jewish people had been exiled to Babylon, and of colonists who had immigrated from Assyria. Ever since their fatal dispute with the Jews after the Babylonian exile, the Samaritans have kept strictly to themselves.[2] With the exception of a small Jewish group they are the only people who have inhabited the country from that ancient period down to the present day. They were not influenced, to any appreciable extent, by the nations who came to dominate the country after the dispersion of the Jews. Even the Arabs whose language they took over for every day use did not cause any substantial change in their manner of life. They still scrupulously observe the teachings of their only sacred book, the Pentateuch. They still use the ancient Hebrew script, and still perform their ancient religious ceremonies, above all, their offerings on Mount Gerizim, on the eve of Passover. Their strict seclusion, maintained almost to the point of self-extinction, has made them easily distinguishable from any other group of the population of Palestine; their outward appearance, tall build, bearded faces, priestly deportment, cannot be mistaken.[3]

---

1. According to British censuses, there were 182 Samaritans in 1932. Their numbers increased through the Mandatory period until by 1948 there were 250 Samaritans in Nablus and a further fifty-eight living in settlements elsewhere (Schur 1989, 125–26). Marriages with Jewish women—allegedly to increase the birthrate and to counter the effects of the disproportionately high ratio of male to female births—were first reported in the late nineteenth century and continued in the twentieth century (Schur 1989, 123, 125, 130).

2. See Mor 1989 for a critical discussion of the various conflicting traditions concerning the origins of the Samaritans and the circumstances leading to their decisive split with the Jews.

3. Lachmann's description tallies with those found in other nineteenth and early twentieth-century writings (see Schur 1989, 124, 127). In 1960 Izhak Ben-Zvi, the second president of the State of Israel (in office 1952–63), described his first encounter with a "real life Samaritan" while residing in Jaffa: "He looked like an old eastern patriarch: his flowing white beard, his movements were slow and controlled, his self-assurance and all his appearance were full of dignity. His face was typically Jewish and only his hair, which still showed traces of its original blond colour, was not in accordance with this impression" (quoted in Schur 1980, 126).

The Englishwoman Mary Eliza Rogers, whose brother Edward Thomas Rogers was a British consular official in the Levant, spent several years in Palestine in the mid to late 1850s. Unusually, her description of the Samaritans of Nablus includes women and children: "On the whole, I was very favorably impressed with the appearance of the Samaritan community. The men were generally handsome, tall, healthy-looking, and intelligent, but very few of them could read or write. The women are modest, and the children very pretty and thoughtful, yet full of life and activity" (Rogers 1862, 248). Later she observes that

> the women do not hide their faces from men of their own community, but they veil themselves closely in the streets and in the presence of strangers.
>
> They were generally very simply dressed, in trousers and jackets of Manchester prints and coloured muslin head-kerchiefs and veils. When out of doors, they shrouded themselves in large white cotton sheets, and though the former were faced and the latter patched, their poorest garments looked clear. I saw very little jewellery, except on the head-dresses of the most recently married women. They nearly all, however, wore glass bracelets; and some of the children had anklets, made of tinkling silver bells. The girls had a few small coins sewn to the edges of their red tarbouches, just in front (Rogers 1862, 251).

The same can be said of their chant. You will presently hear three representative performers of it: the High Priest of the community, Taufiq Kohen, his brother Ibrahim Kohen, and Yisḥaq Amram Kohen, the son of the former High Priest.[4]

When I first heard Samaritan cantillation I was reminded of a certain Englishman's impression of the Japanese Nō, the most ancient form of Japanese drama. There too, an unbroken tradition is being kept up to the present day by singers and actors who, by birth or adoption, belong to the families of those who originated the play. This Englishman says that his first reaction to the extraordinary way in which the actors used their voices was an almost irresistible desire to burst out laughing. But, having, of course, to suppress this impulse he felt during the next half hour or so, how the recitation which at first had seemed to be nothing but a challenge to common sense, slowly grew upon him until he sat listening to it in a kind of quiet rapture like the Japanese themselves. This result, he thinks, was due to the unswerving consistency with which the actors pursued their manner of singing, thus creating a sphere of expression with a reality of its own, however unreal it may appear to us.[5]

It is, perhaps, useful to remember this account of Nō chanting when first hearing Samaritan recitation,—the more so because there is not sufficient time now to let it exercise its own full effect. You will first hear a fragment of the Song of the Sea from Exodus. But you will find it difficult to follow the recitation of the text. Nearly every word is drawn out to considerable length by means of expletives,—a device to be found also in Ancient Indian cantillation.[6] (Recitation 6.1, CD 1, tracks 13–14)[7]

You will agree with me in thinking that this style of recitation sounds highly archaic. How can we verify a general statement of this kind? You may remember that, on a former occasion, I drew your attention to various points of relation, spiritual as well as technical, between the highly developed liturgy of civilised nations and the magic ritual of primitive communities.[8] Now, Samaritan cantillation, more than Jewish, Christian, and Muhammedan, is apt to establish this relationship on a musical basis. The sorcerer or medicine man, in shamanic ritual, pronounces magic formulae for the cure of the sick and for bringing about other desired effects. On these occasions, he works himself up into a state of ecstasy; his soul is supposed to leave his body and to communicate with good and evil spirits and, at a certain stage of his trance, he becomes possessed with a demon who takes the place of his soul during its absence. His voice seems to illustrate the whole process. It ranges from a monotonous recitation to uncanny outcries; and at times, it really seems to belong to a demon rather than to a human being.

Among civilised[9] nations, the nearest approach to magic chanting is found in the Japanese Nō drama and in

4. Lachmann made a total of forty-six recordings (D520–D565) of these three priests on 2 and 3 February 1937.

5. Lachmann's recording diaries from his Berlin years list thirty-seven cylinder recordings of Japanese music and a further ten recordings of Noh drama performed by visiting Japanese artists in 1924–25 (Jewish Music Research Centre, Lachmann Archive, A.I.17). Of these, only the Noh recordings are accompanied by further documentation: Gerson-Kiwi's catalogue lists the music transcriptions and texts in Japanese script and transliteration with German translation (A. 11. 28) that formed the basis of Lachmann 1925 and Lachmann 1926. In the second of his "Four Lectures on Eastern Music" (reproduced in Katz 2003, 386–96) and more extensively in "Orientalische Musik und Antike" (Lachmann 1974, 45–59), he explores specific commonalities between Noh and Samaritan cantillation, claiming that both forms derive from magical incantation. He also discusses similarities between Noh drama and ancient Greek drama, both of which, he claims, "have their roots in ecstatic cult, in the cult of Dionysos and wine harvest which corresponds to Japanese rice harvest" (Lachmann 1974, 57). Finally, he suggests that the two dramatic forms shared a historical link via India and China, concluding that "the No-drama, which has survived until today in Japanese musical life, can give us an idea of the practice of performance and also of the structure and linkage of melodic types of the Greek tragedy" (Lachmann 1974, 56–57).

6. Lachmann is referring here to the sung texts of the Sāmaveda, where individual words are modified and extraneous syllables are inserted within and between words to fit the melodies (Katz 2001; Howard 2000, 242). As previously noted for Coptic chant (see "Editor's Note on the Music" in program 3), these characteristics of Samaritan and Vedic chant apparently contradict Lachmann's principle that the text is the primary determinant of melodic flow in sacred cantillation. They are, however, consistent with George Herzog's observations on the deliberate violation of speech-tones in Navajo ritual songs, rendering the songs virtually unintelligible to lay members of the community. Such obfuscation of the text, Herzog suggests, is typical of much primitive song: "It is not at all easy for the Navaho layman to understand these songs. But that is just as well, since the mysterious in ritual always has its effect on beholder and listener. The language of primitive song texts the world over is a mixture of the poetic and the obsolete, often amounting to a technical jargon, difficult for the average native to follow" (Herzog 1934, 463).

7. The description of this recitation in Lachmann's recording diaries reads, "Sir Miriam, Exodus XV, 1 u. Anf. 2. (nach Barakat Aharon). Zu jedem grossen Fest. Eigentlich von der Gemeinde gesungen, in zwei Halbchoeren" (Song of Miriam, Exodus 15, verse 1 to the beginning of verse 2 after the blessing of Aaron. Sung at every major feast. Actually sung by the community in two half-choruses). In the same diary Lachmann identifies the original radio recording, D536, as "Šir Miryam (Mittelteil)" (Song of Miriam, middle section), equating this with D530 (a continuation of D529, below), titled "Sir Mittelteil (neue Melodie), v. 13–16" (Song, middle section, new tune, v. 13–16). In the biblical source, however, these four verses belong to the Song of Moses (Exod. 15: 1–19), which is followed by the Song of Miriam (Exod. 15:20–22).

8. See Lachmann's discussion of shamanic and magical incantation in program 4.

9. Lachmann's script: *civilized*.

Samaritan cantillation. In the Nō drama, the connection with magic modes of expression is confirmed by the frequent presence of ghosts and demons among the dramatis personae and by the resemblance of certain scenes to magic ceremonies. But both here and in Samaritan cantillation, the magic style of chanting, if we may use this term, has been purified, not only as regards vocal technique, but also in that it has been subjected to a system.

In both cases, the system establishes a definite number of phrases or modulations closely linked up with the text. Leaving the Nō chant aside we find that the Samaritan system assigns the different turns of the voice to different parts of the textual structure. All those striking characteristics of the cantillation, those shakes, glides, sudden stresses, and sudden lapses into ordinary speech which, at first hearing, seem to be spontaneous are, in reality, made to respond and to lend colour to various stereotyped properties inherent in the syntax, rhetoric, and emotional character of the liturgical text. Each of these ten properties has its special name, and is marked by a special sign; and the names give us the exact meaning of the musical sounds or groups of sounds which correspond to them. Some of the names, like conjunction and separation, simply point to structural qualities; others, as, e.g., astonishment, supplication, and exasperation, refer to the contents.[10]

This system, evidently, places Samaritan cantillation in the immediate neighbourhood of Jewish cantillation,—which, considering their close historical connection, is precisely what we should expect. The Jewish system, as well, establishes a restricted number of melodic phrases, and assigns them to certain points of the text; and the Samaritan recitation signs correspond, of course, to the Jewish accent marks, the ta'amim, which they resemble both by their names and graphically.[11]

The similarity of the two systems can be followed up still further. Just like Jewish cantillation, Samaritan as well discerns a number of melodic modes. In Jewish liturgy, each of the modes or neginoth belongs to a special book, or group of books, of the Bible. The Samaritan scriptural canon includes only the Pentateuch; accordingly, all their eleven modes refer to this one book. Each of them is used on a different occasion, one, e.g., on ordinary Sabbaths, four others at different hours of the day of atonement, one for funerals, one on joyous occasions, and so on. The different melodic modes, therefore, represent different moods; but, for a foreign listener, it is difficult, if not impossible, to recognize these moods from the character of the music.

Every liturgical reading is preceded by the recitation of two[12] lines from Moses' song in Deutoronomy;[13] in this recitation, the character of every melodic mode is reduced to a concise formula. You will now hear successively three of these formulae. The first one expresses joy, and precedes the cantillation on festive events such as the celebration of the birth of Moses. (Recitation 6.2)

The second one expresses mourning, and is used for dirges. (Recitation 6.3)

The third mode is used for the cantillation referring to the miracles performed by Aaron before Pharaoh; it is considered to be in a cheerful mood. (Recitation 6.4)

The Samaritan system of eleven modes, like the Jewish system, only applies to liturgical cantillation and neither to sacred nor to secular song. The rhythmic and melodic form of these songs is simpler than that of the cantillation. But here, too, strange accents and glides like those with which the cantillation abounds are woven into the texture and, above all, the general style of recitation is unmistakably the same. As an example you hear a convivial song in Arabic in which a soloist alternates with a chorus. The use of the Arabic language, in this song, makes it particularly clear how far remote it is from genuine Arab song. (Recitation 6.5, CD 1, tracks 15–16)

The investigation of Samaritan song and cantillation has not been carried far enough to yield definite results. One point, I think, may be considered as settled. As regards the evolution of sacred cantillation, the Samaritan style represents a stage intermediary between magic incantation among primitive tribes and the comparatively tame expression of religious feelings in Near Eastern service. It is certainly more ancient than the cantillation preserved in any of the Jewish communities.

This does not necessarily mean that Jewish cantillation, at any time, was identical with Samaritan. While they are closely akin, as we have seen, with respect to their musical system, i.e., the grouping of the cantillation into melodic modes and melodic phrases, they are, on the other hand, wide apart as to their melodic substance and as to the way in which it is delivered. As a matter of fact, no kind of song or cantillation throughout the Near East, as far as I know, resembles Samaritan. This leads us to think that Samaritan chant, apart from representing an earlier stage of development than Jewish, may possibly represent, also, a different racial style. But the style of what race? Can we hope to have discovered, in Samaritan cantillation and song, the music, or vestiges of the music,[14] of one of the nations which, in antiquity, dominated the Near East,—some nation now extinct unless it survives in the Samaritan community? I prefer stopping here to being drawn onto soft ground.

---

10. Idelsohn 1917b, 117 lists the names of the ten Samaritan recitation signs (Samaritan-Aramaic, *sidre miqrata;* Hebrew, *sidre ha-miqra*) and their corresponding properties. He divides the signs into two groups: signs *a* through *c,* whose properties are essentially syntactical, and signs *d* through *j,* which express the emotional content of the text. For a similar list, see Spector 1965, 146.

11. See Idelsohn 1917b, 122 for a comparative table listing the names of the Samaritan signs with their Hebrew and Greek counterparts.

12. Lachmann's script: *tqo.*

13. Deuteronomy 32:3: "For I will proclaim the name of the Lord. Ascribe greatness to our God!"

14. Lachmann's script: *musik.*

Recitation 6.1: Shirat ha-yam *(Song of the Sea, excerpt, Exod. 15:1)*

Original recording numbers: D536–D537 (Exod. 15:13–16)

Substitute recording number: D529 (3 February 1937)

Performer: Ibrahim Kohen (on both original and substitute recordings)

Note: Following the through transcription of recitation 6.1, a tabular transcription shows the cyclic melodic structure that begins at 0:28 and rises progressively in pitch with each repetition. In both transcriptions, roman numerals I–III indicate the beginning of each melodic cycle. Slurs in the tabular transcription indicate melodic phrases.

A. Through Transcription

אָז יָשִׁיר־מֹשֶׁה וּבְנֵי יִשְׂרָאֵל אֶת־הַשִּׁירָה הַזֹּאת לַיי וַיֹּאמְרוּ לֵאמֹר אָשִׁירָה לַיי
כִּי־גָאֹה גָּאָה סוּס וְרֹכְבוֹ רָמָה [בַיָּם׃]

(Exod. 15:1)

aze yašar-*uwanuwa*-are mu-*nu*-uši weba-*wanuwa*-ani-*iyinwi* išira'e-*nwe-e-uwe-e*-li it a-*wanuwa*-aši-*nwi*-ira-*wanuwa* aze-*wenuwe*-e'ot a-*nuwa*-alešema wa-*a-uwawi*-ya-*a-a*-'u-*wunuwu*-ume-*nwe*-eru li-*iwinwi*-limor aširu-*u* a-*nwa*-alešema-*wa-a-uwa-a* ki-*i* gu-*nu*-uwi-*nuwi-i* ga-*nwa* so-*o*-os wiri-*i*-kibu-*u* rama-*nwa*

Transliteration by Ben Outhwaite

Then Moses and the people of Israel sang this song to the Lord, saying, "I will sing to the Lord, for he has triumphed gloriously; the horse and his rider he has thrown [into the sea.]"

(RSV)

B. Tabular Transcription

0:28
1:08
1:53
I
II
III
3

Recitations 6.2–6.4: Three versions of "Ke-ev-sem" (Deut. 32:3)

Recording numbers: D538–D539

Performers: Amram Kohen (solo), Ibrahim Kohen and Taufiq Kohen (chorus)

Recitation 6.5: "Sukkāni dhāk al-wādī"

Recording number: D540

Performers: Ibrahim Kohen (solo), Amram Kohen and Taufiq Kohen (chorus)

Note: Designated "Gesellschaftslied" (communal song) in Lachmann's recording diaries.

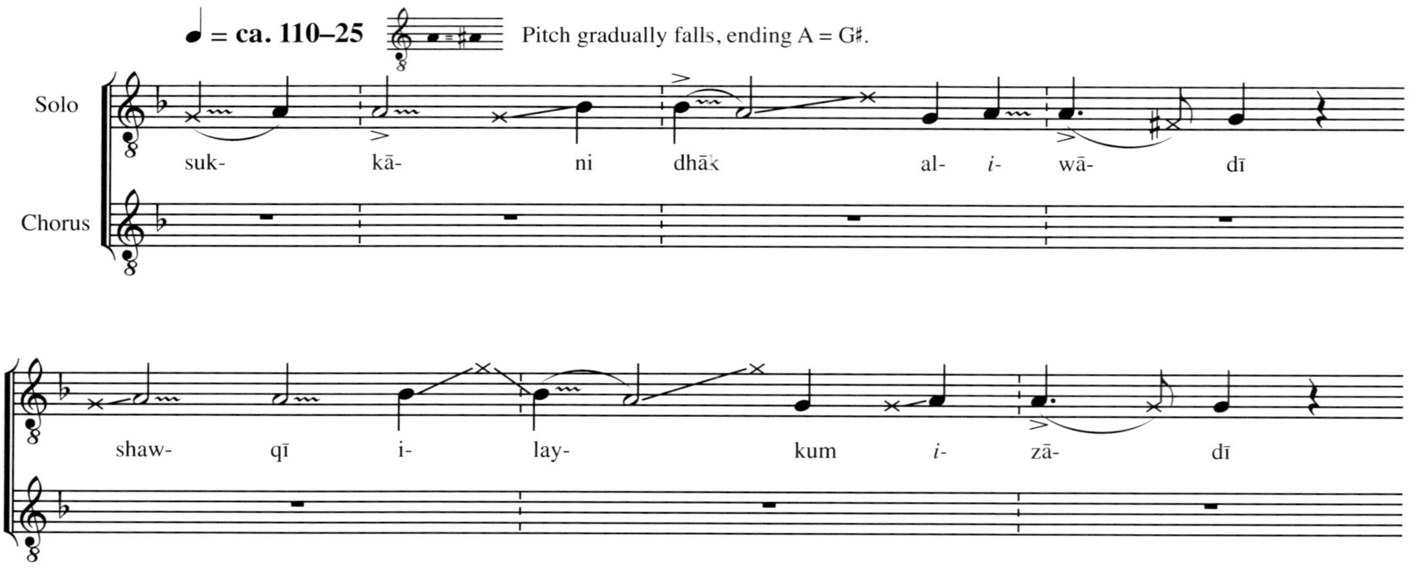

sukkāni dhāk al-*i*-wādī shawqī ilaykum *i*-zādī wal-*i*-qalbu minnī ṣādī
yā ahl il-*i*-wafā ar-*i*-jū ṣafā hādhā shifā jis-*i*-mānī

sub-*i*-ḥān dāyim waḥ-*i*-dānī fīhi-l-*i*-kamāl luh thānī

antum-*i* malādhi l-*i*-fānī fi l-yawm il-akh-*i*-rānī antum ḍiyyā a'yānī
yā ahl il-walā yā ahl al-*i*-malā fīkum ḥilā aw-*i*-zānī

sub-*i*-ḥān dāyim waḥ-*i*-dānī . . .

People of that valley; my longing for you is my food, and my heart aches.
O loyal people, I wish for serenity—this in itself is a physical cure.

Praise be to the Eternal, the Only One: he is perfection, he has no other.

You are my eternal refuge on the Last Day; you are the light of my eyes.
O people of allegiance, O people of the steppes, you are the source of my beautiful tunes.

Praise be to the Eternal, the Only One . . .

Allāh ʻalaykum-*i* dāyim rabbi l-*i*-ʻaẓīm ad-dāyim mā dām u-dīnuh qāyim
bi-l-Muṣ-*i*-ṭafā baḥ-*i*-r al-wafā rīquh shifā jis-*i*-mānī

sub-*i*-ḥān dāyim waḥ-*i*-dānī . . .
Transcribed by Makram Khoury-Machool

May you always be under the eyes of God, for as long as his religion is maintained
by al-Mustafa, the sea of fidelity, whose drops are a physical cure.
Praise be to the Eternal, the Only One . . .
Translated by Makram Khoury-Machool

Editor's Note on Recitation 6.5

With its mixture of *fuṣḥā* and *ʻamiyyā* (literary and colloquial Arabic), strophic refrain structure, and overtly Islamic references, this song evokes the atmosphere of a Sufi *nashīd*. Al-Muṣṭafā (The Chosen) is an epithet for the Prophet Muhammad; *al-dāyim* (the Eternal), while not one of the ninety-nine Qur'anic *'asmā' Allah al-ḥusnā* (the most beautiful names of God), is commonly used as an epithet for God in Sufi contexts, and *baḥr al-wafā* (the sea of fidelity) could be perceived as a reference to the Prophet's tears, which are traditionally considered to heal the sick.

Editor's Commentary

The Samaritans held a peculiar fascination for both Idelsohn and Lachmann. Unlike any Jewish community, they had maintained a continuous presence in the land of Israel since at least the time of Solomon. Crucially, they had not adopted the Masoretic text with its system of accent marks, and their cantillation therefore potentially represented an earlier practice.

In August 1911 Idelsohn made ten recordings of Samaritan biblical cantillation for the Vienna Phonogrammarchiv (Ph 1171–74, Ph 1176–80, Ph 1193; Schüller and Lechtleitner 2005, CD 3, tracks 17–26), and in 1913 he made nine recordings for the Berlin Phonogramm-Archiv (Sammlung Idelsohn, nos. 15–23). His sources on both occasions were priests from Nablus. The Berlin recordings provide the basis of his study "Die Vortragszeichen der Samaritaner" (The Recitation Signs of the Samaritans, 1917b), in which he attempts to decipher, for the first time, the Samaritan system of biblical accents (*sidre miqrata*).[1]

Idelsohn illustrated the individual signs by eight musical transcriptions, including two versions of his first example. Apparently not all the *sidre miqrata* were marked in the biblical texts; some were transmitted orally alone. In contrast to his practice in the *Thesaurus of Hebrew-Oriental Melodies,* where in addition to sharp and flat accidentals he used special signs to represent precise interval measurements obtained by means of a tonometer (see, e.g., figure 2.1), Idelsohn's Samaritan examples use no accidentals at all, and, apart from occasional dynamics, trills, and acciaccaturas, they contain no marks of expression. Only two of the examples include extraneous syllables and are significantly melismatic: the one showing the signs *enged* and *afsak* (conjunction and end of sentence) with *annachu* and *arkenu* (pause and diminuendo at the end of the section), and the other showing *atmehu* (amazement, surprise). The remaining examples are predominantly syllabic and stick faithfully to the biblical text.

Idelsohn's seventh example illustrates the sign *turu* (law, instruction) with a transcription of the introduction to the Song of the Sea (Exod. 15:1) as recited by the priest Yitzhak Cohen (figure 6.1). Idelsohn describes the melodic character of *turu:*

> Their songs are all located in the fourth between c and f. The usual tone series is monotonous, typically in steps of seconds and thirds. The preparation of the end of each sentence is characterized by a jump of a fifth c–g, g being impure and closer to a speechtone. Afterwards a lowering of the tone series occurs, the small third c–A downwards, and it ends on the fundamental tone with a strange tremolo (Idelsohn 1917b, 118).[2]

Idelsohn's transcription generally corresponds to his description of the sign. It is almost entirely syllabic and centers on a single tone, C, with occasional ascents of a whole tone to the final, D. Two leaps of a fourth (C–F and D–G) break the pattern toward the end, and the "strange tremolo" is indicated on the final note. Not only does this transcription bear no relation to Lachmann's recording of Ibrahim Kohen reciting the same text some twenty-four years later (recitation 6.1); it is equally unrelated to Idelsohn's earlier recording of the same passage (Exod. 15:1) recited by a different priest, Abischa Cohen, for the Vienna Phonogrammarchiv (Ph 1171, CD3:17). Idelsohn made no transcriptions of this or any other of his Vienna recordings; it is clear, however, on listening to Abischa Cohen's rendering that it corresponds closely to that of Ibrahim Kohen in recitation 6.1.

Ultimately Idelsohn failed to make sense of Samaritan cantillation, which he regarded as alien and unpleasant:

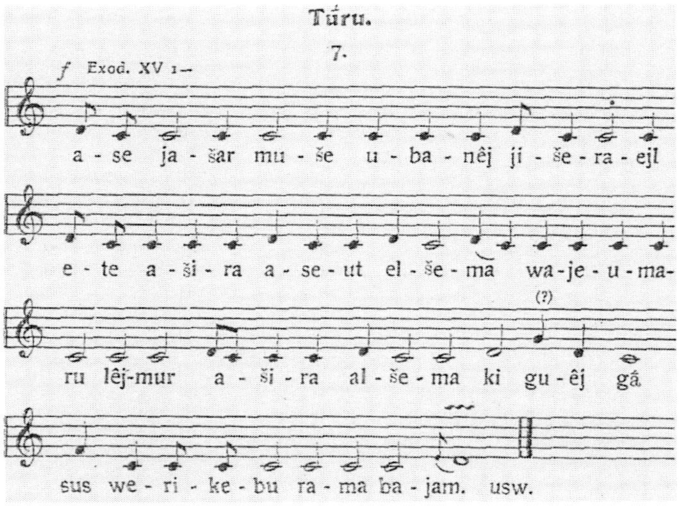

Figure 6.1. Abraham Z. Idelsohn's transcription of the Samaritan cantillation sign *turu*. Idelsohn 1917b, 126.

> Their tonality is—seen from a strictly musical point of view—completely nondiatonic, even in comparison with the Arabic tonality. Their songs are completely different from Jewish-oriental and Mohammedan songs. They sound wild to us and leave a most gruesome impression (Idelsohn 1917b, 119).[3]

Lachmann's fascination with the Samaritan tradition is reflected in the sheer number of recordings he made of it (220 of his 959 Jerusalem recordings, i.e., about twenty-three percent). His description in program 6 of the "ten stereotyped properties," each with its special name and sign, clearly mirrors Idelsohn's account of the *sidre miqrata*. In contrast to Idelsohn, Lachmann found the indefinable tonality and the "wild sound" of their recitation highly significant: for him, Samaritan cantillation represented a unique, living example of a liturgical tradition at an intermediary stage of development between the primitive chant of the magic ceremony and the liturgical cantillation of "civilized" nations. In his musical worldview, the characteristic "shakes, glides, sudden stresses and sudden lapses into ordinary speech" were clearly the legacy of the "disguised voice" of the shaman; the indefinable intonation of Samaritan cantillation, far from baffling him, simply confirmed his conviction that it represented an early stage on a hypothetical continuum from prerational to rational tone conditions. In short, Samaritan cantillation provided the crucial link in Lachmann's theory of the origins and evolution of religious song.

Lachmann recognized that the Samaritans had adopted a system analogous to the Jewish accent signs (*te'amim*). Yet he made no attempt, either in program 6 or elsewhere in his writings, to define the precise relationship between the Samaritan signs and the liturgical text. Nor does he make more than a rudimentary attempt (in recitations 6.2 through 6.4) to identify the eleven "melodic modes" of Samaritan cantillation and the different occasions or "moods" to which they apply. It was not until the end of the 1940s that the American ethnomusicologist Johanna Spector, a holocaust survivor from Latvia, embarked on the first systematic investigation of the relationships between the Samaritan accents and the liturgical texts and between the "modes" or styles of recitation and the circumstances of their performance. Her study was based on fieldwork in Jordan and Israel, and, unlike Idelsohn and Lachmann, who recorded only priests, Spector also recorded lay Samaritans living in the area around Tel Aviv.[4]

Spector illustrates her study with recordings of the High Priest of Nablus, Amram ben Ishaq Kohen, and a lay Samaritan "of great erudition" from Israel, Ratson Sedaqa (Spector 1965, 147). In addition to listing the ten *sidre miqrata* in a table similar to that provided by Idelsohn (Spector 1965, 146), she describes the eleven "modes" (cantillation styles) that may be applied to any liturgical text depending on the circumstances of the performance. The first style, which is confined to the priestly circle, is the most obviously related to Jewish cantillation: "it is wordbound (logogenic), syllabic, and the text is at all times more important than the melody" (Spector 1965, 144). The second style is used when the High Priest or his deputy addresses the entire congregation. In this style the melody predominates over the text; text phrases are lengthened by the insertion of nonlexical syllables and shortened by swallowing of text syllables—practices prohibited at all times in Jewish cantillation but in Samaritan only when the cantillation is confined to the priestly circle. The remaining nine styles, which may be performed by either priests or lay Samaritans, are used at weddings, circumcisions, funerals, individual holidays, and other "special festivities" (Spector 1965, 144).

Idelsohn's recordings, which were taken exclusively from priests, clearly demonstrate the first and second styles. His transcription of the Song of the Sea, illustrating *turu* (figure 6.1), represents the first style with its syllabic, logogenic character. In contrast, his recording for the Vienna Phonogrammarchiv of Abischa Cohen singing the same text—corresponding both in melodic outline and style of delivery to Lachmann's recording of Ishaq Kohen in recitation 6.1—represents the more elaborate second style, used (as Lachmann confirms) when the High Priest or his deputy addresses the lay community.

Spector also discovered differences between the priestly and lay interpretations of the *sidre miqrata*. Her lay informant, Ratson Sedaqa, recognized only the first three signs, which relate to syntax; furthermore, his observation of these signs, while internally consistent, did not always correspond to the positions of the accents in the text. Curiously, he referred to the accents by the unrelated Hebrew names *kaved* (heavy), *hasikaved* (medium heavy), and *qal* (light) instead of the traditional Samaritan-Aramaic names (Spector 1965, 147). The High Priest Amram ben Ishaq, in contrast, reveled in the expressive accents: "The High Priest shouts commands in fortissimo, drops his voice from piano to pianissimo in supplication, and separates every word dramatically in teachings and orders" (Spector 1965, 150). Yet his observation of the relationship between accents and textual syntax seemed to Spector to be even more random than that of the lay Samaritan: "even the major accent *afsaq* is different every time" (Spector 1965, 147). As a possible explanation for these inconsistencies, Spector cites a lay Samaritan who, "after great reluctance," confided that the original interpretation of the *sidre miqrata* had been lost in the latter part of the nineteenth century when a former High Priest died after refusing to hand down the tradition (Spector 1965, 149 and 151–52).[5] Regardless of the authenticity of this tale, it had clearly not taken an onslaught of Western influence for the Samaritans to forget their own tradition, either partially or completely. Indeed, they had done so within the very conditions of isolation that, according to Lachmann and Idelsohn, should have ensured its continuity.[6] For Spector, the loss represented a "reversal in musical development, a deterioration perhaps due to [the] decimation of the Samaritan community as a whole and its general poverty until very recent times" (Spector 1965, 153).

Notes

1. Idelsohn's examples 1a and 1b in this article illustrate different versions of the signs *enged* (conjunction) and *afsak* (end of sentence). The remaining six examples are each devoted to one or more different signs.

2. "Ihre Gesänge bewegen sich in der Quarte c–f. Die gewöhnliche Tonreihe ist monoton, Sekunden- und Terzenschritte. Die Vorbereitung des Satzschlusses charakterisiert ein Quintensprung c–g, wobei g unrein und eher Sprechton ist. Nachher tritt eine Senkung der Tonreihe ein, die kleine Terz c–A abwärts und schließt auf dem Grundton mit einem eigentümlichen Tremolo."

3. "Ihre Tonalität ist in strengem musikalischem Sinne vollständig undiatonisch, auch im Vergleich mit der arabischen Tonalität. Ihre Gesänge sind von den jüdisch-orientalischen und mohammedanischen Gesängen grundverschieden. Sie klingen uns wild und machen einen höchst schauerlichen Eindruck."

4. Lay Samaritans had begun to settle outside Nablus, mostly in the area around Tel Aviv, at the beginning of the twentieth century. With the creation of the State of Israel in 1948 and Jordan's annexing of the West Bank, the lay Samaritans living around Tel Aviv found themselves cut off from the priestly families in Nablus. In 1951 a Samaritan quarter was created in Holon, a southern suburb of Tel Aviv, and most of the lay community settled there. Although in principle Israeli citizens were denied entry to Jordan until the peace treaty of 1994, Samaritans of Israeli citizenship were given permission to reunite with their relatives in Nablus for one week each year to celebrate the Passover on their holy Mount Gerizim (based on Deut. 11:9 and 27:11).

5. It is not clear from Spector's account whether the lay Samaritan in question was Ratson Sedaqa or someone else, possibly one of the three other lay Samaritans—also of the Sedaqa family—named in Spector 1965, 149 n. 22 (Avraham, Israel, and Yefet).

6. Acknowledging his indebtedness to Idelsohn's pioneering work in the lecture "National und International in der orientalischen Musik," delivered in Tel Aviv on 12 February 1936, Lachmann observed that Idelsohn was "the first to study the melodies of the oriental Jews, working from the accurate recognition that the communities least influenced by their environment would have had to have preserved the purest types of musical tradition."

Program 7

Men's Songs for a Yemenite Jewish Wedding
17 February 1937

To-night you will hear some of the main musical items of a Yemenite Jewish wedding. You will thus, by way of example, be enabled to form an idea of the function of music in the life of an Oriental Jewish community. This function cannot easily be overrated. Practically all the important events in Eastern communal life, sacred and secular festivals, as well as events of family life, like birth, marriage, funeral, are permeated with music and song.

This fact is confirmed in every description of the manners and customs of any Oriental people. But most of these descriptions fail to go beyond the bare fact that certain ceremonies and other activities are accompanied by, or even culminate in, music. With few exceptions, we learn nothing from those accounts about the character of the music employed on these occasions; examples of it in staff notation are rare and generally incorrect.[1]

In this respect, the student of Oriental music has an interesting task before him. Going over the principal events in the social life of an Eastern community he can closely attend to the musical features contained in them, and thus add the indispensable element of sound to mute descriptions as given by others. In doing so he will not only render an invaluable service to ethnology, but, at the same time, have a reliable guidance in his own field of research. To make a complete survey of musical forms existing in a social group in the East he can do no better than follow up its manners and customs.

This method, if it were applied to European music of the present day, would yield but scanty results. For about a century, by far the greatest and most important part of the musical production in Central and Western Europe has been conceived independent of special occasions. The legitimate place for this kind of music is the concert hall with its neutral atmosphere where people assemble with the sole object of listening to music and of appreciating its intrinsic qualities. In contrast with this, applied music, i.e., music composed for definite social ends or events, has been pushed into the background.

But it is of little help to insist on the contrast which exists between present day musical practice in East and West. This would easily lead to exaggerations and false generalities. We had better remember that, a few centuries ago, the social functions of European music were not at all unlike those of Eastern. At that time and even more when we go still farther[2] back we find that in Europe as well music fell into groups vastly differing from each other according to their function in social life and to their distribution among different social classes. John Sebastian Bach's Cantatas, to mention one instance, were intended not to figure each as an item in some concert programme irrespective of time and place, but for immediate use at his own church on a particular Sunday.[3] Further: the difference, in style and function, between instrumental and vocal forms of music is not peculiar to the East. The English, with their conservative attitude towards music, still speak of "music and song," thus giving them two separate names.

---

1. A century earlier, the Englishman Edward William Lane had published his classic ethnography *An Account of the Manners and Customs of the Modern Egyptians* (1836; modern edition in Lane [1836] 1986) based on his experiences living in Egypt in the 1820s and 1830s. In separate chapters on music and dance and in passages scattered throughout the text, Lane provides first-hand observations on Egyptian music and musical life, including social attitudes toward music and musicians, the different kinds of music performed and musical instruments played on different occasions, and descriptions of individual musical performances, including the reactions of the audiences. Lane's rudimentary musical transcriptions ([1836] 1986, 375–83) contain no accidentals other than strange-looking key signatures that bear no relation to the notes on the staff and whose function seems purely ornamental.

2. Lachmann's script: *further.*

3. The association of time, place, purpose, and musical style in Bach's cantata output was not quite as exact as Lachmann implies. Stylistically, Bach's sacred cantatas and secular cantatas are indistinguishable: both employ the standard baroque movement types of recitative, aria, and chorale, and many of the sacred cantatas are parodies or reworkings of secular works. Examples include the *Christmas Oratorio* (1734–35, BWV 248), the *Ascension Oratorio* (1735, BWV 11), and the *Easter Oratorio* (1738, BWV 249), all of which reuse the music of earlier secular cantatas; see Wolff 2000, 366 and 383–86.

It would also be a mistake to exaggerate the prevalence, in the East, of applied music, of music for a special situation and incapable of being disconnected from it. The fact that music and song are indispensable features of certain festivals does not necessarily imply that the musical items performed on these occasions are peculiar to them. The frequent use, in Roman Catholic and Protestant service, of secular tunes adapted to religious purposes by simply providing them with a new text has analogies also in the East.[4]

Throughout the East, men's and women's songs are strictly apart from each other. In the domain of music as well as in others, women, with the exception of dancing-girls and other professionals, are kept in seclusion. But even professional female musicians in the urban sphere are allowed only a limited field of activity.[5] I hope that, on a future occasion, I shall be able to let you hear a programme of Oriental Jewish women's songs; at present, we are concerned only with male songs.

Generally speaking, men's songs are less frequently bound up with particular situations of life than women's. This also applies to the wedding songs from which a selection will now be given; the different forms which they represent are not restricted to the wedding.[6] You will hear these songs in the chronological order in which they are recited at the wedding and it will be necessary to point out the precise stage of the festival to which each of them belongs. The present performers are Sa'adiyya Nahum, Yahya Nahari, and Hayyim Mahbub, all of them born in Yemen.

An Oriental wedding, Jewish the same as Arab, extends over a number of days. Most of the ceremonies performed during that time have a magical significance; they serve to protect the young couple from evil spirits. Among these ceremonies those of applying henna to the hands and feet of the bride and bridegroom are of outstanding importance, and are always accompanied with singing. Both henna-ceremonies are performed at night. The bridegroom, according to Yemenite Jewish custom, is first painted by the morē, the scholar, who takes a predominant part throughout the wedding, then by the singers, and lastly by wedding guests[7] who have to buy this privilege with a small money present. The songs recited on this occasion belong to the form called Našīd; here is one of them. (Recitation 7.1, CD 1, tracks 17–18)

On a later day, in the evening, the bridegroom's head is shaved in the presence of his friends and relatives. This, as well, is an occasion for the recitation of songs. The following one which belongs to the form called Hidduya is specially favoured. (Recitation 7.2)

After the act of shaving, the bridegroom is led to the bride's house where the marriage-ceremony takes place. The bridegroom signs the marriage-contract and afterwards hands it over to the bride whom, on this occasion, he sees for the first time. Before this ceremony the following song is recited. (Recitation 7.3)

After the marriage-ceremony, the bridegroom is taken back to his house. On the following day which is the last one of the wedding he returns with his escort to the bride's house early in the morning. On the way his companions sing a song in praise of the bride which belongs to the form called Zaffa. (Recitation 7.4, CD 1, tracks 19–20)

The bride is then conveyed in procession to her future husband's house where the wedding is brought to its close.

The songs that you have been hearing do not by any means exhaust the musical repertoire of a Jewish Yemenite wedding. Above all it must be kept in mind that only the male part of it was represented. My next talk will, I hope, be illustrated by some items from the women's musical programme, and will thus supplement the present one.

A recital of all the musical items occurring in the course of a wedding would acquaint us with some additional forms of secular song. It would very nearly complete the whole series of musical forms extant among Yemenite Jews. In this particular case, therefore, it appears that the method of studying the music of a community in connection with their manners and customs provides us with a full knowledge of their musical production. The same is true of many other cases; so the collaboration of the ethnologist and the musical scholar yields results highly to be welcomed from both points of view.

---

4. Idelsohn describes the process by which Jews introduced the verse meters and music of secular Arab songs into their own secular and synagogue songs "so that by the tenth century . . . rhythmical song among the Jews of the Orient became synonymous with Arabic music" (Idelsohn [1929] 1992, 112). The process was encouraged by the religious authorities, who, "in their zeal to prevent the people's singing words of doubtful morals, would simply substitute texts of religious content, imitating the meter and even the sounds of the vowels of the secular texts" (Idelsohn [1929] 1992, 124). Later Idelsohn cites Israel Najara's diwan *Zemiroth Israel* (Safed, 1587), the first Hebrew-language songbook, in which nearly all the song texts were set to the tunes of Arabic, Greek, Turkish, and Spanish songs. In his preface to the second, enlarged edition, published in Venice in 1599–1600, Najara explained that he set Hebrew texts to foreign tunes in order to prevent the people from singing the vulgar, profane texts of the foreign songs and to encourage them to sing the Hebrew ones instead (Idelsohn [1929] 1992, 363). For more recent examples of this practice among Tunisian Jews, see Davis 2009, Davis 2002, and Davis 1986; among Syrian Jews, Shelemay 1998; and among Babylonian Jews, Rosenfeld-Hadad 2010.

5. See program 8 below.

6. See the editor's commentary below for Idelsohn's description of the different themes and multiple functions of the various song types.

7. Lachmann's script: *quests*.

Recitation 7.1: " 'At ben 'aṣe 'eden" (Judah Halevi, ca. 1080–1141)

Recording number: D588

Performers: Sa'adiya Nahum (solo), Yahya Nahari and Hayyim Mahbub (chorus)

Note: On the recording this song is followed by a "Blessing on the Bride and Groom" recited by Yahya Nahari.

אַתְּ בֵּין עֲצֵי עֵדֶן הֲדַס פֹּרֵחַ
וּבְכוֹכְבֵי שַׁחַק כְּסִיל זֹרֵחַ
שָׁלַח לְךָ הָאֵל צְרוֹר מִמָּר־דְּרוֹר
מִמַּעֲשָׂיו לֹא מַעֲשֵׂה רֹקֵחַ

(Hebrew text from Yitzhary 1992, 115)

’at ben ‘aṣe ‘ed̲an had̲ɔs poreaḥ
uvak̲ok̲ave šaḥag kasil zoreaḥ
šɔlaḥ lak̲ɔ hɔ’el ṣaror mimmɔr *i*-daror
mimma‘sɔw lo ma‘ase rogeaḥ

Transcribed by Ben Outhwaite

You are a flowering myrtle among the trees of Eden
and an Orion rising among the stars of the sky.
God has sent you a bundle of flowing myrrh
of his own making, not the work of a perfumer.

Translated by Ben Outhwaite

Recitation 7.2: "Lefelaḥ ha-rimmon" (Judah Halevi)

Recording number: D589

Performers: Hayyim Mahbub (solo), Yahya Nahari and Sa’adiya Nahum (chorus)

Recitation 7.3: "Sha‘ar asher nisgar Shelomo" (Solomon ben Judah Ibn Gabirol, ca. 1021–58)

Recording number: D590 (=D586)

Performers: Yahya Nahari (solo), Hayyim Mahbub and Sa’adiya Nahum (chorus)

Recitation 7.4: " ’Ayelet ḥen" (Shalem Shabazi, 1619–1720)

Original recording number: D591

Substitute recording number: D587

Performers: Sa’adiya Nahum (solo), Hayyim Mahbub and Yahya Nahari (chorus)

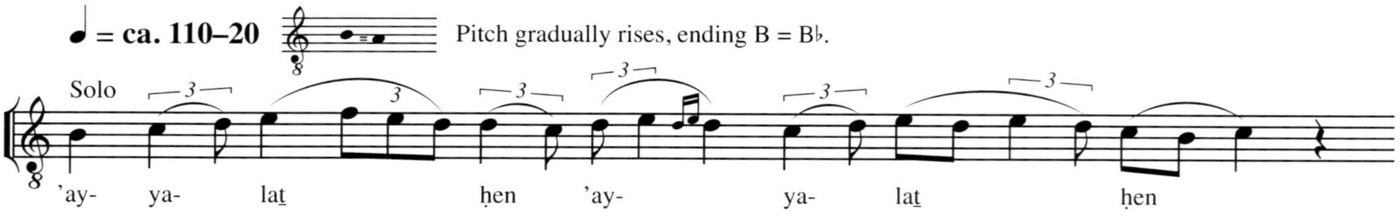

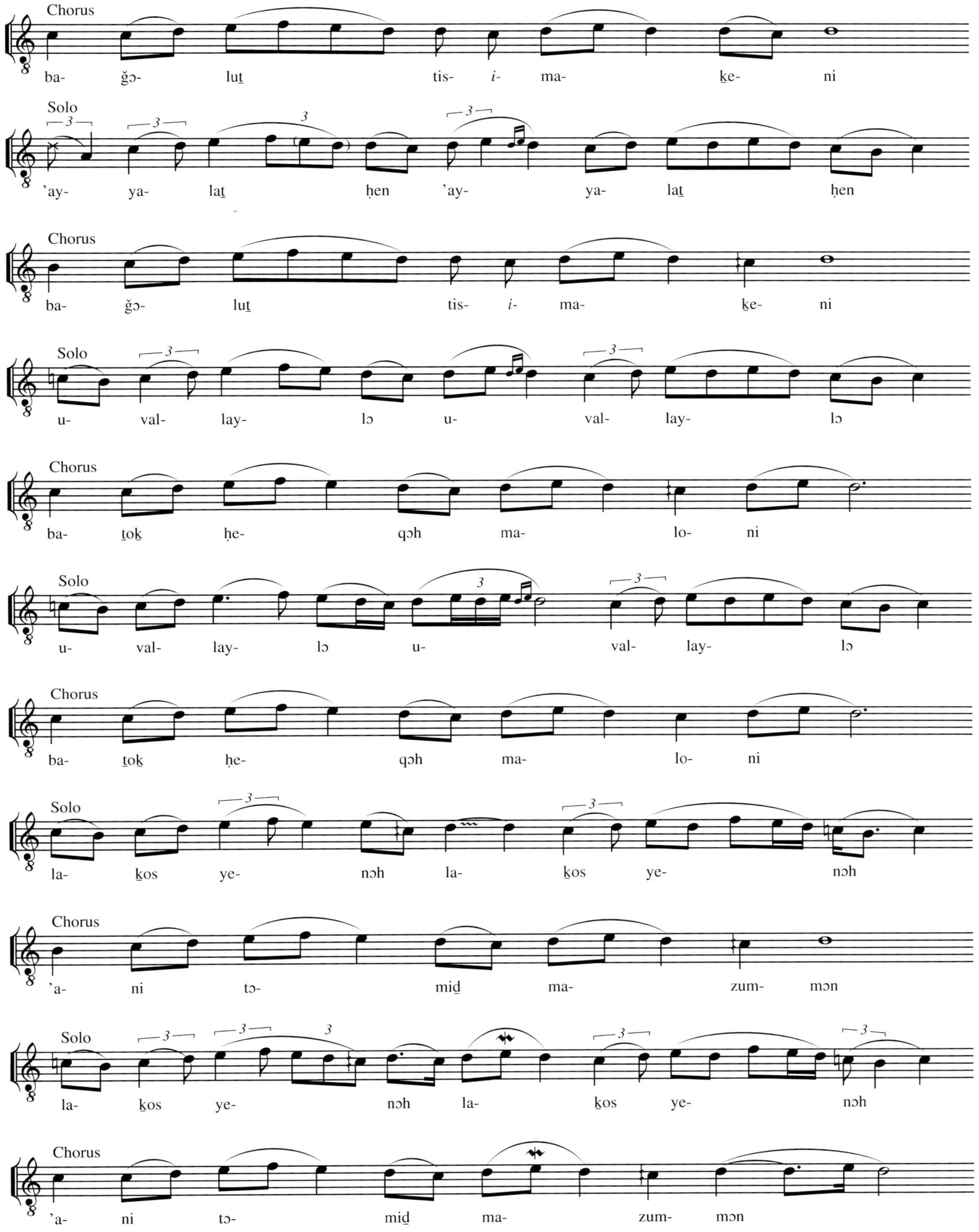
Chorus
ba- ğɔ- luṯ tis- i- ma- ḵe- ni
Solo
'ay- ya- laṯ ḥen 'ay- ya- laṯ ḥen
Chorus
ba- ğɔ- luṯ tis- i- ma- ḵe- ni
Solo
u- val- lay- lɔ u- val- lay- lɔ
Chorus
ba- ṯoḵ ḥe- qɔh ma- lo- ni
Solo
u- val- lay- lɔ u- val- lay- lɔ
Chorus
ba- ṯoḵ ḥe- qɔh ma- lo- ni
Solo
la- ḵos ye- nɔh la- ḵos ye- nɔh
Chorus
'a- ni tɔ- miḏ ma- zum- mɔn
Solo
la- ḵos ye- nɔh la- ḵos ye- nɔh
Chorus
'a- ni tɔ- miḏ ma- zum- mɔn

אֲיֶלֶת חֵן בְּגָלוּת תִּסְמְכֵנִי
וּבַלַּיְלָה בְּתוֹךְ חֵיקָהּ מְלוֹנִי:
לְכוֹס יֵינָהּ אֲנִי תָמִיד מְזֻמָּן
וְנִתְעָרַב חֲמַד יֵינָהּ בְּיֵינִי:

(Hebrew text from Yitzhary 1992, 109)

'ayyalat ḥen bağɔlut tis-*i*-makeni
uvallaylɔ batok ḥeqɔh maloni
lakos yenɔh 'ani tɔmid mazummɔn
wanit'ɔrav ḥamad yenɔh biyeni

Transcribed by Ben Outhwaite

The graceful doe sustains me in exile,
and at night I lodge in her breast.
For a glass of her wine I am always invited,
and it is mixed—the loveliness of her wine with mine.

Translated by Ben Outhwaite

Editor's Note on the Music

Idelsohn's transcriptions of " 'At ben 'aṣe 'eden" (recitation 7.1), "Lefelaḥ ha-rimmon" (recitation 7.2), and " 'Ayelet ḥen" (recitation 7.4) appear in the first volume of the *Thesaurus* (Idelsohn [1914–32] 1973, vol. 1, nos. 154, 145, and 156). None of these transcriptions is associated with a recording. Idelsohn classifies both no. 154, " 'At ben 'aṣe 'eden" (Lachmann's example of *nashid*) and no. 156, " 'Ayelet ḥen" (Lachmann's example of *zaffa*) as *nashid,* with the qualification that "No. 156, like No. 145, is sung at haircutting" (Idelsohn [1914–32] 1973, 1:42).

Like Lachmann, Idelsohn classifies no. 145 ("Lefelaḥ ha-rimmon") as a *ḥidduyah.* In his commentary, however, Idelsohn notes that the melody of the first part of no. 145 is the same as that of "Platte 1952" (i.e., Vienna Phonogrammarchiv, Ph1952; Schüller and Lechtleitner 2005, CD 1, track 25), where "Lefelaḥ ha-rimmon" appears as a *piyyut* (festive liturgical poem) for Passover, sung by a choir of three Yemenites. Noting that the same melody also appears as no. 57, sung in the synagogue for the festival of Simchat Torah (Rejoicing in the Law), he observes that it is "probably the only melody that has been transferred from the secular chant into the synagogue service" (Idelsohn [1914–32] 1973, 1:41).

Editor's Commentary

O dancer,
A cane in a field of grain.
When the wind blows
You move like the waves.
O belt of Hubeish,[1]
Its edges beautifully embroidered.
Oh, you are a field on many creeks
With a bountiful harvest.

—Extract from a Yemenite Jewish women's wedding song (Caspi 1985, 61)

Program 7 is the first of Lachmann's three programs devoted to wedding songs, and of these it is the only one for which Idelsohn provides a precedent. In his essay introducing the first volume of the *Thesaurus of Hebrew Oriental Melodies,* Idelsohn includes substantial chapters on the different types of "non-synagogal song" sung by Yemenite Jewish men to celebrate the Sabbath, religious holidays, and major life-cycle events, especially weddings (Idelsohn [1914–32] 1973, 1:10).[2] The texts of these songs are included in the unique anthology of poems known as the Jewish-Yemenite diwan (modern edition in Yitzhary 1992). Idelsohn replicates much of his account in *Jewish Music: Its Historical Development* in the chapter "The Folk Song of the Oriental Jews" (Idelsohn [1929] 1992, 364–76). As Lachmann's examples reveal, not all the poems are of Yemenite origin: Idelsohn's Yemenite "folk songs" include poems by the celebrated Spanish-Jewish poets of the eleventh and twelfth centuries, such as Solomon Ibn Gabirol (recitations 7.2 and 7.3) and Judah Halevi (recitations 7.1 and 7.4), and poems by the renowned Palestinian mystics of the sixteenth century, such as Isaac Luria, Solomon Ha-Levi Alkabeẓ, and Israel Najara. The diwan does, however, also include more recent poems by Jews of local origin, of whom by far the most prolific was the seventeenth-century rabbi Shalem Shabazi (1619–1720; recitation 7.4). Yet the uniqueness of the Yemenite collection, Idelsohn explains, consists not so much in the identity of the poems themselves as in their selection and arrangement, the tunes to which they are sung, and the way they are performed.

Like Lachmann, Idelsohn introduces the different song types according to their function in the wedding rituals. Unlike Lachmann, however, his starting point is not their social but their spiritual function, interpreted according to the kabbalistic tradition in which marriage symbolizes the troubled relationship between God and the Jewish people: thus the bridegroom, or husband, represents God; his bride, or wife, the people of Israel; and their home, the Temple in Jerusalem. As Idelsohn explains:

> The pair, designated now as engaged, now as married, quarrels and separates. It goes without saying that in this conflict the bride, i.e., wife, is the guilty party. The result is that the bridegroom, i.e., husband, banishes his beloved from his house—Palestine, especially the Temple. But now he feels unhappy to be alone in the house, and he too abandons his home, which thereupon remains desolate. However, as soon as the reconciliation between the angered husband and his beloved will take place, the pair will return to their old home (Idelsohn [1929] 1992, 366).

According to Idelsohn, the different poetic forms were originally intended to express the different phases of the story:

> Thus songs in which the longing and complaints of the bride are pictured, received the form *Neshid;* the love songs of the bridegroom were couched in the form *Shira;* the march to reconciliation was treated in the form *Zafát,* and the joyful effusions after the reconciliation in the form *Chidduyoth,* while the *Haleloth* served as interlude, overture, or postlude (Idelsohn [1929] 1992, 366).[3]

Yet in his more detailed commentary Idelsohn associates only three of the five song types (*ḥalelot, zafat,* and *ḥidduyot*) with specific parts of the wedding ritual, and even these types have multiple and interchangeable functions (see below). Their tunes, moreover, are "few in number, for no great importance was attached to these songs which used to be sung on no other occasion than at the dressing of the bridegroom or during his passage (procession) from his home to the neighbouring house of the bride" (Idelsohn [1929] 1992, 367). Thus the processional songs, or *zafat,* are all sung to one of two closely related tunes (Idelsohn [1914–32] 1973, vol. 1, nos. 144 and 145). Likewise, the *ḥidduyot,* recited immediately after the marriage ceremony, are all sung to one of two tunes (Idelsohn [1914–32] 1973, vol. 1, nos. 141 and 142), of which the first is effectively a synthesis of the two *zafat* melodies (Idelsohn [1914–32] 1973, vol. 1, 40–41).

The vast majority of the songs—those that Idelsohn calls "the wedding songs proper"—belong to the types known as *nashid* and *shirah* and are sung during the nightly festivities during the week following the marriage. Modeled on the literary Arabic poetic forms of *qaṣīda* (*nashid*) and *tawshīḥ* (*shirah*), these songs are multilingual: in addition to the poems in Hebrew, "approximately the fifth part of their poems is purely Arabic, and about half of them are Hebrew-Arabic. There are also trilingual poems, namely Hebrew-Arabic-Aramaic" (Idelsohn [1914–32] 1973, 1:11 n. 1).[4] And in addition to songs relating specifically to marriage, "many songs of a purely secular nature such as songs about conviviality, songs about dispute of rank, and epistles to friends, are couched now in the form of Nešid, now in that of Šira" (Idelsohn [1914–32] 1973, 1:13).

Unlike the numerous Middle Eastern song collections that identify melodies either by *maqām* or by the name of a popular song tune, the Jewish-Yemenite diwan gives no musical information. Idelsohn tentatively assigns *maqām* scales to his transcriptions of the Yemenite songs, yet he qualifies his designations:

> To be sure, this [*maqām*] identity applies only to the scales and characteristic tone-steps, but by no means to their modes, for the modes of the Yemenite melodies completely diverge from those of the Maqamāt current in Egypt, Syria, Mesopotamia, and Persia. . . . It should be added that the Yemenite-Jewish singers themselves were entirely ignorant of the theory of the oriental Maqamāt and Usulāt (rules of rhythm), nay, they are even unaware of the use of the term "Maqama" in the sense of Arabic music (Idelsohn [1914–32] 1973, 1:43–44, 45).

Idelsohn closes his essay with transcriptions of four Arab songs from different parts of Yemen, recorded in Jerusalem by Hajj Muhammad of Ibb (Idelsohn [1914–32] 1973, 1:46–47; Vienna Phonogrammarchiv, Ph 2046, Ph 2056, Ph 2057; Schüller and Lechtleitner 2005, CD 3, tracks 30, 32, and 33). Comparing the four Arab melodies with his much larger sample of Jewish melodies, he concludes that the Jewish songs from Aden, a major seaport and commercial hub, and those from the surrounding countryside, were "strongly influenced by Arabic song. Even entire melodies were borrowed" (Idelsohn [1914–32] 1973, 1:39). The Jews of the mountain city of Sana'a, in contrast, who were confined to ghettos, supposedly developed a unique melodic repertory untouched by the surrounding Arabic tunes (ibid.).[5]

Yet the most remarkable aspect of the Yemenite wedding songs is the way they are performed. Sung antiphonally by a group of four or more men, nearly all the songs are in definite rhythm and are accompanied by hand clapping, percussion, and dancing:[6]

> The dance is executed by one pair, sometimes two pairs, naturally only men, and it has the well-known Oriental character. It starts with an adagio tempo, but the more the excitement rises the quicker becomes the tempo until finally it becomes a whirling prestissimo. There are among the Yemenites very skillful dancers, and their movements are easy and graceful. Aged and worn-out men dance with an astonishing celerity and alacrity. Women are excluded from dancing; the festivities take place only in the sphere of men. Women are allowed to participate only in the chanting of the

> Zafat, by beating the kettledrum or emitting the well-known Oriental trill, which resembles a howling (Idelsohn [1914–32] 1973, 1:40).[7]

Meanwhile, the women celebrated the male dancers in their own wedding songs, which they sang and danced to in gatherings from which the men were excluded. Passed down orally in colloquial Arabic, their themes reflect not kabbalistic allegory but on the women's own real-life yearnings:

> O the one named Ya-Sin,
> The handsome one rose to dance,
> When he is adorned,
> The heart bursts into flames.
>
> Look at the grace of the handsome one
> When he steps out on the floor,
> He moves lightly as on a thread
> Of silk and embroidery. (Caspi 1985, 129)

Notes

1. "Ḥubeish is in the southern part of Yemen, known for its excellent craftsmen" (Caspi 1985, 239).

2. Idelsohn (1914–32) 1973, 1:9–15 (texts); 39–47 (music). Seventy-three of Idelsohn's two hundred transcriptions of Yemenite song in the first volume of his *Thesaurus* are of "non-synagogal song"; several more examples taken from recordings feature in an appendix to this volume.

3. For a similar description, see also Idelsohn (1914–32) 1973, 1:10. For descriptions of these song types, see Idelsohn (1929) 1992, 367–68.

4. See also Idelsohn (1929) 1992, 371.

5. See also Idelsohn (1914–32) 1973, 1:47.

6. Exceptions are the *halelot* and a few older poems (e.g., " 'At ben 'aṣe 'eden" in recitation 7.1), whose melodies are sung in an unmeasured recitative style. The *halelot* are sung in unison by the entire congregation.

7. A slightly condensed description is given in Idelsohn (1929) 1992, 370: "During the singing of *Neshid* and *Shirah*, dancing is obligatory. The dance is executed by one pair, sometimes two pairs, of men only; and it has an Arabic character. The dance starts with a slow tempo, but the more the excitement rises the quicker becomes the tempo, until finally it becomes a whirling prestissimo. There are among the Yemenite Jews very skillful and graceful dancers. Aged and worn-out men dance with an astonishing celerity and agility. Women are excluded from dancing; the festivities take place among groups of men alone."

Program 8

Women's Songs for a Yemenite Jewish Wedding
3 March 1937

As suggested during my last talk which dealt with the music at a Yemenite wedding, I propose to give you, tonight, the supplement to it, namely, the women's part in it.

This is the first occasion on which women and women's songs have been introduced into this series of Oriental music and it may remain the only one. It therefore seems to be the proper place to stop for a moment and consider the woman's part in Oriental music, generally.

On the whole, we can discard women as creative musicians. In this, there is hardly a difference between Oriental and European women except for the fact that, in Europe more often than in the East, ambition stirs women to try and assert themselves as composers. I should not like to draw any rash conclusions as to their being excluded from this field of artistic production by the nature of things. But if we can cherish any hopes of future women composers these hopes can hardly be built on their achievements, in this direction, during the last and the present centuries when their production—scanty as it was—seemed to proceed from a tendency to compete with men in this field as well as in others, very much remote from music, rather than from a genuine outburst of musical imagination. In the past, anyhow, their musical talents have, with rare exceptions, lain elsewhere and I think we can, in our present survey, pass over these exceptions of which the famous ancient Greek poetess Sappho has remained the most outstanding—although her music has not come down to us.[1]

Far more can be said about women as executants of music, vocal and instrumental. From antiquity onward there has been, in most Eastern countries, a class of professional female musicians. We can see pictures of them with their instruments on reliefs and vases playing, for the most part, stringed instruments or hand-beaten drums, but not, as far as I know, wind instruments.[2] This is confirmed by present day practice. One need only remember the Geishas in modern Japan who have to undergo a full training in vocal and instrumental music, and the Indian nautch-girls with their reputation for music and dancing. In Arab musical history as well, distinguished female musicians have been on record ever since the rise of Islam, and have formed an integral part of noble households, together with their male colleagues.[3] While these women, in the Middle Ages, mostly

1. Curiously, Lachmann's consideration of the ethical attitudes toward music propagated by the "three great religions which originated in the Near East" (outlined in program 2) does not extend to their implications for the role of women in music. His contemporary Henry George Farmer, in contrast, not only devotes substantial sections of his *History of Arabian Music* (1929) to accounts of female musicians and singers; in so doing, he presents sharply contrasting accounts of the status of music in general, and of the role of female musicians in particular, before and after Islam was well established, drawing mostly from the tenth-century *Kitāb al-aghānī* by Abū al-Faraj al-Iṣfahānī. Farmer notes that "during the 'Days of Idolatry' music, as a profession, was in the hands of the women-folk and slave-girls for the greater part" (Farmer [1929] 2001, 44), and that women particularly excelled in laments and elegies (Farmer [1929] 2001, 10). Among the famous female singers of the Umayyad (early Islamic) period at least one, a freewoman named Jamīla (d. ca. 720), was also a composer and counted many famous male musicians and poets among her pupils (Farmer [1929] 2001, 85–86). But the negative attitudes of Islamic clerics eventually ensured that any such creative activity among women was either stifled or at least concealed. According to al-Iṣfahānī, the Abbasid caliph al-Mu'taṣim (d. 842) was furious to discover that it was common knowledge among musicians that his relative, the princess 'Ulayyah bint al-Mahdī, was a composer (al-Iṣfahānī 1963–73, 10:167–68; cited in Sawa 1985, 73).

2. Edward William Lane confirms that "in many of the tombs of the ancient Egyptians we find representations of females dancing at private entertainments, to the sounds of various instruments, in a manner similar to the modern Ghawazee but even more licentious" (Lane [1836] 1986, 385–86). He surmises from this evidence that "the dance of the women who perform unveiled in the public streets . . . with castanets of brass" has continued uninterrupted since antiquity; and that "perhaps the modern Ghawazee are descended from the class of female dancers who amused the Egyptians in the times of the early Pharaohs" (Lane [1836] 1986, 386).

3. *Qaynāt* or *qiyān* (lit. "singing-girl," "songstress"; sing. *qayna*) were found in the household of every Arab of social standing in pre-Islamic times and are mentioned in several hadith (Farmer [1929] 2001, 10; Shiloah 1995, 32–33).

had the standing of slaves, with the change of social conditions during the 19th century they have come to be independent professionals, the foremost of them keeping bands of male instrumentalists as an accompaniment for their singing.[4]

Women singers, even Umm Kalthoum, the great contemporary Egyptian singer, have their poems and the tunes to which they sing them specially composed for them. The same is true of most of to-day's prominent men singers; still, a few of them "melodise," as the Arabs express it, that is to say, they compose their tunes themselves, which, in the old times, they were expected to do as a matter of course, and which women were not. Another difference is that, among the various kinds of urban music, not all are practised by women while none of them are peculiar to them. But the general style of urban melody is the same with male and female professionals.[5]

To find an exclusively female type in Oriental music we have to turn to the domestic sphere of life. Here, the music belonging to men and to women is as strictly separate as their social functions. Women's songs, in this sphere, are as far removed from any other kind of music as is, for instance, sacred cantillation from secular singing, and it is, therefore, possible to enumerate the qualities—positive and negative—which establish it.[6] All through the Near East, women, irrespective of race or creed, sing their domestic songs to the sole accompaniment of hand-clapping or hand-beaten drums; among the Berbers of Algeria, women's songs are actually named "hand-clapping," this, evidently, being considered to be the outstanding feature of these songs. The characteristic scales of string- and wind-instruments, therefore, are absent in this class of music. Nor are women's songs subjected to any of the modal systems evolved by these instruments and by the position of the notes on them.

While unimpaired by instrumental influences, women's songs, on the other hand, do not receive their melodic shape from the words as liturgical cantillation does. Although purely vocal like liturgical cantillation they are in character more remote from it than from any other type of vocal music. Above all, they are never in free rhythm, as the practice of hand-clapping and drumming shows. On the contrary, they are invariably built on the simplest rhythmical scheme conceivable. They consist of two sections which may be described as "up and down," "to and fro," or "question and answer." This pendular motion shows them as belonging to that large class of songs which is connected with regular bodily movement, and which is represented in its simplest form by children's songs and nursery rhymes like "Ring-a-ring-a-roses." These nursery rhymes, by the way, in spite of all the usual protestations as to music being an international language, are really the only tunes which seem to be common to all nations, Eastern and Western, civilized and primitive.

Women's songs represent the same type in a more elaborate, but still simple, way.[7] They, too, consist mainly of one melodic line, with a half-close in the middle, and this line is repeated to innumerable verses. Obviously, the words, and especially the sequence of the sentences are

4. Lane extols the female professional singers, called *'awālim* (lit. "learned female," sing. *'ālima*), hired to entertain the women of nineteenth-century Egyptian households: "Some of them are also instrumental performers. I have heard the most celebrated 'Awālim in Cairo, and have been more charmed with their songs than with the best performances of the Ālāteeyeh [ensembles of male musicians]. . . . They are often very highly paid. . . . There are, among the 'Awālim in Cairo, a few who are not altogether unworthy of the appellation of 'learned females,' having some literary accomplishments" (Lane [1836] 1986, 366). Unlike the male instrumentalists, however, the *ghawāzī* and *'awālim* typically only played percussion (Racy 1977, 24–25). The introduction of commercial recording in the early twentieth century and the rise of new venues for public music making in major Middle Eastern cities such as Baghdad, Cairo, and Tunis contributed to the increasing emancipation of women as singers (Danielson 1997, 46–48; Davis 2009, 194–97; Kojaman 2001, 45–47). In 1926 the Egyptian diva Umm Kulthūm replaced her chorus of male family members with a band (*takht*) of leading male instrumentalists, resulting in a transformation of her artistic status as well as her musical style (Danielson 1997, 61–62).

5. As Jihad Racy has shown, the scant documentation available on the repertory of the *'awālim* before and including World War I does in fact make a clear distinction between the styles of male and female professional musicians (Racy 1977, 53). Moreover, as male and female repertories began to merge after World War I, it was often the women's repertory that was taken up by the men rather than vice versa. With the rise of commercial recording in Cairo in the 1920s, for example, the *ṭaqṭūqah*—a simple strophic song genre in colloquial Arabic formerly associated with the *'awālim*—"shed its female associations as many prominent male singers began to incorporate it into their repertories" (Racy 1977, 54).

6. Despite their physical segregation, men and women found opportunities to hear each other's music. Lane describes how, in the homes of Cairene families, the male guests of the husband would be treated to the sound of the *'awālim* hired to perform for his wife's party: "The female singers who are called "Awālim' . . . sit in one of the apartments of the harem, generally at a window looking into the court. The wooden lattice-work of the window, though too close to allow them to be seen by persons without, is sufficiently open to let them be distinctly heard by the male guests sitting in the court or in one of the apartments which look into it" (Lane [1836] 1986, 506). Similarly, Baron Rodolphe d'Erlanger described Tunisian women listening "behind grilles" to the concerts of Andalusian music held in the gardens and jasmine-scented rooms of their villas (d'Erlanger 1917, 92–94, cited in Davis 2004, 48).

Confined to the home, Middle Eastern women cultivated rich oral musical repertories that they passed down to their children. Cheykh el-Afrit, the legendary Jewish media star of 1920s and 1930s Tunis, acknowledged his Tripolitanian mother as a primary source of his repertory (Abassi 2000, 9; el-Melligi 2000, 21). El-Afrit's songs were in turn reabsorbed via the phonograph into the domestic song repertories of both men and women (Davis 2009, 189).

7. The idea that women's songs generally represented a relatively early stage of musical development was commonplace among Lachmann's contemporaries; see, for example, Hornbostel 1927, 425; Sachs 1943, 91; and Bartók 1951 (all cited in Gerson-Kiwi 1965, 102).

more or less immaterial in this class of song. Here it is not the melody which carries the text, but, on the contrary, the text simply helps to keep the tune and its pendular movement going, and is often replaced by mere senseless syllables. The regular movement inherent in this kind of melody may or may not serve to accompany an actual bodily occupation. Some of these songs accompany the rocking of the cradle, the turning of the hand-mill, or games and dances. But even when this is not the case the singers can hardly help swaying their bodies.

This description holds good of practically all the different forms of women's songs in the Near East, and so applies also to their wedding songs. There is one curious exception for which I cannot account, but which I would mention for the sake of completeness. Berber women of Algeria sing one song, in the middle of their Henna ceremony which entirely deviates from the usual type both in its melody and by being in free rhythm. I never came up against any song of this kind either in Arab or in Jewish surroundings.

Arab and Jewish women's songs are closely related to each other and this relation is stressed by the fact that Jewish women, as well, sing in Arabic without exception. Shall we suppose that this approximation to the Arab style has narrowed down the range of Ancient Jewish women's songs? Certainly, if you have fed your expectations of what Jewish women's songs might be, on Miriam's or on Deborah's song, you will be disappointed in the modest little tunes that you are going to hear. But then it is unfair to conjure up musical feats which mark climaxes in Scriptural history, as models for everyday use. And, on the whole, what we hear of women's music in biblical times does not contradict the observations that we can make with regard to their Oriental descendants. Miriam, in Exodus, after all, only takes up the men's words and her companions accompany her song with percussion, just as is done to-day.[8]

Parallel to the men's wedding songs that you heard last time, the women, too, have songs peculiar to the Henna ceremony and the other stages of the wedding. First you will hear one of the songs sung while the henna is applied to the bride's hand and feet.[9] (Recitation 8.1, CD 1, tracks 21–22)

The second song is performed during the act of cutting the bride's front locks. This is on the day preceding the night on which the marriage contract is read and the blessing pronounced. (Recitation 8.2)

Apart from songs like those that you have just heard and which have their definite place in the respective ceremonies there is another group including songs which may be sung at any time of the wedding, and serve to entertain the bride and her companions during the long hours which separate the various ceremonies. These songs, in contrast to those of the first group, accompany dances. They are also distinguished from the first group musically. Instead of slow beats at equal distances, the drum here accompanies the tunes with vivid patterned figures. You will now, in conclusion, hear a series of such songs. (Recitations 8.3, 8.4, and 8.5, CD 1, tracks 23–24, 25–26, 27–28)

8. While it is true that the brief Song of Miriam (Exod. 15:20–21) takes its cue from the Song of Moses (Exod. 15:1–19), echoing its opening words, it is hardly representative of biblical women's songs "on the whole." The Songs of both Hannah (1 Sam. 2:1–10) and Deborah (Judg. 5:1–31) are lengthy poems with their own words. Deborah's song, which occupies almost the entire fifth chapter of Judges, celebrates the victory of the Israelites over the Canaanite army, making special mention of the death of the Canaanite general Sisera at the hands of Jael (Yael), the wife of Heber (Judg. 5:24–27). Lachmann includes a performance of the opening verses of Deborah's Song in Program 4 (recitation 4.2).

9. For a slightly different version of the song text in transliteration and English translation, see Caspi 1985, 85–86. Gerson-Kiwi gives a musical transcription of the first two lines of the song taken from her own recording in Gerson-Kiwi 1965, 101.

Recitation 8.1: "Sāʿat ʾr-raḥmān dalḥīn"

Original recording number: D604

Substitute recording number: D596 (23 February 1937)

Performers: Two Yemenite Jewish women with percussion. In his diary entry for the Yemenite Jewish women's songs recorded on D596–D609, Lachmann specifies, "die eine mit daff (mittel-grosse Handtrommel ohne Schellen), die andere mit Metallteller" (one with daff [medium-sized frame drum without jingles], the other with cymbals).

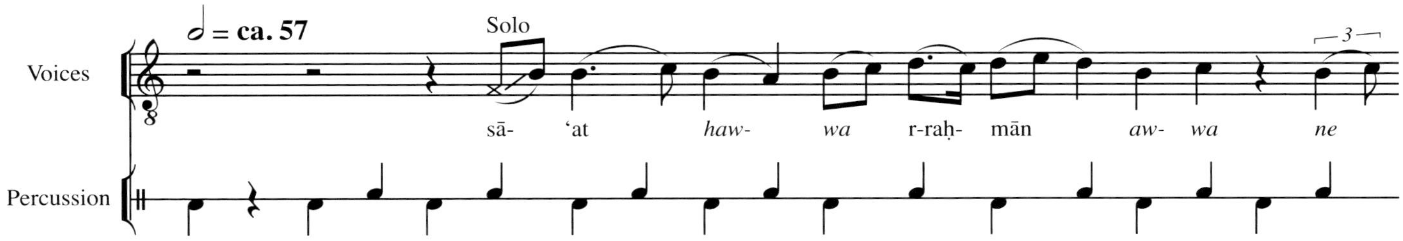

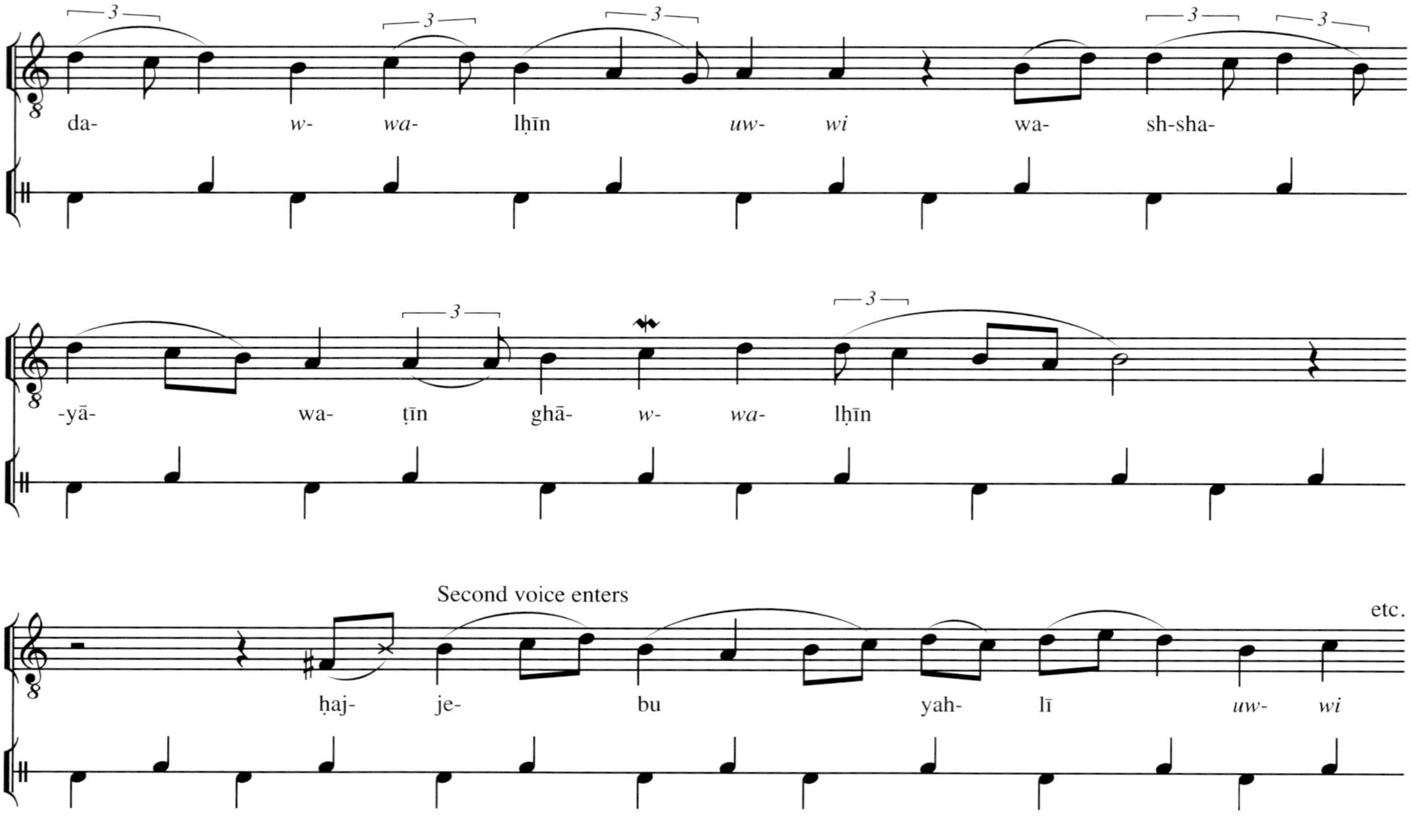

sā'at *hawwa* r-raḥmān *awwa ne* da-*wwa*-lḥīn *uwwi*
wa-sh-shayāwaṭīn ghā-*wwa*-lḥīn

ḥajjebu yahlī *uwwi* 'alayya *uwwa*
wa-shterū lī bi-l-ḥijāb

al-ḥijāb qad ḥa-*wwa*-jabaw lī-*uwwi*
wa-th-thirayya sāyera

'iḥira li yya-*wwa* khawātī *uwwe*
ya jamī'a l-ḥaḍāra
[*zaghrūda*]

Transcribed by Avi Shivtiel

It is the hour of mercy,
and the devils are not here.

My family, screen me
and cover me with many veils.

The veils have veiled me,
and the lights are lit.

Hail me, my sister,
all you who are present.
[*zaghrūda*]

Translated by Avi Shivtiel

Recitation 8.2: " 'Alā na 'īm yā beda"

Recording number: D605 (=D597)

Performers: Same as recitation 8.1

Recitation 8.3: "Allāh yā Allāh, yā 'ālem bi-ḥālī"

Original recording number: D606

Substitute recording number: D599 (23 February 1937)

Performers: Same as recitation 8.1

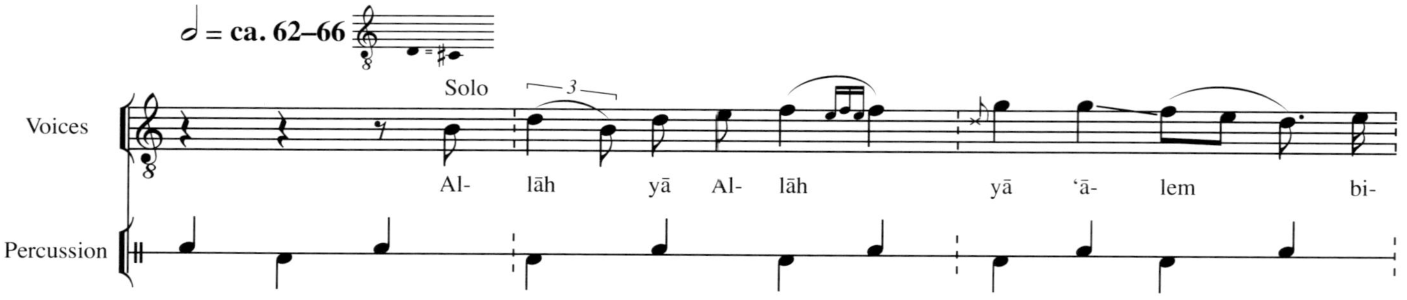

Allāh yā Allāh yā ʻālem bi-ḥālī
teḥannen qalb maḥbūbī ʻalayyī

habībī ʻādana l-layla we-bāker
wa ba'da l-bakrī we-ʻenni mesāfer

wa-'inno li-baker wa-*dda'*tak tafarraq
wa-'inno li-firāq ya ghārat Allāh

Transcribed by Avi Shivtiel

O God, who knows my situation,
fill my lover's heart with compassion for me.

My love, we have tonight and dawn,
and in the morning he is leaving me.

And if you leave at dawn, may God be with you,
and if we do separate, I pray for God's salvation.

Translated by Avi Shivtiel

Recitation 8.4: "Yā Allāh hal-yōm"

Original recording number: D607

Substitute recording number: D600 (23 February 1937)

Performers: Same as recitation 8.1

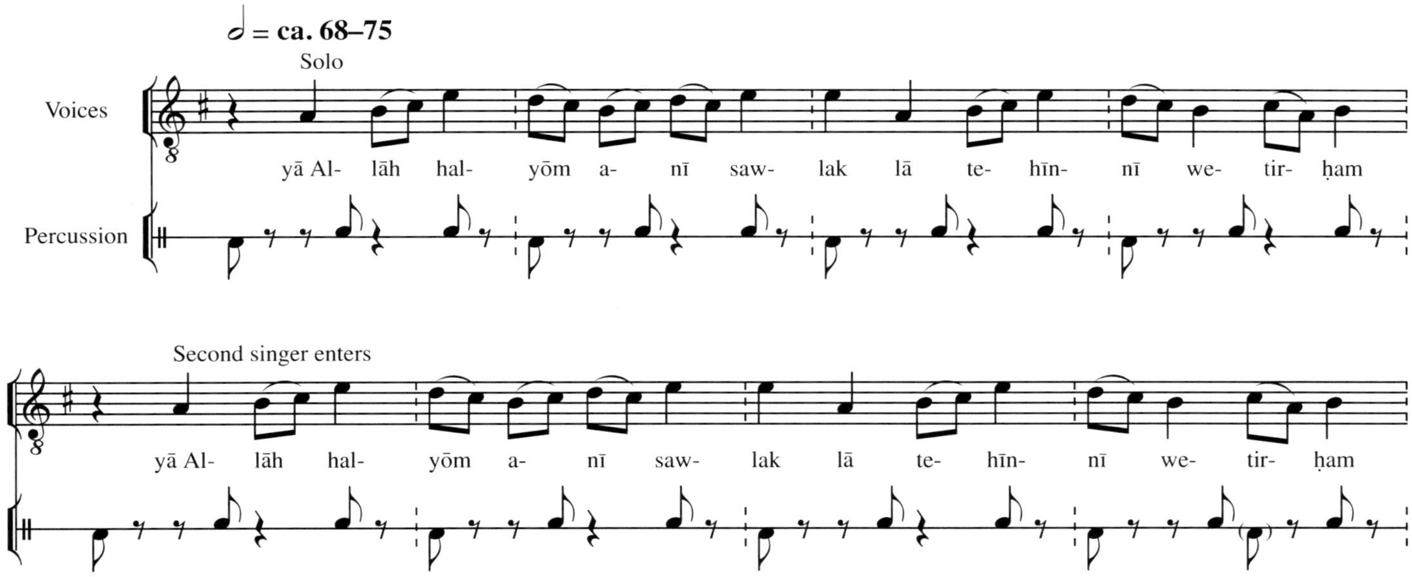

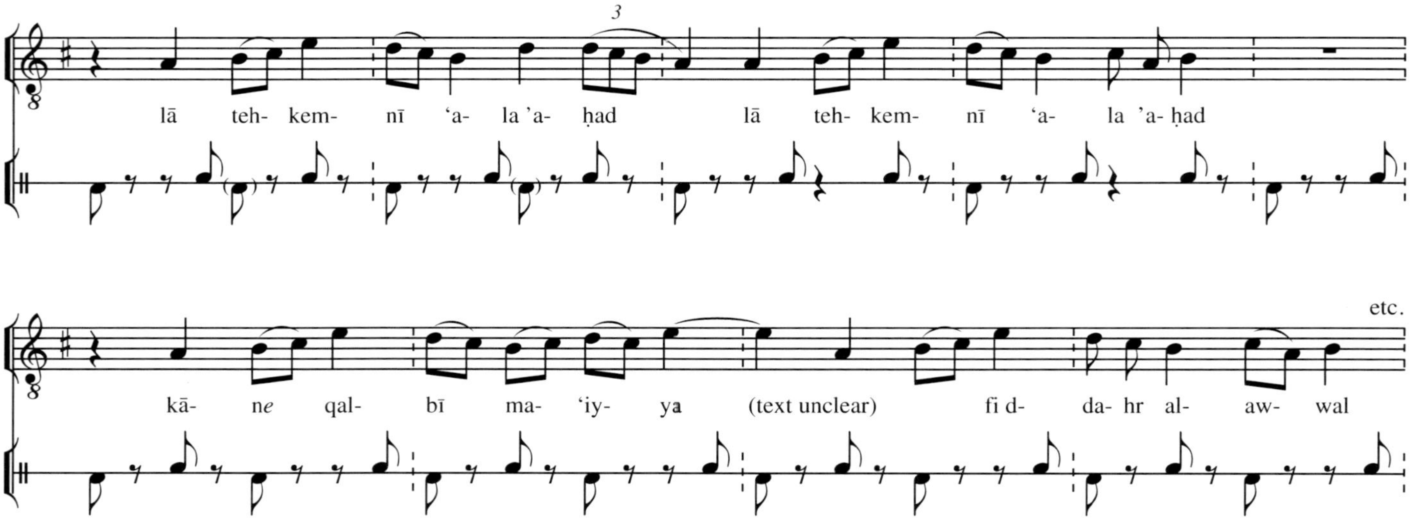

yā Allāh hal-yōm anī sawlak lā tehīnnī we-tirḥam	O God, today I ask you not to humiliate me and have mercy on me;
lā tehkemnī ‘ala ’aḥad	do not judge me before anyone.
kān*e* qalbī ma‘iyya fi d-dahr al-awwal qumti malakt kullī	My heart was with me as before; I gave it completely.
wa-n-nabi was-l-qasam lawma tesā‘ed we-tirḥam	I swear by the Prophet you should help me and have mercy upon me;
la-’aqat‘ak bi-r-rasam wa-’aqaydak qayd mubham	I will imprison you and fetter you in sealed shackles.
yā ‘awayla le-qalbī la‘an abūh man yalūmo ’in ṣabar ma qadar wa-’in ṣāḥ sā‘at ’alūmah [cough]	Anyone who blames me will be cursed; his suffering will be unbearable, and if he shouts his state will be known [cough].
yā rayt asāmrec yā bint fī ḍaw sham‘a we-’aḥrrosec fī manāmec	I wish I could stay up with you all night talking by the light of the candle to protect you when you are asleep.
Transcribed by Avi Shivtiel	Translated by Avi Shivtiel

Recitation 8.5: "Yā-llāh ’na salak"

Recording number: D601 (23 February 1937)

Performers: Same as recitation 8.1

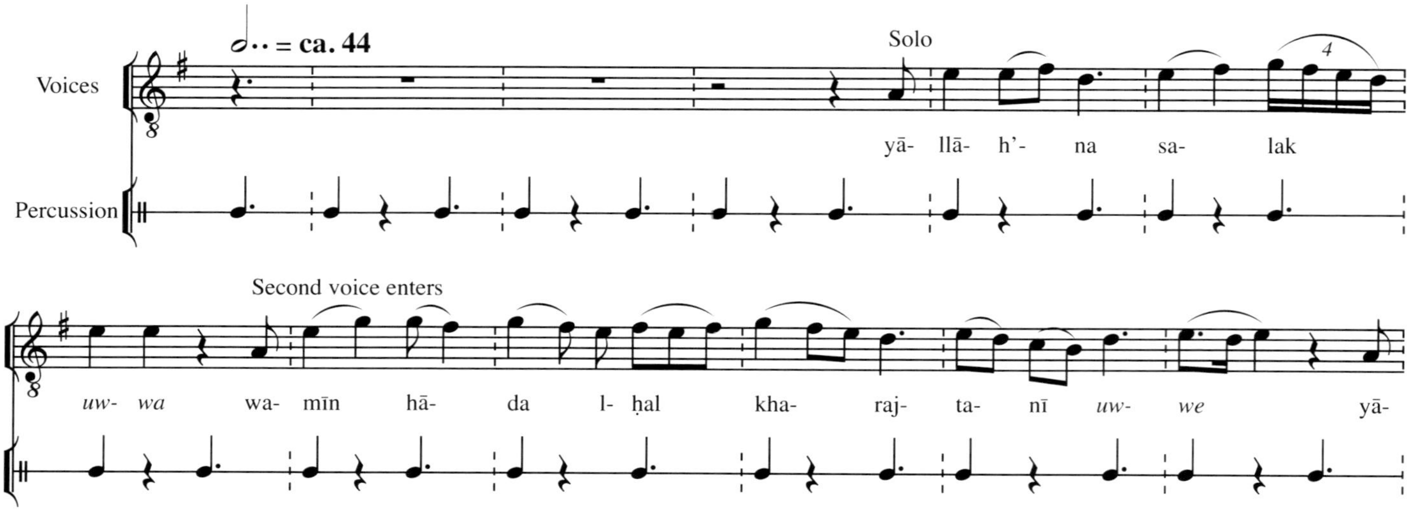

llā- h'- na sa- lak uw- wa wa- mīn hā- da l- ḥal
kha- raj- ta- nī uw- we yā nī- nī yā a'i-ya- ni
etc.
uw- wi yā ghā- fel al- zal- la- uw- wa-t wa-

yā-llāh 'na salak *uwwa*
wa-mīn hāda l-ḥal kharajtanī *uwwe*
yā nīnī yā a'iyani *uwwi*

yā ghāfel al-zalla-*uwwa*-t
wa-lā ghar al-khetā samaḥtanī *uwwe*
yā nīnī yā a'iyani *uwwi*

rūḥū lakum minnī *uwwe*
adaytunī adiyye balighe *uwwe*
yā ghuṣnī yā ḥāli *uwwe*

Transcribed by Avi Shivtiel

O God, I beseech you to save me
from this situation,
O my Exalted One, the pupil of my eye.

O the One who overlooks my stumbling,
and who has forgiven me if my sins are heavy,
O my Exalted One, the pupil of my eye.

Go away from me,
you have hurt me severely,
O my twig, O my beauty.

Translated by Avi Shivtiel

Editor's Commentary

> Whereas men's poems sometimes sound like artifacts produced by scholars poring over ancient volumes and dictionaries in search of recondite expressions, women's songs—whether of love, of jealousy, of a newly wed bride's fears and homesickness, of family problems—really sing.
>
> —William M. Brinner, foreword to Caspi 1985, xiii–xiv

In a report for the Hebrew University's *Information Bulletin,* dated 4 May 1937, Lachmann proposed to publish collections of melodies representing all the different musical traditions of individual communities. Outlining his progress to date, he reports that "a very full collection of Yemenite Jewish records has been made." He continues:

> The songs and recitations collected make it possible to furnish a complete musical supplement to the study of the manners and customs of the Yemenite Jews. . . . The Archives possess examples of every kind of song involved in the different events and ceremonies of their social life—a fact which should be greatly appreciated by students of ethnology (quoted in Katz 2003, 192).

Referring specifically to the women's songs, he notes that "these very simple types of song represent an early stratum in oriental musical development and have been recorded for the first time" (quoted in Katz 2003, 192).

The prototype for Lachmann's Yemenite collection is his study of the songs of the Jews on the island of Djerba, Tunisia, based on the recordings he made in the village of Hara Sghira in 1929 (Lachmann 1940 and Lachmann 1978; see also "The Djerba Monograph" in the introduction). In this study Lachmann establishes a clear correlation between social functions of the different song types he recorded and their musical systems: "As we have seen, the three types vary not only in their social function, but also in their technical musical elements: each of them has its particular scale, melodies and rhythmical forms—in short, its particular musical system" (Lachmann 1940, 84; see also Lachmann 1978, 82).

Lachmann's interest in women's songs, whether on Djerba or among the Yemenite Jews of Jerusalem, consisted not so much in their gender associations as in the fact that they exemplified what he considered to be a fundamental musical type "which—like the recitation of magic or liturgical texts—goes back to prehistoric times" (Lachmann 1940, 84). As he explains in program 8, the women's songs belong to "that large class of songs which is connected with regular bodily movement, and which is represented in its simplest form by children's songs and nursery rhymes." In the second of his "Four Lectures on Eastern Music," he includes in the same category

> lullabies sung by mothers while they rock the cradle . . . occupation songs as those of women turning a handmill or pounding seeds in a mortar . . . boatmen's songs on the Nile and elsewhere . . . refrains sung by a community in response to a priest's or another protagonist's solo; songs sung to primitive dances; and many others. . . . Most of these kinds of song address themselves to an audience; they grow out of the common spirit of a group and everybody present is supposed to join in (quoted in Katz 2003, 393).[1]

Such song types, he argues represent "one of the main tendencies in music. . . . a perfect equilibrium, in rhythm and tune, between tension and relaxation, closely connected with some regular bodily motion whereas the words matter much less" (quoted in ibid.).[2]

Indeed, Lachmann makes no mention of the words of the songs sung in program 8, nor does he mention the women singing them, despite their presence with him in the studio. In his Djerba study, in contrast, he draws special attention to the women's song lyrics, which, with their focus on biblical and festive themes and above all themes relating to marriage, he considers as a specifically feminine form of expression: "The songs in our collection are concerned with the main events in the life of Oriental Jewish women: in this way they give a lively insight into their sphere of thought and feeling" (Lachmann 1940, 67). And while his recording sessions with the Djerban men go virtually unmentioned, Lachmann gives a vivid account of his single session with the Djerban women, which took the form of a communal gathering (Lachmann 1940, 67–68; and Lachmann 1978, 154–56).

It was not until the 1970s, when the way of life they represented had vanished and the entire repertory seemed on the verge of disappearing, that the texts of the Yemenite Jewish women's songs began to attract scholarly attention. Recognizing their value as a unique oral literature, complementing the songs of the Jewish-Yemenite diwan, certain Israeli scholars of Yemenite descent—notably Nissim Benyamin Gamli'eli and Mishael Maswari Caspi—set about transcribing and publishing collections of the lyrics in Hebrew (Gamli'eli 1975) and in English translation (Caspi 1985). As Caspi and Deborah Lipstadt write in their introduction to Caspi's volume:

> Male poetry can be described as elevating man to a sacred level, to the illusion of being a participant in the process of redemption. In sharp contrast, women's songs are the very mirror of life, the reflection of their own roles in society. The woman sings of grinding the grain, of her husband leaving her, of his travelling to distant places to sell his goods; she sings of love and hatred and she sings of both with great intensity. Her poetry is earthly and her songs are imbued with the harshness of life and its many disappointments. . . . Unlike male poetry, noted for its elusive metaphorical language, women's poetry is intended to be understood precisely as it is conveyed (Caspi and Lipstadt 1985, 4–5).[3]

No single theme inspired a greater outpouring of song among the women than that of marriage and its associated events. Yemenite Jewish girls traditionally married between the ages of ten and fourteen. The betrothal, which included negotiations over the bride-price, was arranged by the couple's parents, and a bride almost never had the opportunity to meet her future husband before the wedding day. After the marriage the bride moved to her husband's home, where she spent the rest of her life with only limited opportunities for contact with her birth family. The loss might be as unbearable for the mother as for the bride:

> Said the mother of the daughters,
> "O I wish I would die,
> I raised the daughters—
> They were plucked from my garden" [whilst they were still blooming]. (Caspi 1985, 23)

Other songs describe the homesickness of the newly married girl:

> If the one who bore me
> My sobs and cries could hear,
> If you would know your infant's life
> The one you nursed and reared.
>
> O the one who bore me,
> My heart is burnt and dark
> Like black ink
> On plain paper. (Caspi 1985, 73)

For the bride, the most desirable match was with a scholar; for the groom, with a daughter of a scholar:

> O daughter of the Mori,[4]
> Honey stored in jars,
> He who desires you
> Will pay thousands . . . (Caspi 1985, 17)

Less fortunate girls might have to marry a widower:

> I do not want an old man
> His flesh is crumbled
> And good for nothing,
> Not even for a shoelace. (Caspi 1985, 155)

There are songs of yearning:

> I wish I were a dove
> On top of your roof
> To peek through the chimney
> And to listen to your words. (Caspi 1985, 137)

Songs of passion and boundless love:

> My beloved,
> You are like perfume in a flask.
> You are the light of my eyes
> In the evening.
>
> My beloved,
> I love you in the open and in hiding,
> Like the serpent
> Hides the pearls. (Caspi 1985, 115);

Songs that are overtly erotic:

> You kissed me once—in turn I kissed you five.
> The first one—on top of your head,
> The second—between your eyebrows,
> The third—between your lips and teeth,
> The fourth—I drowned between your breasts,
> The fifth—hush, tell no one. (Caspi 1985, 165);

And, finally, songs of revenge, as in this verse addressed to an unfaithful husband who took another wife on a journey to a distant land:

> I wish for you, husband of two,
> That a serpent, viper's venom
> Coiled around you
> In seventeen windings,
> Will bite you in the middle of the day
> And at twilight you shall die! (Caspi 1985, 197)

Notes

1. Lachmann effectively includes in the same category the rhythmic songs of the Yemenite Jewish men discussed in program 7; see, for example, recitation 7.4.
2. Lachmann is of course referring here not to the words themselves but rather to their role in determining the melodic flow. In the song types he lists, this is shaped by a regular pendular motion rather than the spontaneous flow of a text.
3. As the examples below and in program 8 reveal, the women's songs are in fact rich in metaphor and simile, albeit drawn from lived experience rather than from erudite texts.
4. On the role of the *morē* (scholar) in the Yemenite-Jewish wedding ceremony, see program 7.

Program 9

Arab Urban Music: Maqām
16 March 1937

Arab urban music is often alluded to as *the* music of the Arabs. Henry George Farmer's History of Arabian Music [Farmer 1929], e.g., the only comprehensive work on the subject, deals exclusively with urban music; in the same way, the Congress of Arabian Music held in Cairo in 1932 took hardly any notice of other kinds besides urban.[1] This seems to imply that, in Arab music, the urban kind is held to be the only one worth discussing. Now, this is obviously wrong, for two reasons. In the first place, Arab rural music, the music of the Bedouins and the peasants, can claim to occupy a considerable part of the entire field of Arab music. Secondly, urban music in Arab countries is representative of the Arab spirit in music only with some reservations. If, on one hand, it undoubtedly is one of several kinds of music practised among Arabs, on the other hand it also belongs to a large class of music of which other varieties are Turkish, Persian, and even Indian.[2] As a racial expression, therefore, it is less entitled to being called Arab music than the rural kinds of song.

It would be too much to say, however, that urban music, in contradistinction to rural, is international as far as the Near and Middle East are concerned, and that rural is not. Arab urban music is clearly distinguishable, especially by its delivery, from Persian, Turkish and Indian although their musical system is more or less the same. Nor can it be maintained that Arab rural music is incapable of being accepted by, or of absorbing influence from, people not belonging to the Arab race.

The difference between Arab urban and rural music lies elsewhere. They belong to different social groups which, at the same time, represent different stages of civilisation. This is clearly reflected in their structure and design. Rural music is simple and straightforward; it ranges over a small number of notes; it uses a comparatively small number of melodic phrases and rhythmical devices, and only a small number of instruments. Naturally, music of this description would not be subjected to theory and analysis. There are systems of scales both in the practice of the fiddle (rabāba) and of the reed flute; but these systems can be shown to have originated in the urban sphere.[3] Rural music is entirely a thing of oral practice, so much so that not even the names of prominent singers (who, at the same time, are poets) are recorded in writing.

Arab urban music, on the other hand, has developed an increasing number of notes, of melodic modes, and of rhythms, a variety of complex vocal and instrumental forms, and diverse and elaborate musical instruments. This corresponds to its different social standing. It has been, as it still is, among the chief entertainments of the higher classes since the rise of Islam[4] and before. Many of

---

1. Among the delegates to the Cairo Congress were ensembles representing urban musical traditions of Morocco, Algeria, Tunisia, Egypt, Turkey, Syria, Lebanon, and Iraq. The recording committee, however, which was headed by Lachmann, took a special interest in rural music (Racy 1993, 73), and recordings made at the congress also include performances of folk music by ensembles from Egypt and neighboring Sudan. According to Bartók, the folk music ensembles were added as an afterthought at the request of the European members of the committee, and most performed not rural but urban popular music (Bartók 1933, 46–48; cited in Simon 1992, 159–60); see Simon 1992 for details of the folk music ensembles and the repertory they performed. More than 170 double-sided 78-rpm discs were produced at the congress by His Master's Voice, England, fourteen of which document folk music. Two complete sets of recordings made at the congress were donated to the Musée Guimet and the Musée de la parole et du geste (subsequently Phonothèque nationale) in Paris by King Fu'ad of Egypt. A selection of these recordings, including seven tracks of Egyptian "musique populaire," have been reissued on compact disc (Institut du monde Arabe 1988).

2. Lachmann illustrates these other varieties of music in program 11. Like Arab music, Persian music and Turkish music are based on the modal system known as *maqām* (Arabic; Turkish *makam*). Indian music, in contrast, is based on the modal system known by the Sanskrit term *rāga*. Although there are clearly similarities between *rāga* and *maqām*, they are in fact distinct modal systems, and, as Lachmann himself indicates in program 11, they are not conventionally grouped together. For similarities and differences between *rāga* and *maqām*, see Powers and Widdess 2001a and Powers and Widdess 2001b, sections (i), (ii), and (iii).

3. See the editor's commentary to program 5 for Lachmann's account of the origins of these scale systems.

4. Lachmann's script: *Islem*.

the khalifs, during the most splendid periods of Islamic rule, were ardent music lovers and the courts of Damascus, of Baghdad, and of Moorish Spain were centres of musical competition. Evidently, the musical taste of this society and the music created to suit this taste was as different from that of Nomads as a Moorish palace is from a tent, although each of them may be perfect in its own way.

Owing to the literary and scientific renaissance in medieval Arab civilisation urban music became an object of interest with scholars. Through chroniclers we are informed, sometimes in minute detail, as to the lives and personalities of many medieval urban musicians, their particular musical talents, and even the extraordinary fees which some of them received from patrons of their art.[5] What is even more valuable for present students of the subject than these records of musical personalities and of the position of music at court and in town is the large number of writings, from the 9th century onward, dealing with the musical system underlying urban music and with its spiritual background.[6] Considering that the music itself has not been preserved any more than Bedouin music, these writings are the only evidence which to form an idea as to characteristics in the past and from which to judge to what extent present day urban music may have retained them.

The theory and philosophy of Arab urban music, like most other branches of medieval learning, was derived from Ancient Greek and Hellenistic[7] thought. According to ancient ideas, music is not an isolated product of the human mind, but is closely connected with the elementary forces of the universe of which it is considered to be one. Thus, a system of cosmic harmony was established in an attempt to determine the precise mutual relations between these forces, the relations, e.g., between sounds, colours, human temperaments, times of the day, seasons of the year, and celestial bodies. It is easy to see that this system is nothing but a more coherent and more rational expression of the belief, prevailing in primitive societies, that magic forces govern both the universe and human fate. And in the same way as the influence of those irrational magic beliefs can be recognized in ritual music,[8] so can the influence of the cosmological system as worked out at a higher stage of civilisation be shown to pervade secular urban music.

The cosmological system, in being handed down from antiquity to the Middle Ages, and in passing from one country to another, has undergone changes which it would be impossible to follow up here. There are characteristic differences between Chinese, Indian, and Hellenistic tradition; the Hellenistic came to be the basis for medieval writings both in Europe and the Near East. A few examples may illustrate the system. In China, the five principal notes were identified with five planets, with the four seasons and the whole year, the four cardinal points and the centre, and so forth. The seven notes of the Ancient Greek scale were coordinated with five planets to which the sun and the moon were added, and, hence, with the seven days of the week which bear their names. The starting notes of the Dorian mode, e.g., corresponds to the planet Mars, that of Hypolydian to Venus; this accounts for Plato recommending the former as promoting manly virtues and a warlike spirit and condemning the latter for its erotic and wanton character.

There are other and cruder instances, both in ancient and medieval writings, of the belief that music, as represented by its different notes, rhythms, and melodic modes, can act upon public and private life as well as on external nature, much in the same way as the stars do according to astrological doctrines. It was essential for musicians to know the magic forces inherent in music. A certain tune played or sung at an inappropriate time and in adverse circumstances was held to shake the harmony of the universe whereas music employed in the proper way was relied upon as bringing about all kinds of favourable effects such as curing the sick, fertilizing barren soil or taming wild animals, a feat with which Orpheus was credited.

A great number of these beliefs survive among Arab urban musicians of the present day. The different modes or melody types of this music are still supposed not only to correspond to different humours, but also to belong to different days and hours. The system of melody types is first mentioned in the 11th century. It embraces a great many melodic modes each of which is defined by its scale and by a number of typified melodic phrases peculiar to it.[9] On a later occasion we shall have to go more deeply

---

5. See, for example, the vast sums of gold and silver bestowed on virtuosi by the early Abbasid caliphs including the legendary Hārūn al-Rashīd (r. 786–809, of *One Thousand and One Nights* fame), cited by Farmer in the fifth chapter of his *History of Arabian Music* (1929). Farmer's account draws copiously from al-Iṣfahānī's *Kitāb al-aghānī* (see editor's commentary to program 5) among other contemporary sources, including tales from the *Kitāb alf laylah wa-laylah (Book of the One Thousand and One Nights)* itself.

6. The first major Arab theorist whose works survive is Abū Yūsuf Ya'qūb al-Kindī (see Lachmann and el-Hefni 1931), who was attached to the Abbasid court in Baghdad at the time when Greek philosophical works began to be translated into Arabic. Al-Kindī established the convention in medieval Arab music theory of presenting intervals and scales in terms of frettings and strings of the *'ūd* (short-necked four-stringed lute), and he developed a musical cosmology based on Pythagorean concepts of number and numerical relationships, which was taken up by the Ikhwān al-Safā' (Brethren of Purity), a group of Islamic philosophers based in Basrah, in the tenth-century (see Wright 2001). Numerical associations remained the basis of subsequent Arab musical cosmologies through the Ottoman era to the early twentieth century. In the Maghreb (Arab lands west of Egypt) the term *ṭab'* (lit. "character, nature," pl. *ṭubū'*) was applied to a modal entity equivalent to *maqām*; the various *ṭubū'* were classified according to cosmological criteria and presented in a symbolic *shadjarat al-ṭubū'* (tree of modes; see Guettat 2000, 137–39 and XIV–XV).

7. Lachmann's script: unclear, possibly *Hellanistic.*

8. Lachmann elaborates on this topic further in program 4.

9. In his *Kitāb al-shifā'* (Book of Healing), the eleventh-century scholar Avicenna (Ibn Sīnā) presents an exhaustive analysis of intervals, tetrachords, and tetrachordal combinations,

into the nature of these melody types; a melody tune (in Arabic, maqām) is a musical category which has no exact equivalent in European music. The character of each of them is best represented by the instrumental solos in free rhythm which preface, as it were, recitals of urban music. Only a small collection can be played to-night; but it includes some of the most important melody types. They will be performed on the 'Ud, the Arab lute (the ancestor of the European) by Mr. Ezra Aharon from Baghdad whose playing is typical of the 'Iraqian style of urban music.[10]

The first item is a prelude (in Arabic, taqsīm) in the mode of Ḥigāz the name of which suggests that it originated in that country.[11] The mode is considered to express cheerfulness; its appropriate time is Thursday night. (Recitation 9.1, CD 2, tracks 1–2)

The second prelude is in the mode of Ṣabā. The name signifies a soft North wind greatly appreciated in the Arabian desert. This melody type has a sad character; it is played at dawn, but is not connected with any particular day. (Recitation 9.2, CD 2, tracks 3–4)

The third and last melody type in tonight's performance is Sīkā. This name, unlike the preceding ones, is Persian, and thus points to the fact that Persian musicians contributed greatly towards creating the system of melody types. The mode itself is quite common among Arabs. Sīkā means the third degree, i.e., the third note of the Arab fundamental scale which lies between European mi and mi♭,[12] and is the tonic of the mode. It is considered to be moderate in character, but is apt to lend itself to various moods. Its allocated time is Monday night. (Recitation 9.3)

According to orthodox believers in the magic significance of the melody types, it has certainly been a mistake to perform these three at the same time of the day and two of them on a different day from those to which they are attributed. I hope you will not be afraid of harmful consequences arising from this transgression of time-honoured rules. There are musicians in the Near East even nowadays who would refuse to break these rules. One of them told me that he once omitted to respect the character of a certain melody type which ought to have been performed in the open, by performing it in-doors. This offence, he added, was promptly punished; three days after it had been committed, burglars broke into his house and robbed him of all his property.

After having dealt with the cosmological and magical aspect of Arab urban music a number of other points concerning it will have to be raised; they will be the subject of my next talk.

Editor's Note on the Music

The transcriptions of recitations 9.1 and 9.2 that follow are based on the tetrachordal system of *maqām* analysis outlined by Baron Rodolphe d'Erlanger (1872–1932) and the Syrian Shaykh 'Alī al-Darwīsh in their report on the melodic modes of Arab music presented to the Congress of Arab Music held in Cairo in 1932. This report formed the basis of d'Erlanger's posthumously published fifth volume of his six-volume work *La musique arabe* (1930–59). In this volume, d'Erlanger claimed to present for the first time in modern Arab music a systematic classification and analysis of the melodic modes (*maqāmāt*) according to the methods advocated by the medieval Arab theorists. His source for the Eastern Arab modes was Shaykh 'Alī, who had been sent to Tunisia in 1931 by the Egyptian government to serve as d'Erlanger's assistant (d'Erlanger 1930–59, 5:xiv).

The main body of d'Erlanger's fifth volume consists of an exposition of the melodic modes in current use, grouped according to their final (tonic) degree. The individual *maqāmāt* are presented as ascending and descending scales made up of named tetrachordal (also pentachordal and occasionally trichordal) units called *'uqūd* (sing. *'iqd*), which are arranged in conjunct, disjunct, or overlapping sequence. Following each scale, d'Erlanger provides a brief description of the melodic characteristics of the *maqām*, which are illustrated by a *taqsīm* (solo instrumental improvisation in free rhythm, pl. *taqāsīm*) transcribed by Shaykh 'Alī (d'Erlanger 1930–59, 5:xiv, 381).[13]

---

concluding with examples of several common modes. Tetrachords remained a fundamental concept of Arab and Turkish music theory until the sixteenth century, when they dropped out of use. They were reintroduced into Turkish music theory in the early twentieth century by Raūf Yektā and Sādeddin Arel (see Yektā 1921) and to Arab music theory by Baron Rodolphe d'Erlanger and the Syrian Shaykh 'Alī al-Darwīsh in their report to the 1932 Cairo Congress (see Davis 2002, 502–3; and Davis 2004, 46; see also "Editor's Note on the Music" below). Tetrachords first appear in modern Arab music theory in the 1932 Cairo Congress publications (*KMM'A* 1933 and *Recueil* 1934).

10. See editor's commentary below.

11. The region of Ḥijāz (al-Ḥijāz), which lies to the west of the Arabian peninsula bordering the Red Sea, includes the holy Islamic cities of Mecca and Medina.

12. Lachmann's script has a blank space in place of the ♭ symbol.

13. Crucially, d'Erlanger claims to be neither definitive nor comprehensive in his presentation of the *maqāmāt:* "Le nombre, la composition et le mouvement melodique ou métrique des diverses combinaisons modales ou rhythmiques, sont . . . trop controversées pour que nous pretendions présenter toutes ces combinaisons, sans aucune omission et dans des formules définitives" (The number, makeup, and melodic or rhythmic movement of the different modal and rhythmic combinations are too controversial for us to pretend to present every combination, without omission, in its definitive form; d'Erlanger 1930–59, 5:viii). Nor does he comment on the aesthetic and psychological properties of the *maqāmāt,* feeling at a loss to decide between the diverse, often contradictory explanations provided by his informants (ibid.). Nevertheless, the authority of d'Erlanger's and Shaykh 'Alī's work was sanctioned at the 1932 Cairo Congres by the Committee on Melodic and Rhythmic Modes and Composition, whose members included the most eminent musicians of Cairo headed by the Turkish musicologist Raūf Yektā Bey (d'Erlanger 1930–59, 5:xiv; Racy 1991, 73–74). The Arabic version of the committee's report became an extremely influential source of modern Arab music theory of its time (Marcus 1989, 48).

In his commentary to the fifth volume, d'Erlanger identifies as the defining attributes of a *maqām* (1) its overall ambitus; (2) its constituent tetrachords; (3) its starting degree (*al-mabdā*); (4) its final degree (*qarār*); (5) the degrees on which the internal phrases close (*al-marākiz*—typically, degrees that frame the constituent tetrachords); and (6) the dominant, or degree to which the melody gravitates (*gammāz*—typically, the fifth above the final; d'Erlanger 1930–59, 5:100). While concepts such as *al-mabdā*, *al-marākiz*, and *gammāz* have largely dropped out of use, the definition of the individual *maqāmāt* according to their constituent tetrachords has remained a fundamental principle of *maqām* theory to the present day (Marcus 1989, 487–587).

In the transcriptions of recitations 9.1 and 9.2 below, I map the melodic trajectories of Ezra Aharon's improvisations according to their tetrachordal structure. Preceding each transcription, the complete set of *'ūqud* for each performance is identified and presented as a single ascending scale; in Aharon's performances, *maqām ḥijāz* and *maqām ṣabā* have been transposed from their regular final D to final G. In both *taqāsīm* the melody unfolds in phrases of irregular length, each concluding on the final of the *maqām*. The summary transcriptions indicate the tetrachordal content of each successive phrase and its opening and closing riffs. Table 6 identifies the special notational conventions used.

Table 6
Special Symbols Used in Recitations 9.1 and 9.2

Symbol	Description
0:00	CD track timing (minutes:seconds)
ø	final degree, tonal center
•̄	prominent degree
• ~~~~~~	rapidly repeated note
(•)	leading tone
⁝•	occasional pitch inflection

Unlike Shaykh 'Ali's carefully crafted transcriptions of *taqāsīm* in volume five of *La musique arabe,* which present complete (albeit compressed) interpretations of the individual *maqām* trajectories, Aharon's performances are constrained by the limitations of the recording medium. Furthermore, the recordings themselves are truncated because of damage to the discs. As a result, recitations 9.1 and 9.2 represent merely the opening sections of performances whose overall trajectories remain unknown.

Recitation 9.1: Taqsīm ḥijāz

Recording number: D623

Performer: Ezra Aharon, *'ūd*

A. Scale

Maqām ḥijāz on G showing *'uqūd* used:

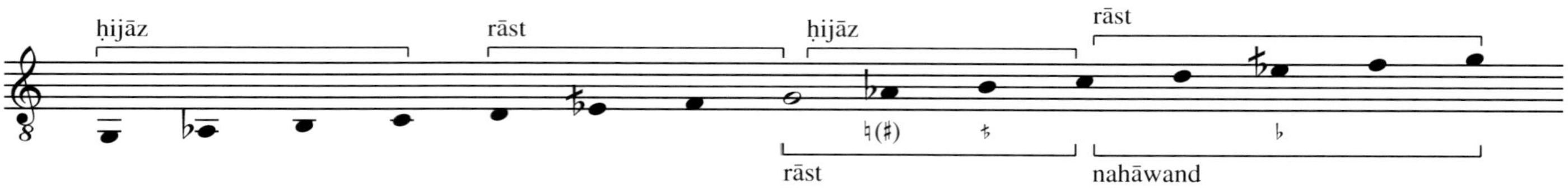

B. Summary Transcription

Taqsīm ḥijāz as performed by Ezra Aharon:

0:08–0:42

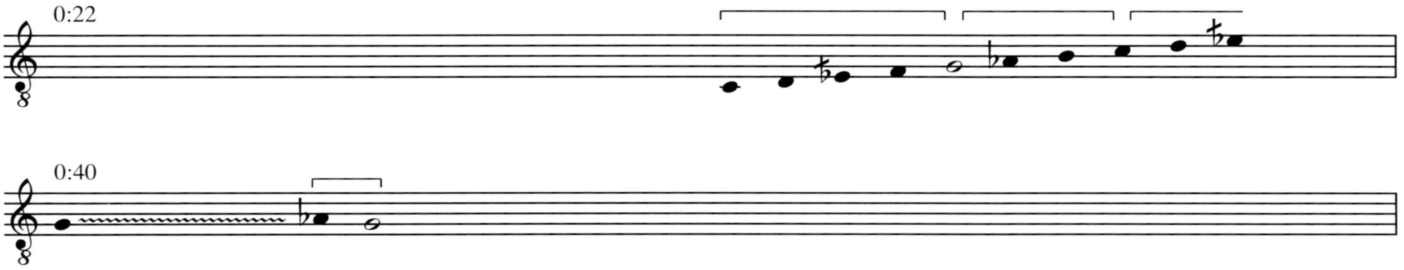

0:43–1:16

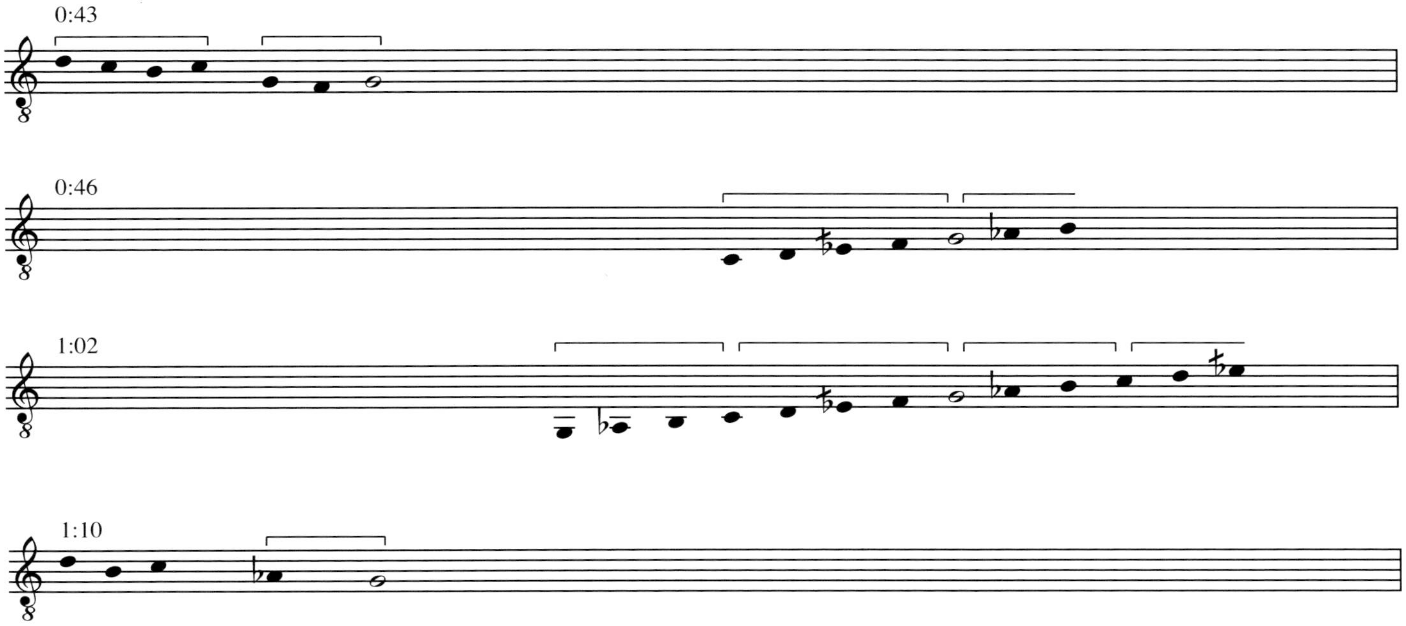

1:17–2:41

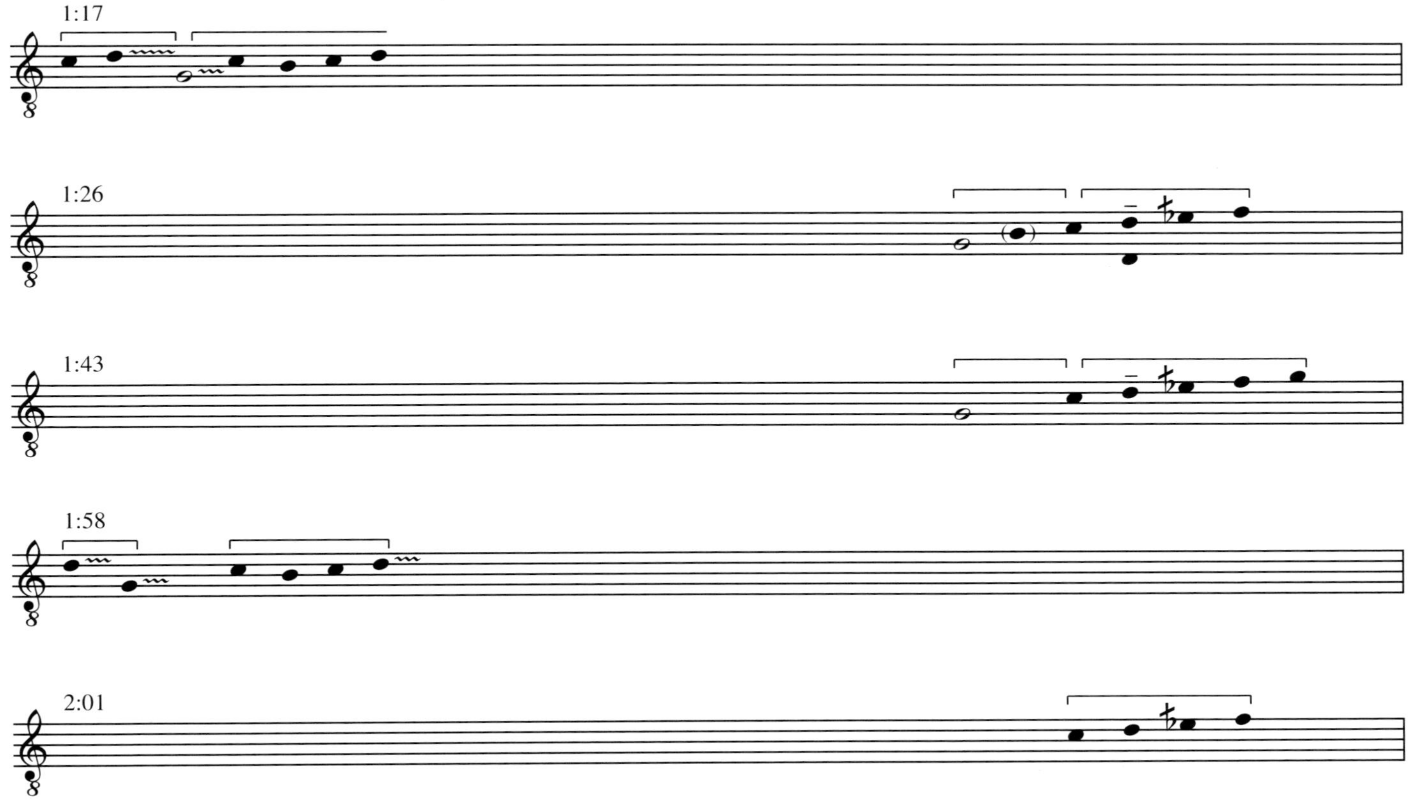

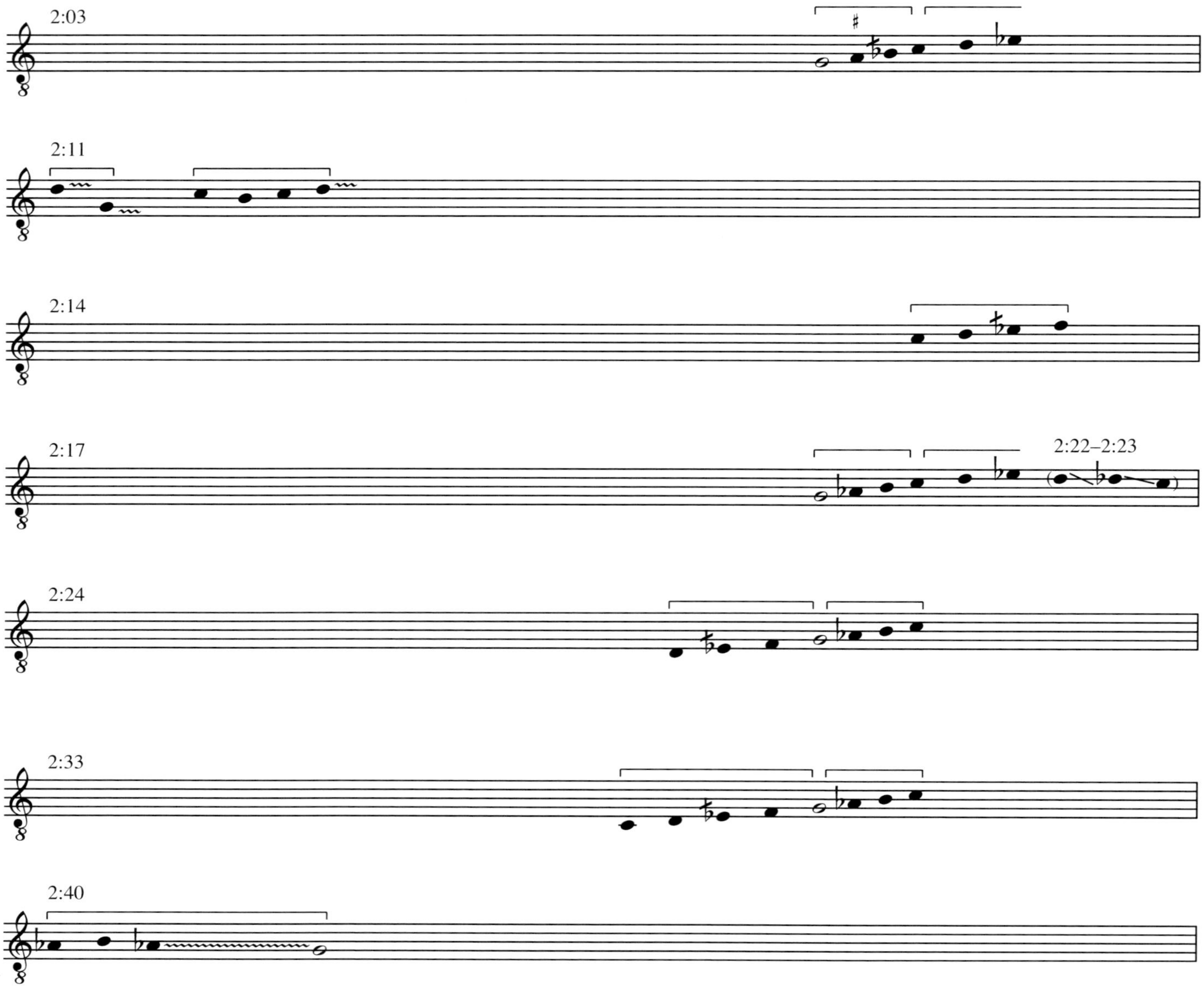

2:42–3:01

Recitation 9.2: Taqsīm ṣabā

Recording number: D624

Performer: Ezra Aharon, *ʿūd*

A. Scale

Maqām ṣabā on G showing *ʿuqūd* used:

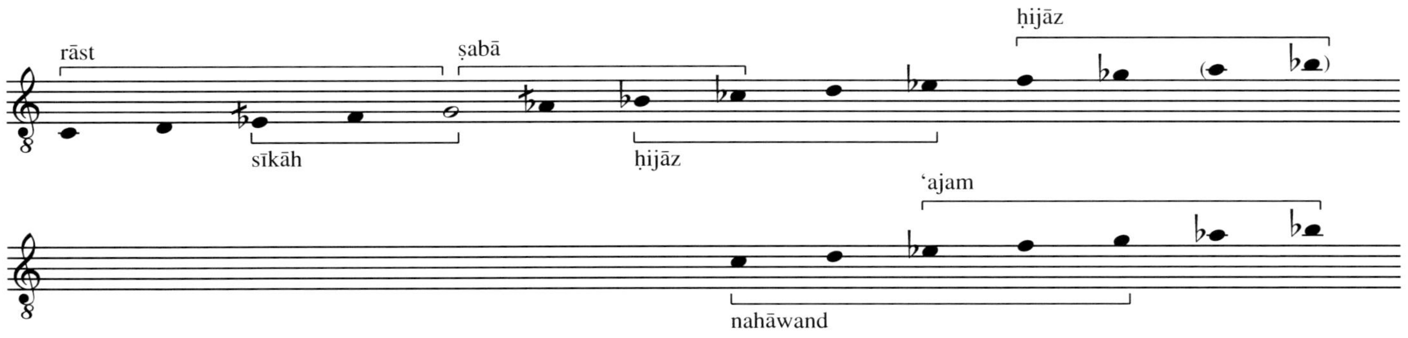

B. Summary Transcription

Taqsīm ṣabā as performed by Ezra Aharon:

0:02–0:40

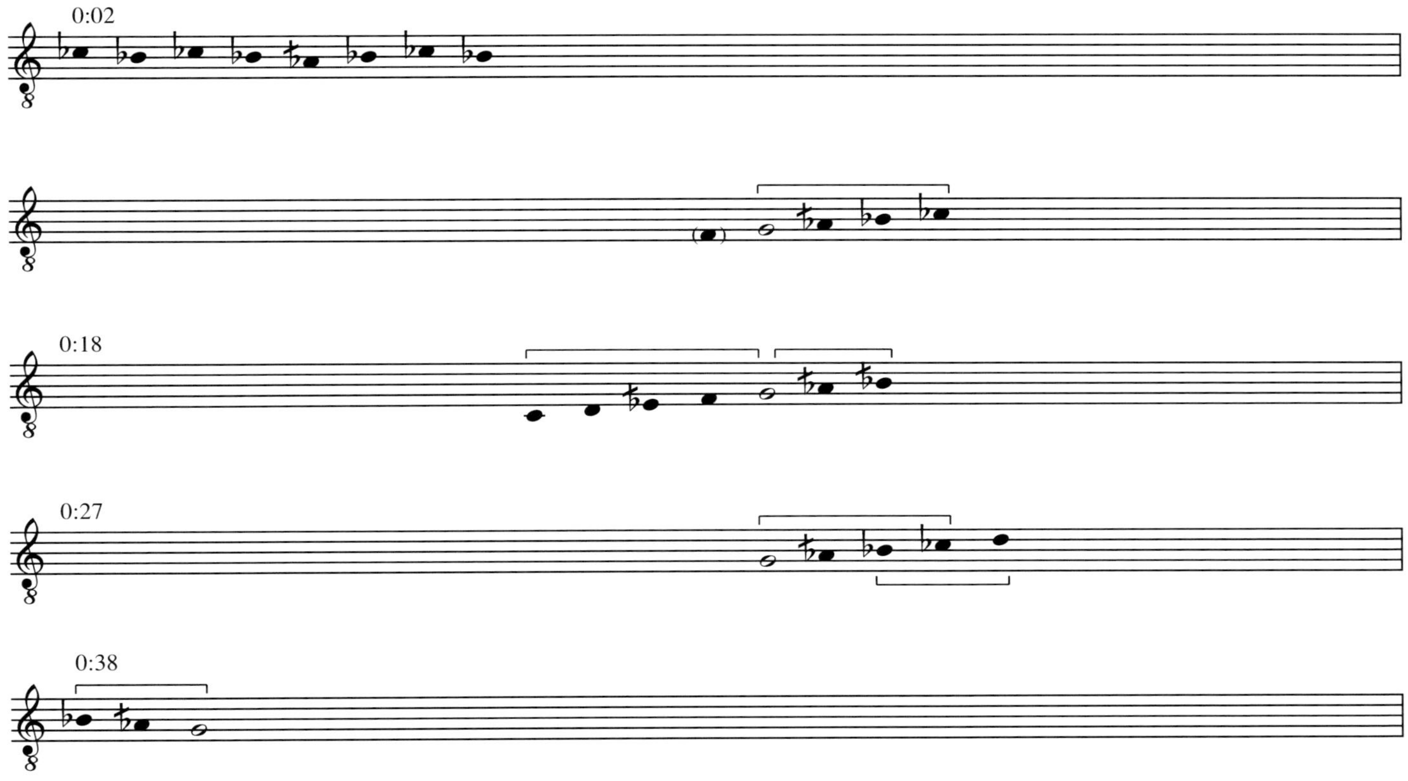

0:42–1:20

1:21–1:53

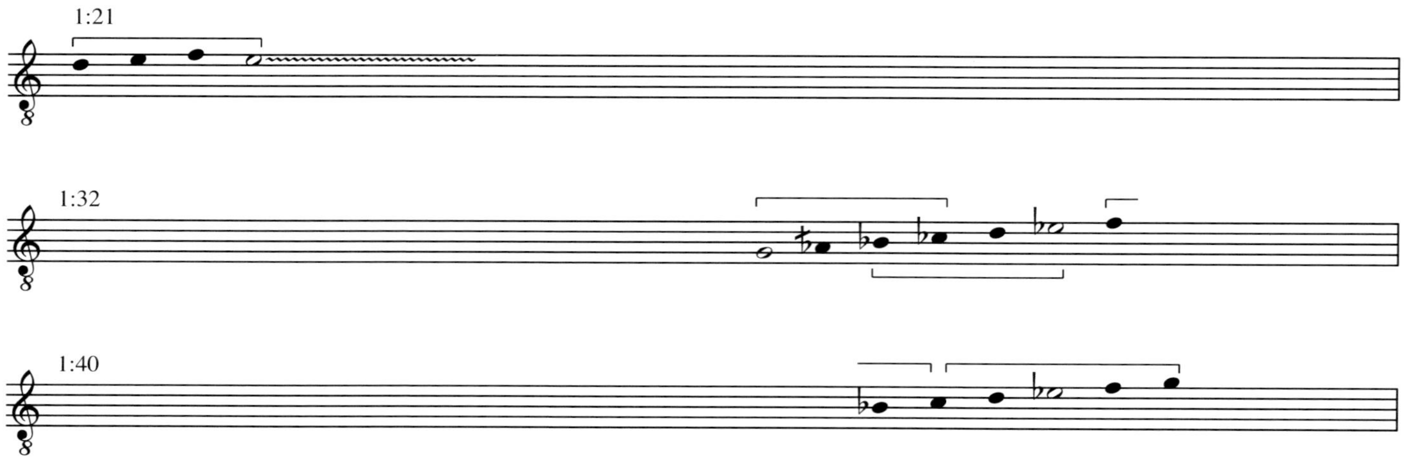

1:53–2:16 (original recording only)

Recitation 9.3: Taqsīm sīkā

Recording number: D625

Performer: Ezra Aharon, *'ūd*

Editor's Commentary

Lachmann first met Ezra Aharon, the Jewish *'ūd* player from Baghdad, at the 1932 Cairo Congress, where he was performing with the ensemble from Iraq under his Arabic name of 'Azzūri Hārūn. In addition to recording the ensemble as a whole, Lachmann recorded the individual musicians playing solo improvisatory preludes (*taqāsīm*, sing. *taqsīm*) in the different melodic modes (*maqāmāt*).[1] Toward the end of 1934, Aharon fled to Palestine, apparently following a threat to his life from the pan-Arab movement. Jehoash Hirshberg recounts how Lachmann, shortly after his arrival in Palestine, chanced upon Aharon on a street in Jerusalem, whereupon the two seamlessly resumed their work together (Hirshberg 1995, 198–99).[2]

Lachmann made a total of sixty-seven recordings of Aharon in Jerusalem, of which all but eighteen are marked as missing. He describes the full scope of this project in his report of 4 May 1937 for the *Information Bulletin* of the Hebrew University:

> The Archives are making a complete study of the musical modes or melody types of Oriental urban music . . . by recording, analyzing and transcribing into staff-notation the preludes in "free rhythm" of all the musical modes now in practice. . . . This collection, which is being recorded from musicians belonging to the different schools of tradition, will be completed toward the end of this year (quoted in Katz 2003, 193).

Clearly Lachmann considered Aharon as representing the Iraqi "school of tradition." In reality, however, he was hardly a typical representative of that tradition. In her account of the Iraqi contribution to the Cairo Congress, Schéhérazade Qassim Hassan discerns a fundamental misconception among both the European and the Egyptian participants about the nature of the Iraqi *maqām* tradition, which the majority were encountering there for the first time. None of the participants, she contends, understood the distinction between *maqām* in the general sense of mode or melody type (as represented by the *taqāsīm* performed by Aharon) and the Iraqi *maqām*, or *maqām al-'irāqī*, a large-scale vocal genre with a distinctive performance style, peculiar to Iraq (Hassan 1992, 133–34). Typically, the *maqām al-'irāqī* featured a solo vocalist, or *qāri' al-maqām* (lit. "*maqām* reciter"; pl. *qurrā al-maqām*) accompanied by an instrumental ensemble called *chalghī al-maqām*.[3] This comprised a *joza* (spiked-fiddle), a *santūr* (dulcimer), a *dunbuk* (goblet drum), and a *daff* (tambourine); it did not traditionally include Aharon's instrument, the *'ūd sharqī* (lit. "eastern *'ūd*"). And while solo improvisatory passages (also called *taqāsīm*) featured as part of the overall instrumental texture of the *maqām al-'irāqī*, the very notion of the *taqsīm* as a freestanding genre—as in Lachmann's recordings of Aharon—was alien to the Iraqi tradition.

In 1930s Baghdad, the *'ūd sharqī* was emblematic of the new pan-Arab musical style emanating from Egypt. The Iraqi-Jewish musicologist Yeheskel Kojaman has recounted how, in the years after World War I, musical life in Iraq was transformed by the impact of Egyptian mass media such as phonograph records, musical films, and broadcasting, and the influx of foreign singers and composers steeped in the new style. Gradually, the imported music came to surpass the *maqām al-'irāqī* in popularity and status. Particularly influential in bringing about this shift were the two Jewish brothers Salah and Daoud al-Kuwaiti, who virtually monopolized Iraqi composition through the 1930s (Kojaman 2001, 100). Jewish musicians, who had long dominated instrumental performance in Baghdad, were quick to forge links with the visiting celebrities, and Aharon was allegedly the first Iraqi to compose in the new style (Warkov 1986, 13–14; Kojaman 2001, 100).

In contrast to the *maqām al-'irāqī*, which was traditionally performed in special coffee houses and in private homes, the new music was associated with the new performance venues that proliferated after World War I, such as nightclubs where alcohol was served and the audience, seated in rows, watched staged performances by female singers and dancers called *banāt* (lit. "girls"). Their performances were accompanied by an ensemble called *takht sharqī* (lit., "eastern ensemble") or simply *takht*, comprising an *'ūd sharqī*, a violin, an optional *qānūn* (zither), and at least one *daff* (tambourine; Kojaman 2001, 100).

In 1929 the record company Baidaphon invited the young *qāri' al-maqām* Muhammad al-Qubbānjī to Berlin to record the *maqām al-'irāqī* using state-of-the-art technology. In an extraordinary break with tradition, al-Qubbānjī took to Berlin not the traditional *chalghī* but a *takht sharqī*, with Ezra Aharon (as 'Azzūri Hārūn) on *'ūd*.[4] When, however, on the eve of Iraqi independence, al-Qubbānjī was selected to represent Iraq at the 1932 Cairo Congress, he agreed to a compromise: the regular *chalghī* instrumentalists would be joined by an *'ūd sharqī* and a *qānūn*, thus effectively creating a new hybrid ensemble.[5] As a result, the recordings of the *maqām al-'irāqī* made at the congress, far from representing traditional Iraqi practice, document a novel lineup consisting of the merging of the traditional Iraqi and the modern Egyptian styles (Hassan 1992, 126).

In Jerusalem, Aharon's propensity for modernization took a new turn. In an attempt to attract new audiences, he began to compose settings of modern Hebrew poetry in a synthesis of Arab and Western musical styles with accompaniment on traditional Arab instruments (Hirshberg 1995, 198; Warkov 1986, 17). Remarkably, Lachmann reacted positively to Aharon's efforts, discerning in them a phenomenon of profound socio-cultural significance. In his lecture "National und International in der orientalischen Musik," delivered in Tel Aviv in February 1936 (Lachmann 1936a), Lachmann introduced Aharon performing his setting of Ḥayyim Naḥman Bialik's poem "Bein nehar Perat ve-nehar Hidekel" (Between the River Euphrates and the River Tigris), with the observation that

> a fundamental change can occur in the musical situation when Jews from many lands are concentrated in one; that in place of compositions representing the individual styles of different environments, a new style with a resonance of its own could become possible. . . . Mr Azuri [*sic*] has taken it upon himself, from the perspective of a musician trained in the Arab tradition, to set to music a poem in modern Hebrew. It was not enough for him to simply place the texts atop melodies that remain strictly in the *maqām* system. . . . You will certainly recognize in this music a seeking after a new style that is up to the new task (Lachmann 1936a).[6]

With the founding of the Palestine Broadcasting Service in March 1936, Aharon found a wider platform for his new style; with Lachmann's support, he was appointed head of a special section for Oriental Jewish music (Shiloah 2007b). That his efforts were widely appreciated is evident from the remarks of Karl Salomon, Musical Director of the PBS, in an article in *Musica Hebraica*, the journal of the World Centre for Jewish Music in Palestine:

> In the domain of oriental music, special mention deserves to be made of the Iraqi Jew Ezra Aharon, composer, singer, *'ūd* player, and leader of a choir and a small oriental orchestra. His concerts may well represent a landmark in the history of Palestinian and Jewish music in that they offer for the first time Oriental music with vocal accompaniment in Hebrew, the whole being in a form which, without pandering to popular taste, appeals to a very wide circle, including listeners who are not Orientals (Salomon 1938, quoted in Bohlman 1992, 196; and Bohlman and Davis 2007, 117).[7]

Yet Aharon's experimental phase was short-lived. In 1943 he founded a larger, Egyptian-style ensemble called al-Firqa al-Ḥadītha (The New Ensemble) that specialized in the Egyptian mainstream style he had pioneered in Baghdad. And in contrast to the "small oriental orchestra" described by Salomon, which had consisted of immigrant Jewish musicians from different Middle Eastern countries, Aharon's new ensemble consisted primarily of Palestinian Arab and German Jewish musicians (Warkov 1986, 16, 19).

The effects of Aharon's reorientation were far-reaching. With the creation of the State of Israel in 1948, he was appointed head of Eastern music in Kol Israel (Voice of Israel), the Israeli public broadcasting service. In this capacity he played a crucial role in establishing institutional policies toward Arab music in the early years of statehood. Effectively, al-Firqa al-Ḥadītha paved the way for the almost exclusive patronage of the mainstream Egyptian style by the Israeli mass media and cultural policy makers and their neglect and discouragement of the individual ethnic Arab styles introduced by Jewish immigrants from Arab lands (Warkov 1986, 25).

These homogenizing policies toward Arab music formed part of a wider policy to promote a unitary national culture based on European models epitomized by the *shirei eretz Israel* (lit. "songs of the land of Israel")—the invented Israeli folk song tradition pioneered by European immigrant poets and composers (Hirshberg 1995, 146–56; and Regev and Seroussi 2004, 49–70; see also Nathan 1994).[8] Yet, as Amnon Shiloah and Erik Cohen observed in their groundbreaking survey of Arab music in Israel at the end of the 1970s, ethnic Arab music continued to play a vital role in the family and communal rituals of the immigrant communities themselves, both within and beyond the liturgical and paraliturgical domains. As a result, traditional musical activities were "not completely interrupted but merely curtailed" (Shiloah and Cohen 1983, 23).

By the time Aharon retired from his radio position in the late 1960s, the homogenizing policies of the Israeli cultural establishment had begun to crumble in the face of the multiethnic realities of Israeli society. Within the following decade, *musiqa mizraḥit* (lit. "Eastern music")[9]—an umbrella term for the spectrum of ethnic rock and popular musical styles promoted by the Israeli-born offspring of the marginalized Eastern communities—had exploded onto the Israeli musical scene, eventually to become absorbed into the popular musical mainstream (Regev and Seroussi 2004, 191–212; Horowitz 2010).[10] Meanwhile, Arab music, in both traditional forms and multiple fusions—the latter often associated with new political and identity movements—continued to revitalize an increasingly varied Israeli musical soundscape.[11] At the beginning of the second decade of the twenty-first century, Aharon is remembered not only for his legendary musical accomplishments but also for his unique role, sustained over three decades, in maintaining a serious profile for Arab music on the pre-state and Israeli airwaves at a time when European cultural models prevailed and the Arab dimension of Jewish cultural identity was typically either ignored or deliberately marginalized. More fundamentally, he is celebrated in Israel for his enduring contribution to Iraqi music and his participation in the 1932 Cairo Congress. As such, he symbolizes the lost era before the mass exodus of Jewish communities from their ancient Arab homelands, when Jewish musicians played vital roles in mainstream Arab musical life.

Notes

1. For details of the Iraqi recordings, see Hassan 1992, 138–40.

2. Lachmann mentioned that he had commenced working with Aharon in his report of 7 July 1935.

3. *Qurrā al-maqām* generally doubled as Qur'anic reciters or synagogue cantors and were respected members of their communities. The *chalghī* instrumentalists who accompanied them, in contrast, were socially less well regarded (Kojaman 2001, 17–21).

4. In Berlin, Aharon also recorded independently of the *takht*, playing *'ūd, joza,* violin, and piano (Moussali 1988, 119).

5. Schéhérazade Qassim Hassan suggests that al-Qubbānjī's preference for the *takht sharqī* was motivated primarily by artistic considerations. Whereas in the

chalghī the instrumentalists traditionally led the melody, anticipating the *qāri' al-maqām*, the instrumentalists of the *takht sharqī* typically played a subordinate role, highlighting the solo voice (Hassan 1992, 126). Kojaman, in contrast, emphasizes sartorial factors, arguing that the shabby appearance of the *chalghī* musicians, in their traditional clothes and sandals, would have been considered unacceptable for an official visit to a European capital (Kojaman 2001, 36). Before leaving for the Cairo Congress, however, the *chalghī* musicians were persuaded to don Western-style suits and shoes topped by the *sidara*, the Iraqi conical hat (Kojaman 2001, 36–37; Hassan 1992, 126–27). Kojaman cites an interview with Aharon in which he recounts how he was summoned to the office of the Iraqi prime minister, Nuri al-Said, only to be informed that his main duty in Cairo was to make sure the *chalghī* musicians dressed properly (Kojaman 2001, 36–37).

6. ". . . daß die musikalische Situation sich mit der Konzentrierung der Juden verschiedener Länder in ein Einziges einen grundlegenden Wandel erleben kann; daß statt individuelles Schöpfungen im Stil einer anderen Umwelt ein eigenes Stil mit eigener Resonanz möglich werden könnte. . . . Herr Azuri hat vom Standpunkt eines in arabischer Tradition ausgebildeten Musikers unternommen, neuhebräische Gedicht zu vertonen. Er hat sich nicht begnügt, den Texten einfach Melodien unterzulegen, die streng im Meqām-System verharren. . . . Ein Bestreben um einen neuen Stil, der der neuen Aufgabe gerecht werden will, werden Sie gewiß selbst darin erkennen" (Lachmann 1936a).

Aharon subsequently performed "Bein nehar Perat ve-nehar Hidekel" in the last of Lachmann's "Four Lectures on Eastern Music," given on 3 March 1936. On that occasion, Lachmann described Aharon's composition as: "a 'monologue,' a form recently developed in Egypt. Contrary to older forms, each stanza is supplied here with its own music and coherence is not arrived at by a refrain or ritornello, but merely by a certain conformity of melodic invention" (Katz 2003, 415).

7. Longer excerpts of Salomon's article with further commentary are given in Bohlman 1992, 192–96; and Bohlman and Davis 2007, 117–19.

8. Bohlman's essay appears as an afterword to a collection of fifteen *shirei eretz Israel* arranged for voice and piano in the late 1930s by composers Aaron Copland, Arthur Honneger, Darius Milhaud, Ernest Toch, Kurt Weill, and Stefan Wolpe, edited by Hans Nathan. The songs were originally published on postcards and distributed by the Zionist organization Keren Kayemeth in the early 1930s.

9. Also known as *musiqa yam tikhonit* (Mediterranean music).

10. For a nuanced account of these later developments in their wider socio-political context, see Warkov 1986.

11. The rise of *musiqa etnit Yisraelit* (Israeli ethnic music), in which ensembles consisting of Israeli Jews and Israeli and Palestinian Arabs engage in creative musical collaborations, is associated with the peace process of the 1990s (see Brinner 2009). In the twenty-first century, the *piyyut* revival, in which *piyyutim* (sacred Hebrew poems set to popular vernacular melodies; see program 7 above) are arranged in a wide spectrum of traditional and contemporary styles, reflects the reengagement of third-generation Mizraḥi Israelis with their eastern roots and a renewed interest in spirituality. See, for example, Raz, forthcoming; and the websites *Hazmanah le-piyyut* (Invitation to *Piyyut*; http://www.piyut.org.il) and *Kehilot sharot* (Singing Communities; http://www.kehilotsharot.org.il).

Program 10

Music from the Western Arab World
31 March 1937

Last time, we were concerned with the spiritual background of Arab urban music. It was shown that the doctrine of cosmic harmony as handed down from antiquity is still present in the musicians' minds even nowadays and that superhuman forces are still held to be largely responsible for the effects that music can produce.

We now pass on to the music itself. However little Europeans may know about it, they generally have some vague notion of its being in quartertones. This hardly seems attractive, and is not even accurate. So it may be worth while saying a few words about the real function of those quartertones.

The scale system of Arab music has been taken over from Ancient Greek theory. Like every scale system among Ancient and Oriental nations it is based on numerical relations as applied to string instruments and pipes, and is not based, as people often believe, on observations of intervals as executed by the human voice. It would lead too far to elaborate this point now. In support of it, it may only be said that in the whole domain of purely vocal music, and especially in liturgical cantillation, there exists no original system of scales and no musical notation establishing standard notes and intervals; where there is any notation at all, it only gives vague indications as to the rise and fall of the voice.[1]

The different scale systems of Ancient and Oriental urban music are all demonstrated on a specially favoured instrument. In Arab theory, this instrument is the ʿUd which, together with its name, also passed into European musical practice where it is known, in English, as lute.

The first Arab treatise on music which has come down to us dates from the 9th century.[2] It establishes a system of twelve notes within the octave, that is to say, the same number of notes as that represented, in later times, by the white and black keys of the European piano. In European theory, this series of twelve notes is called a chromatic scale. But it is not really a scale. In Arab music as well as in European, scales consist, at most, of seven notes and the set of twelve notes merely provides a supply from which to choose seven note scales of varying structures.

While in European music the system of twelve notes has remained the final stage of development down to the present day, Arab theory, soon after its start, increased the number of notes available and, from the 10th century onward, recognized seventeen notes within the octave until about two centuries ago when the number of notes was again increased, and the present system of twenty-four notes was established. With regard to this modern system, we can indeed speak of quartertones, the octave now being divided into double the number of sections than the European chromatic scale.[3]

---

1. See "The Djerba Monograph" in the introduction for a summary of Lachmann's arguments for the instrumental origins of the musical scale. On the different notational systems used in the Christian, Jewish, Muslim, and Vedic liturgies, see program 4, footnote 15. On the Samaritan recitation signs and their relationship to the Jewish signs, see program 6, footnotes 10 and 11.

2. The earliest extant treatises are by Abū Yūsuf Yaʿqūb al-Kindī; see program 9, footnote 6.

3. Lachmann introduces here the purely theoretical concept of a general scale, comprising the repository of pitch degrees from which the particular scales of a musical system are drawn. The general scale of Arab, Persian, and Turkish music derives from the seventeen-note-per-octave scale of medieval Persian and Arab theorists as described by Safī al-Dīn in the *Kitāb al-adwār* (Book of Cycles), where it is shown as frets on the *ʿūd*. The seventeen-degree scale was reconceptualized as a scale of twenty-four quarter tones per octave in Syria in the late eighteenth and early nineteenth centuries. The first comprehensive presentation of the twenty-four-tone scale appears in the *Risāla al-shihābiyya fi al-sināʿa al-musiqiyya* (Essay on the Art of Music for the Emir Shahab, 1840) by the Lebanese theorist Mīkhāʾīl Mushāqa (1800–1880), who effectively made up the number by filling in the gaps in the earlier scale. See Davis 2001.

The general scale of Arab music comprises forty-nine named pitch degrees spanning two octaves, from G to g′. It is based on a two-octave fundamental scale of fifteen degrees whose Arabic and Persian names correspond to those of the equivalent degrees in the medieval Arab scale. At the core of the fundamental scale is the fundamental octave, from c to c′, of which six degrees (*rāst, dūkā, jahārkā, nawā, husaynī,* and *kirdān*) correspond to the notes c, d, f, g, a, and c′, of the Western scale; the third degree (*sīkā*) falls between e and e♭, and the sixth degree (*nawā*) falls between b and b♭. The fundamental scale repeats

But in alluding to the Arab system as including, successively, twelve to twenty-four notes we must always remember that the actual scales consist of no more than seven degrees. Why, then, you might ask, should the number of notes available have been raised? The answer is that Arab urban music aims at a finer differentiation of melodic steps than European and that, in order to achieve this, it required to have an increasing supply of notes at its disposal. So some of the steps used in Arab melody are unknown in European music; one of them, e.g., is about midway in size between the tone and the semitone, another midway between the major and the minor third, and so forth. But the quartertone itself as a musical interval does not occur any more than in European music.[4]

Arab urban melody, thus, possesses niceties of intonation absent from European. On the other hand, it lacks, and has always lacked, that system of harmony which European music has gradually evolved and which, with its consonant and dissonant chords, has come to be one of its chief means of expression.

There is another and equally important point on which the musical conception of the Near East differs from European. The classification of melodies, in Arab urban music, does not rest solely on their difference in scale. Beyond its own scale, every melodic category or mode has its own melodic turns and phrases; and it is this traditional melodic material which ultimately determines the character of the respective mode. This means that musicians are not at liberty to invent any kinds of tune in a given scale. They must use the melodic material that they have received from their masters and it is difficult to say how much freedom they are allowed in handling this material.[5]

The melodic character of each mode (in Arabic: maqām) can be recognized, more clearly than in other forms[6] of song, in the introduction which precedes every recital and of which several examples were played in my last talk. In contrast with these introductions which may be sung as well as played, all the pieces following it are in strict time. The melodic connection between them and the introduction is of supreme importance for the understanding of the melodic mode or maqām. All these pieces draw upon the melodic material as exposed in the introduction, but they sometimes transform it[7] in such a manner that, at a first hearing, the relation is but dimly perceived by outsiders.

In the following example, a vocal and instrumental introduction is immediately followed by a song in strict time. In this example, I think, it is easy to notice that the melodic material is common to both.

I must apologise for the fact that, in illustration of to-night's talk, I am compelled to use records instead of collaborating with musicians, and that some of the records are a little worn. But the particular types of music that I want to show you are not practised in this country. (Record 10.1)

The melody in strict time is accompanied, as you have heard, by a drum. This practice of drumming, a typical feature of the music of the Near East and India, does not merely serve to mark the time. The beats of the drum have quite a different function from those in military marches; they constitute a rhythmical phrase repeated throughout and thus forming a steady background as against the fluctuations of the melody. In Arab urban music, a number of such rhythmical types or patterns are distinguished. This as well as the grouping of melodies into melody types or maqāmāt is characteristic of the Oriental mind fixing on concrete configurations of melody and rhythm rather than on abstract tabulations of scales and time-values.[8]

---

the degrees of the fundamental octave through the lower octave to G and through the upper octave to g′ (see Davis 2001).

4. The twenty-four-tone scales of Arab and Persian music were originally conceived as equal-tempered. In contrast, the Turkish twenty-four-tone scale is conceived according to the Pythagorean system of commas. In practice, however, the intervals in all three scale types are variable, depending on regional tradition, musical context, and individual preference.

5. Elaborating on this concept of mode in the last of his "Four Lectures on Eastern Music," presented in early 1936, Lachmann observed that this "stability of [melodic] types which also extends to rhythm is the backbone of oral tradition" (quoted in Katz 2003, 409). Both here and in program 10, Lachmann's conception of mode clearly echoes that of Idelsohn in *Jewish Music:* "A MODE . . . is composed of a number of MOTIVES (i.e., short music figures or groups of tones) within a certain scale" (Idelsohn [1929] 1992, 24). Idelsohn's definition is itself a compression of his pioneering 1913 definition of the Arabic term *maqām* as "a musical type [*Musikart*] that makes use of its own proper degrees of the scale [*Tonstufen*] and motivic groups [*Motivgruppen*]. . . . in *maqām* both scale type and melody type [*Tonleiter und Tonweise*] are comprised, and pre-eminently the latter" (Idelsohn 1913–14, quoted in Powers and Widdess 2001a, 830). In their report on the melodic modes of Arab music to the 1932 Cairo Congress, Baron Rodolphe d'Erlanger and Shaykh 'Alī al-Darwīsh introduced a more abstract concept of *maqām,* which nevertheless included melodic characteristics, based on the medieval concept of the tetrachord as the fundamental melodic unit. In the fifth volume of *La musique arabe* (1949), d'Erlanger describes and illustrates the distinctive melodic characteristics for each *maqām* scale in current use in the Arab Near East (d'Erlanger 1930–59, 5:117); see also "Editor's Note on the Music" in program 9.

6. Lachmann's script: *form.*

7. Lachmann's script: *if.*

8. In the sixth volume of *La musique arabe* (1959), based on his report to the 1932 Cairo Congress, d'Erlanger illustrates 111 named rhythmic-metric patterns characterizing the "Oriental tradition" of Arab music (d'Erlanger 1930–59, 6:29–140). The transcriptions, provided by Shaykh 'Alī al-Darwīsh, effectively represent Syro-Egyptian urban practice. In the same volume, d'Erlanger represents the "Occidental," "Andalusian," or "Hispanic-Arab" tradition (see footnote 9 below) with nine rhythmic-metric patterns and their variants, taken from Tunisian urban practice (d'Erlanger 1930–59, 6:145–52).

The melodic as well as the rhythmic types in Arab urban music are traditional; but the tradition has not remained, if ever it was, uniform. Above all, there is a strong difference between an Eastern and a Western style, the latter extending from Tripoli westward to Tunis, Algeria, and Morocco. Each of the two styles, the Eastern and the Western, again falls into several groups. The Eastern style may be reserved for future discussion; we are now concerned with the West.[9]

In Western North Africa we should expect to find one common tradition. The names of the melody types and the texts of the musical répertoire are mostly the same. Moreover, musicians of all the three countries, from Tunis to Morocco, claim to have preserved the musical inheritance of Moorish Spain. But in reality, there are three traditions instead of one as you may judge for yourselves.[10] The introduction and song which you heard before is a good specimen of the Tunisian style; the next example is from Algeria. (Record 10.2)

The Moroccan[11] style, again, is obviously different. Its peculiar character may be due to the fact that the population in Morocco, more than in the two other countries, has retained its Berber qualities. A large proportion of the country has not even accepted the Arabic language; so it is quite possible that the Berber element may have influenced the tradition of urban music in Morocco.[12] (Record 10.3, CD 2, tracks 5–6)

The question as to which of the three Western styles may be nearest to the Original Moorish music, the music of Andalus, has to remain open until further investigations. These investigations will have to extend also to the remnants of Moorish song in Spain. As a matter of fact, a certain manner of song practised in Southern Spain, the Flamenco, no doubt bears traces of the Moorish past. It is in free rhythm like the preludes of Arab urban music and its melodic style is Arab and not Spanish. But, as compared to North African urban music, the Flamenco conveys a picture of distortion and decay. The rhapsodic vocal part does not, like the introductions that you have heard, deliberately expose the outlines of a melody type; it has retained the mannerisms, and lost the meaning and function, of those introductions. It has, moreover, been placed in a most unsuitable setting consisting of a few typical chords on the Spanish guitar.[13] I will close the present talk with an example of this curious hybrid kind of music. (Record 10.3)[14]

---

9. Lachmann's notion of a "strong difference" between Eastern and Western styles of Arab urban music corresponds to the distinction made by d'Erlanger in volume 5 (on the melodic modes) and volume 6 (on the rhythms and compositional forms) of *La musique arabe,* where the two styles are treated in separate sections. Both scholars present the Western style as divided into distinct national traditions and the Eastern Arab style as one general tradition, the Syro-Egyptian.

Echoing popular belief, d'Erlanger portrays the North African repertories as the legacy of medieval Andalusia, imported by Muslim and Jewish refugees fleeing the Reconquista (d'Erlanger 1930–59, 5:335–36). He attributes the origins of the Occidental Arab style to the early ninth-century musician Ziryāb ('Alī ibn Nāfi'), a freed Persian slave, who was ousted from the court of Baghdad by his jealous teacher and rival Isḥāq al-Mawṣilī (d. 850), court musician and companion (*nadīm*) to Hārūn al-Rashīd. Fleeing westward, Ziryāb found refuge at the court of the Umayyad caliph 'Abd al-Raḥmān II (r. 822–52) in Cordoba, where he founded a music conservatory and developed a distinctive school of Andalusian Arab music (d'Erlanger 1930–59, 5:388–91). Ziryāb is traditionally credited with inventing new techniques of constructing and playing the *'ūd,* developing a distinctive musical cosmology, and creating a system for classifying and ordering compositions in twenty-four large-scale song cycles called *nūbat* (sing. *nūba*), each of which corresponded to a different melodic mode, or *tab'* (lit. "character, nature"; pl. *tubū'*). For the historical background and overview of the present-day North African traditions, see Guettat 2002; for an exhaustive treatment, see Guettat 2000.

10. The differences between the three national traditions (the Libyan closely resembles the Tunisian) are believed to reflect the original pattern of migration from Spain, where each city cultivated its own school of Andalusian music. This belief has been challenged, however, by Mahmoud Guettat, who points to the long history of interraction between Al-Andalus and the Maghreb, arguing that the refugees served only to refine and enrich pre-established traditions of Andalusian music (Guettat 2000, 212–16).

11. Lachmann's script: *Moroccon.*

12. Morocco was also the only North African country that did not come under Ottoman (Turkish) rule.

13. Lachmann's script: *quitar.*

14. The origins of *cante flamenco* are widely disputed. Its early history is generally associated with the gypsies of southern Andalusia, who are believed to have originated in northwest India and migrated through Persia, Egypt, Eastern Europe, and the Balkans before crossing into Spain in the early fifteenth century. The extent to which flamenco reflects the gypsies' eastern origins and migration history or the various musical styles they encountered in Spain, however, remains an open question. The Andalusian composer Manuel de Falla (1876–1946) identified the chief foreign sources of flamenco as Byzantine, Moorish, and Indian (Falla 1922, cited in Leblon [1994] 2003, 69–72). Bernard Leblon, in contrast, disputes claims of direct Moorish influence on the grounds that the style did not begin to develop until long after the expulsion of the Moors from Andalusia (Leblon [1994] 2003, 72). Like Lachmann, Falla considered the commercialized flamenco of his time degenerate, and in 1922 he and several other artists and intellectuals organized a flamenco competition in Granada, partly as a means of rediscovering the pure art among unknown rural performers (Hess 2001).

Record 10.1: Tunisian song: "Ya saki al-houmeya" (Odeon 93324)

Recording number: F131, Odeon 93324

Performer: Cheikh Hassen ben Amran

Note: The catalogue entry for record F131 includes the note "Disc broken."

Record 10.2: Algerian song: "Oua men li bidjesmi"(Odeon 93571)

Recording number: F98, Odeon 93571

Performer: Sfinda

Record 10.3: Moroccan song: "Ṣaḥbi l-awwal" (Baidaphon 093364)

Recording number: F83, Baidaphon 093364

Performer: al-Touhami bin Omar

ah ṣaḥbi l-awwal, m'ḥabbto fi galbi, wa-'alih n'awwal,
'amri ba'd ash akheye

ah ṣaḥbi th-thāni, lli m'ḥabbto fi galbi, msha wa-khallani,
'amri ba'd ash akheye

ah ṣaḥbi th-thālet, lli m'ḥabbto fi galbi, qalūli fālet,
'amri ba'd ash akheye

ah ṣaḥbi r-rābe', 'la m'ḥabbto fi galbi, khallani ṣāber,
'amri ba'd ash akheye

ah ṣaḥbi l-khāmes, 'la m'ḥabbto fi galbi, qalūli fālet,
'amri ba'd ash akheye

ah ṣaḥbi s-sādes, 'la m'ḥabbto fi galbi, qalūli tālef,
'amri ba'd ash akheye

ah ṣaḥbi es sābe', 'la m'ḥabbto fi qalbi, qalūli wāle',
'amri ba'd ash akheye

ah ṣaḥbi th-thāmen, 'la m'ḥabbto fi qalbi, qalūli ghāmel,
'amri ba'd ash akheye

ah ṣaḥbi et tāse', 'la m'ḥabbto fi qalbi, qalūli wāse',
'amri ba'd ash akheye

ah ṣaḥbi l-'āsher, 'la m'ḥabbto fi galbi, qalūli daṣṣer,
'amri ba'd ash akheye

Transcribed by Saad Souissi and Mohamed Kharbach

Ah my first friend, the one whose love is in my heart, and on whom I rely, that's life, my friend.

Ah my second friend, the one . . . , he/she has gone and left me, that's life, my friend.

Ah my third friend, the one . . . , they told me he/she is worthless, that's life, my friend.

Ah my fourth friend, the one . . . , he/she left me in a state of resignation, that's life, my friend.

Ah my fifth friend, the one . . . , they told me he/she is worthless, that's life, my friend.

Ah my sixth friend, the one . . . , they told me he/she is lost and confused, that's life, my friend.

Ah my seventh friend, the one . . . , they told me he/she is really sharp, that's life, my friend.

Ah my eighth friend, the one . . . , they told me he/she is really stale, that's life, my friend.

Ah my ninth friend, the one . . . , they told me he/she is really lax,* that's life, my friend.

Ah my tenth friend, the one . . . , they told me he/she is really impertinent, that's life, my friend.

Translated by Saad Souissi and Mohamed Kharbach

*Literally "very wide" (sexual innuendo).

Record 10.4: Southern Spanish flamenco song (Gramófono 262608)

Recording number: Gramófono 262608

Performer: unknown

Note: There is no entry for this record in Lachmann's catalogues (see "Dating and Cataloguing of Lachmann's Recordings" in "About the Edition").

Program 11

Music from the Eastern Arab World
14 April 1937

When I was dealing with Moorish music, i.e., Arab urban music in Western North Africa I hinted at the possible influence that Berber song may have exercised on it, especially in Morocco. This influence would account for the general difference between an Eastern and a Western style which is so strongly marked in the practice of urban music in the Near East.

We are now going to study the Eastern group extending from Egypt to Persia, and even to India. Here, the musical style is far less uniform than in the West. This is due to the fact that, in these parts, the nations which have contributed to the system and practice of what we call Arab urban music are highly dissimilar in race and customs, and are connected with each other only through their common adherence to Islam and their common political fortunes in certain periods of the past.[1]

The musical elements common to these nations may therefore be expected to lie in the theory and system of music rather than in melody and rhythm and least of all in musical delivery. The system of music as being purely a product of the intellect is hardly restricted by racial and national boundaries. As to musical practice, it is generally believed that tunes are fully characteristic of the nations in which they originate. But this is hardly more than half true. There is, of course, an obvious difference between the melodies of nations vastly differing in race and civilisation as, e.g., the English and the Turks. On the other hand, it is a well-known fact that we can easily embarrass even a trained musician by playing a tune and asking him to decide to which of two European countries it belongs. Which elements in Chopin's music are French and which are Polish? Which, in Handel's later compositions, English and which, German? Or which, in Mendelssohn's, German, and which, Jewish?[2] Questions similar to and as puzzling as these arise as to the music of the different nations in the Near East.

---

1. Lachmann was not alone in extending the scope of Arab music to include traditions beyond the Arab world. D'Erlanger, for example, writes, "This classical music is not specifically Arab: it is cultivated throughout the Islamic New East, in Turkey, Syria, Lebanon, Palestine, Egypt, and even in Greece" (Cette musique classique n'est pas spécifiquement arabe; elle est cultivée dans tout le Proche-Orient musulman: en Turquie, en Syrie, au Liban, en Palestine, en Égypte, et même en Grèce; d'Erlanger 1930–59, 6:29). Lachmann's inclusion of Indian music, however, seems to be exceptional; see program 9, footnote 2.

2. Lachmann virtually lifts this passage from his lecture "National and International in der orientalischen Musik," in which he proposes to demonstrate that "the question about the essence of Jewish music, like that of any other music, cannot be answered so long as one seeks to isolate a music from its environment" (Die Frage nach dem Wesen der jüdischen Musik, wie irgendeiner anderen, kann nicht beantwortet werden, solange man sie aus ihrer Umwelt herauszulösen versucht). Attempts to isolate specifically Jewish traits in the work of European Jewish composers, he argued, were particularly futile, because of the long history of interaction between Jews and non-Jews in Europe. He concluded:

> Deshalb ist es so schwer, bei europäischen Komponisten jüdischer Abstammung, bei Mendelssohn, Meyerbeer, Offenbach, Mahler, Schönberg, den gemeinsamen jüdischen Nenner aufzuzeigen. Die meisten, die es versuchen, bewegen sich dabei in einem Circulus vitiosus: aus der biographischen Kenntnis heraus, daß es sich um Juden handelt, nehmen sie die Züge, die einen dieser Komponisten von seinen Zeitgenossen unterscheidet als jüdisch an; sie vergessen aber, daß der Unterschied zwischen dieser Zeitgenossen untereinander oft ebenso groß oder größer ist als der Unterschied eines jeden von ihnen zu dem jüdischen Komponisten (Lachmann, 1936c).
>
> [This is what makes it so difficult to look for a common Jewish denominator among European composers of Jewish origin, in Mendelssohn, Meyerbeer, Offenbach, Mahler, Schoenberg. Most of those who try to do so move in a *circulus vitiosus*: from the biographical knowledge that the composer was a Jew, they assume to be Jewish the traits that distinguish one of these composers from his contemporaries; yet they forget that the difference between these contemporaries were often just as large or larger than the difference between any one of them and the Jewish composer.]

Lachmann might have extended his argument to include much of the Jewish sacred music composed in the wake of reforms in synagogue worship in the nineteenth century, which looked to church music for models. Idelsohn devotes substantial sections of *Jewish Music* to an analysis of the musical reforms in Central and Western Europe and in North America (Idelsohn [1929] 1992, 232–95 and 316–36, respecitively); see also Frühauf 2013 for a critical study of the interaction of "Jewish" and "non-Jewish" traditions in nineteenth- and early twentieth-century German-Jewish organ music.

We do very little towards characterising a melody by taking down its main steps and time-values in staff-notation from direct hearing. We may try this method, e.g., on an Arab song and then have the written tune sung by a European. Let us suppose that his rendering of our notation will be scrupulously correct; still, it will sound hopelessly wrong as compared to the Arab's own rendering.

The unmistakeable genuine colour of a tune is[3] due to subtler elements of it than to the mere sequence of notes. A foreign tune may, e.g., be in common time and its rhythm, therefore, may sound quite familiar to us; but the stresses, in the original rendering, will be distributed in a way slightly different from our own, or there may be an almost imperceptible difference in the relative length of the four time-units as against that to which we are used. In the same way, the tune may proceed in musical intervals roughly identical with those of our own tunes; but the transition from one note to another may be slightly smoother than with us, or the contrary; or the final note of a phrase may be broken off abruptly instead of dying away, or the reverse. These and other delicate shades in the delivery of a tune make all the difference in its effect. They are not the result either of training or of aesthetic judgment. They proceed from unconscious physiological impulses and cannot, therefore, be imitated. These traits, then, and not the bare facts which we can ascertain about the scale and the melodic outline of a tune are characteristic of the deepest elements at work in music.[4]

These general remarks are intended to direct your attention towards the difference between the following examples chosen from the Eastern group of Arab urban music.

They are all based on the same musical system. This system of melody types or maqāmāt can be traced back as far as the 10th century. From the outset, it contained both Arab and Persian elements as borne out by the names of the melody types, the Ḥiǧāzī mode figuring side by side with the 'Irāqī and Isfahan modes. The theorists were of various origin; al-Fārābī, e.g., the most eminent among them, was a Turcoman by birth.[5]

The present musical system, therefore, cannot be claimed as the exclusive property of any one of the nations concerned; they have all contributed towards it. But this does not apply to the music itself. Egyptian music, during the last century, and especially instrumental music, has been largely influenced by Turkish. But besides this, traditional Arab forms of song have maintained themselves. The following example is representative of one of these forms, the Tauśīḥ.[6] The musical mode of the song is Sika, with the note mi as its tonic; its rhythmical pattern, al-Nawaht, consists of seven time-units.[7] The singer, Sheikh Said as-Safti, was held in high esteem as a conservative interpreter of this style.[8] (Record 11.1, CD 2, tracks 7–8)

The next item is an example of the Turkish urban style of instrumental music. It is played on the ṭanbur, a long-necked lute which, like the short-necked 'Ūd,[9] goes back to the Middle Ages and even, under its correct name of pandura, to antiquity.[10] The ṭanbur is specially favoured

---

3. Lachmann's script: *id.*

4. In comparing the Jewish music of Djerba with that of the Tunisian Arab environment, Lachmann distinguishes between musical traits that may be "learned" (international) and those that are "inherited" (national); see Lachmann 1940, 85–86; and Lachmann 1978, 199–200. He observes that

> characteristics are all the lighter to transmit, the more technical and material they are in nature and therefore the more easily learned: to this category belong primarily the melodic and rhythmic principles of division, also scales and time-forms, and to a certain extent, the melodic and rhythmic material. . . . Hereditary qualities introduce us into more deep-lying strata of musical expression. They are expressed less in the musical material as such than in what is made of it. . . . The individuality of the interpretation has as yet baffled analysis; we are reduced here to relying on impressions (Lachmann 1940, 85–86).

Thus in his lecture "National und International in der orientalischen Musik" of 12 February 1936, Lachmann differentiates between recordings of an Arab song from Tunis and a Jewish song from Djerba in the same *maqām*, according to nuances of interpretation:

> Vielleicht ist es auch gar nicht die Melodiebildung, die den verschiedenen Eindruck ausmacht. Mir selbst scheint, wenn nicht *der*, so doch *ein* wesentlicher Unterschied in der *Verschiedenheit des Vortrags* zu bestehen. Ein solches Moment ist aber schwer greifbar, schwer in Worten auszudrücken. Mir klingt das jüdische Melodiesingen intensiver, eindringlicher, das arabische unbekümmerter, monologhafter. Aber das ist ein persönlicher Eindruck, der keinen Anspruch auf Allgemeingültigkeit erheben will (Lachmann 1936c).
>
> [Perhaps it is not the melodic formation at all that is behind the difference in impression. My own view is that, if not the, then at least one, essential difference is in the difference in performance. Such a moment, however, is difficult to grasp, difficult to express in words. To my ear the Jewish melodic singing is more intensive, more urgent, the Arab more carefree, more monologue-like. But that is a personal impression with no claim to general applicability.]

5. The early tenth-century Islamic philosopher and theorist al-Fārābī was born in the Farab district of Turkestan and died in Syria around 950. His *Kitāb al-mūsīqī al-kabīr* (Great Book on Music) is the earliest extant work to give detailed descriptions of the various tetrachordal types, which he defines as the basic melodic units and shows as frets on the fingerboard of the *'ūd*.

6. The Arabic term *tawshīḥ* has different meanings in different musical contexts. Here it denotes a rhythmical song in the poetic form of *muwashshaḥ*, a type of strophic poetry in literary Arabic that originated in Andalusia.

7. *Sīkā* is the third degree of the Arab scale, conventionally notated as E𝄳; see program 10, footnote 3. For a contemporary representation of *maqām sīkā*, see d'Erlanger 1930–59, 5:306–7 (where *sīkā* is spelled *sahgāh*); for a contemporary representation of the rhythm *nawāḥt*, see d'Erlanger 1930–59, 6:58.

8. The famous Egyptian singer Shaykh Sayyid al-Ṣafṭī (1875–1939) recorded prolifically for various labels, including Gramophone, Odeon, Polyphon, Baida (subsequently renamed Baidaphon), and Favorite (Racy 1976, 30, 36, 41, and 45). An extract from Lachmann's transcription of al-Ṣafṭī performing the same song is given below for record 11.1.

9. Lachmann's script: *Ūd* (lacking 'ayn).

10. The Greco-Roman lute known as the *pandura* (*pandoura*) appeared after Alexander's conquest of Persia, toward the end of the fourth century BCE (McKinnon 2001). Much earlier

by the Turks, but hardly ever used by Arabs. The melody is played on the highest string only; the other strings are used for occasional chords.

I believe that Turkish music, in comparison with Arab, tends towards smoothness, delicacy of tone, and the display of emotion. It has a preference for quick triplets and for expressive pauses stressed by chords. Both these traits are unusual in, or absent from, the Arab style which might be described as restrained, but, at the same time, as highly strung.

The piece belongs to the melody type Shet arabau; its form is known as Saz Samai.[11] The performer is Djemil Bey who, in his time, was the best ṭanbur player in Turkey.[12] (Record 11.2, CD 2, tracks 9–10)

The Persians have largely contributed to the urban music of the Near East as regards both theory and practice. Among the musicians at the splendid courts of the early Arab dynasties, many singers and players of rank were of Persian origin, above all Ishaq al-Mausili, the famous court musician of the Abbasid Khalifs, Harun ar-Rashīd, Al-Ma'mūn, and their successors.[13]

Present day Persian music has scarcely been investigated as yet.[14] The following item, a typical example of its style, may serve to show that it would be worth while being studied. It is characterised by curious fluctuations of the voice and by an equally curious instrumental drone and its impassioned delivery produces an unfailing effect on Oriental listeners. (Record 11.3)

It is doubtful whether a specimen of Indian music may be legitimately included in this group.[15] Indian music, certainly, is a unity clearly distinguishable from the music of the Near East. It has scales and rhythmic patterns of its own. Its melodies seem to come from a far distance, an impression which is enhanced by the unsubstantial sound of sympathetic strings attached to Indian viols and zithers.

Figure 11.1. "Rāga Malkaus." Fyzee-Rahamin 1925, 68, reproduced in Lachmann 1929, 134.

examples of long-necked lutes are depicted in seals and reliefs found in Iraq from the Akkadian period (third millennium BCE) and in Egypt during the New Kingdom (second millennium BCE; Hassan 2002, 409).

11. The *saz semai* (also *saz semaisi*) is a composed instrumental form with four sections (*hāne*), each of which is followed by a refrain. Each section presents a different range or modulates to a new *makam*, returning to the "home" *makam* in the refrain. The *saz semai* is distinguished from the related instrumental genre *peşrev* by its use of *semai* rhythmic patterns—typically a ten-beat cycle and a faster six-beat cycle (Reinhard 2002, 773; Signell [1973] 1986).

12. Tanburî Cemil Bey (ca. 1871–1916) was a composer, theorist, and virtuoso soloist on several different instruments, including *tanbur, yayli tanbur* (bowed tanbur), *kemençe* (bowed lute), *lauta* (lute), cello, and clarinet. His innovative style, which combined classical, folk, and Western elements, reflected the cosmopolitan mix of modernizing and westernizing trends in Turkish culture at the end of the Ottoman empire. Between 1910 and 1914 Cemil Bey made 180 recordings on several different labels (including Blumentahl, Orfeon, and Regent), a selection of which—including record 11.2—have been reproduced by Traditional Crossroads (Tanburî Cemil Bey 1994–95). See Hagopian and Aksoy 1995; and O'Connell 2002, 757–58.

13. Hormoz Farhat provides a list of eminent musicians and music scholars of Persian origin with Muslim-Arab names who wrote in Arabic (Farhat 1990, 4–5). Isḥaq al-Mawṣilī (d. 850) was a court musician and companion (*nadīm*) to the Abbasid caliph Hārūn al-Rashīd (786–809) and subsequently to five successive caliphs up to and including al-Mutawakkil (847–61).

14. Lachmann seems unaware of the efforts of the modernizing scholar, teacher, composer and theorist 'Alī Naqī Vazīrī (1886–1981). Trained in the Persian classical tradition, Vazīrī spent five years in Europe studying at the École supérieure de musique in Paris (1918–21) and the Hochschule für Musik in Berlin (1921–23). On his return to Teheran he founded the Madrasa-ye 'āli-e musiqi (Superior School of Music)—the first music school in Iran—where he established a curriculum that combined Western and Persian classical music. In the introduction to his *Dastor-e Tār* (1922), a primer for learning to play the *tār* (Persian long-necked lute with three double courses of strings), Vazīrī was the first to apply the theory of the twenty-four-quarter-tone scale to Persian music. He elaborates on this theory in *Musiqi-e nazari* (1934) where he also provides an account of the twelve *dastgāhs*, the distinctive modal system of Persian music.

15. On Lachmann's inclusion of Indian music as a class of Arab music, see footnote 1 above and program 9, footnote 2.

On the other hand, Indian music is connected with that of the Near East by a number of common features. It has taken over from it some instruments with their Persian names and at least one musical form, the Ghazal.[16] But above all it is divided into melody types like Arab urban music. One might say against this that the grouping of melodies into melody types can be traced back, in Indian music, to times prior to the rise of Islām. But the present Indian system of melody-types or rāgas is very probably due to Muhammedan influence in the 12th and 13th centuries. Arab urban music, in its Persian variety, would thus have influenced Indian music with regard to its system and other external features without, however, affecting its melodic substance or its peculiar mode of expression.

The present specimen of North Indian song is in the Rāga Malkus[17] which is supposed to express love and laughter, and to belong to the hours from midnight to the early morning,—exactly in the same way as Arab musicians claim a certain emotional character and a special hour of the day for each of their melody types or maqāmāt.[18] (Record 11.4; see figure 11.1)

---

16. Examples of instruments common to Eastern Arab and Indian musical traditions include the sitar, a much enlarged and adapted derivative of the Persian *setār* (*se-tār,* lit. "three strings")—a small, pear-shaped lute with a long thin neck and four strings (the fourth was added in the early twentieth century); the *shahnāī,* a shawm-like reed instrument derived from the Persian *sornā* (Uzbek, Tajik, and Kyrgyz, *surnāy, sornā*); and the *tabla,* or drum pair, derived from the Persian-Arab *tabl.* The *ghazal* is the form of Persian lyrical poetry on which performances of Persian art music (*dastgāh*) are based. It was introduced to India by the Mughals, where it developed into a form of Urdu poetry with sensual and erotic content in the tradition of Sufi mysticism. This type of *ghazal* flourished from the eighteenth through the early twentieth centuries in the courts of Delhi, Lucknow, and Rampur, where it was performed by courtesans who danced as well as sang. With the advent of sound film in the 1930s, a new popular form of *ghazal* emerged that was widely disseminated on mass media.

17. Also written as *malkaus* (Fyzee-Rahamin 1925; see figure 11.1), *malkauns,* and *malkaush.*

18. See program 9 on the cosmological associations of the Arab *maqāmāt.*

Record 11.1: Egyptian song: "Qad ḥarrakat aydī n-nasīmi" (Shaykh Sayyid al-Ṣafṭī; Odeon O-5168b)

Recording number: F65, Odeon O-5168b; reissued on Hornbostel 1931, no. 20[1]

Performer: Shaykh Sayyid al-Ṣafṭī

Note: Lachmann includes a transcription of a recording of the same song performed by al-Ṣafṭī for the Odeon label, but with a different catalogue number (Odeon 47099), in *Musik des Orients* (1929, 121–23), where it is designated "Kunstlied" (art song). In this transcription, the opening of which is reproduced in figure 11.2, *maqām sīkā* has been transposed from its regular final E♮ to a final of B (Lachmann uses only unaltered sharp and flat accidentals in his transcriptions). In all other respects, the transcription essentially corresponds to the performance on record 11.1, from the beginning of the second strophe (the instrumental introduction, first strophe, and instrumental interlude are omitted). The vocal line is given without text, and the *qānūn* ("Zither") and *'ūd* ("Laute") are notated separately on one staff. The metered sections are divided into measures of $\frac{4}{4}$, $\frac{6}{4}$, and $\frac{8}{4}$ by dotted *Mensurstriche* and without time signatures. In a footnote in his Djerba monograph, however, Lachmann takes the opportunity to correct these divisions, claiming that he made the transcription "without knowledge of the authentic drum-figure . . . the rhythm of the composition is called al-faḥtī and extends over seven half-notes" (Lachmann 1940, 63 n. 42; see also Lachmann 1978, 206, n. 43). Both *al-faḥtī* and *nawāḥt* (the rhythm given in program 11) have a seven-beat cycle; for *nawāḥt*, see d'Erlanger 1930–59, 6:58. D'Erlanger gives no examples of *al-faḥtī*.

قد حركت أيدي النسيم
تلك الغصون الميس
فانهض وبادر يا نديمي
إلى رياض السندس

(Arabic text from Lajnah al-Mūsīqīyah [1959?], vol. 4, unpaginated)

qad ḥarrakat aydī n-nasīmi
tilka l-ghuṣūni l-mayyisi
fanhaḍ wa bādir yā nadīmī
il riyāḍi s-sundusī

Transliteration by Ali Jihad Racy

The hands of the breeze set
those swaying branches into motion.
Oh! My boon companion, go forth
to the silk-like gardens.

Translated by Ali Jihad Racy and Yousef Meri

Record 11.2: "Shet araban saz semaisi" (Tanburî Cemil Bey, Orfeon 10524)

Recording number: F66, Orfeon 10524

Performer: Tanburî Cemil Bey (*tanbur*)

Record 11.3: Persian popular song (Odeon O-5168a)

Recording number: F65, Odeon O-5168a, reissued on Hornbostel 1931, no. 19.

Performer: unidentified male singer accompanied by violin and "lute" (*Laute*)[2]

Note: Designated "Volkstümlicher Gesang" in Hornbostel 1931, no. 19.

Record 11.4: Hindustani song in rāga malkus *(Odeon 95113)*

Recording number: F138, Odeon 95113

Performer: Gulzar Begum, from Lahore[3]

Figure 11.2. Opening of Lachmann's transcription of *tawshīḥ* in *maqām sīkā* as performed by Shaykh Sayyid Al-Ṣafṭī' on Odeon 47099. Lachmann 1929, 121.

Notes

1. In the catalogue of Lachmann's commercial recordings, F65 is identified as a double-sided disc containing nos. 19 (F65a) and 20 (F65b) of Hornbostel 1931; a note states that "Lachmann made a zinc copy from this record." In 1934 Hornbostel's compilation was released on twelve double-sided 78-rpm records by the British Parlophone label under the title *Music of the Orient*, with Hornbostel's accompanying notes in English. The Parlophone compilation was subsequently released in the USA on the Decca label, first as 78-rpm discs and, in 1951, as a two-record LP set (Decca DX-107). In 1979 the Parlophone compilation was released as a double LP on Folkways (FE 4157) and reissued by Smithsonian Folkways (FW 04157 and FW 04157-CCD). See the entry for Erich von Hornbostel on the *Recording Pioneers* website (http://www.recordingpioneers.com/RP_HORNBOSTEL1.html).

2. Information taken from Hornbostel 1931, no. 19.

3. Information taken from Lachmann's "F" recording catalogue (see "Dating and Cataloguing of Lachmann's Recordings" in "About the Edition").

Program 12

Men's Songs for an Arab Village Wedding in Central Palestine
28 April 1937

After some excursions to other countries of the Near East, I am now coming back once more to song and music as practised in Palestine. On former occasions, you heard the traditional songs performed at Yemenite Jewish weddings. This time, a number of songs from an Arab peasant wedding will be recited. I would lay particular stress on the fact that it is not the purpose of the recital to present to you extraordinary feats of professional skill on the part of musicians and singers, but rather to give you an idea of what is ordinarily heard at a village wedding in central Palestine. The vocal parts will be performed by Mḥammed Abu Msellem and others* and the flute will be played by Aḥmed Smīr.[†][1]

In order to appreciate the songs and dance tunes of an Arab villagers' wedding it is necessary to know the circumstances surrounding them. A wedding, with them as with rural populations all over the world, consists of a long chain of events and ceremonies each of which has its fixed place and time. It is a public feast; the whole village and even the neighbouring villages share in the rejoicings of the families concerned.[2]

The musical programme of the wedding consists both of men's and women's songs; but at the present recital we must content ourselves with the men's part. The first section of it takes place on an evening after the marriage has been definitely agreed upon and after the bridegroom's family have bought new clothes for the marriage. This part of the musical programme precedes the marriage by one day or a number of days and, in the latter case, is repeated every night until the marriage.

At dusk the bridegroom lights a wood fire on an open space, mostly in front of the guesthouse, and different groups of villagers successively assemble for dance and song. The first who come are boys about 8 to 15 years of age. Their singing is a sign for a second group to appear; these are young men up to the age of 25. Lastly, after the evening prayer, they are joined by older men and notables.

The performers of the dance range themselves in one line in front of the fire or in two lines with the fire between them, everybody keeping tightly to his neighbours. The closeness of the line is a particularly striking feature in Arab dances of this kind; both peasants and Bedouins, on these occasions, although they have a wide space at their disposal, behave as if not an inch could be spared to right or left. While dancing and singing they stretch their arms forward and clap their hands; hence, this form of song is called saḥgā which means clapping.[3]

---

* Mḥammed 'Abd ar-Raḥūn Abu Msellem, of the Beni Murra tribe, from Ain Yabrūd, Ramallah district; 'Abd al-Fattaḥ as-Sahāda, of the Beni Mālik tribe, from Qaṭanna near Jerusalem, &c.

† From Qaṭanna.

1. The notes identifying the musicians are given as they appear in Lachmann's typescript. He recorded the same program with the same musicians a week earlier on 21 April 1937. The lead singer is variously designated in the catalogue taken from Lachmann's recording diaries as "Mhd. 'abderrahim AbuMullem" (9 April), "Mhd. 'Abd er-rahmim" (21 April), and "Mhd. Abd er-rahim" (28 April).

2. Ḍirghām Ḥ. Sbait describes a comparable sequence of songs in his account of the musical program of traditional Palestinian weddings, both Muslim and Christian, around Haifa and in the Galilee, based on his field research in the 1970s (Sbait 2002; selected examples are given on the audio CD included with Danielson, Marcus, and Reynolds 2002). In November 1994 the Palestine Popular Art Centre (PAC) in Ramallah, West Bank, launched the Palestinian Traditional Music and Song Archive project to document performances in the field. The resultant recordings, photographs, and film footage collected in the West Bank are held in the audiovisual library of the PAC. A selection of recordings, including wedding songs, is featured on Shammout and Boss 1997; for detailed notes on the recordings, see Boulos 2002. The PAC is home to the leading Palestinian dance troupe El-Funoun (founded 1979), one of many such troupes specializing in modern staged versions of Palestinian folk songs and dances. El-Funoun has recorded a contemporary interpretation of a traditional Palestinian wedding based on arrangements of Palestinian folk tunes accompanied by an ensemble of traditional Arab musical instruments (El-Funoun 1999).

3. According to Sbait, the line of men who dance and sing in chorus is called *ṣaff saḥjih*. Sbait also describes various types of *ṣaff saḥjih* improvised songs led by a pair of professional poet-singers (Sbait 2002, 583; and track 17 on the audio CD included with Danielson, Marcus, and Reynolds 2002).

The dance consists of stamping on the ground with a certain kind of rhythmical steps. The two rows of performers alternately advance towards, and retreat from, the fire. But the way in which the dance is performed is variable in character and pace. The young men violently rush forward and backward; they work themselves up into a passion and it sometimes occurs that instead of retreating they stop at the fire with their knees bent and challenge those opposite by throwing their headgear at their feet, similarly as medieval knights threw down their gauntlet. This impetuous form of the dance, with corresponding words, takes its name from the word ḥamāsa which means bravery and a warlike spirit. You will hear a song in a similar style later on.

The dance in which the older men partake has a moderate character; the dancers move on the spot and the song is slower. Here is an example of it. (Recitation 12.1)

After the various stages of this dance, refreshments as coffee, milk, tea, or cinnamon (qirfa)[4] are served. Then, all the performers, old and young, form one row, everybody, again, keeping close to his neighbours. A singer walks along the row and sings verses every one[5] of which is answered by them with a burden, as, e.g., yā ḥalālī yā mālī or yā halābak yā halābu.[6] This song is immediately followed by what is called a daḥḥiyya consisting of almost breathless repetition of this word. Then[7] the performance breaks off. (Recitation 12.2)

The women, all through the evening, attend from a distance, from time to time spurring the dancers and singers with their well-known penetrating trills.[8]

On the marriage day, there are, again, various occasions for dancing and singing. About the middle of the day, the bridegroom takes a bath and then dresses in his wedding clothes. This ceremony is preceded, accompanied, and followed by various songs. When he reappears in his new dress the women besprinkle him with salt, barley, and perfume to protect him from the evil eye and sing in order to bless his bath. The young men, before and after the bath, recite songs belonging to a kind called zaffa; these, too, like the young men's songs in front of the fire at night, have an impetuous character.[9] (Recitation 12.3, CD 2, tracks 11–12)

The bridegroom then rides or walks to a place outside the village and the young men follow him in procession. He rests in the shade, under a tree, and watches horsemen performing games, and riflemen aiming at a target, in his honour. At this time, the programme of music and dancing reaches another climax by the performance of a debka.[10]

The word debka refers to treading and stamping, various kinds of accentuated steps being a main feature of the dance. It is not performed in rows, but in a circle, one man behind another, and a piper and a singer in the middle. The instrument may be a śubbāba,[11] a reed flute with six holes in front and one at the back and without a mouthpiece, or a double-clarinet, in Arabic miǧwiz (but Palestinian peasants also call it a nayya), or an arghūl, a kind of clarinet with a long drone pipe attached alongside of it.[12] In the present example, it will be a śubbāba or reed-flute. Various songs may be sung on this occasion, such as ala del'ūna, yā hwēdalī or others. (Recitation 12.4, CD 2, tracks 13–14)

An hour or half an hour before sunset, the bridegroom is conducted back to the village, either to the guesthouse or to the house of a villager who acts as his host on that day. In the meantime, the women of his family, above all,

4. Arabic, lit. "cinnamon," also "cinnamon tea."

5. Lachmann's script: *everyone* (without space).

6. "Yā ḥalālī yā mālī" (O rightfully mine, O my wealth); "yā halābak yā halābu" (O welcome to you, O welcome to him). The *daḥḥiyya*, or *dabkat al-daḥḥiyya*, typically involves a line of men, simultaneously clapping and swaying from side to side in a wave-like motion, while repeating the word *daḥḥiyya* or *diḥḥiyya*.

7. Lachmann's script: *The*.

8. Arabic, *zaghārīd*, sing. *zaghrūda*; see recitation 12.5.

9. Sbait describes a type of song called *zaffih* sung at the groom's shaving ceremony (*zaffit il-'aris*, "the shaving of the groom"). Usually the singing at this ceremony is led either by the groom's mother or by a professional female singer (Sbait 2002, 589; and track 18 on the audio CD included with Danielson, Marcus, and Reynolds 2002).

10. The *dabke* (*debka*) is a popular communal folk dance of the Arab Levant, danced to a sequence of different melodies based on contrasting rhythmic cycles of strong and weak beats. The dancers mark the beats by "treading and stamping" (see below). The *'ala dal'ūnā dabke* is a very common type of *dabke* song in which each musical phrase, corresponding to a line of verse, is set to the twelve-beat rhythmic cycle *dum taka taka dum dum taka taka dum dum* [rest] *tak* [rest], where *dum* represents a strong beat and *taka* or *tak* represents a weak beat. In recitation 12.4, the *'ala dal'ūnā* cycle is shown for the opening phrase. In *dabke* songs, the name of the song type signals the end rhyme of each four-line stanza. Thus, in the *'ala dal'ūnā dabke*, the typical rhyme scheme may be represented *aaax*, *bbbx*, *cccx*, etc., where *x* rhymes with the last two syllables of *'ala dal'ūnā* (see text of recitation 12.4). For further examples of the *'ala dal'ūnā dabke* in performance, see track 16 on the audio CD included with Danielson, Marcus, and Reynolds 2002 (traditional interpretation); and El-Funoun 1999, track 8 (modern interpretation). Since the emergence of the modern, staged *dabke* (see note 2 above), the term has come to stand for Palestinian and other Levantine folk dance and song generally and is often associated with nationalism and resistance movements; see, for example, Ladkani 2001; McDonald 2009, 65–72; Davis 2013 (for Palestine); and Silverstein 2012a and 2012b (for Syria).

11. Lachmann's script: *śubbba* (with macron above third *b*).

12. In her study of the Palestinian *dabke*, Jennifer Lee Ladkani gives detailed descriptions of these and other instruments, both traditional and modern, associated with the *dabke* (Ladkani 2001, 80–94; see also Hassan 2002, 413–14). In his cross-cultural study of the *mijwiz*, Racy describes this instrument as a "double reedpipe" or "specifically, the single-reed double-pipe, sometimes called 'double-clarinet' . . . consisting of two pipes played simultaneously by the same person with each pipe fitted with a single-reed apparatus" (Racy 1994, 38). Racy also mentions "drone-and-chanter types of double-pipes, such as the Palestinian *yarghul* and the Egyptian *arghul*" and "the *minjayra* or *shabbāba*, an open-ended reed or metal flute also associated with shepherds and typically used for accompanying dance" (Racy 1994, 39). The *shabbāba* is featured in recitation 12.4.

his mother have fetched the bride to his house. The bride, on the eve of the marriage day, has undergone the henna ceremony, i.e., the application of henna to her hands and feet, in her parents' house. She is now placed in the bridal room, in the company of her mother-in-law and of other women and girls who entertain her with dancing and singing.

At nightfall, the bridegroom comes to meet her. On his way to the house he is accompanied by his friends; they stop in front of the door, and announce his arrival by a short song called hāma. After this, they fire a shot and the women inside answer with a trill of joy. (Recitation 12.5, CD 2, tracks 15–16)

With this, the men's part in the musical programme of the wedding is ended. They retire and the bridegroom enters. He sits down next to the bride. Refreshments and sweets are served and the newly married must drink from one glass. Dances and songs continue for some time, usually two or three hours; then the women successively leave the room.

This is only a rough sketch of the musical items of a peasant wedding in Palestine. It must be remembered that the programme is subject to certain variations according to the different regions of the country. There exists, e.g., a kind of dialogue in which two singers enter upon a dispute in improvised stanzas; but this form of song, as far as I know, is special to Galilee.[13]

[Epilogue]

I am now at the end of my series of talks.[14] In conclusion, I may rightly be expected to sum up its main results. The immediate purpose of the series was to let you hear as many and as various specimens of unadulterated Oriental music as possible and to try and show you ways towards understanding them and towards understanding, through them, Oriental music generally.

You have been hearing specimens of very different kinds of music: religious and secular, urban and rural, vocal and instrumental, male and female songs, lyrical recitation and choral entertainment songs. It has been one of my chief endeavours to show that these kinds differing in their social functions also have musical systems and forms of their own. Remember, e.g., the difference between religious cantillation, male songs, and female songs in Oriental Jewish communities and the difference between the urban and the rural style in Arab music. The melodic steps in sacred cantillation are fundamentally different from the scales used on a viol in accompaniment of epic or lyric recitation, and both of them from the scales of urban music.

Another distinction had to be made with regard to national and racial styles in music. Urban music in the Near East differs owing to its Berber element in North Africa and to the predominance of Arab, Turkish, and Persian elements respectively, in the Eastern group. But this division is not superior to the division according to the social functions of music. Religious cantillation, e.g., as performed in one nation, may have more features in common with that of another nation than it has with other groups of music belonging to the same nation.[15]

These principles of division, the national style and the social function of music, have both to be considered in determining the precise character of a song or a piece of music. Nor must we forget that they do not present themselves as clearly separate; historical developments have blended them in various ways. In urban music and in liturgical cantillation, international relations are more active, and national characteristics, therefore, less obvious, than in rural music. Further, urban music, again and again, has influenced liturgical cantillation and the music of more primitive classes of society. This is specially interesting as permitting us to recognize different historical strata[16] in cantillation and in rural forms of song.

The immense variety of Oriental music resulting from its various racial, social, and historical conditions has been illustrated, in these talks, almost exclusively by singers and musicians belonging to communities in this country. This is all the more worth remarking since it has not been possible to include specimens of all the kinds extant. Unfortunately, there are influences at work towards destroying this diversity and towards Europeanizing Oriental music. European influence should not be considered as similar to those processes which, as I mentioned, have brought about changes in Eastern music in the past. It is not stimulating like them, but destructive. Nor can this influence be welcomed, as some are inclined to think, as part of modern technical progress. A motor tourist will certainly be delighted at finding, even in remote corners of the East, standardized[17] parts to fit his damaged car. But there is no reason to delight in hearing, in the same remote corners, dance tunes of fashionable European bars echoed by a gramophone or played on a shepherd's flute. The only effect of modern standardization on music is to deprive it of its characteristic power of expression and to turn it into a tedious noise. This process may be inevitable; still, we should, instead of promoting it, try to counteract it by encouraging genuine local music. Its practice is, as the illustrations of this talk may have shown, still fully alive in this country. To further it, means, at the same time, to further the development of more ambitious kinds which, throughout history, have relied on folk-music as their true and natural basis.[18]

---

13. See Sbait 2002, 584 for a brief introduction to this tradition of improvised poetic dueling; and Sbait 1993 for a more substantial study.

14. In Lachmann's typescript this section is separated from the main part of program 12 by a line drawn across the page.

15. For a summary of the ideas presented here, see "*Oriental Music*" in the introduction.

16. Lachmann's script: *atrata.*

17. Lachmann's script: *standardised.*

18. Comparative musicologists and composers of national music alike placed a special value on folk music as a repository of melodic archetypes; hence the insistence of the recording committee on including rural traditions among the recordings made at the 1932 Cairo Congress (Racy 1993, 73; see also pro-

gram 9, footnote 1). In Mandatory Palestine and Israel, the ten volumes of "Hebrew-Oriental" melodies collected by Abraham Z. Idelsohn (1914–32), which he himself characterized as "folk song" (Idelsohn [1929] 1992, 27), provided a repository of melodic archetypes for Jewish immigrant composers: Philip V. Bohlman, interviewing Israeli composers in the early 1980s, discovered that each of them, in seeking to compose "Israeli" music, had turned to Idelsohn's *Thesaurus of Hebrew Oriental Melodies* as their common source (Bohlman 2008, 7).

Recitation 12.1: Slow saḫgā

Recording number: D693

Performers: Mḥammed Abd ar-Raḥūn Abu Msellem and group

Note: Designated "Ruhige saḫgā" in Lachmann's recording diaries.

Recitation 12.2: Tasgia *(followed by* daḫḫiyya*)*

Recording numbers: D694 (beginning of *tasgia*), D695 (end of *tasgia, daḫḫiyya*)

Performers: Same as recitation 12.1.

Recitation 12.3: Zaffa hamasiyya

Recording number: D696

Performers: Same as recitation 12.1.

yā ʻayni ṣ-ṣalā ʻa-n-nabī
wi-l-wārid-*i* fattaḥ-*a* li-n-nabī

kurmāl i-Maḥammad uw ʻAlī
ij-*i*-nayneh w'-ḥamleh sarrīs
wi-ṣ-ṣābir-*i* b'Allāh-*a* yā ʻarīs

ij-*i*-nayneh w'-ḥamleh rummān
wi-ṣ-ṣābir-*i* b'Allāh-*a* yā ʻizbān

wi-nikhkh yā jamalnā
uw yā bū kaff imḥannā

ʻalaynā bi-radd al-khayl
fī ṭaʻn il-qanā wi-syūf

wi-llī mā yiṣaddiqnā
yiṭlaʻ ʻa'l-khalā wi-yshūf

ʻalaynā bi-radd al-khayl . . .
Transcribed by Makram Khoury-Machool

O magnificent prayers for the Prophet,
roses bloomed for the Prophet.

For the sake of Muhammad and Ali,
a garden bears saris.
O groom, be patient, for God's sake.

A garden bears pomegranates.
O bachelors, be patient, for God's sake.

Kneel, our camel,
you with the henna-tinted palm.

Our duty is to stop the horses
with spears and swords.

And he who does not believe us
can come out into the open and see.

Our duty is to stop the horses . . .
Translated by Makram Khoury-Machool

Recitation 12.4: ʻAla dalʻūnā dabke

Recording number: D697

Performers: ʻAbd al-Fattaḥ es-Sahāda (voice) and Aḥmed Smīr (*shabbāba*)

Note: The *ʻala dalʻūnā* rhythmic cycle is shown in the music for the opening phrase (D = *dum*, T = *taka*, with *dum* representing a strong beat and *taka* a weak beat).

ṣā- rat ad- dab- keh w-in- zilt at- far- raj
w'-la- gā- nī khū- ya uw 'a- lay- yi ḥar- raj
3

w-ir- ji‘t al- magh- rib ‘a- dār ad- dar- raj
yā ‘ī- nī btib- kī gal- bī maḥ- zū- nā

w-
-Al- lāh yā būn w- 'hā- dhā māy- wā- tī w-
-ib- ti- thim bī- nā w-i- ḥi- nā ba- nā- tī

w’-ṣ- ḥāb al- ‘i- ris ’il- hin ‘ā- dā- tī *tī*
yi- ghan- nū li-sh- shābb wi- yid- bi- kū- nā

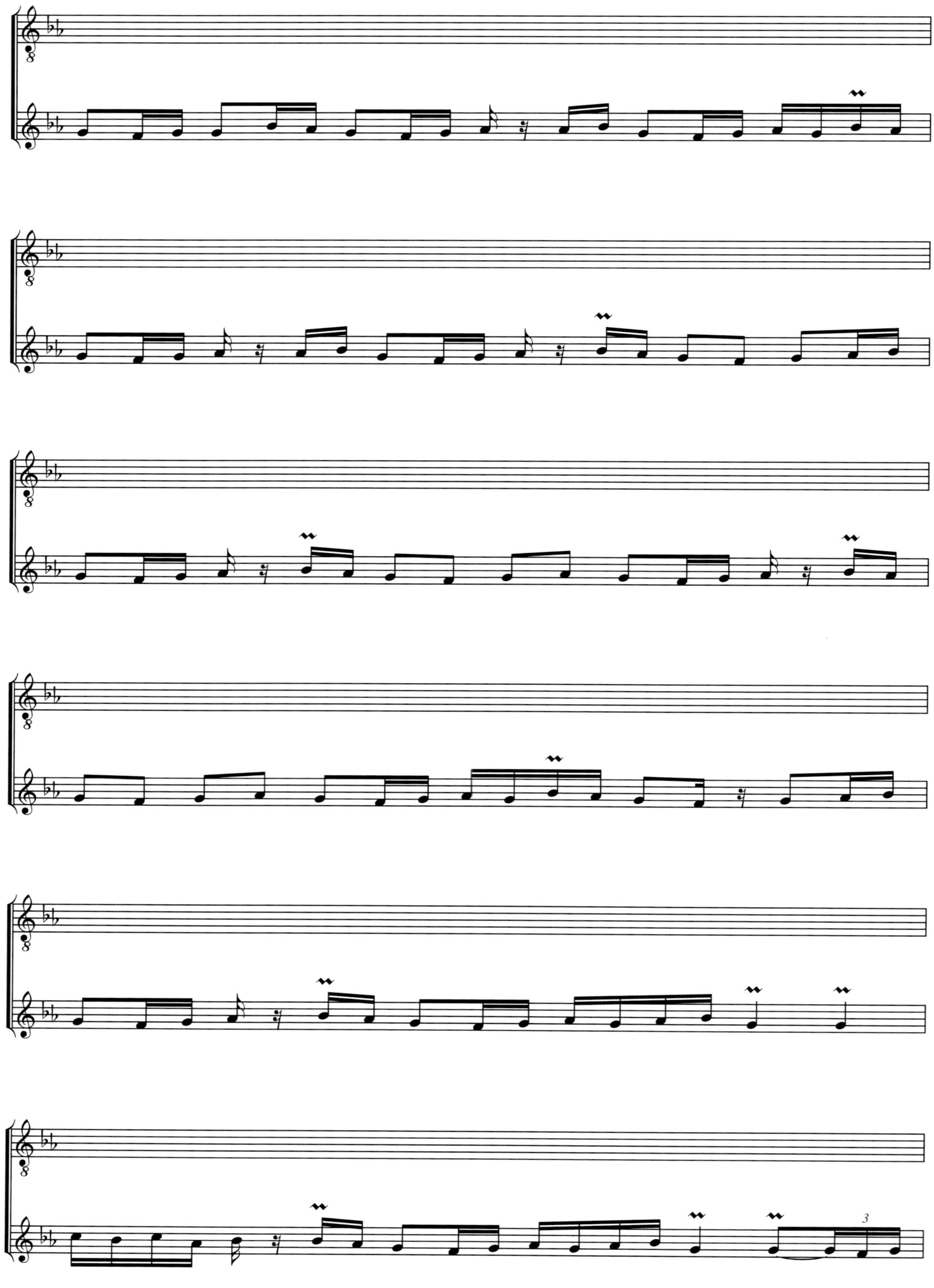

‘a- lā da- lā- lik ‘a- lā da- lā- lik w-
-in- ti li-’m- hay- ra w-a- na khay- yā- lik

law ṣir- ti ja- mal a- nā jam- mā- lik w'-
nu- khu- ṭur 'a Yā- fā ni- ḥa- am- mil lay- mū- nā

ṣārat ad-dabkeh w-inzilt atfarraj
w'-lagānī khūya uw 'alayyi ḥarraj

w-irji't al-maghrib 'a-dār addarraj
yā 'īnī btibkī galbī maḥzūnā

w-Allāh yā būn w'-hādhā māywātī
w-ibtithim bīnā w-iḥ-*i*-nā banātī

w'-ṣḥāb al-'iris 'ilhin 'ādātī *tī*
yighannū li-sh-shābb wi-yidbikūnā

'alā dalālik 'alā dalālik
w-inti li-'mhayra w-ana khayyālik

law ṣirti jamal anā jammālik
w'-nukh-*u*-ṭur 'a Yāfā niḥ-*a*-ammil laymūnā

Transcribed by Makram Khoury-Machool

They were dancing the *dabke* and I went down to look.
My brother met me and told me: never again!

I trudged home at dusk
with tears in my eyes and a broken heart.

By God, father, this is unacceptable,
you are accusing us because we are girls.

The wedding family has its own customs:
they sing, so the youngsters can dance the *dabke.*

Be coquettish, be coquettish,
for you are the filly and I am your knight.

If you be the camel, I'll be your rider,
and we'll go to Jaffa and carry citrus.

Translated by Makram Khoury-Machool

Recitation 12.5: " 'A l-hāma 'a l-hāma"

Recording number: D698

Performers: Same as recitation 12.1; *zaghrūda* (ululation) by Ahmed Smīr.

'a-l-hāma 'a-l-hāma
dakhal ẓarīf il-qām[a]

yā bū 'uyūn adh-dhablāna
mabrūka hā-l-'arūs
[*zaghrūda*]

[spoken]
mabrūk yā 'arīs!
Allāh yibārik fīkum!

Transcribed by Makram Khoury-Machool

What stature, what stature,
the man with the handsome physique has entered!

O you with the languid eyes,
we congratulate you on your bride!
[*zaghrūda*]

[spoken]
Congratulations, groom!
May God bless you, too!

Translated by Makram Khoury-Machool

Editor's Commentary

In his report of 21 June 1935, Lachmann describes his first recording session outside Jerusalem:

> Mr D. N. Barbour had the kindness of conveying ourselves and the recording machine to Artas, a village near the ponds of Solomon, in his motor-car. He introduced us to Madam Louise Baldensperger who occupies a singular position in the village, having spent a life-time among the natives, and enjoying their full confidence. Being herself a Student of Arab manners and customs she readily used her influence to make people play and sing for us at her house (quoted in Katz 2003, 114).[1]

The only daughter of Alsatian missionaries, Louise Baldensperger, known locally as "Sitt Louisa" (Miss Louisa), was in her early seventies at the time of Lachmann's visit. A collector of wild plants and a repository of local knowledge and lore, she is best remembered in scholarly circles for her various collaborations, most famously with the Swedish-Finnish ethnographer Hilma Granqvist.[2] A graduate of the University of Helsinki, Granqvist originally came to Jerusalem in 1925 to research "Women of the Old Testament."[3] Frustrated by the paucity of information available in the written sources in European libraries, she hoped that

> the chance of observing life and conditions in the Holy Land would throw a clearer light on the problems connected with them, give quite another conception of them and the possibility of absorbing oneself in and going deeply into the subject (Granqvist 1931, 1).

Granqvist began her research by joining an archeological course for theologians in Jerusalem.[4] It was while traveling around Palestine by car and on horseback visiting the various archeological sites that she realized her project required an altogether different approach:

> It was most valuable to have obtained an insight into the nature and life of the different parts of the country . . . but I required more than could possibly be seen and observed while travelling about. I needed to live among the people, hear them talk about themselves, make records while they spoke about their life, customs, and ways of looking at things. For that reason I decided to remain in Palestine after the close of the course, and as specially favorable conditions offered themselves in Artas, a Muhammadan Arabic village south of Bethlehem at the edge of the Judean desert, I decided to begin there the folkloric studies necessary for my work (Granqvist 1931, 2).

Nestling in a spring-fed valley in the Judean Hills, about twelve miles south of Jerusalem, Artas is laden with biblical associations: the young King David is said to have tended his flocks there, and cut into the rock face on the outskirts of the village are the three giant reservoirs known as Solomon's Pools. With its vineyards, orchards, and cultivated fields, Artas is also traditionally identified with the "enclosed garden" in the Song of Songs (4:12). Yet the "specially favorable conditions" that attracted Granqvist to Artas refer above all to the presence of Sitt Louisa, whose home she shared and whose "inestimable help and value" she would amply acknowledge in her writings (Granqvist 1931, 19).

Granqvist soon realized that, in order fully to understand the situation of the women, she would need to undertake a comprehensive study of the society as a whole. She explains her methodology in the introduction to the first volume of *Marriage Conditions in a Palestinian Village*, published in 1931. Drawing an analogy with archeological practice, which advocates systematic excavations of individual sites, Granqvist vigorously defended the need for in-depth, comprehensive research of individual societies to supplement the wide-ranging comparative studies that formed the backbone of nineteenth and early twentieth century ethnography.[5] Writing at a critical moment in social anthropology, when the evolutionary theory and comparative methods espoused by her teacher and compatriot, Edward Westermarck, were giving way to new theoretical approaches, particularly the functional anthropology of Bronislaw Malinowski, Granqvist provides a penetrating critique of contemporary ethnography, its problems, and its debates.[6] Emphasizing the need for concrete and, above all, reliable evidence as a basis for abstract theory, she criticized the superficial, biased, and decontextualized data on which she claims too many comparative studies were based. Among the specific problems associated with Palestine, she warns above all of "the biblical danger," namely:

> the temptation to identify without criticism customs and habits and views of life of the present day with those of the Bible, especially of the Old Testament. Only too often one has been tempted to build a bridge from the past to the present by combining modern parallels with Bible verses. . . . But in any case one must remember the whole time that it is Muhammadan Arabs, not Jews, whose traditions are being studied, and that there is a period of 2000 years and more between then—a gap which cannot be explained away merely by citing "the immovable East" (Granqvist 1931, 9).

Between 1926 and 1931, Granqvist spent nearly three years in Artas carrying out the first systematic ethnography of a Palestinian village. Her research resulted in five books on the different phases of the life cycle. The first, *Marriage Conditions in a Palestinian Village,* volume 1 (1931), explores the customs associated with betrothal; the second, *Marriage Conditions in a Palestinian Village,* volume 2 (1935), describes the wedding events themselves. Together, the two volumes present "a comparative examination of all the marriages in the village of Artas during a hundred years; so far back could the memory of the people reach, that is to say 4–5 generations" (Granqvist 1931, 12).[7]

In his various writings and reports to the Hebrew University, Lachmann repeatedly draws attention to the potential value of his work to ethnographers.[8] Nowhere does he do so more explicitly than in program 7, in which he describes the musical rituals performed by Yemenite Jewish men at weddings:

> Going over the principal events in the social life of an Eastern community [the student of Oriental music] can closely attend to the musical features contained in them, and thus add the indispensable element of sound to the mute descriptions as given by others. In so doing he will not only render an invaluable service to ethnology, but, at the same time, have a reliable guidance in his own field of research.

Working independently of one another yet almost contemporaneously, both Granqvist and Lachmann undertook pioneering studies of weddings as celebrated in Arab villages in central Palestine. Clearly, there are fundamental differences between their accounts. Lachmann's brief commentary merely summarizes the events of a typical wedding, providing a framework for the musical performances he presents. Granqvist's detailed descriptions of the equivalent events, in contrast, are woven into a sustained, richly textured ethnography of the community as a whole. And whereas Lachmann describes only the events in which men participate, Granqvist's descriptions alternate between the men's and women's celebrations, which generally occur in parallel. Her attention to the women's events is particularly striking on the wedding day itself, all of whose activities revolve around the transporting of the bride from her father's home to that of the groom. Lachmann provides no sources for his commentary, nor does he state his own participation in the events. His account is more likely a composite of information provided by the few musicians he recorded, who themselves came from different villages.[9] Granqvist's account, in contrast, is based on her own participant observation during the three years she lived in Artas; this included extensive conversations with numerous villagers, all of whom she came to know well and whose words permeate her commentary (Granqvist 1931, 12, 22). And whereas Lachmann addresses a general audience, Granqvist wrote for the scholarly community: *Marriage Conditions in a Palestinian Village* was published by the Finnish Society of Sciences and Letters (Societas Scientiarum Fennica), and the first volume earned her a doctorate from the Åbo Akademi in Finland.[10]

Yet there are clearly correspondences between Lachmann's and Granqvist's accounts. Local variations notwithstanding, Granqvist's detailed descriptions of the equivalent events in Artas lend substance, depth, and authority to Lachmann's "rough sketches," while his musical recordings may indeed "add the indispensable element of sound" to her "mute descriptions."

The appendix below presents extracts from Lachmann's commentary alongside extracts from Granqvist's account of the corresponding events in Artas, including the associated women's activities when relevant. The material is arranged under Granqvist's chapter headings: "Preparations and Preliminary Festivals for Weddings," "The Fetching of the Bride," and "In the Bridegroom's Home." The subheadings in Granqvist's column are her own. Numbers in square brackets in the right-hand column refer to page numbers in Granqvist 1935.

Appendix: Correspondences between Program 12 and Granqvist 1935

... At dusk the bridegroom lights a wood fire on an open space, mostly in front of the guesthouse, and different groups of villagers successively assemble for dance and song. . . .

Chapter 4: Preparations and Preliminary Festivals for Weddings

The Evenings of Joy

[35] Directly after the moon rises, one hears trilling and singing of women in the village; that is the signal that the festival has begun. If one goes to [36] the bridegroom's house, one can see a little group of women standing in a ring and singing with their heads together. In the darkness they look like large birds with their dark dresses and the white head cloths which fall down behind; the wide sleeves remind one of folded wings.

After this preliminary grouping, the inhabitants of the village collect; the women go into the house where they dance the whole evening; the men stand outside and make big fires to boil the coffee . . . it is also men who carry round and offer coffee to those present; often the bridegroom himself waits upon his guests. . . .

Meantime the dance of the men has begun. Young men stand up in two rows and begin the introductory dance. While they dance they sing:

The performers of the dance range themselves in one line in front of the fire or in two lines with the fire between them, everybody keeping tightly to his neighbours. . . . While dancing and singing they stretch their arms forward and clap their hands. . . .

The dance consists of stamping on the ground with a certain kind of rhythmical steps. The two rows of performers alternately advance towards, and retreat from, the fire. . . .

The dance in which the older men partake has a moderate character; the dancers move on the spot and the song is slower. Here is an example of it.

"All ye sitting ones! May God salute you!
Beside a garden a green bird twitters to you. . . ."

It is a very monotonous song which accompanies the dance, but it is a beautiful dance with swaying movements. One thinks of [37] reeds murmuring and swaying with the wind. The dance continues until late in the night; the women dance alone, and the men dance alone. . . .

Recitation 12.1: Slow *saḥgā*

After the various stages of this dance, refreshments as coffee, milk, tea, or cinnamon (qirfa) are served. Then, all the performers, old and young, form one row, everybody, again, keeping close to his neighbours. . . .

Recitation 12.2: *Tasgia* (followed by *daḥḥiyya*)

On the joyful evenings which preceded the wedding of 'Isa Halīl, . . . the first after my arrival in 1925 at Arṭās, I was fortunate in that the men's dance took place under my window; a lantern had been hung up in an olive tree to supplement the moonlight; the later it became in the night the more animated grew the dancing. They danced, stamping and clapping in a ring or alone to the notes of a flute (*nāye*) played by a young man; the older men sat or half lay with dignity in a semi- [38] circle; they looked at the dance, they talked, they drank coffee, and smoked the waterpipes, and were waited upon by the young men. . . .

The women, all through the evening, attend from a distance, from time to time spurring the dancers and singers with their well-known penetrating trills.

[39] The dance evenings take place three to seven days before the wedding-day itself; every evening after the moon has risen one hears the trilling and singing and dancing in the village till far into the night.

Chapter 3: The Fetching of the Bride

Preparations in the Morning

[51] On the wedding day there is the ceremonial bringing of the bride from her father's house to the bridegroom's house.

In the morning the bride is bathed by her mother and her sisters. . . .

. . . About the middle of the day, the bridegroom takes a bath and then dresses in his wedding clothes. . . .

[52] The bridegroom undergoes a similar process [53] and is shaved; then he puts on new clothes, if he has bought some for his wedding. . . .

[55] On the morning of the day when Mḥammad Yūsef was to fetch his bride Sa'da Derwīš from el-Haḍr near Solomon's Pools, when I reached my little village, I at once noticed the bridegroom, who sat outside a house higher up the mountain being shaved by Halīl Šahīn. . . .

The young men, before and after the bath, recite songs belonging to a kind called zaffa. . . .

Recitation 12.3: *Zaffa hamasiyya*

On the morning of the wedding-day the bridal camel is made ready. The custom is that a bride, if a virgin, goes from her father's house to her husband's house on a camel or a horse. . . .

Procession from the Bridegroom's Home to the Bride's

[56] When Sa'da Derwīš' [the bride's] bridal camel was ready, two small girls were placed among the cushions.

'Alya said once:

> Before the bride rides on the camel, they place either a boy or a girl on it according to their wish that the first-born may be either a boy or a girl. [In the latter case] the woman relatives of the bridegroom cry: "O ye, why have you placed a girl on the camel!" [The answer is given:] "Let it be a girl!"[11]

[60] The two little girls, in this case nearly related to the bridegroom, were delighted to ride on the camel. The animal was made to rise, the women began to trill, to clap their hands and sing; the procession started; up from the village came the men. . . . The older and more prominent men were riding on horses or mules; the bridegroom that time went very simply on foot, last in the row of young men. He came forward to me and said: "It is my wedding to-day, Sitt Ḥalīme [Granqvist's moniker among the villagers]." I congratulated him. . . . As always, the children followed the women; the smallest ones were carried in the arms or on the backs in little hammocks. . . . Other mothers or sisters let the children ride on their shoulders or led them by the hand. One of the women carried on her head the red bundle with the bride's outfit. . . .

The bridegroom then rides or walks to a place outside the village and the young men follow him in procession. He rests in the shade, under a tree, and watches horsemen performing games, and riflemen aiming at a target, in his honour.

[61] Arrived at Solomon's Pools all the men on horseback went down to the open place which is beside the road on the left when one comes from Hebron to Jerusalem, and there began racing. They arranged themselves two or three in a row at one end of the open place and off they went. Having reached the winning-post at the other end, they arranged themselves again and raced back to the starting point; they delighted in showing their skill on horseback; the rest of the men stood and watched but the women sang:

> Thy prayer, O Muhammad!
> Thou disgraced one, O Satan!
> The horses went down to race in the racing place of the bridegrooms. . . .

[62] These words were to blunt the force of evil power; now and again the women would repeat "Shame the devil (ihzi blīs)."

When it again moved forward the men began to dance; someone played the flute (*nayē*) and they danced in a ring, or alone, with a sword, or without a sword. Many Arṭās men now showed their skill in dancing. . . .

[63] They were boisterous and jolly. . . .

At this time, the programme of music and dancing reaches another climax by the performance of a debka.

The word debka refers to treading and stamping, various kinds of accentuated steps being a main feature of the dance. It is not performed in rows, but in a circle, one man behind another, and a piper and a singer in the middle. The instrument may be a śubbāba . . . or a double-clarinet, in Arabic miǵwiz (but Palestinian peasants also call it a nayya). . . .

Recitation 12.4: *'Ala dal'ūnā dabke*

Chapter 5: In The Bridegroom's Home

Preparations for the Meeting of the Bridal Pair in the Evening

. . . In the meantime, the women of his family, above all, his mother have fetched the bride to his house. . . . She is now placed in the bridal room, in the company of her mother-in-law and of other women and girls who entertain her with dancing and singing.

[112] [T]he women prepare the bride for the meeting with the bridegroom. . . .

[113] One of the women sits in front of the bride holding in her hand a piece of wood in which there are small wells for the colours with which she paints the face of the bride. . . .[12]

[114] The women sing:

The window of thy jar [i.e., the bride's mouth] is sweetness,
love for girls has caused enmity.
The window of thy jar is a mulberry leaf,
love for girls hurts unto death.
The window of thy jar is a fig leaf,
love for the girls means stabbing with knives. . . .

Another song for that occasion runs:

Oh woman, who paints, I recommend my bride to thee!
I did not see her until I had emptied my treasure.
Oh woman who paints, thou with the ear-rings, I recommend her to thee!
I did not see her until I had emptied [myself of all my garments even] the old skirt.
O woman who paints I recommend my bride to thee!
I did not see her until I had given my money. . . .[12]

[115] These colours are really only the foundation for the gilding. When the painting is finished, the woman who engraves, takes the gold leaf which she lays all over the face of the bride, who the whole time sits with closed eyes. As soon as this is done, the bride must rise, her face is again covered with the thick veil and the women call out that the bridegroom shall now come.

Recitation 12.5: " 'A'l-hāma 'a'l-hāma"

The Bridegroom Comes to His Bride

At nightfall, the bridegroom comes to meet her. On his way to the house he is accompanied by his friends; they stop in front of the door, and announce his arrival by a short song called hāma. After this, they fire a shot and the women inside answer with a trill of joy. . . .

[The men] retire and the bridegroom enters. He sits down next to the bride.

The bridegroom is standing ready with some hear relatives outside the door. He comes, sword in hand and presses with it, or as the expression runs "threatens" with it, three times against the bride's face: first over her nose and forehead then on each cheek. According to the people he does this in order to make her respect him. Then he folds the edge of her veil over three times with the point of the sword and her face is uncovered.

[Several pages earlier, Granqvist writes, "Sometimes, as I myself have observed, guns are fired off on the entering of the bridal pair into the home of the bridegroom" (Granqvist 1935, 107).]

By the warmth under the veil the gold leaf has stuck closely to the face of the bride, so that the bridegroom sees a golden face. She looks like an Indian idol. The bridegroom wipes away the gold from the face with a handkerchief and so makes her look human again; but she still stands with her eyes closed. It would be very unfitting, if she were curious and bold enough to open her eyes and look at him. There are cases when the bridegroom sees his bride first at this time. . . .

[118] The bridegroom has placed himself beside his bride and stands there sword in hand. . . .

Congratulations

[119] Before the guests go away congratulations are exchanged. . . .

Refreshments and sweets are served and the newly married must drink from one glass.

[121] I was among the last guests who left the house and the bride was sitting on a pillow with her eyes still closed, but before her was the basin with rice and meat which she would eat with the bridegroom. Sometimes their nearest relatives: father, mother, sisters and brothers take part in the meal.

Seclusion of the Bridal Pair

Dances and songs continue for some time, usually two or three hours; then the women successively leave the room.

Later on when the nearest relatives have left the bridal pair, it is said of them that they are in seclusion (*fi helwe*).

Notes

1. Lachmann further reports that he recorded "a romance (qusida) about the invasion of Tunisia by the Beni Hilal, sung by a young villager to the accompaniment of the Rabab al-shair" and "women's songs, partly ritual, partly profane, sung by a blind elderly woman" (quoted in Katz 2003, 114).

2. Louise's father, Henry Baldensperger, was among a group of European and North American Christian visionaries who, attracted by the biblical associations of the site, bought land in Artas and settled there in the middle of the nineteenth century with the aim of establishing an agricultural colony (Granqvist 1931, 14n). Her five brothers were all, at various times, itinerant beekeepers; the eldest, Philip Baldensperger, wrote *The Immovable East: Studies of the Peoples and Customs of Palestine* (Baldensperger 1913). One by one the brothers either died or left the country, leaving their sister to live alone in the family home in Artas. In his "Biographical Introduction" to Philip Baldensperger's monograph, Frederic Lees gives a detailed account of the Baldensperger family and their various missionary and agricultural projects in Palestine (Lees 1913, viii–xii). Another of Louise Baldensperger's collaborations was with Grace Crowfoot, a British archeologist, botanist, and expert on textile and ceramics, with whom she coauthored a book on local plants and folklore (Crowfoot and Baldensperger 1932).

3. Granqvist graduated with a master's degree from the University of Helsinki, where she studied pedagogy, child psychology, and philosophy; she subsequently took courses in biblical literature and archeology in Leipzig and Berlin. Her original thesis topic was chosen for her by Gunnar Landtman, her supervisor at the University of Helsinki and a student of Edward Westermarck.

4. The course was run by the Deutsches Evangelisches Institut für Altertumswissenschaft des Heiligen Landes.

5. She cites as an example James George Frazer's classic study *Folklore in the Old Testament: Studies in Comparative Religion, Legend and Lore* (1918; Granqvist 1931, 5, 8–9).

6. In the introduction to *Birth and Childhood among the Arabs* (Granqvist 1947), Granqvist claims that she came to similar conclusions quite independently of the functional anthropologists. She notes that she wrote her introduction to *Marriage Conditions* (1935) before she was exposed to their teachings, which occurred on a visit to London in the summer term of 1938. During that term she attended seminars by Bronislaw Malinowski and Raymond Firth and attended a discussion between A. R. Radcliffe-Brown and Malinowski (Granqvist 1947, 14).

7. Granqvist's documentation of life in Artas included over one thousand black and white photographs of which only twenty were published in her lifetime, all in the second volume of *Marriage Conditions in a Palestinian Village* (1935). On Granqvist's death in 1972, her notes, manuscripts, photographs, and other documents were presented by her family to the library of the Palestine Exploration Fund in London. Karen Seger (1981) has published a selection of 226 photographs with commentary based on Granqvist's writings.

8. In his report of April 1937, for example, he states: "It is evident that a work of this nature is of foremost importance not only from the point of view of Musical History, but also from the sociological, ethnological and philological standpoint, and will throw considerable light on the historical and cultural life of the peoples in question" (reproduced in Katz 2003, 182). On this source, see "The 'Oriental Music Archive' and Outreach Projects" in the introduction.

9. As indicated in Lachmann's typescript, the musicians in program 12 came from 'Ain Yabrūd and Qaṭanna, both in today's central West Bank; see footnote 1 above.

10. Granqvist's innovative methods and especially her refusal to pursue comparative studies may have cost her

an academic career in Finland; despite international critical acclaim, she remained an independent scholar throughout her life. Even within the context of contemporary trends, several aspects of her research—including her intensive focus on a single village, reliance on participant observation, and extensive direct citation of informants—were novel and controversial; her research relating to women and children in particular was pioneering. Yet her work was highly regarded by her contemporaries. For scholarly appreciations of her work by E. E. Evans-Pritchard, Moses Gaster, and Margaret Mead, among others, see Weir 1989, 9; and Suolinna 2000. For more recent evaluations of Granqvist's work and its contemporary significance, see Moors 2006; Rothenberg 1999; and Suolinna 2000.

11. Granqvist makes no comment on the women's call for the first-born to be a girl, which contradicts traditional birth preferences for boys in Arab society. In *Birth and Childhood among the Arabs* (1947), she explains that the gender of the newborn is believed to be decided by God at conception, and that no thought or action on the part of man or woman has the power to influence the matter (Granqvist 1947, 34–37). Later, however, she describes various postnatal customs that clearly illustrate the communal preference for sons (Granqvist 1947, 76–79).

12. Granqvist goes on to describe the colors (red, white, green, yellow) and patterns (palm tree, rose, jar, moon) used in the henna painting: the palm tree represents the groom, the rose the bride (Granqvist 1935, 114).

References

Recordings

El-Funoun. 1999. *Zaghareed: Music from the Palestinian Holy Land.* Boulder, Colo.: Sounds True DIS-MM00109D, compact disc.

Hornbostel, Erich M. von, ed. 1931. *Musik des Orients.* Berlin: Carl Lindström Kulturabteilung, twelve 33⅓ rpm discs (previously recorded on commercial labels) with accompanying booklet.

Institut du monde arabe. 1988. *Congrès du Caire 1932: musqiue arabe savante et populaire.* Paris: Édition Bibliothèque nationale / l'Institut du monde arabe APN 88–9 and 88–10, 2 compact discs with booklet.

Schüller, Dietrich, and Gerda Lechtleitner, eds. 2005. *The Collection of Abraham Zvi Idelsohn (1911–1913).* With comments by Philip V. Bohlman and Edwin Seroussi. Tondokumente aus dem Phonogrammarchiv der österreichischen Akademie der Wissenschaften: Gesamtausgabe der historischen Bestände 1899–1950, ser. 9. Vienna: Österreichische Akademie der Wissenschaften OEAW PHA CD 23, 3 compact discs with booklet and CD-ROM.

Shammout, Bashar, and Gidi Boss. 1997. *Traditional Music and Songs of Palestine.* Popular Art Center PAC-1001, compact disc.

Tanburî Cemil Bey. 1994–95. *Tanburi Cemil Bey.* 5 vols. New York: Traditional Crossroads CD 4264, CD4274, and CD 4308, compact discs.

Literature

Abassi, Hamadi. 2000. *Tunis chante et danse: 1900–1950.* Tunis: Editions du Layeur.

Abert, Hermann. 2007. *W. A. Mozart.* Translated from the German by Stewart Spencer. Edited by Cliff Eisen. New Haven, Conn.: Yale University Press.

Adler, Israel, Bathja Bayer, Eliyahu Schleifer, and Lea Shalem, eds. 1986. "The Abraham Zvi Idelsohn Memorial Volume." Special issue, *Yuval* 5. Jerusalem: The Magnes Press.

Atalla, Magda Wadie, trans. n.d. Introduction to Ghubriyāl 1916. E. dited by Carolym M. Ramzy. *Performing Arts Encyclopedia,* The Library of Congress (http://memory.loc.gov/diglib/ihas/loc.natlib.ihas.200155976/default.html).

Baldensperger, Philip J. 1913. *The Immovable East: Studies of the People and Customs of Palestine.* Edited with an introduction by Frederic Lees. Boston: Small, Maynard & Co.

Bartók, Béla. 1933. "Zum Kongress für arabische Musik, Kairo 1932." *Zeitschrift fur vergleichende Musikwissenschaft* 1:46–48.

Bartók, Béla, and Albert B. Lord. 1951. *Serbo-Croatian Folk Songs: Texts and Transcriptions of Seventy-Five Folk Songs from the Milman Parry Collection and a Morphology of Serbo-Croatian Folk Melodies.* New York: Columbia University Press.

Beardsley, Theodore. 1989. "The Spanish Musical Sources of Bizet's *Carmen.*" *Inter-American Music Review* 10 (2): 143–46.

Becking, Gustav Wilhelm. 1933. "Der musikalische Bau des montenegrischen Volksepos." *Archives néerlandaises de phonétique expérimentale* 8–9:144–53.

Bentwich, Norman. 1961. *The Hebrew University of Jerusalem, 1918–60.* London: Weidenfeld and Nicolson.

Blum, Stephen. 1991. "European Musical Terminology and the Music of Africa." In Blum, Bohlman, and Neuman 1991, 3–36.

Blum, Stephen, Philip V. Bohlman, and Daniel M. Neuman, eds. 1991. *Ethnomusicology and Modern Music History.* Urbana: University of Illinois Press.

Bohlman, Philip V. 1987. "The European Discovery of Music in the Islamic World and the 'Non-Western' in 19th-Century Music History." *The Journal of Musicology* 5:147–63.

———. 1992. *The World Centre for Jewish Music in Palestine, 1936–1940: Jewish Musical Life on the Eve of World War II.* Oxford: Clarendon Press.

———. 2005. "Abraham Z. Idelsohn and the Re-Orientation of Jewish Music History." In Schüller and Lechtleitner 2005, 18–51.

———. 2008. *Jewish Music and Modernity.* Oxford: Oxford University Press.

———. 2011. *Music, Nationalism, and the Making of the New Europe.* Second Edition. New York and London: Routledge.

Bohlman, Philip V., and Ruth Davis. 2007. "Mizrakh, Jewish Music and the Journey to the East." In *Portrayal of the East: Music and Orientalism in the British Empire, 1780s–1940s,* edited by Martin Clayton and Bennett Zon, 95–125. Aldershot: Ashgate.

Boulos, Issa. 2002. Review of Shammout and Boss 1997. *Music and Anthropology* 7 (http://www.muspe.unibo

.it/wwcat/period/ma/index/number7/boulos/palesti.htm).

Brinner, Benjamin. 2009. *Playing Across a Divide: Israeli-Palestinian Musical Encounters*. Oxford: Oxford University Press.

Caspi, Mishael Maswari. 1985. *Daughters of Yemen*. Berkeley: University of California Press.

Caspi, Mishael Maswari, and Deborah Lipstadt. 1985. "Introduction." In Caspi 1985, 1–11.

Castelo-Branco, Salwa El-Shawan. 2002. "Western Music, Colonialism, Cosmopolitanism, and Modernity in Egypt." In Danielson, Marcus, and Reynolds 2002, 607–13.

Clark, Jane. 1980. "Les folies françoises." *Early Music* 8:163–69.

Crowfoot, Grace M., and Louise Baldensperger. 1932. *From Cedar to Hyssop: A Study in the Folklore of Plants in Palestine*. London: The Sheldon Press (SPCK); New York: Macmillan Company.

Crown, Alan D., ed. 1989. *The Samaritans*. Tübingen: J. C. B. Mohr.

Danielson, Virginia. 1997. *The Voice of Egypt: Umm Kulthūm, Arabic Song, and Egyptian Society in the Twentieth Century*. Chicago: University of Chicago Press.

Danielson, Virginia, Scott Marcus, and Dwight Reynolds, eds. 2002. *The Garland Encyclopedia of World Music*, vol. 6, *The Middle East*. New York: Routledge. Includes compact disc with audio samples.

Davis, Ruth F. 1986. "Some Relations between Three *Piyyutim* from Djerba and Three Arab Songs." *The Maghreb Review* 11 (5–6): 134–44.

———. 2001. "Mode, §V, 2: Middle East and Central Asia: 'maqām,' 'makom.' " In *The New Grove Dictionary of Music and Musicians*, 2nd ed., edited by Stanley Sadie, 831–37. London: Macmillan.

———. 2002. "Music of the Jews of Djerba, Tunisia." In Danielson, Marcus, and Reynolds 2002, 523–31.

———. 2004. *Ma'luf: Reflections on the Arab Andalusian Music of Tunisia*. Lanham, Md.: Scarecrow Press.

———. 2009. "Time, Place, and Jewish Music: Mapping the Multiple Journeys of 'Andik bahriyya, ya rais.' " In *The Musical Anthropology of the Mediterranean: Interpretation, Performance, Identity*, edited by Philip V. Bohlman and Marcello Sorce Keller, 47–58. Bologna: CLUEB.

———. 2013. "Music in the Mirror of Multiple Nationalisms: Sound Archives and Ideology in Israel and Palestine." In *The Cambridge History of World Music*, edited by Philip V. Bohlman. Cambridge: Cambridge University Press.

Densmore, Frances. 1926. *The American Indians and Their Music*. New York: The Woman's Press.

d'Erlanger, Rodolphe, Baron. 1917. "Au sujet de la musique arabe en Tunisie." *Revue tunisienne* 24:91–95.

———. 1930–59. *La musique arabe*. 6 vols. Paris: Paul Geuthner.

Eliade, Mircea. 1989. *Shamanism: Archaic Techniques of Ecstasy*. London: Arkana.

Falla, Manuel de. 1922. *El "cante jondo" (canto primitivo andaluz)*. Granada: Editorial Urania.

Farhat, Hormoz. 1990. *The Dastgah Concept in Persian Music*. Cambridge: Cambridge University Press.

Farmer, Henry George. 1929. *A History of Arabian Music to the XIIIth Century*. London: Luzac and Co.

al-Faruqi, Lois Ibsen. 1985. "Music, Musicians, and Muslim Law." *Asian Music* 17 (1): 3–37.

Forry, Mark. 2000. "Serbia." In *The Garland Encyclopedia of World Music*, vol. 8, *Europe*, edited by Timothy Rice, James Porter, and Chris Goertzen, 940–56. New York: Garland.

Fox Strangways, Arthur Henry. 1914. *The Music of Hindostan*. Oxford: Clarendon Press.

Frischkopf, Michael. 2009. "Mediated Qur'anic Recitation and the Contestation of Islam in Contemporary Egypt." In *Music and the Play of Power in the Middle East, North Africa and Central Asia*, edited by Laudan Nooshin, 75–114. Farnham, Surrey: Ashgate.

Frühauf, Tina, ed. 2013. *German-Jewish Organ Music: An Anthology of Works from the 1820s to the 1960s*. Recent Researches in the Music of the Nineteenth and Early Twentieth Centuries, vol. 59. Middleton, Wis.: A-R Editions.

Fyzee-Rahamin, Atiya Begum. 1925. *The Music of India*. London: Luzac and Co.

Gamli'eli, Nissim Benyamin. 1975. *The Love of Yemen: Popular Yemenite Women's Poetry*. Tel Aviv: Afikim.

Gerson-Kiwi, Edith. 1938. "Jerusalem Archive for Oriental Music." *Musica Hebraica* 1:40–42.

———. 1963. "The Legacy of Jewish Music through the Ages." *In the Dispersion* 3:149–72.

———. 1965. "Women's Songs from the Yemen: Their Tonal Structure and Form." In *The Commonwealth of Music: Writings on Music in History, Art, and Culture in Honor of Curt Sachs*, edited by Gustave Reese and Rose Brandel, 97–103. New York: Free Press.

———. 1971. "The Music of Kurdistan Jews: A Synopsis of Their Musical Styles." *Yuval* 2:59–72.

———. 1974. "Robert Lachmann: His Achievement and His Legacy." *Yuval* 3:100–108.

Gherardi, Evaristo. 1683. *Le théâtre italien de Gherardi, ou Le recueil général de toutes les comédies & scènes françoises jouées par les comédiens italiens du Roy, pendant tout le temps qu'il ont été au service*. Paris: Jean-Baptiste Cusson and Pierre Witte.

Ghubriyāl, Kāmil Ibrāhīm. 1916. *Al-tawqī'āt al-mūsīqīyah li-maraddāt al-Kanīsah al-Murqusīyah* [The musical notation of the responses of the Church of St. Mark]. Cairo: al-Maṭaba'ah al-Miṣrīyah al-Ahlīyah bi-al-Qāhirah.

Gilbert, Martin. 1992. *The Arab-Israeli Conflict: Its History in Maps*, 5th ed. London: Weidenfeld and Nicolson.

Godsill, Simon J., and Peter J. W. Rayner. 1998. *Digital Audio Restoration: A Statistical Model-Based Approach*. London: Springer.

Goren, Arthur A., ed. 1982. *Dissenter in Zion: From the Writings of Judah L. Magnes*. Cambridge, Mass.: Harvard University Press.

Granqvist, Hilma. 1931. *Marriage Conditions in a Palestinian Village*, vol. 1. Societas Scientiarum Fennica: Com-

mentationes Humanarum Litterarum, vol. 3, no. 8. Helsingfors: Akademische Buchhandlung.
———. 1935. *Marriage Conditions in a Palestinian Village,* vol. 2. Societas Scientiarum Fennica: Commentationes Humanarum Litterarum, vol. 6, no. 8. Helsingfors: Akademische Buchhandlung.
———. 1947. *Birth and Childhood among the Arabs: Studies in a Muhammadan Village in Palestine.* Helsingfors: Soderstrom & Co.
Guettat, Mahmoud. 2000. *La musique arabo-andalouse: L'empreinte du Maghreb.* Paris: Éditions El-Ouns.
———. "The Andalusian Musical Heritage." In Danielson, Marcus, and Reynolds 2002, 441–54.
Hagopian, Harold G., and Ercument Aksoy. 1995. Liner notes to Tanburî Cemil Bey 1995, vol. 2.
Hassan, Schéhérazade Qassim. 1992. "Choix de la musique et de la représentation irakiennes au Congrès du Caire: Vers une étude de contexte." In Vigreux 1992, 123–46.
———. 2002. "Musical Instruments in the Arab World." In Danielson, Marcus, and Reynolds 2002, 401–23.
Hebrew University. 1925. *Inauguration of the Hebrew University of Jerusalem, April 1st 1924, Nisan 7th 5685.* Jerusalem: Universitah ha'Ivrit bi-Yerushalayim (The Hebrew University of Jerusalem).
Herder, Johann Gottfried. (1778; 1779) 1975. *"Stimmen der Völker in Liedern"; Volkslieder,* edited by Heinz Rölleke. Stuttgart: Reclam.
Herzog, George. 1934. "Speech-Melody and Primitive Music." *Musical Quarterly* 20:452–66.
Hess, Carol A. "Falla, Manuel de." In *Grove Music Online,* Oxford Music Online (http://www.oxfordmusiconline .com).
Hirshberg, Jehoash. 1995. *Music in the Jewish Community of Palestine, 1880–1948: A Social History.* Oxford: Oxford University Press.
Hornbostel, Erich M. von. 1927. "Musikalische Tonsysteme." In *Handbuch der Physik,* vol. 8, edited by H. Geiger and K. Scheel, 425–49. Berlin: J. Springer.
———. 1928a. "African Negro Music." *Africa* 1:30–62.
———. 1928b. "Die Massnorm als kulturgeschichtliches Forschungsmittel." In *Festschrift: publication d'hommage offerte à P. W. Schmidt,* edited by Wilhelm Koppers, 303–23. Vienna: Mechitharisten-Congregations-Buchdruckerei.
Horowitz, Amy. 2010. *Mediterranean Israeli Music and the Politics of the Aesthetic.* Detroit: Wayne State University Press.
Howard, Wayne. 2000. "Vedic Chant." In *The Garland Encyclopedia of World Music,* vol. 5, *South Asia: The Indian Subcontinent,* edited by Alison Arnold, 238–45. New York: Garland.
Idelsohn, Abraham Z. 1913–14. "Die Maqamen der arabischen Musik." *Sammelbände der Internationalen Musikgesellschaft* 15:1–63.
———. 1917a. *Phonographierte Gesänge und Aussprachsproben des Hebräischen der jemenitischen, persischen und syrischen Juden.* Sitzungsberichte der philosophisch-historischen Klasse der kais. Akademie der Wissenschaften in Wien, vol. 175:4; Mitteilung der Phonogramm-Archivs-Kommission, vol. 35. Wien: In Kommission bei A. Hölder.
———. 1917b. "Die Vortragszeichen der Samaritaner." *Monatsschrift für Geschichte und Wissenschaft des Judentums* 61:117–26.
———. (1914–32) 1973. *Thesaurus of Hebrew Oriental Melodies / Hebraisch-orientalischer Melodienschatz.* 10 vols. Berlin: B. Harz. Reprint, New York: Ktav Publishing House.
———. (1935) 1986. "My Life: A Sketch." In Adler et al. 1986, 18–23. Originally published as "My Life." *Jewish Music Journal* 2 (2): 8–11. Page numbers refer to Adler et al. 1986.
———. (1929) 1992. *Jewish Music: Its Historical Development,* edited with an introduction by Arbie Orenstein. Mineola, N.Y.: Dover.
al-Iṣfahānī, Abū al-Faraj. 1963–73. *Kitāb al-aghānī.* 21 vols. Cairo: Dār al-Kutub.
Jeffery, Peter. 1992. *Re-Envisioning Past Musical Cultures: Ethnomusicology in the Study of Gregorian Chant.* Chicago: University of Chicago Press.
Katz, Jonathan. 2001. "India, §V, 2: 'Sāmavedic' Chant." In *Grove Music Online,* Oxford Music Online (http://www.oxfordmusiconline.com).
Katz, Ruth. 2003. *"The Lachmann Problem": An Unsung Chapter in Comparative Musicology.* Yuval Monograph Series, vol. 12. Jerusalem: The Magnes Press.
al-Khulā'ī, Kāmil. 1904. *Kitāb al-mūsīqā al-sharqī* [The Book of Eastern Music]. Cairo: Maṭba'at al-Taqaddum.
KMM'A. 1933. *Kitā'b al-mu'tamar al-musiqa al-'arabiyya* [Book of the Arab music conference]. Cairo: al-Matba'a al-Amiriyya bi Bulāq.
Kojaman, Yeheskel. 2001. *The Maqam Music Tradition of Iraq.* London: Y. Kojaman.
Kotzin, Daniel P. 2000. "An Attempt to Americanize the Yishuv: Judah L. Magnes in Mandatory Palestine." *Israel Studies* 5 (1): 1–23.
Lachmann, Robert. 1923. "Die Musik in den tunisischen Städten." *Archiv fur Musikwissenschaft* 5:136–71.
———. 1925. "Das No und seine Musik." *Vossische Zeitung* 38, 19 September. Musikblatt.
———. 1926. "Musik und Tonschrift des No." In *Bericht über den musikwissenschaftlichen Kongress der Deutschen Musikgesellschaft in Leipzig,* 80–93. Leipzig: Breitkopf & Härtel.
———. 1929. *Musik des Orients.* Breslau: Hirt.
———. 1935a. "Remarks on Broadcasting Music from the Jerusalem Station." Unpublished manuscript, 2 June. Hebrew University of Jerusalem, Lachmann Archive, no shelfmark.
———. 1935b. Review of Wünsch 1934. *Zeitschrift für vergleichende Musikwissenschaft* 3:45–46.
———. 1936a. "National und International in der orientalischen Musik." Lecture presented at the College of Music "Beth Levi'im," Tel Aviv, February 12. Hebrew University of Jerusalem, Lachmann Archive, A. III. 48.
———. 1936b. "Musikkulturen des vorderen Orients." Series of six lectures presented at the University of Basel, May 11–16. Hebrew University of Jerusalem, Lachmann Archive, A. III. 47.3.

———. 1936c. "Musical Systems among the Present Arab Bedouins and Peasants." Lecture presented to the Palestine Oriental Society, Jerusalem, December 17. Hebrew University of Jerusalem, Lachmann Archive, A. III. 46.1.

———. 1940. *Jewish Cantillation and Song in the Isle of Djerba.* Jerusalem: Azriel Press and Archives of Oriental Music, Hebrew University.

———. 1974. *Posthumous Works,* vol. 1, *Zwei Aufsätze: "Die Musik im Volksleben Nordafrikas," "Orientalische Musik und Antike,"* edited by Edith Gerson-Kiwi. Yuval Monograph Series, vol. 2. Jerusalem: The Magnes Press.

———. 1978. *Posthumous Works,* vol. 2, *Gesänge der Juden auf der Insel Djerba,* edited by Edith Gerson-Kiwi. Yuval Monograph Series, vol. 7. Jerusalem: The Magnes Press.

Lachmann, Robert, and Mahmoud el-Hefni, eds. 1931. *Ja'qūb Ibn Isḥāq al-Kindi: Risāla fī Khubr tā'līf al-alhān: Über die Komposition der Melodien, Veröffentlichungen der Gesellschaft zur Erforschung der Musik des Orients.* Leipzig: Fr. Kistner and C. F. W. Siegel.

Ladkani, Jennifer Lee. 2001. "Dabke Music and Dance and the Palestinian Refugee Experience: On the Outside Looking In." Ph.D. diss., Florida State University School of Music.

Lajnah al-Mūsīqīyah al-'Ulyā [The Higher Music Committee]. [1959?]. *Turāthunā al-Mūsīqī* [Our musical heritage], 4 vols. Cairo: Lajnah al-Mūsīqīyah al-'Ulyā.

Lane, Edward William. (1836) 1986. *An Account of the Manners and Customs of the Modern Egyptians.* Reprint, London: Darf Publishers Ltd.

Laufer, Bernard. 1917. "Origins of the Word Shaman." *American Anthropologist* 19 (3): 361–71.

Leblon, Bernard. (1994) 2003. *Gypsies and Flamenco: The Emergence of the Art of Flamenco in Andalusia.* Hatfield, Hertfordshire: University of Hertford Press.

Lees, Frederic. 1913. "Biographical Introduction." In Baldensperger 1913, vii–xix.

Locke, Ralphe P. 2009. *Musical Exoticism: Images and Reflections.* Cambridge: Cambridge University Press.

Lord, Albert B. ed. 1953. *Serbocroatian Heroic Songs Collected by Milman Parry.* Cambridge, Mass.; Belgrade: Harvard University Press; Serbian Academy of Sciences.

———. (1960) 2000. *The Singer of Tales.* Cambridge, Mass Harvard University Press. Reprint edited by Stephen Mitchell and Gregory Nagy. Cambridge, Mass.: Harvard University Press.

Lot-Falck, Éveline. 1977. "À propos du terme chamane." *Études mongoles et sibériennes* 8:7–18.

Marcus, Scott Lloyd. 1989. "Arab Music Theory in the Modern Period." Ph.D. diss., University of California, Los Angeles.

———. 2007. *Music in Egypt: Experiencing Music, Expressing Culture.* Oxford: Oxford University Press.

McClary, Susan. 1992. *Georges Bizet: "Carmen."* Cambridge: Cambridge University Press.

———. 1997. "Structures of Identity and Difference in Bizet's *Carmen.*" In *The Work of Opera: Genre, Nationhood, and Sexual Difference,* edited by Richard Dellamora and Daniel Fischlin, 115–89. New York: Columbia University Press.

McDonald, David A. 2009. "Poetics and the Performance of Violence in Israel/Palestine." *Ethnomusicology* 53 (1): 58–85.

McKinnon, James W., ed. 1987. *Music in Early Christian Literature.* Cambridge: Cambridge University Press.

———. 2001. "Pandoura." In *The New Grove Dictionary of Music and Musicians,* 2nd ed., edited by Stanley Sadie, 30–31. London: Macmillan.

el-Melligi, Tahar. 2000. *Les immortels de la chanson tunisienne.* Carthage Dermech: Les Éditions MediaCom.

Moftah, Laurence. 2006. "A Musical Resurrection." *Al-Ahram* 79 (20–26 April), http://weekly.ahram.org.eg/2006/791/cu4.htm.

Moftah, Ragheb. 1975. "The History of Recording Coptic Hymns and the History of Moalem Mikhail." *El-Keraza Magazine.* Translated by Shenouda Mamdouh. 1996. Coptic Music Website, http://www.coptic.org/music/keraza75.htm.

Moftah, Ragheb, Martha Roy, and Margit Tóth, eds. 1998. *The Coptic Liturgy of St. Basil with Complete Musical Transcription.* Cairo: The American University in Cairo Press.

Moors, Annelies. 2006. "From Travelogue to Ethnography and Back Again? Hilma Granqvist's Writings and Photographs." In *Uncertain Territories: Boundaries in Cultural Analysis,* by Inge E. Boer; edited by Mieke Bal, Bregje van Eekelen, and Patricia Spyer, 219–37. Amsterdam: Rodopi.

Mor, Menachem. 1989. "The Persian, Hellenistic and Hasmonaean Period." In Crown 1989, 3–18.

Moussali, Bernard. 1988. Liner notes to Institut du monde arabe 1988.

Nathan, Hans, ed. 1994. *Israeli Folk Music: Songs of the Early Pioneers.* With foreword and afterword by Philip V. Bohlman. Recent Researches in the Oral Traditions of Music, vol. 4. Madison: A-R Editions, Inc.

Nelson, Kristina. 2001. *The Art of Reciting the Qur'an,* 2nd ed. Cairo: American University in Cairo Press.

Neubauer, Eckhard. 1985. "Der Essai sur la musique orientale von Charles Fonton (Textteil)." *Zeitschrift für Geschichte der arabisch-islamischen Wissenschaften* 2:277–324.

———. 1986. "Der Essai sur la musique orientale von Charles Fonton mit Zeichnungen von Adanson (Einleitung und Indices)." *Zeitschrift für Geschichte der arabisch-islamischen Wissenschaften* 3:335–76.

Newlandsmith, Ernest. 1927. *A Minstrel Friar: The Story of My Life and Work.* London: The New Life Movement.

O'Connell, John Morgan. 2002. "Snapshot: Tanburī Cemil Bey." In Danielson, Marcus, and Reynolds 2002, 757–58.

Parakilas, James. 1993–94. "The Soldier and the Exotic: Operatic Variations on a Theme of Racial Encounter." Pts. 1 and 2. *The Opera Quarterly* 10 (2): 31–56; 10 (3): 43–69.

Powers, Harold S., and Richard Widdess. 2001a. "Mode, §V, 1: Introduction: Mode as a Musicological Concept." In *Grove Music Online,* Oxford Music Online (http://www.oxfordmusiconline.com).

———. 2001b. "Mode, §V, 3: South Asia: 'rāga.'" In *The New Grove Dictionary of Music and Musicians*, 2nd ed., edited by Stanley Sadie, 837–44. London: Macmillan.
Powers, Harold S., and Frans Wiering. 2001. "Mode, §II: Medieval Modal Theory, 1: The Elements." In *Grove Music Online*, Oxford Music Online (http://www.oxfordmusiconline.com).
Racy, Ali Jihad. 1976. "Record Industry and Egyptian Traditional Music: 1904–1932." *Ethnomusicology* 20 (1): 23–48.
———. 1977. *Musical Change and Commercial Recording in Egypt, 1904–1932*. Urbana-Champaign: University of Illinois Press.
———. 1981. "Music in Contemporary Cairo: A Comparative Overview." *Asian Music* 13 (1): 4–26.
———. 1991. "Historical Views of Early Ethnomusicologists: An East-West Encounter in Cairo, 1932." In Blum, Bohlman, and Neuman 1991, 68–91.
———. 1994. "A Dialectical Perspective on Musical Instruments: The East-Mediterranean *Mijwiz*." *Ethnomusicology* 38 (1): 37–57.
Ramzy, Carolyn M. 2008. "Ernest Newlandsmith: Biography." *Performing Arts Encyclopedia*, The Library of Congress (http://lcweb2.loc.gov/diglib/ihas/loc.natlib.ihas.200155648/default.html).
Raz, Carmel. Forthcoming. "Tafillalt's 'Soulmate': A Snapshot on the Israeli Piyyut Revival." In *Musical Exodus: Al-Andalus and its Jewish Diasporas*, edited by Ruth F. Davis. Lanham, Md.: Scarecrow Press.
Recueil. 1934. *Recueil des travaux du congrès de musique arabe qui s'est tenu au Caire en 1932 (Hég. 1350) sous le haut patronage de S. M. Fouad 1er, roi d'Egypte*. Cairo: Imprimerie National, Boulaq.
Regev, Motti, and Edwin Seroussi. 2004. *Popular Music and National Culture in Israel*. Berkeley: University of California Press.
Reinhard, Ursula. 2002. "Turkey: An Overview." In Danielson, Marcus, and Reynolds 2002, 759–77.
Reynolds, Dwight Fletcher. 1995. *Heroic Poets, Poetic Heroes. The Ethnography of Performance in an Arabic Oral Epic Tradition*. Ithaca: Cornell University Press.
Robertson-Wilson, Marian. 2001. "Coptic Church Music." In *Grove Music Online*, Oxford Music Online (http://www.oxfordmusiconline.com).
Rogers, Mary Eliza. 1862. *Domestic Life in Palestine*. London: Bell and Daldy.
Rosenfeld-Hadad, Merav. 2010. "The Paraliturgical Songs of Babylonian Jews in the Context of Arabo-Islamic Culture and Religion." Ph.D. diss., University of Cambridge.
Rothenberg, Celia. 1999. "Who Are We for Them? On Doing Research in the Palestinian West Bank." In *Feminist Fields: Ethnographic Insights*, edited by Rae Bridgman, Sally Cole, and Heather Howard-Bobiwash, 137–56. Peterborough, Ontario: Broadview Press.
Rouget, Gilbert. 1985. *Music and Trance: A Theory of the Relations between Music and Possession*. Chicago: University of Chicago Press.
Rousseau, Jean-Jacques. 1998. *"Essay on the Origin of Languages" and Writings Related to Music*, translated and edited by John T. Scott. The Collected Writings of Rousseau, vol. 7. Hanover, N.H.: University Press of New England [for] Dartmouth College.
Roy, Martha. 1992. "La liturgie copte et les enrégistrements du Congrès du Caire de 1932: l'enseignement musical en Égypte." In Vigreux 1992, 37–39.
Sachs, Curt. 1921. *Die Musikinstrumente des alten Ägyptens*. Mitteilungen aus der ägyptischen Sammlung, vol. 3. Berlin: K. Curtius.
———. 1940. *The History of Musical Instruments*. London: Dent.
———. 1943. *The Rise of Music in the Ancient World, East and West*. New York: W. W. Norton & Co.
Sachs, Curt, and Jaap Kunst. 1962. *The Wellsprings of Music: An Introduction to Ethnomusicology*. Leiden: M. Nijhoff.
Salomon, Karl. 1938. "Kol Yerushalayim: Music Programmes for Jewish Radio Listeners in Palestine," *Musica Hebraica* 1–2:36–39.
Sawa, George Dimitri. 1985. "The Status and Roles of the Secular Musicians in the Kitab al-Aghani (Book of Songs) of Abu al-Faraj al-Isbahani (D. 356 A. H./967 A. D.)." *Asian Music* 17 (1): 69–82.
———. 1989. *Music Performance Practice in the Early 'Abbāsid Era 132–320 AH/750–932 AD*. Toronto: Pontifical Institute of Mediaeval Studies.
Sbait, Dirgham H. 1993. "Debate in the Improvised-Sung Poetry of the Palestinians." *Asian Folklore Studies* 52 (1): 93–117.
———. 2002. "Palestinian Wedding Songs." In Danielson, Marcus, and Reynolds 2002, 579–92.
Schleifer, Eliahu. 1986. "Introduction to Idelsohn's Autobiographical Sketches." In Adler et al. 1986, 15–17.
Schur, Nathan. 1989. "The Modern Period (from 1516 A.D.)." In Crown 1989, 113–34.
Seger, Karen. 1981. *Portrait of a Palestinian Village: The Photographs of Hilma Granqvist*. London: Third World Centre for Research and Publishing.
Seroussi, Edwin. 2005. "The Content and Scope of Abraham Zvi Idelsohn's Recordings." In Schüller and Lechtleitner 2005, 52–57.
Shehadi, Fadlou. 1995. *Philosophies of Music in Medieval Islam*. Leiden: Brill.
Shelemay, Kay Kaufman. 1998. *Let Jasmine Rain Down: Song and Remembrance Among Syrian Jews*. Chicago: Chicago University Press.
Shelemay, Kay Kaufman, and Peter Jeffery. 1993–97. *Ethiopian Christian Liturgical Chant: An Anthology*. Recent Researches in the Oral Traditions of Music, vols. 1–3. Madison, Wis.: A-R Editions.
Shiloah, Amnon. 1991. "An Eighteenth-Century Critic of Taste and Good Taste." In Blum, Bohlman, and Neuman 1991, 181–89.
———. 1992. *Jewish Musical Traditions*. Detroit: Wayne State University Press.
———. 2007a. *Music and its Virtues in Islamic and Judaic Writings*. Farnham, Surrey: Ashgate.
———. 2007b. "Aharon, Ezra." In *Encyclopaedia Judaica*, edited by Michael Berenbaum and Fred Skolnik, 2nd ed., 1:531. Detroit: Macmillan Reference USA.

Shiloah, Amnon, and Edith Gerson-Kiwi. 1981. "Musicology in Israel, 1960–1980." *Acta Musicologica* 53 (2): 200–216.

Shiloah, Amnon, and Erik Cohen. 1983. "The Dynamics of Change in Jewish Oriental Ethnic Music in Israel." *Ethnomusicology* 27 (2): 227–52.

Signell, Karl L. (1977) 1986. *Makam: Modal Practice in Turkish Art Music.* New York: Da Capo Press.

Silverstein, Shayna. 2012a. "Mobilizing Bodies in Syria: Dabke, Popular Culture and the Politics of Belonging." Ph.D. diss., University of Chicago.

———. 2012b. "Syria's Radical Dabke." *Middle East Report* 263:33–37.

Simon, Artur. 1992. "Les enrégistrements de musique populaire égyptienne au Congrès du Caire." In Vigreux 1992, 155–61.

Spector, Johanna. 1965. "The Significance of Samaritan Neumes and Contemporary Practice." *Studia Musicologica* 7 (1): 141–53.

Spoer, H. H. 1923. "Five Poems by Nimr Ibn 'Adwān." *Journal of the American Oriental Society* 43:177–205.

Spoer, H. H., and Elias Nasrallah Haddad. 1945. "Poems by Nimr Ibn 'Adwān." *Journal of the American Oriental Society* 65 (1): 37–50.

St. Mark Coptic Orthodox Church. 1997. *The Three Masses According to the Three Saints: Basil, Gregory, and Cyril.* Montreal: St. Mark Coptic Orthodox Church.

St. Mary and St. Shenouda Coptic Orthodox Church. 2002. *The Holy Kholagy of the Three Liturgies of the Coptic Orthodox Church.* Rickman Hill, Coulsdon: St. Mary and St. Shenouda Coptic Orthodox Church.

Stanton, Andrea. 2012. "Jerusalem Calling: The Birth of the Palestine Broadcasting Service." *Jerusalem Quarterly,* no. 50 (http://www.jerusalemquarterly.org/ViewArticle.aspx?id=409).

———. Forthcoming. *This is Jerusalem Calling: State Radio in Mandate Palestine:* Austin, Tex.: University of Texas Press.

Suchoff, Benjamin. 1972. "Bartók and Serbo-Croatian Folk Music." *The Musical Quarterly* 58 (4): 557–71.

Suolinna, Kirsti. 2000. "Hilma Granqvist: A Scholar of the Westermarck School in its Decline." *Acta Sociologica* 43:317–23.

Treitler, Leo. 1982. "The Early History of Music Writing in the West." *Journal of the American Musicological Society* 35 (2): 237–79.

Vigreux, Philippe, ed. 1992. *Musique arabe: le congrès du Caire de 1932.* Cairo: CEDEJ.

Warkov, Esther. 1986. "Revitalization of Iraqi-Jewish Instrumental Traditions in Israel: The Persistent Centrality of an Outsider Tradition." *Asian Music* 17 (2): 9–31.

Williams, Peter. 1993. *The Organ in Western Culture.* Cambridge: Cambridge University Press.

Wolff, Christoph. 2000. *Johann Sebastian Bach: The Learned Musician.* New York: W. W. Norton & Co.

Wright, Owen. 2001. "Arab Music §I, 2, iv: Early Theory." In *Grove Music Online,* Oxford Music Online (http://www.oxfordmusiconline.com).

Wünsch, Walter. 1934. *Die Geigentechnik der südslawischen Guslaren.* Brünn: R. M. Rohrer.

Yektā, Raūf. 1921. "La musique turque." In *Encyclopédie de la musique et dictionnaire du conservatoire,* edited by Albert Lavignac, 1945–3064. Paris: Delagrave.

Yitzhary, Mordechai. 1992. *Ha-divan ha-meforash: mivḥar shirat yehude teman* [The annotated diwan: a selection of Yemenite Jewish poetry]. Netanyah: Assocation for Society and Culture, Documenting and Research in Israel.

Ziegler, Susanne. 1994. "The Collection of Wax Cylinders (former Berlin Phonogram Archive)." Paper presented at the IASA Conference, Berlin-Bogensee, September.

Zipperstein, Steven J. 1993. *Elusive Prophet: Ahad Ha'am and the Origins of Zionism.* London: Halban.

Recent Researches in the Oral Traditions of Music
Philip V. Bohlman, general editor

Vol.	Title
1–3	*Ethiopian Christian Liturgical Chant*
4	*Israeli Folk Music*
5	*Celestial Airs of Antiquity*
6	*The Folk Songs of Ashkenaz*
7	*Deutsche Lieder für Jung und Alt*
8	*Chinese Buddhist Monastic Chants*
9	*Emily's Songbook*
10	Robert Lachmann: *The "Oriental Music" Broadcasts, 1936–1937*